A Politics of Grace

T&T Clark Studies in Edward Schillebeeckx

Series editors
Frederiek Depoortere
Kathleen McManus O.P.
Stephan van Erp

A POLITICS OF GRACE

Hope for redemption in a post-Christendom context

Christiane Alpers

LONDON • NEW YORK • OXFORD • NEW DELHI • SYDNEY

T&T CLARK
Bloomsbury Publishing Plc
50 Bedford Square, London, WC1B 3DP, UK
1385 Broadway, New York, NY 10018, USA

BLOOMSBURY, T&T CLARK and the T&T Clark logo
are trademarks of Bloomsbury Publishing Plc

First published in Great Britain in 2018
Paperback edition first published 2020

A catalogue record for this book is available from the British Library.

Library of Congress Cataloging-in-Publication Data
Names: Alpers, Christiane, author.
Title: A politics of grace : universal redemption forpolitical theology in a
post-Christendomcontext / Christiane Alpers.
Description: 1 [edition]. | New York : Bloomsbury T&TClark, 2018. | Series:
T&T Clarkstudies in Edward Schillebeeckx | Includes bibliographical
references andindex.
Identifiers: LCCN 2017036886 (print) | LCCN 2018006149 (ebook) | ISBN
9780567679864 (ePUB) | ISBN 9780567679857 (ePDF) | ISBN
9780567679840 (hardback)
Subjects: LCSH: Political theology. | Postliberaltheology. | Schillebeeckx,
Edward,1914-2009. | Radicalism–Religious aspects–Christianity.
Classification: LCC BT83.59 (ebook) | LCC BT83.59 .A472018 (print) | DDC
261.7–dc23
LC record available at https://lccn.loc.gov/2017036886

ISBN: HB: 978-0-5676-7984-0
PB: 978-0-5676-9249-8
ePDF: 978-0-5676-7985-7
eBook: 978-0-5676-7986-4

Series: T&T Clark Studies in Edward Schillebeeckx

Typeset by Deanta Global Publishing Services, Chennai, India

To find out more about our authors and books visit
www.bloomsbury.com and sign up for our newsletters.

CONTENTS

ACKNOWLEDGEMENTS

This book is based on my doctoral project, which began in October 2013 under the supervision of Professor Stephan van Erp and Professor Christoph Hübenthal, on whose insights, critique and incessant encouragement, I could always rely – an invaluable support without which I could not imagine having written this book. I would also like to thank my Master's supervisor, Dr Marcus Pound, not only for the theological training he provided, but also for having encouraged me to apply to work at this doctoral project.

Prior to settling in Nijmegen in 2013, I was prepared to spend the next three-and-a-half years in the city in which Edward Schillebeeckx had lived for over half of his life. I had the pleasure and privilege of encountering many people whose paths had crossed with that of Schillebeeckx, which allowed me to get glimpses into the life of the person whose work I was beginning to study. Little did I know then, that this book's journey would lead me onto further, unknown places. From January 2015 onwards, when Professor Stephan van Erp moved to Belgium in order to become a professor of fundamental theology at KU Leuven, I started visiting Leuven on a monthly basis. This led to the provisioning of a six-month stay in Leuven, from January to July 2016. Prior to that, I had just finished enjoying a four-month research period from August to December 2015 at the University of Notre Dame, Indiana. This was a great opportunity afforded by Professor Mary Catherine Hilkert whom I would like to thank for the dedicated effort she put into inviting and accommodating me there, but most of all for the time and care she took to supervise my work during my stay at Notre Dame. I benefitted greatly, not only from her unparalleled knowledge of Edward Schillebeeckx's theology, but also from the encouraging interest she took in my work. Special thanks also go to Professor John Betz who arranged for me to present my work to graduate students of the faculty and whose availability to discuss critically the theology of Radical Orthodoxy contributed positively to the present shape that this book has taken.

Very special thanks go to Professor Kathryn Tanner and Professor John Milbank who both generously made themselves available to meeting and discussing my work on their theologies with me; these opportunities proved to be greatly stimulating. At this point, I would also like to thank Professor Erik Borgman for discussing with me on several occasions my thoughts about Edward Schillebeeckx's theology, as well as Professor Robert Schreiter, Professor Gavin D'Costa and Professor Karen Kilby, who all offered helpful comments on my work-in-progress during Master classes organized by the Netherlands School for Advanced Studies in Theology and Religion (NOSTER). I am particularly grateful to Eleonora Hof and Jos Moons who organized monthly NOSTER meetings for doctoral students in systematic theology from the Netherlands, as well as to Professor Stephan van Erp and Professor Marcel Sarot for chairing these meetings and for sharing their expertise. The opportunity to share our work during these meetings proved immensely helpful and I would like to thank all of the members of that group for their critical comments on my emerging dissertation. Likewise, I would like to thank the members of the Research Group Theology in a Postmodern

Context at KU Leuven for inviting me to participate in their monthly meetings, the members of the chair of systematic theology at Radboud University Nijmegen for our monthly discussions about public theology and the members of the weekly Schillebeeckx reading groups, both at Nijmegen and at KU Leuven, for all the stimulating discussions.

I would not have been able to write this book without the boundless support of my friends. Primarily, I thank Dorothea Dechau, not only for never getting tired of listening to my theological ponderings, but most of all for allowing me to discover a little more of life's beauty every day. I would also like to thank the Carmelites from the Titus Brandsma Gedachteniskerk in Nijmegen whose prayerful stillness carried me through the heights and depths of past years. Furthermore, I would like to thank John Bosco Kamoga, Marijn de Jong and Marije Marijs, Inigo Bocken, Trevor Maine and Lindsey Bryant, Joanne Vrijhof, Anne Siebesma, Anne van den Berg, Josh and April Furnal, Morris Ibiko, Julia Feder, Karthikeyan Pakriswamy, Stephan Sahm and Sreemoyee Roy Chowdhury. I would also like to thank my brothers Dominik and Josef, and my parents, who, in their very distinct ways, each continued to spur my interest in God and in people.

In particular, I would like to thank John O'Neill and Susann Kabisch who proofread and commented upon various drafts of this book and who, amazingly, managed to voice their fine criticisms in the most encouraging of ways. Their generous help and friendship was all in the service of the great improvement of this text.

Last, but not least, I would like to thank the congregation of All Saints Middlesbrough. Their gentle welcome helped me to rediscover my fascination for the mysteries of the Christian faith; a grace without which this book would never have been written.

Christiane Alpers
June, 2017

INTRODUCTION

There is widespread consensus among the otherwise oftentimes divided community of Western European and North American theologians that, when theologically responding to the political issues of the day, one particular move is to be avoided: falling prey to the lures of the cultural mainstream. Whether attributed to lazy slumber, cowardice or unfaithfulness – accommodating the Christian tradition to its secular surroundings is regularly criticized for being, not only unorthodox, but also politically irresponsible. A sociopolitical catastrophe is believed to have dawned already on the horizon, and its eruption is predicted if Christian theology does not draw on its most distinct resources, in order to turn away the disaster and deliver the cultural mainstream from its most grievous problems.

Yet, perhaps, this powerful tide of heroic theological reactions to the northern hemisphere's contemporary political situation risks burying under its weight a more gentle and hesitant hope; a hope that keeps alive and nourishes a certain optimism that there is already an abundance of resources, spread across the diverse and multifaceted composition of post-Christendom societies, believed to provide itself sufficient means to enhance the contemporary political scene. So let me ask quite simply the muted hopeful counter-question, posed to the theological despisers of contemporary political trends: Could it not be that trusting in secular society's ability to solve its own problems, and thus accommodating Christian theology, to quite a considerable degree, to the surrounding culture's politics, might after all comprise a genuine development of the Christian tradition? When faced with the, at times, overpowering misery of a fallen world, the accommodationist posture, in all its craven timidity, perhaps whispers most honestly its stammering confession, that today's world does not need a theological hero, because the only trustworthy hero, is the one on whose redemptive mercy we all equally depend. And, when asked for the reasons why one belongs to Christ's gathered flock, not being able to name anything else but God's abundant offer of mercy to sinners, a Christian theologian might be allowed to trust less hesitantly that also those outside the Christian fold embody what it means to follow God's mysterious ways in this world.

Thus, all those heroic prophets of doom, theological harbingers of the world's complete redemption, might overlook that their hope for redemption has already been wrought, albeit in perhaps less glorious splendour than they might have expected. In their incessant search for solutions to society's political problems, they might be too quick in discarding the broken treasures hidden in their surroundings. Instead of identifying ever more problems in need of solutions, an alternative political theology might want to recover these treasures, trying its best not to crush them any further. To these, theologians can, then, add ever more broken pieces, until the world's redemption will be gloriously completed at the eschatological feast.

As such, I join contemporary political theologians in asking the question: How can Christian theology contribute to the enhancement of the political life of post-Christendom societies? Yet, while there is currently an unspoken agreement to associate such enhancement with solving whatever is being defined as politically problematic, and with completing the work of redemption that Christ has left undone, I seek to dig deeper to recover the hidden alternative underneath this near consensus. This book can be read as an invitation to accompany me as far as you wish on this hunt for discarded treasures. My own findings rely heavily on precious insights, found in already existing strands of contemporary public and political theology, insights which I seek to assemble in my alternative proposal. In case that you find already even more value than I do in that which I critique and leave behind, of course, you do not have to join me in digging deeper. Concerning all those who accompany me to the end, I hope that one day, you will tell me of all the graces that I, from my limited perspective, was unable to see.

I will set out by introducing, in the first chapter, the specificity of the post-Christendom context as it is connected to an unprecedented situation for political theology. Inasmuch as post-Christendom societies are no longer marked by a monolithic Christian culture, it is no longer unanimously accepted that the Christian tradition should be resourced for an enhancement of the whole society's political life. The three most prominent theological responses to this situation have been proffered by Radical Orthodoxy, post-liberal Protestantism and a certain strand of public theology, all of which will be discussed in some more detail throughout the course of this book. The journey begins by showing how public theology seeks to maintain a sincere commitment to contributing to the whole society's common good, while simultaneously respecting the post-Christendom demand to refrain from dominating the political sphere with specifically Christian theological contributions. Whereas this approach comes under critique, from the Radical Orthodox and the post-liberal Protestant camp, for supposedly accommodating the Christian tradition to the surrounding culture when subscribing to secular notions of the common good, I highlight a certain blind spot that appears if matters are being assessed from the opposite angle. When public theologians have sought to defend the public relevance of Christian theology apologetically, by crafting theological solutions for problems appertaining to the whole of society, they have tended to re-ascribe to Christian theology a more dominant political role than a post-Christendom society might be willing to accept. This can be interpreted as the symptom of an insufficient recognition of the theological significance of the specific post-Christendom context, and the particular graces mediated therein. The discussion then moves to Radical Orthodoxy; first by explaining in more detail why public theologians have distanced themselves from the Radical Orthodox approach to politics, due to the latter's supposed aspiration to regain Christianity's lost dominance, its construction of a church–world dualism, and its blindness to the theological significance of the non-Christian public.

Seeking to excavate the value of Radical Orthodoxy's response to the post-Christendom context from underneath all three reproaches, Chapter 2, then, serves to expose that, most fundamentally, Radical Orthodoxy shares with public theologians a desire to enhance the political life of their societies. Furthermore, all agree that such endeavour is best realized through providing theological solutions to certain societal problems. On this shared basis, public theologians and Radical Orthodoxy merely disagree at the level of what is diagnosed as problematic, and of what is consequently suggested as appropriate cure. Highlighting the differences between John Milbank's and Graham Ward's respective political theologies throughout, I show that, while public theologians have criticized Radical Orthodoxy for upholding a remnant of Christendom, the movement returns the criticism by accusing secularism, and any commitment to a secularly defined common good, of perpetuating Christianity's lost cultural and political dominance in a new guise. Regarding public theology's criticism of Radical Orthodoxy's church–world dualism, I explain how Milbank's and Ward's theologies seek to embrace and perfect, rather than to exclude, the world, and how this offers a much more dynamic picture of the church's relation to the world than public theologians might expect. Concerning the theological significance of the non-Christian public, an examination of Milbank's and Ward's respective understandings of grace will lead me to question the Radical Orthodox promise that Christian theology will further Christ's redemption of the world. In search of an alternative to this move, I then turn to political theologies that have been more Christocentric in their approach; specifically, those marked by a more emphatic stress on Christ's uniqueness.

In Chapter 3, I introduce first John Howard Yoder's Christology as representative post-liberal Protestant response to the post-Christendom context, and second Kathryn Tanner's political theology as already paving the way for my alternative theological approach to post-Christendom politics. Yoder will be presented as a particular representative of post-liberal theologies, who principally rejects theological contributions to a secularly defined common good as well as any remnant of Christendom, both for the sake of Christianity's integrity. While appreciative of certain aspects of Yoder's Christocentrism, I distance myself from this principled rejection, inasmuch as I criticize Yoder for paralleling Radical Orthodoxy in conflating the role of Christian theology with that of Christ concerning the completion of the world's redemption. Kathryn Tanner is then introduced as deflecting attention away from Christian theology, concentrating more on the redemption uniquely won by Christ, a redemption upon which Christian theology and any non-Christian position equally rely. This leads her to reject the necessity for theology to adopt a central political role in post-Christendom societies, in favour of confessing theology's own entanglement in sin. I part ways with Tanner at the point at which she offers theological solutions to contemporary political problems, thus still working with a fundamentally problem-centred approach to politics, because I want to craft a political theology that builds more radically on grace, rather than on the lack thereof.

My constructive work consists in systematically elaborating how Edward Schillebeeckx's engagement with the surrounding public of his time exhibited a certain understanding of grace in terms of mercy. While I began Chapters 1 and 2 with public theology's and Radical Orthodoxy's apologetic defences of Christian theology's political relevance in a post-Christendom context, then going on to explain how this is related to their respective understandings of grace, Chapter 4 begins with an explanation of Schillebeeckx's *unapologetic* approach to those he may have considered to be theology's opponents, namely the growing number of atheists in his own context. I argue, in the remainder of Chapter 4, that Schillebeeckx's optimistic reception of atheism corresponds to a Christology that is better able to distinguish between Christ's uniqueness and the sinful shortcomings of Christian theology than those of public theology, Radical Orthodoxy or post-liberal Protestantism. While the others associate the Christian faith in redemption with theology's ability to solve political problems, Schillebeeckx is more pessimistic regarding theology's ability to solve problems and more optimistic concerning the reality of redemption in which the whole world always already participates nonetheless; this reflects a pessimism concerning humankind's liability to sin and an optimism regarding God's forgiveness.

In Chapter 5, I assess the contemporary relevance of Schillebeeckx's Christology to answering the question of how Christian theology can contribute to the enhancement of the political life in post-Christendom societies, by tracing the way in which he continuously modified his own theology in accordance with what he understood to be contemporary mediations of God's forgiveness. Arguing from the perspective of an ontological vision that bears great similarities with the Radical Orthodox ontology of peace, Schillebeeckx at the same time shared public theology's rejection of any remnant of Christendom, and paralleled post-liberal Protestantism in its Christocentrism. I argue that Schillebeeckx was able to balance the three because he understood grace as pure positivity, uniquely mediated by Christ, while mediated by the church as well as by the extra-ecclesial public to a similarly imperfect degree. This interpretation of the extra-ecclesial public as mediating God's mercy for the redirection of a sinful church to God, and of the church as being called to approach the extra-ecclesial public's failures with mercy, can be retrieved for an alternative public theology, in a post-Christendom context. Overall, thus joining existing debates concerning the political importance of theologies of nature and grace, this book adds a focus on Christology as a corrective to stress the usually overlooked importance of recognizing the ways in which grace might be mediated in a post-Christendom context as well as of confessing Christianity's own entanglement in sin.

Chapter 1

PUBLIC THEOLOGY: SOLUTIONS FOR POLITICAL PROBLEMS IN POST-CHRISTENDOM SOCIETIES

1.1 Political Theology in a Post-Christendom Context

One of the most important characteristics of the contemporary West European context, in respect to political theology, is the increasing loss of Christianity's social and political dominance. The current situation can be referred to as the 'collapse of Christendom',[1] if Christendom denotes the era in which Christianity was more or less identical with the whole of organized society, and the Christian tradition had the silently accepted privilege of significantly influencing, if not determining, the politics of the day.[2] Theologians would have engaged in politics when studying the Christian tradition in relation to contemporary political questions or in relation to the social order as a whole, and their deliberations would at least have been heeded, even if they did not always meet unanimous acceptance. Christian theologians of quite a different persuasion would have advocated for a stark split between 'religious' and 'political' matters, but as they would have done so on the basis of their particular interpretation of the Christian tradition, the very assumption of this split remained thoroughly Christian. And, given that most inhabitants of Western Europe used to be Christians of one or the other inflection, the Christian tradition would have influenced the political

---

1. William Storrar, '2007: A Kairos Moment for Public Theology', *International Journal of Public Theology* 1 (2007): 6. Elaine Graham speaks of the passing away of Christendom (Elaine Graham, 'The Unquiet Frontier: Tracing the Boundaries of Philosophy and Public Theology', *Political Theology* 16 (2015): 44).

2. R. W. Southern, *Western Society and Church in the Middle Ages* (Middlesex: Penguin Books 1970), 16, cit. by Paul G. Doerksen, *Beyond Suspicion: Post-Christendom Protestant Political Theology in John Howard Yoder and Oliver O'Donovan* (Milton Keynes: Paternoster, 2009), 1 n.1; William Cavanaugh, 'Church', in *Blackwell Companion to Political Theology* (Oxford: Blackwell Publishing, 2004), 397, cit. by Doerksen, *Beyond Suspicion*, 1 n.1.

sphere, also beyond this split, at least implicitly.[3] Thus, in former eras, even if there had been heated debates and disagreements concerning the correct interpretation of Christianity's impact on specific political questions or on the realm of politics as a whole, the Christian tradition would have functioned, at least implicitly, as common reference point. Today, however, in the less monolithically Christian set-up of West European societies, it has become far more debatable whether the Christian tradition should be allowed to have even the most delicately implicit impact on contemporary politics, or whether such societies should not focus their political energy most wholeheartedly on finding ways to leave their Christian past behind, and become more fully secular and pluralist than anyone might have previously dared to imagine. In this sense, the current situation provides for an unprecedented theological context, one which deserves particular attention.

a) Enhancing Post-Christendom Democracies

Currently, one can distinguish three major strands of theological responses to the loss of Christianity's privileged position in Western Europe. Radical Orthodoxy,[4] as one such response, promotes the re-establishment of Christianity's lost dominance in political matters, while post-liberal Protestantism, as another, suggests that an adequate response would be to withdraw, as Christian theologians, from political discussions concerning the whole of society. As a third alternative to these two existing theological reactions to the current loss of Christianity's dominant political position in Western Europe, public theology emerges on the scene. As an emerging theological sub-discipline, public theology is still engaged in an ongoing process of establishing itself, so that its areas of research, its methodologies and its purposes would be clearly defined and communicable to the interested questioner.[5]

---

3. Else one would promote the idea that human beings are capable to believe one thing privately and, totally disconnected thereof, another when it comes to political affairs; an understanding of the human constitution that has lost its credibility in recent decades.

4. Radical Orthodoxy is a theological movement that was inaugurated with the publication of John Milbank's, Catherine Pickstock's and Graham Ward's co-edited volume *Radical Orthodoxy: A New Theology* (London: Routledge, 1999) (David Grumett, 'Radical Orthodoxy', *The Expository Times* 122(6) (2011): 261). Milbank's *Theology and Social Theory: Beyond Secular Reason* (Oxford: Blackwell Publishing, 1990), Pickstock's *After Writing: On the Liturgical Consummation of Philosophy* (Oxford: Blackwell Publishing, 1997), and Ward's *Barth, Derrida, and the Language of Theology* (Cambridge: Cambridge University Press, 1995) can be seen as precursors of Radical Orthodoxy as a movement (R. R. Reno, 'The Radical Orthodoxy Project', *First Things*, February 2000, http://www.firstthings.com/article/2000/02/the-radical-orthodoxy-project (accessed 03 May 2016)).

5. As prominent, slightly divergent, examples of such endeavours, see Sebastian Kim, *Theology in the Public Sphere: Public Theology as a Catalyst for Open Debate* (London: SCM Press, 2011), 3; Ronald F. Thiemann, *Constructing a Public Theology: The Church in a Pluralistic Culture* (Louisville, KY: Westminster/ John Knox Press, 1991); Elaine L. Graham,

The purpose of the present study is, however, neither to join discussions about what most distinguishes the emerging sub-discipline of public theology from others, nor to search for an adequate definition of what precisely the term 'public theology' stands for. I will not present or clarify what public theology is, taken as a whole. Instead, I engage constructively with a distinct set of public theologians, namely those who address, in an unparalleled manner, the challenges for political theology posed by the current collapse of Christendom. With these public theologians, I share the conviction that political theology must orient itself anew in this changed cultural climate. They seek to construct political theologies suited to post-Christendom contexts on the one hand, and faithful to the Christian tradition on the other. Welcoming this much-needed re-contextualization of political theology within post-Christendom societies, this research contributes to the search for an adequate Christian theological response to the sociopolitical situation in Western Europe today.

Public theologians reject both the Radical Orthodox and the post-liberal Protestant response to the post-Christendom context, due to a supposedly one-sided reaction to the relative newness of this context, on both sides. Supposedly leaning towards favouring continuity over newness, Radical Orthodoxy is being accused of aspiring to return to Christianity's political dominance, thereby failing to appreciate, as an unprecedented opportunity, the theological significance of cultural pluralism.[6] The post-liberal Protestant approach, on the contrary, is rejected due to its favouring of newness over continuity. Where Radical Orthodoxy strives to reattain Christianity's political dominance, post-liberal Protestants erroneously interpret the context of post-Christendom as an incentive to withdraw altogether, as Christian theologians, from answering political questions concerning the whole of society, and to limit theological reflection instead only to questions concerning the organization of the church.[7] While oftentimes agreeing with the post-liberal conviction that churches should be morally outstanding communities as compared to the rest of society, public theologians still hold fast to the idea that Christian

Between a Rock and a Hard Place: Public Theology in a Post-Secular Age (London: SCM Press, 2013), xviii.

6. Graham, *Between a Rock and a Hard Place*, 106–7; Jeffrey Stout, *Democracy and Tradition* (Princeton: Princeton University Press, 2003), 115. This criticism has also been voiced by theologians who do not associate themselves with public theology. See, for example, Laurence Paul Hemming, 'Introduction: Radical Orthodoxy's Appeal to Catholic Scholarship', in *Radical Orthodoxy? – A Catholic Enquiry*, ed. Laurence Paul Hemming (Aldershot: Ashgate, 2000), 7; 13; Sean Larsen, 'The Politics of Desire: Two Readings of Henri de Lubac on Nature and Grace', *Modern Theology* 29(3) (2013): 301–2; Christopher Insole, 'Against Radical Orthodoxy: The Dangers of Overcoming Political Liberalism', *Modern Theology* 20 (2004): 234.

7. Storrar, '2007: A Kairos Moment for Public Theology', *International Journal of Public Theology*, 8–9.

theology should search for solutions to the problems that concern the society as a whole, even in the relatively new situation of cultural pluralism.

As a middle path between these two responses to the post-Christendom context, public theologians seek to pave new ways of engaging politically, as Christians, in affairs that concern the whole of society. Thus, the most distinct feature of public theology, in this regard, is its attempt at doing justice to both Christianity's situatedness in an inherently diverse and pluralistic political forum, on the one hand and the Christian faith that, however diverse a society may be, Christian theology, due to its belief in universal redemption, cannot enclose and limit itself to engage solely with internal ecclesial matters, on the other.[8] Instead of restricting their theological reflections to internal ecclesial issues, public theologians still address political questions concerning the whole of society. They define themselves as 'public' precisely inasmuch as they commit themselves to the common good that unifies an entire society, that is, to that which unifies different 'private' interests – interests pertaining only to specific sociocultural groups.[9]

To acknowledge the loss of Christianity's dominance, nevertheless, means that public theologians understand 'the public' as a pluralist political forum, in contrast to the monolithically Christian political forum of previous eras.[10] The public, in this political sense, is identified with the democratic forum in which theologians can voice their opinion as representatives of one sociocultural group among many others.[11] Public theologians thus evaluate as positive that political debates are no

8. Kim, *Theology in the Public Sphere*, ix; 7.

9. Others have observed that public theologians may use the term 'public' as synonym for 'universal' or as a synonym for 'common', depending on their national context (Eneida Jacobsen, 'Models of Public Theology', *International Journal of Public Theology* 6 (2012): 21–2).

10. The public is always distinct from a larger global, as well as from a smaller intimate, community (William A. Barbieri Jr., 'Introduction', in *At the Limits of the Secular: Reflections on Faith and Public Life*, ed. William A. Barbieri Jr. (Grand Rapids, MI: Eerdmans, 2014), 7). A great deal of public theological literature has inherited the understanding of the public in terms of universal accessibility from Jürgen Habermas' discourse theory (Sebastian Kim, 'Editorial', *International Journal of Public Theology* 6 (2012): 131–3; Graham, *Between a Rock and a Hard Place*, 87–8; 97; Barbieri Jr., 'Introduction', in *At the Limits of the Secular*, 8–9).

11. Storrar, '2007: A Kairos Moment for Public Theology', *International Journal of Public Theology*, 16. Defining the public as a democratic forum, public theology is also closely tied to the nation state. Thus, public theologians seek to converse with 'citizens on issues wider than religious matters' (Sebastian Kim, 'Editorial', *International Journal of Public Theology* 1 (2007): 1; Malcolm Brown, Stephen Pattison and Graeme Smith, 'The Possibility of Citizen Theology: Public Theology After Christendom and the Enlightenment', *International Journal of Public Theology* 6 (2012): 184). Also Jeffrey Stout understands the public in close connection to the nation state. His American context, however, is evidenced in his association of the nation state, not so much with a specific geographical territory, but with a

longer dominated by influences from the Christian tradition, but rather shaped by politicians from a plurality of cultural backgrounds and outlooks. Welcoming the newly developing internal plurality of West European societies, the public theological approach is fundamentally dialogical. 'Public theology is theology engaging with the main bodies in the public sphere and the Church's attempt to contribute to wider society.'[12] In order to permit the mutual exchange, characteristic of any genuine dialogue, much public theological research is dedicated to rendering Christian theological claims not only publicly accessible but also assessable by the scrutiny of all.[13] The basic trust that discussions concerning the whole of society can take place also within a context of internal plurality evidences that public theologians seek to balance their respect for sociocultural plurality with their Christian theological aspiration to address issues wider than those pertaining to the organization of ecclesial life alone.[14]

b) Cooperating with Existing Democratic Structures

A further distinguishing characteristic of public theologians operating in a post-Christendom context is their acceptance of the existing democratic orders of their countries, as constituting an adequate political framework for the needs and challenges of internally diverse societies.[15] There is a basic trust that what the Christian social order of former times was for monolithically Christian societies is now adequately being replaced by liberal or social democratic orders, for internally pluralistic societies. Public theologians admit that existing democracies could benefit from some enhancements, such as more support for the greater interaction between representatives of different sociocultural groups, where issues related to the whole of society are concerned. And, driven by their Christian ethical motivation, public theologians commit themselves to contributing actively to such an enhancement of existing democracies.[16] When it comes to the question of whether existing democratic orders are to be fundamentally accepted or rejected, however, public theologians are most distinct from Radical Orthodoxy, on the one hand, and from post-liberal Protestants, on the other.

group which is constituted whenever any number of people address each other as citizens. This address is allegedly marked by a shared responsibility for the common good (Stout, *Democracy and Tradition*, 113).

12. Kim, *Theology in the Public Sphere*, 230.

13. Graham, *Between a Rock and a Hard Place*, 69–70; 98.

14. Their commitment to the Christian tradition thus distinguishes public theologians from those contemporaries who think of the particularity of each sociocultural group as inevitably conflicting with the particularities of others.

15. Dirkie Smit, 'Notions of the Public and Doing Theology', *International Journal of Public Theology* 1 (2007): 436–8.

16. Kim, 'Editorial', *International Journal of Public Theology*, 1.

Public theologians opt for the former and understand theology's task as one of refining existing democracies, whereas Radical Orthodoxy and post-liberal Protestants are more critical with regard to this overall positive evaluation of existing democratic systems. Highlighting the embeddedness of existing democratic systems within the Christian tradition, Radical Orthodox theologians argue that the contemporary democratic order is the result of erroneous theological decisions in the past, which is why they advocate for the replacement of existing democratic systems by an alternative social order, one that is supposedly theologically more justifiable, and politically more advantageous.[17] Post-liberal Protestants, on the contrary, might criticize the public theological alliance with liberal democracy for perpetuating a remnant of Christendom, namely the close entanglement of church and state. Again, this alliance is rejected on theological grounds as such an entanglement is regarded as departure from genuine Christianity.[18]

If public theologians thus seek to reconfigure the role of Christian theology in response to the demands of a post-Christendom context, and in faithfulness to the Christian tradition, some would regard this project as failed, due to the public theological alliance with existing democratic systems. It is being criticized that this alliance undermines, from the outset, public theology's faithfulness to the true Christian tradition. It is at this point that my own research intervenes and opens up the discussion by presenting a fourth alternative of being faithful to the Christian tradition in the contemporary West European context. In this and the two subsequent chapters, I will show how public theology, Radical Orthodoxy and post-liberal Protestantism all foreclose a certain alternative theological response to the post-Christendom context, because they fundamentally interpret the Christian call to enhance contemporary political life as a call to solve some identified societal problems. In other words, while disagreeing with regard to what precisely is most problematic in the current political scene, public, Radical Orthodox and post-liberal Protestant theologians silently agree that political theology is primarily called to solve problems. Where public theologians identify problems within current democratic systems, to which they then offer solutions as further enhancement, Radical Orthodox theologians identify problems concerning existing democratic systems, taken as a whole, to which they then propose, as a solution, an alternative political system. Post-liberal Protestant theologians identify political problems in society, in response to which the church is then called to instantiate a counterculture, geared to solve these problems within its own ranks, and thus embody a better societal alternative.

This fundamental agreement that Christian theology's political role is primarily one of enhancing post-Christendom societies by way of solving certain problems

---

17. I shall explain this criticism in more detail in Chapter 2.

18. The reason underlying this position will be explored in more depth in Chapter 3, when I discuss the work of John Howard Yoder.

has largely remained unquestioned to this day, and, thus, this book opens up the debate of whether a response to the contemporary post-Christendom context, that is faithful to the Christian tradition, might not start from an altogether different outlook, and be more humble in its aspirations and its promises, as a result. As will become clear in Chapter 4, it is from my close observation of how Edward Schillebeeckx engaged theologically with the political concerns of his day, that I have learnt to appreciate that faithfulness, to the God of love and grace who has revealed Godself in Jesus Christ, might open up ways for political theology to enhance contemporary democracies which do not primarily rely on the identification of some supposed societal problems, but which seek to appreciate and build upon that which is already good. As will become clear, my own approach is based on the assumption that if the Christian tradition is most distinct through its faith that the whole world has already been redeemed through Christ's Resurrection, a Christian political theology should be most distinct through its search for signs of redemption in the contemporary context, not for its identification of political problems and its provision of solutions thereof. This approach shares with public theology the conviction that Radical Orthodoxy and post-liberal Protestant theologies insufficiently appreciate the theological significance of the contemporary context of societal pluralism. However, I will turn this criticism, to some extent, against public theologians themselves and show that they can be equally accused of clinging to a remnant of Christendom, due to the particular theology of grace operative in their approach. While resembling the post-liberal Protestant position on the surface, it will become clear that my theological reasoning for a more complete overcoming of Christendom provides a clear alternative to theirs.

In the following, I thus join public theologians in their attempt to contribute to the political enhancement of the societies in which they live, and to remain, in so doing, faithful to the Christian tradition. However, I question the preference of a problem-centred approach, which as I will argue is closely tied to the dominance of apologetics in contemporary public theology. It will be shown that such an approach might tend to perpetuate, rather than abandon, Christianity's former dominant position in society. This tendency originates in a certain underestimation of the abundance of God's offer of grace and a certain underestimation of one's own reliance on this offer, underestimations that are symptomatic of apologetics.

1.2 Theological Solutions for Societal Problems

What I mean by public theology's problem-centred approach to political questions can be illustrated when we look at how public theologians have responded to the situation of the sociocultural pluralism that constitutes a relatively new context for societies that have been long dominated by a monolithic Christian culture. Public theologians usually take it as their political responsibility, in such contexts, to focus on problems with contemporary pluralist cultures and to offer Christian theological solutions to these problems.

a) Public Theology's Problem-Centred Approach

A first problem identified by public theologians is a lack of common ground as to what the common good, for which all people should strive, actually is.[19] A second problem that public theologians associate with pluralist societies is that of the existence of antagonistic religious groupings that refuse to collaborate for the common good, defining themselves as in a fundamental conflict with specific other sociocultural groupings or with the liberal democratic framework, as a whole.[20] As a solution to this problem, public theologians seek to convince Christians that faithfulness to their tradition does not allow for such a fundamentally antagonistic stance vis-à-vis the surrounding society, and the plurality of groups that constitute it. Moreover, they envision the churches to act as places for dialogue and as mediators between conflicting positions.

As a solution to the first problem, some public theologians seek to excavate the shared cultural foundations of contemporary post-Christendom societies, as these are regarded capable to provide the common ground for political discussions also in pluralist societies. In a sense, this solution negates the essential reality of pluralism in Western societies. The plurality of world views is interpreted as a surface phenomenon of a society which is, however, still held together by the same cultural foundation. Here, it is argued that theology is able and responsible to excavate this shared moral fundament, which might then be implemented more explicitly to unify the plurality of world views within a society more effectively. Representative of this solution is Max Stackhouse's trust that our present society is still based on the Christian heritage that led to modernity and which simply needs to be recovered from overzealous secularization.[21] It sometimes goes unnoticed that Stackhouse, and those who follow in his footsteps, still advocate a central place for theology in democratic life, associating Christian theology with the responsibility of developing a normative vision for the whole of democracy.[22] This is not so much phrased in terms of providing the social order, as it is in terms of providing ethical guidance to the entire society.[23]

However, the entire argument that Christian ethics could and should be accepted by all relies on the implicit assumption that the lack of common ground in pluralist societies is a problem, and that Christian theology can provide a

---

19. Graham, *Between a Rock and a Hard Place*, xviii.

20. See, for example, Graham's critical chapter on evangelical identity politics (ibid., 140–75).

21. Max Stackhouse, 'Reflections on How and Why we go Public', *International Journal of Public Theology* 1 (2007): 421–2.

22. Smit, 'Notions of the Public and Doing Theology', *International Journal of Public Theology*, 443.

23. Harold E. Breitenberg Jr., 'What Is Public Theology?' in *Public Theology for a Global Society: Essays in Honor of Max L. Stackhouse*, eds. Deirdre Hainsworth and Scott R. Paeth (Cambridge: William B. Eerdmans Publishing Company, 2010), 5.

solution. This approach fails to attend seriously to those contemporaries who interpret from the opposite direction what counts as problem and what counts as solution. Some might understand it precisely as the problem that contemporary post-Christendom societies are still anonymously supported by a Christian past, inherited by the majority of people, and consider it as sole viable solution to encourage a more radically pluralist future that leaves this common moral ground more seriously behind. In other words, what counts as problem in pluralist societies is less unanimously accepted than public theologians seem to believe. Whatever public theologians regard as problem might not so much be a problem for society as it is one for themselves, when they assess the state of affairs from their particular theological perspective. Consequently, also the solutions envisaged by public theologians might not so much enhance the shared democratic life in pluralist societies, as it might serve all those who share certain specific public theological interests.

However, there is also an alternative current within public theology that understands the plurality of world views to be more fundamentally real. They regard Christianity as one world view among other equally legitimate world views, and seek to discern the appropriate place for theology in this mélange. These theologians seek to discern the common ground between different positions, not in the sense of a buried leftover from the past that needs to be excavated, but more in the sense of that which emerges as medium between opposing or complementary political outlooks. This strand of public theology wants the Christian churches to be responsible for the facilitation of dialogue needed in order to overcome conflicts in a democratic culture.[24] Enhancement of democratic life is promised in association with acting as the mediator for conflicting or otherwise alienated parties. Although apparently ascribing to political theology a more humble role in pluralist societies than the aforementioned outlook, this current also illustrates what I call a public theological focus on solving problems.

For example, when considering the public theological reaction to the increasing globalization of the world, it is remarkable that public theologians attest to a supposed need to define the common good of such a globalized world.[25] It is claimed that the problem of identifying the common good for the entire world community has become more urgent than at any other previous point in human history. In other words, public theologians again start their endeavour of enhancing the contemporary political scene with the identification of a lack. As proposed solution, public theology seeks to contribute to a more inclusive globalization, by connecting different contextual theologies in such a way that they enrich each other.[26] In the face of the whole world's increasing economic, infrastructural and political interconnectedness, public theology seeks to establish a theological

---

24. Smit, 'Notions of the Public and Doing Theology', *International Journal of Public Theology*, 445; Graham, 'The Unquiet Frontier', *Political Theology*, 44.

25. Kim, *Theology in the Public Sphere*, 18.

26. Ibid., 40.

discourse which reflects upon and harnesses this interconnection. In this way, public theologians strive towards a more inclusive globalization.[27] Thus, public theology is a self-consciously international discipline, in which the West European and North American contexts are not meant to be privileged over others.[28]

However, also this ascription of a mediating position to public theology, in a sense, still implicitly promotes a central political role for Christian theology also in post-Christendom societies. Public theologians assess, from their specific perspective, that global disconnectedness and certain conflicts are to be regarded as problematic, and the proposed solution exhibits a certain Christian theological bias for dialogue and reconciliation. As a Christian, I welcome this incentive, but I think it is important to acknowledge that certain non-Christians might evaluate these matters differently, and thus not welcome the public theological solution, as they might fundamentally disagree on what is truly problematic.

b) Apologetic Defences of Theological Solutions

Thus, one may wonder, whether the public theological identification of societal problems really discovers problems of post-Christendom societies. The suspicion that this might not be the case arises especially when attention is paid to contemporaries who reject Christian theology's involvement in the politics of post-Christendom societies. At this point, public theologians opt to counter this opposition to their own endeavour by defending themselves. They interpret this partial questioning of the appropriateness of political theology in post-Christendom contexts as incentive to revive Christianity's tradition of apologetics. Public theologians are aware that, unlike in previous eras, theology's relevance for the public is no longer presupposed and unanimously accepted by society.[29] They then seek to defend the legitimacy of their endeavours to those contemporaries who think of 'religion'[30] as a merely private affair, and to those who vehemently

---

27. William Storrar, 'The Naming of Parts: Doing Public Theology in a Global Era', *International Journal of Public Theology* 5 (2011): 23.

28. This is manifest in the *International Journal of Public Theology*, which has established a theological debate that includes authors from a wide range of nationalities. Sebastian Kim highlights that most contributions stem from the United Kingdom, the United States, Australia and South Africa (Sebastian Kim, 'Editorial', *International Journal of Public Theology* 8 (2014): 121–2). For a critique that 'the public' in public theological literature often remains a specifically Western concept, however, see Peter Casarella, 'Public Reason and Intercultural Dialogue', in *At the Limits of the Secular*, 51–84.

29. Kim, 'Editorial', *International Journal of Public Theology*, 1.

30. I avoid the term 'religion', following William Cavanaugh's argument that the term 'religion' has been constructed in the interest of Western colonialism in order to separate a people's faith from the political organization of their societies. This allowed colonial powers to govern, while allowing the peoples to practice their 'religion' (William T. Cavanaugh, 'The

reject any Christian theological contributions to public politics. Public theologians opt for an apologetic approach in order to enable members of post-Christendom societies to trust and respect Christian theological attempts at enhancing public life once again.[31] This is perceived, on the one hand, as a practical issue insofar as some of the mistrust against Christianity has arisen due to the churches' past political failures to meet their own propagated ideals. In this respect, Christian theology has to win the wider public's trust back by motivating churches to follow their calling more faithfully. If theologians promise, for example, a reduction of poverty, the churches have to be motivated to do their best to put this ideal into practice. On the other hand, public theologians also seek to respond argumentatively to the questioned legitimacy of Christian theological contributions to public political matters, by way of highlighting the public relevance of such contributions.

Public theologians thus see themselves faced with the question concerning how, in a context in which Christian theology has lost its privileged position, theologically motivated involvement in public politics might be defended apologetically.[32] Not questioning whether everyone agrees with the public theological identification of certain societal problems, the public theological apologetic defence of theological contributions to post-Christendom politics largely centres on the solutions public theologians offer. They seek to convince everyone of the legitimate place of political theology also in post-Christendom societies by demonstrating that public theological solutions to certain self-identified problems are publicly relevant, in the sense of enhancing the democratic life of the whole of society. The definition of public theology as 'the study of public relevance of religious thought and practice, normally within Christian tradition',[33] suggests that Christian public engagement is measured against whatever is defined as 'publicly relevant'. This core concern in public theological literature, namely the 'relevance' of public theology,[34] has been

Invention of the Religious-Secular Distinction', in *At the Limits of the Secular: Reflections on Faith and Public Life*, ed. William A. Barbieri Jr. (Grand Rapids, MI: Eerdmans, 2014), 105–28).

31. Kim, 'Editorial', *International Journal of Public Theology*, 1; Sebastian Kim, 'Editorial', *International Journal of Public Theology* 4 (2010): 133.

32. The privileging of an apologetic approach to public theology can be traced back to the influence of Max Stackhouse on the sub-discipline (Jacobsen, 'Models of Public Theology', *International Journal of Public Theology*, 16–17). For recent examples of this preference for apologetics see: Kim, 'Editorial', *International Journal of Public Theology*, 3; John W. De Gruchy, 'Public Theology as Christian Witness', *International Journal of Public Theology* 1 (2007): 26–41; Graham, *Between a Rock and a Hard Place*, 104–14; 177–233; Terrence Reynolds, 'A Closed Marketplace: Religious Claims in the Public Square', *International Journal of Public Theology* 8 (2014): 201–22; Christoph Hübenthal, 'Apologetic Communication', *International Journal of Public Theology* 10 (2016): 7–27.

33. Graham, *Between a Rock and a Hard Place*, xviii.

34. Smit, 'Notions of the Public and Doing Theology', *International Journal of Public Theology*, 445.

met with the criticism that 'typically, "public theologies" are self-destructively accommodationist: they let the '"larger" secular world's self-understanding set the terms, and then ask how religious faith contributes to the purposes of public life, so understood'.[35]

My own hesitancy to embrace this apologetic approach, however, does not stem from any concern regarding the legitimacy to contribute, as Christians, to that which non-Christians regard as relevant or good. To the contrary, I think that a Christian understanding of the good must include, rather than exclude that which the larger public understands as relevant and good. My concern with this public theological apologetic approach stems from the opposite direction. I contend that, due to their apologetic approach, public theologians are insufficiently aware of what is publicly relevant in a pluralist, post-Christendom society. I am concerned with the way in which public theologians, by highlighting Christian theological contributions to the common good in order to defend the Christian faith in a sometimes adversarial context, have been an obstacle to public theology's attempt at overcoming Christianity's political dominance of bygone ages. Instead of appreciating the theological significance of post-Christendom pluralism, including some people's opposition to the reliance of West European societies on the Christian heritage, public theology's apologetic approach has tended to re-advocate, via this path, a privileged political position for Christian theology. It is precisely their focus on supposed societal problems, which I question, inasmuch as it might prevent public theologians from seeing the possibility that Christian theology's most significant political contribution to post-Christendom societies might not consist in solving problems, but in recognizing and embracing the graces that are currently offered, in order to understand what really is publicly relevant at the moment.

Once again, look at the way in which public theologians have sought to contribute to the enhancement of contemporary democratic life. Beginning with the attestation of a supposed problem, such as the lack of a shared normative vision, existing conflicts between different sociocultural groups or the marginalization of some to the advantage of others in pluralist societies, public theologians offer their theological considerations as contributions to the whole of society, by promising to solve these exact problems. Public theologians promise to provide ethical guidance to an otherwise morally disoriented society,[36] to establish Christian theology as mediator between conflicting political groupings[37] or to empower

---

35. Charles Mathewes, *A Theology of Public Life* (Cambridge: Cambridge University Press, 2007), 1.

36. Smit, 'Notions of the Public and Doing Theology', *International Journal of Public Theology*, 443; Breitenberg Jr., 'What Is Public Theology?' in *Public Theology for a Global Society*, 5.

37. Smit, 'Notions of the Public and Doing Theology', *International Journal of Public Theology*, 445; Graham, 'The Unquiet Frontier', *Political Theology*, 44.

those who are currently marginalized.[38] The problem of this apologetic approach via problem-solving is that it returns to a position of advocating a central role for Christian theology in these matters, implicitly remaining within the problems associated with Christianity's former political dominance. Irrespective of whether Christian theology is advocated in relation to its supposed capacity of offering the overarching normative vision or ethical guidance for society or of facilitating and enhancing democratic dialogue, such argumentation effectively ascribes a more central role to Christian theology, than that of being just one equal contributor to the democratic forum.

1.3 Justifying Public Theology

As my concern with public theology's problem-centred, apologetic approach stems from a theological perspective, it is important to exhibit the theological rationales that public theologians themselves provide when they argue for the necessity of apologetically defending the relevance of Christian theological contributions to post-Christendom societies. One can distinguish three ways in which public theologians justify their own approach: the first concerns the argument that Christianity's distinctiveness in a pluralist public context allows Christian theologians to offer unique contributions to public discussions. Since the defenders of this justification would claim that it is not necessary to be Christian in order to be convinced by this justification, I will call this a secular justification for theology's public relevance. This justification is most distinct from the two that follow, insofar as it is, from the outset, meant to be intelligible to anyone who evaluates societal pluralism as something good, whereas the other two primarily appeal to Christians. A second justification defends the task of contributing specific Christian insights to the wider public on the grounds that Christian theology is inherently public; it is not solely confined to serve the churches.[39] In other words, theology's public relevance is defended in association with the universality of the Christian message. Due to this assumption of the Christian perspective, I will call this a theological justification for theology's public relevance. A third justification for the relevance of public theology concerns the argument that insights from the wider public can enhance the Christian self-understanding.[40] I will call this an argument for the theological significance of the public. This is then no longer an apologetic defence of theology's political relevance, but it is an argument for the

---

38. Elaine Graham, 'Power, Knowledge and Authority in Public Theology', *International Journal of Public Theology* 1 (2007): 61.

39. Sebastian Kim, 'Editorial', *International Journal of Public Theology* 3 (2009): 140.

40. I would like to thank Christoph Hübenthal for sharing his unpublished paper 'Public Theology – A Humble Project Outline' upon which my own systematization partly depends.

necessity of a kind of public theological research, one which concerns Christian theology's attentiveness to a pluralist post-Christendom context. Let me examine all three arguments in some more detail.

a) *The Common Good: Secular Justifications for Theology's Public Relevance*

Many public theologians justify the relevance of their own sub-discipline with reference to the common good; this can take weaker or stronger forms. For Sebastian Kim, theology can contribute alternative and otherwise unknown solutions to public problems.[41] A contribution to the common good can be made by drawing upon the resources that the Christian tradition provides for this undertaking.[42] Some public theologians have highlighted that Christianity should not be given any privilege over other world views in the search for the common good.[43] These are weaker and not explicitly theological reasons for the pursuit of public theology in the sense that they, as mentioned above, presuppose that the public defines the common good, and that theology can contribute to the realization thereof as one of many groups in the public sphere. Again it is in connection to theology's supposed ability to solve certain societal problems that public theologians present theological insights as an enrichment of public life.[44] One problem with this position concerns the very assumption that the public is still striving towards the common good, such as Christian theologians understand it, as this might still be an unjustifiable holdover from Christendom. In other words, the problem with this justification is not so much, as argued by others, that it runs the risk of accommodating the Christian faith to a secular agenda, as it runs the risk of imposing the Christian perspective onto the public, instead of permitting the public to develop in genuinely different directions.

The latter risk is evidenced in the writings of those public theologians who see public theology not just as one contributor to a publicly defined common good, but who position Christian theology at a more central place in debates of public concern. Again associating Christian theology's political task with problem-solving, these public theologians regard the public as being in such a dire need of theology that the whole of society would collapse if it did not draw upon theological

---

41. Kim, *Theology in the Public Sphere*, 3.

42. De Gruchy, 'Public Theology as Christian Witness', *International Journal of Public Theology*, 27. For an argument that declining church membership no longer allows the Church of England to define the common good, but forces it to ally with other groups, see Mark Chapman, 'The Common Good, Pluralism, and the Small Church', *Political Theology* 16 (2015): 61–77. Elaine Graham shows a similar tendency, to use a declining church membership as an argument against Christianity's ability to challenge the majority opinion in any substantial manner (Graham, 'The Unquiet Frontier', *Political Theology*, 36–36; 41–2).

43. De Gruchy, 'Public Theology as Christian Witness', *International Journal of Public Theology*, 39.

44. Kim, *Theology in the Public Sphere*, 8.

resources. It is argued that secularism is unable to provide the values necessary to managing a harmoniously shared public life.[45] Therefore, contemporary Western societies need religion in order to secure public discourse and to provide the platform on which consensus can be founded. This justification of public theology follows in Jürgen Habermas's footsteps. Following his defence of secular reason, Habermas came to detect the insufficiency of secular argumentations to the task of establishing a harmonious society, which is why he came to reconsider the public relevance of theological arguments. Habermas now claims that moral and metaphysical ideals are necessary in order to argumentatively maintain the dignity of human beings as a universal reference point.[46] Max Stackhouse, in a similar vein, has argued that public theology has to remind society that truth, beauty, justice and honesty transcend the realm of that which can be materially accounted for.[47] This presents the secular as itself barren of values and exclusively consisting of material realities.

It is worth mentioning at this point that Radical Orthodoxy shares this problematization of secularism's ability to unify a society around the common good.[48] However, Radical Orthodox theologians identify a different problem with secularism, and consequently offer a different solution. Far from being valueless, and in need of theology in order not to collapse, secularism is presented as working with a very specific metaphysical vision of material reality. Consequently, Radical Orthodox theologians put more effort in disclosing the insufficiency of purely immanent accounts of reality than public theologians would think is necessary.[49] In other words, Radical Orthodoxy understands cultural critique as

45. Graham, *Between a Rock and a Hard Place*, xvi–xvii.

46. Ibid., 49–52. Habermas interprets it as a problem that the Christian vision of the realization of the Kingdom of God on earth has been lost as unifying ideal for societies.

47. Max Stackhouse, *Globalization and Grace: A Christian Public Theology for a Global Future. God and Globalization: Theological Ethics and the Spheres of Life*, vol. 4 (London and New York: Continuum, 2007), 78.

48. Grumett, 'Radical Orthodoxy', *The Expository Times*, 261.

49. Steven Shakespeare, *Radical Orthodoxy: A Critical Introduction* (London: SPCK, 2007), 7. Their opposition to modern secularism is connected to Radical Orthodoxy's leading authors' familiarity with French post-structuralist thinkers, which is why their jargon has been called 'filled postmodernism' (Reno, 'The Radical Orthodoxy Project' *First Things* (2000)). The adjective 'filled' refers to Radical Orthodoxy's aim to disclose secular postmodernism's presumed emptiness. Radical Orthodox authors, thus, speak a postmodern language, while at the same time criticizing that same postmodernism (James K. Smith, *Introducing Radical Orthodoxy: Mapping a Post-secular Theology* (Grand Rapids, MI: Baker Academic, 2004), 23). Radical Orthodoxy is concerned with a *constructive* criticism of modernity, in contrast to one-sidedly deconstructive versions of postmodernism (Reno, 'The Radical Orthodoxy Project' *First Things* (2000)). Those in support of Radical Orthodoxy have called the movement a more consistent postmodernism which perpetuates the critique of Enlightenment reason instead of halting at the point of liberal politics (Smith,

part of the solution to the problem of secularism's supposedly flawed metaphysical underpinnings, where public theologians assume that the latter are merely lacking, which is why they can offer their solution more straightforwardly, as a direct filling of this lack.

As solution, Radical Orthodox authors examine the realities, which one might always have assumed to be unambiguous or self-evident, from a different perspective.[50] Their aim is to provide a comprehensive account of every aspect of the world from the Christian perspective.[51] More precisely, as constructive alternative to a secular understanding of reality as purely immanent, Radical Orthodox theologians uphold the idea of the participation of all of reality in God.[52] The idea of reality's participation in God highlights, on the one hand, that immanent reality is other than God and that immanent reality can only be adequately understood in relation to God on the other.[53] This analogical relation of the world to God is, for Radical Orthodoxy, not merely some static theory, but 'it is a living way of relating to God, best expressed in Christian life and worship'.[54] When arguing that such an analogical reading of reality in relation to God is better able to orient a pluralist society towards the common good than a purely immanent account of reality, Radical Orthodoxy effectively presents its own interpretation of reality as the solution to all problems associated with secularist cultures. Those who agree that the entire cultural landscape of contemporary post-Christendom societies has become problematic, praise Radical Orthodoxy for offering helpful resources for imagining an alternative way of being in the world.[55] They welcome Radical Orthodoxy's retrieval of Christian tradition as a fertile resource for constructing a better future for contemporary church and society.

In sum, certain public and Radical Orthodox theologians thus agree that a purely secular outlook is insufficient to unify a pluralist society around the common good. While public theologians, however, identify a lack of a shared metaphysical vision that would be necessary to unify any society, Radical Orthodoxy identifies as problematic precisely that secularism conceals its reliance on such a vision and pretends to access materiality purely in its immanence. As an alternative to this fundamental agreement, I contend that both the public theological understanding of secularism as valueless and the Radical Orthodox countering of the specific values and metaphysics of secularism ascribe a questionably central political role in post-Christendom societies to Christian theology. Both positions point to a problem within secularism (namely, its inability to organize a society well,

---

Introducing Radical Orthodoxy, 61). The relation of both Milbank and Ward to postmodern philosophies will be analysed further in Chapter 2.

    50. Smith, *Introducing Radical Orthodoxy*, 66.

    51. Ibid., 69; 73–4.

    52. Shakespeare, *Radical Orthodoxy*, 22.

    53. Ibid., 22–3.

    54. Ibid., *Radical Orthodoxy*, 23.

    55. Smith, *Introducing Radical Orthodoxy*, 68.

which public theologians associate with secularism's supposed valuelessness and Radical Orthodox theologians associate with secularism's supposedly erroneous metaphysics) in order to, then, apologetically present Christian theology as a solution to this problem. This apologetic approach readily becomes circular, inventing a problem associated with secularism, to which Christian theology is then offered as solution. Moreover, this apologetic approach forecloses the possibility of acknowledging that Christian theology itself could be a problem for the common good of post-Christendom societies, at this point of time. Such an acknowledgement would demand of public theologians to begin at quite a different point in their attempts at enhancing contemporary democratic life. This first apologetic justification of public theology with regard to theological contributions to the common good of internally pluralist societies thus circumvents the task of being sufficiently self-critical, because the focus is one-sidedly on the secularist perspective's supposed need of theological correction. This conflicts with the public theological self-claimed sensitivity to the theological significance of the public, explained in greater detail below (under c).

b) Universality: Theological Justifications for Theology's Public Relevance

Concerning the more straightforwardly theological justifications of the relevance of Christian theological contributions to the politics of post-Christendom societies, Christianity's relevance for the wider public is associated with the Christian mission to proclaim the gospel to the whole world in word and deed.[56] This is primarily based on the fact that Christianity has no concept of some secret revelation for a select few, but that it confesses a God who has revealed Godself publicly.[57] Since the God Christians believe in has revealed Godself in the midst of the world, the Christian message should not be passed on as some type of secret wisdom, belonging only to the faith community. Whatever Christians have to say should be as publicly manifested as God's own self-revelation. Although this claim is hardly contested by any other Christian theologian, not all of them argue for the need of public theology. Moreover, this justification of Christianity's publicness does not yet cover any questions concerning the degree to which the public appreciates the Christian proclamation in its midst.

In this regard it is important to note that public theologians often associate this publicness of Christianity's message with the need to translate the Christian faith into the language of the surrounding culture.[58] Elaine Graham even claims that public theology is distinct from both post-liberal Protestantism and Radical Orthodoxy due to its contrasting answer to 'the question of the extent to which

---

56. Jacobsen, 'Models of Public Theology', *International Journal of Public Theology*, 10.

57. Ibid., 7.

58. Kim, *Theology in the Public Sphere*, 9; Stackhouse, *Globalization and Grace*, 107, cit. by Graham, *Between a Rock and a Hard Place*, 151; Reynolds, 'A Closed Marketplace', *International Journal of Public Theology*, 203.

public theology should "translate" Christian language into speech acceptable and intelligible to a non-Christian audience in order to make any significant impact'.[59] As will become apparent in the course of this book there is, however, no necessary association between theological utterances, which are public in the sense of not being kept secret, and the translatability of Christian theology into a publicly accessible language. The refusal of some Christian theologians to translate the Christian faith is connected to their denial of the existence of some neutral, universally intelligible language. They regard such a neutral language to be a particularly modern conception, which is suspected of concealing its own rootedness in a particular tradition, and of thereby disguisedly perpetuating Christianity's dominance of former times. Consequently, other theologians envision different ways of conceptualizing Christian universality, in order to overcome the problems of Christendom more successfully.

c) Grace: The Theological Significance of the Public

Apart from these apologetic defences of theology's political relevance in post-Christendom societies, public theologians also justify the necessity of their newly established sub-discipline with reference to Christian theology's reliance on insights from the public realm. This justification is primarily associated with the relatively new context of cultural pluralism, in societies in which Christianity has lost its dominant position. In a society that is no longer monolithically Christian, Christian theologians have now been given the opportunity of discerning the theological significance of non-Christian political positions, insights and practices and are invited to modify their own theologically informed politics accordingly. In this regard, public theologians have, thus far, presented the pluralist public either as new opportunity to expand the grasp of Christianity's already existing political claims or as somehow contributing original insights – insights which theology could not otherwise gain on its own.

The reception of the public as opportunity to expand already existing Christian theological claims is implicitly advocated by Max Stackhouse, according to whom the universality of theological claims is tested and proven by theology's ability to create greater inclusiveness, greater justice and greater mercy in society at large.[60] The public would then serve as empirical evidence (or falsification) of the Christian proclamation. This conception evidently still has Christian theology as the centre of society, when simply assuming that the Christian understanding of, justice, for instance, is publicly acceptable. Appreciating the public's true plurality might imply that the Christian understanding of justice is much more radically challenged by the way in which other traditions understand the term or do not even use it.

59. Graham, *Between a Rock and a Hard Place*, 107.
60. Stackhouse, *Globalization and Grace*, 84.

As more than just an incentive to expand theological ideals, David Tracy, another forefather of public theology, understands the public as more significantly expanding the Christian tradition, by not only reaffirming it but also leading it into genuinely new directions. For Tracy, Christian theologians must not simply repeat the Christian tradition in contemporary culture, but must recreate it in ever new contexts.[61] The tradition has to be manifested anew in each historical circumstance. In other words, doing exactly the same as what has been done in the past would be a distortion, because the past activity belonged as much to a past context as the present activity has to belong to a present context. Conversation with the environment and a hermeneutics of suspicion which unmasks the distortions of the Christian tradition are inherent components of Christian theology. The public is, thus, a constitutive aspect of the faithful transmission of the Christian tradition within the contemporary context.

While Tracy's proposal could be termed a philosophical hermeneutical reflection on the transmission of the Christian tradition throughout history, Graham translates this argument about the relevance of the public for theology in doctrinal terms. She argues that common grace and natural law theory oblige Christian theologians to discern God's presence outside of the confines of the churches.[62] If the acceptance of God's offer of grace is central to the Christian life and the rejection of the self-same offer is regarded as being sinful, then Christian theology must attend to the public in order not to reject the offer of God's grace prematurely. Apart from common grace, Graham also refers to 'the seeds of ... redemption' that are scattered throughout the world, in need of further cultivation by Christian theology.[63] Noticeably, this presents the public as needing Christian theology for its 'seeds of redemption' to bloom. Combined with public theology's emphasis on dialogue, instead of 'one-way preaching', this means that the public is not just a passive field lying in front of theologians to be studied.[64] In order to nourish the public seeds of redemption, public theology wants to provide a platform in which the public can actively contribute to theological discussions and receive the theological completion of its contributions. Again, this understanding of the public as showing forth genuinely new, but incomplete graces, exhibits the pattern of identifying a problem, namely incompleteness, and of presenting theology as offering the solution, namely the platform where completion can take place.

Overall agreeing with public theology's attentiveness to the theological significance of the post-Christendom public, I will advance a slightly different theology of grace, resulting in a different conception of the relation between Christian theology and the non-Christian public constitutive of post-Christendom societies. More precisely, I shall radicalize the public theological understanding

---

61. Gaspar Martinez, *Confronting the Mystery of God: Political, Liberation and Public Theologies* (New York and London: Continuum, 2001), 200.

62. Graham, *Between a Rock and a Hard Place*, xxi–xxii.

63. Ibid., 129–30.

64. Kim, 'Editorial', *International Journal of Public Theology*, 140.

of pluralist societies as graced. By 'radicalize' I mean that I will refrain from searching for problems in non-Christian political positions, in need of a Christian theological solution. This will also allow me to evaluate the questioned relevance of Christian theological contributions to the politics in post-Christendom contexts not primarily as a threat against which Christian theology would have to guard itself apologetically. I will not regard this questioned relevance as a problem in need to be solved, but as itself a grace to be embraced, rather than countered, by Christian theology.

1.4 Public Theology versus Radical Orthodoxy

As has already been indicated, public theology and Radical Orthodoxy are not as opposed to each other as is commonly believed, if looked at from my perspective. Also Radical Orthodoxy seeks to counter the privatization of faith, which is why the movement has been characterized by some as essentially a 'world-oriented' theology.[65] Radical Orthodoxy is in agreement with public theology that the privatization of Christianity is a problem that is in need of a solution. What concerns the proposed solution, however, Radical Orthodoxy points into a different direction than public theology. In order to defend Christianity's public relevance, Radical Orthodoxy is much more critical of secular culture, and aims to disclose the insufficiency of purely immanent accounts of reality.[66] In order to highlight the existing differences between public theology and Radical Orthodoxy, within their shared adaption of an overall problem-centred approach to politics,

65. Smith, *Introducing Radical Orthodoxy*, 68. See also Grumett, 'Radical Orthodoxy', *The Expository Times*, 261.

66. It is noteworthy that, over the years, Radical Orthodox authors have become more nuanced and less confrontational with respect to those whose ideas they oppose (Grumett, 'Radical Orthodoxy', *The Expository Times*, 268–70). Graham Ward has distanced himself from the movement in recent years completely and refers to Milbank's project as a 'nostalgic' retrieval of the ontology prior to Christianity's supposed departure from the true theological tradition in the Middle Ages (Graham Ward, 'The Weakness of Believing: A Dialogue with de Certeau', *Culture, Theory and Critique* 52 (2011): 235. At the same time, however, Ward still published in Radical Orthodoxy's recently launched journal: Graham Ward, 'Affect: Towards a Theology of Experience', *Radical Orthodoxy: Theology, Philosophy, Politics* 1 (2012): 55–80. In his most recent work, Ward is more hesitant to reproach Milbank with nostalgia, but still seeks to distance his own theology from any such nostalgic reproaches, and in the same vein also from Milbank's theological project (Graham Ward, *How the Light Gets In: Ethical Life I* (Oxford: Oxford University Press, 2016), 70–4). Nevertheless, Ward shares Radical Orthodoxy's opposition to an exclusivist secularism and purely immanent understandings of reality (Graham Ward, 'The Myth of Secularism', *Telos* 167 (2014): 162–79).

let us look at certain public theological reservations vis-à-vis Radical Orthodoxy. The table will then be turned around in Chapter 2, when I investigate how public theology could be criticized by Radical Orthodoxy.

a) Contesting Secular Notions of the Common Good: The Radical Orthodox Remnant of Christendom

Among the many reservations held against Radical Orthodoxy by the theological community, those aimed at Radical Orthodoxy's uncompromising cultural critique are especially important in reference to the present discussion about public theology. Overall, public theologians are sceptical of Radical Orthodoxy's refusal to accept the prevailing secular ontology.[67] Public theologians perceive this countercultural outlook as obstacle to their endeavours, as they warn Radical Orthodox theologians from losing any foothold in the public realm when propagating their particular Christian interpretation of reality. It is argued that Radical Orthodoxy's animosity vis-à-vis atheist secularism might restrain many Christians from sufficiently engaging in the democracies in which they live.[68] Public theologians contend that Christians could contribute more effectively to public discussions if they accept that, in a 'de facto' pluralist public realm, Christian arguments are best heeded where the theological presuppositions remain implicit.[69]

The issue thus concerns how to contribute, as Christian theologians, to the common good of internally diversified societies. As already mentioned, public theologians embrace the existing democratic orders of their societies, as these are believed to constitute an adequate political framework for pluralist societies. Public theologians then seek to contribute to the common good by operating as best as they can within this framework. Radical Orthodox theologians, on the contrary, contest the suitability of existing democratic orders for pluralist societies, equally in the name of the common good. Consequently, the much more pointed public theological criticism, in respect to contributions to the common good, accuses Radical Orthodoxy of propagating the re-establishment of an oppressive Christian imperialism.[70] Radical Orthodoxy's aspiration to retrieve and reconstruct a particularly Christian reading of all of reality is associated with the desire to re-establish a privileged position for Christian theology in political debates. Radical Orthodoxy is criticized for seeking to restore the political primacy of

---

67. Graham, *Between a Rock and a Hard Place*, 116–17, Stackhouse, *Globalization and Grace*, 83. This can be connected to the observation that Milbank denies the existence of a neutral common ground between Christianity and the surrounding public, which has been assumed in much of modern apologetics (Hübenthal, 'Apologetic Communication', *International Journal of Public Theology*, 7–8).

68. Stout, *Democracy and Tradition*, 92–4.

69. Ibid., 99.

70. Shakespeare, *Radical Orthodoxy*, 150.

Christendom, evidenced most prominently in Milbank's advocacy of his Christian ontology as the only true and adequate interpretation of reality.[71]

As subsequent chapters will show, public theology's own alliance with existing democracies could, in turn, be accused of subscribing to the disguised dominance of secularism. This would render the public theological endeavour of enhancing the democratic life of their societies itself suspect of perpetuating the problematic aspects of the Christendom past, which would mean that an altogether different approach is needed for political theologies in contemporary Western Europe.

b) Problematic Universality: Radical Orthodoxy's Refusal of Dialogue

This first public theological reservation vis-à-vis Radical Orthodoxy already hints at a second, related, criticism. Whereas public theologians interpret Christianity's universality as equalizing factor between Christians and non-Christians, inasmuch as the Christian message is believed to appeal to everyone equally, they criticize Radical Orthodoxy for drawing a dualistic split between the Christian churches and the extra-ecclesial public, between Christian theology and all non-Christian dialogue partners.[72] In connection to their defence of a particularly Christian ontology as better alternative to purely immanent interpretations of reality, Radical Orthodoxy is criticized for being too concerned with upholding a distinct Christian identity over and against the non-Christian public.[73] As should by now be obvious, this split manifests itself in Radical

---

71. Hemming, 'Introduction', in *Radical Orthodoxy? - A Catholic Enquiry*, 7; 13; Larsen, 'The Politics of Desire', *Modern Theology*, 301–2; Kathleen Roberts Skerrett, 'Desire and Anathema: Mimetic Rivalry in Defense of Plenitude', *Journal of the American Academy of Religion* 71 (2003): 800–2. Roberts Skerrett claims that there is an inner contradiction between the postulated content of Milbank's ontology (peace) and the exclusivist way in which he presents it. At times, these criticisms are thus not as much aimed at the content of Milbank's ontological vision as they are at his exclusivist rhetoric (Romand Coles, 'Storied Others and Possibilities of *Caritas*: Milbank and Neo-Nietzschean Ethics', *Modern Theology* 8 (1992): 333; John C. McDowell, 'Theology as Conversational Event: Karl Barth, the Ending of "Dialogue" and the Beginning of "Conversation"', *Modern Theology* 19 (2003): 483–509; Oliver Davies, 'Revelation and the Politics of Culture: A Critical Assessment of the Theology of John Milbank', in *Radical Orthodoxy? - A Catholic Enquiry*, 116).

72. Shakespeare, *Radical Orthodoxy*, 150; Stout, *Democracy and Tradition*, 114–15; James K. Smith, 'Will the Real Plato Please Stand Up? Participation versus Incarnation', in *Radical Orthodoxy and the Reformed Tradition: Creation, Covenant, and Participation*, eds James K. Smith and James H. Olthuis (Grand Rapids, MI: Baker Academic, 2005), 61–72; Adrienne Dengerink Chaplin, 'The Invisible and the Sublime: From Participation to Reconciliation', in *Radical Orthodoxy and the Reformed Tradition*, 90.

73. Shakespeare, *Radical Orthodoxy*, 176; Larsen, 'The Politics of Desire', *Modern Theology*, 301–2; Graham, *Between a Rock and a Hard Place*, 111–12. Especially Radical Orthodoxy's opposition to modernity in the wake of the Enlightenment has been criticized

Orthodoxy not in the sense of any sectarian withdrawal from the world back to the safe confines of the Christian churches.

The gist of this second criticism becomes clearer when applied to Graham Ward, as the Radical Orthodox author who displays the most amicable stance towards the non-Christian public.[74] Ward's theology has been appreciated for treading 'on a similar territory to that conventionally occupied by public theology'.[75] He also asks how contemporary culture might be transformed, how public institutions generate truth and meaning and how Christian practices relate to these truths. Public theologians appreciate that Ward refrains from the Radical Orthodox claim that Christian theologians can understand the whole of reality better than others, and Ward's explicit acknowledgement of the limitedness and finiteness of Christian theological insights into reality is welcomed.[76] In contrast to other proponents of the movement, Ward is praised for respecting the otherness of his dialogue partners by suspending judgement on them.[77] This more positive understanding of the non-Christian public might be what allows Ward to reflect on the cultural influences which co-condition any theological thinking much more than the rest of Radical Orthodoxy, an acknowledgement for which Ward has received positive critique.[78] Ward then argues that theological sensibilities resurface in late-modern culture and that the sacred reappears within the public, which aligns Ward more closely to public theological sensibilities than Milbank.[79]

And yet, Ward has been criticized for still advocating a position of Christian superiority, stopping halfway in his respect for non-Christian dialogue partners, thus illustrating the gist of the criticism concerning Radical Orthodoxy's world–church dualism. Directing his research primarily at the transformation of

---

for undermining the gains the Enlightenment has brought to humanity (Douglas Hedley, review of *Radical Orthodoxy. A New Theology*, by John Milbank, Catherine Pickstock and Graham Ward, *Journal of Theological Studies* 51 (2000): 405–8).

74. David Ford, 'Radical Orthodoxy and the Future of British Theology', *Scottish Journal of Theology* 54 (2001): 389; Graham, *Between a Rock and a Hard Place*, 124; Grumett, 'Radical Orthodoxy', *The Expository Times*, 264; Christopher Newell, 'Communities of Faith, Desire, and Resistance: *A Response to Radical Orthodoxy's Ecclesia*', in *The Poverty of Radical Orthodoxy*, eds Lisa Isherwood and Marko Zlomislic (Eugene, OR: Wipf and Stock, 2012), 181; Maarten Wisse, 'Introduction to the Thinking of Graham Ward', in *Between Philosophy and Theology: Contemporary Interpretations of Christianity*, eds Lieven Boeve and Christophe Brabant (Farnham: Ashgate, 2010), 65–6; Mary Doak, 'The Politics of Radical Orthodoxy: A Catholic Critique', *Theological Studies* 68 (2007): 368–93.

75. Graham, *Between a Rock and a Hard Place*, 124–5.

76. Grumett, 'Radical Orthodoxy', *The Expository Times*, 266.

77. Shakespeare, *Radical Orthodoxy*, 142.

78. Ibid., 36.

79. Graham, *Between a Rock and a Hard Place*, 124; Graham Ward, *Cultural Transformations and Religious Practice* (Cambridge: Cambridge University Press, 2005), 5, cit. by. Graham, *Between a Rock and a Hard Place*, 108.

contemporary culture, not of Christian doctrine, Ward allegedly does not allow Christian theology to be sufficiently criticized by others.[80] Ward has been criticized for simply presupposing traditional Christian orthodoxy's authority, despite contemporary cultural currents (such as feminism) that put certain doctrines into question.[81] Consequently, Ward, like Milbank, has been criticized for his refusal to approach non-Christians in a dialogue that refrains from the use of non-theological vocabulary. This is linked to Ward's Radical Orthodox preference of a Christian interpretation of reality over a purely immanentist one.[82] Contrary to some secularist assumptions, Ward seeks to show that the particularity of different faith traditions is not primarily problematic, but constitutes an enrichment of any shared public. On this basis, he embraces the Christian faith tradition whole-heartedly, while probably supposing that adherents of other faith traditions are doing the same. In this sense, Ward's theological approach might be more suitable for a pluralist context than Elaine Graham's criticism, concerning his unwillingness to learn anything from the public, would suggest.[83] The issue will be reconsidered in my more nuanced examination of Ward's position in the following chapter.

On the whole, it can be noted, at this point, that the public theological criticism concerning Radical Orthodoxy's world–church dualism is connected to a different conceptualization of universality. In some way, public theologians suspect Radical Orthodox theologians for associating the universality of the Christian message with Christian superiority, elevating Christian theologians to a position from which they can assess others, while remaining immune of any such assessment from the opposite direction. Having explained how Radical Orthodox understandings of the political role of Christian theology in post-Christendom societies have been criticized for still exhibiting certain problems associated with Christianity's cultural and political dominance in Christendom societies, problems which public theologians strive to overcome, it is now time to turn to reassess these criticisms in their relation to theological discussions about grace.

---

80. Graham Ward, 'Response to: Rivera, Joseph M., "Review: Ward, Graham, Christ and Culture"', *Conversations in Religion & Theology* 6 (2008): 33; Graham, *Between a Rock and a Hard Place*, 108.

81. Virginia Burrus, 'Radical Orthodoxy and the Heresiological Habit', in *Interpreting the Postmodern: Responses to 'Radical Orthodoxy'*, eds Rosemary Radford Ruether and Marion Gau (London: T&T Clark, 2006), 38, FN 5. For a similar criticism, see also Linn Marie Tonstad, *God and Difference: The Trinity, Sexuality, and the Transformation of Finitude* (New York and London: Routledge, 2016), 70, who argues that 'the story Ward tells is surprisingly familiar'. Tonstad criticizes Ward for maintaining 'a standard theology of marriage' which he then merely expands to also include same-sex couples.

82. Wisse, 'Introduction to the Thinking of Graham Ward', in *Between Philosophy and Theology*, 67–8.

83. Graham, *Between a Rock and a Hard Place*, 128.

c) Ignoring Grace: Radical Orthodoxy's Failure to Appreciate a Pluralist Public

Regarding the question of the theological significance of the internally diverse set-up of post-Christendom societies, John Milbank has been criticized for prematurely discarding all non-Christian insights as either irrelevant or even outright hostile to Christian theology.[84] Milbank's exclusivist rhetoric has been criticized for breaking with the content of his own ontology insofar as he is unable to conceive of how those with whom he disagrees participate at all in God.[85] Doctrinally, public theologians relate this underestimation of the revelatory value of non-Christian insights to an erroneous understanding of the doctrine of common grace.[86] Presumably, the presence of God's grace within the Christian tradition is overemphasized at the expense of an adequate acknowledgement of non-Christian mediations of God's grace.[87] Radical Orthodoxy's rejection of the idea of the public as a neutral realm is associated with the denial of the existence of any shared space in which common grace operates.[88] Non-Christian conversation partners are either construed as being neutrally un-graced or as sinfully rejecting God's offer of grace.[89] Against this, public theologians hold that the doctrine of common grace implies that Christian theology cannot fully understand the implications of grace if it solely discerns how Christians are moved by grace. It should be acknowledged that grace moves non-Christians in different, but important and supplementary ways.

In contradistinction to Milbank's ambitions of offering an all-encompassing theological account of reality, Elaine Graham moreover appeals to the doctrine of grace in order to argue that public theology should confidently remain fragmentary and partial in its contemporary proclamations, in the hope that God's grace will fulfil the work.[90] Ward's opposition to any presumption of speaking from a God's-eye perspective suggests that his understanding of grace might be closer to that of Elaine Graham than it is to that of Milbank, at least in this respect. Nonetheless, in his criticism of purely immanent ontologies, Ward postulates Christ as the ordering principle of reality and seeks to account for how all cultural occurrences exist in Christ.[91] This

84. Shakespeare, *Radical Orthodoxy*, 155; 176; Larsen, 'The Politics of Desire', *Modern Theology*, 301–2; Graham, *Between a Rock and a Hard Place*, 111–12.

85. Mathewes, *A Theology of Public Life*, 125; 127, FN 32.

86. Graham, *Between a Rock and a Hard Place*, 107; 116–17.

87. Shakespeare, *Radical Orthodoxy*, 176.

88. This is connected to Radical Orthodoxy's supposed failure to acknowledge that the theological tradition has always appropriated resources from the surrounding culture as providential partners for the construction of Christian doctrine (Graham, *Between a Rock and a Hard Place*, 137).

89. Graham, *Between a Rock and a Hard Place*, 111–12; Stout, *Democracy and Tradition*, 103.

90. Graham, *Between a Rock and a Hard Place*, 101.

91. Wisse, 'Introduction to the Thinking of Graham Ward', in *Between Philosophy and Theology*, 67; Graham Ward, 'Spiritual Exercises: A Christian Pedagogy', in *Christ and Culture* (Oxford: Blackwell Publishing, 2005), 220.

means that all beings must be interpreted in terms of their submission to Christ.[92] This could suggest that Christian theologians possess an overarching vision of reality more akin to Milbank's ambitious project than to Graham's fragmentary public theology.[93]

In defence of both Milbank and Ward, more subtle critics have observed that it does not follow from Radical Orthodoxy's cultural criticism that Radical Orthodox theologians would think that there is nothing of value in the secular public.[94] As will become clearer in Chapter 2, they do not simply distinguish between grace and sin, but work with a more subtle distinction between natural aspirations for grace – which are not evil, but good to some extent – and the perfection or fulfilment of these through grace. It might be more appropriate to associate Milbank's and Ward's respective treatments of non-Christian insights with a discernment of how these aspire for grace than with a judgement on them as purely sinful. Christian theology is then presented as the fulfilment of this initial and fragmentary goodness. In other words, when their critics suggest that Radical Orthodox authors should interpret those with whom they disagree not as those who reject the True and the Good, but as those who distort it,[95] both Milbank and Ward might very well agree.

Regarding Radical Orthodoxy's understandings of the doctrine of grace, it also deserves mention that, in contrast to those who criticize Radical Orthodoxy's use of theological vocabulary in post-Christendom societies' public forums, both Milbank and Ward have also been repeatedly criticized for their intensive engagement with postmodern thought.[96] They are said to merely draw on theological resources in the interest of furthering philosophy. It has been claimed that Radical Orthodoxy is more grounded in a post-foundationalist philosophy, which aims at a deconstruction of modernity, than it is grounded in Christian

---

92. Graham Ward, 'The Schizoid Christ', in *Christ and Culture*, 89.

93. How Ward combines these two, somewhat divergent, strands of thought in his theology will be examined in Chapter 2.

94. Mike Higton, review of *Radical Orthodoxy: A Critical Introduction*, ed. Steven Shakespeare, *International Journal of Systematic Theology* 12 (2010): 240–2.

95. Mathewes, *A Theology of Public Life*, 125. This criticism is only directed against Milbank, but the logic of the criticism would also apply to Ward's opposition to secularism.

96. Wayne J. Hankey, '*Theoria Versus Poesis*: Neoplatonism and Trinitarian Difference in Aquinas, John Milbank, Jean-Luc Marion and John Zizioulas', *Modern Theology* 15 (1999): 387–415; Laurence Paul Hemming, '*Analogia non Entis sed Entitatis*: The Ontological Consequences of the Doctrine of Analogy', *International Journal of Systematic Theology* 6 (2004): 119–20, 129; Ford, 'Radical Orthodoxy and the Future of British Theology', *Scottish Journal of Theology*, 394, 397–8; Kathryn Tanner, review of *Christ and Culture*, by Graham Ward, *Modern Theology* 23 (2007): 483–4; Davies, 'Revelation and the Politics of Culture', in *Radical Orthodoxy? – A Catholic Enquiry*, 114; Lucy Gardener, 'Listening at the Threshold: Christology and the "Suspension of the Material"', in *Radical Orthodoxy? – A Catholic Enquiry*, 144.

orthodoxy.[97] In this vein, Radical Orthodox theologians have been criticized for not exhibiting the same respect for Christian Scripture and practices that has marked the Christian tradition throughout the centuries.[98] Radical Orthodox authors appear to be speaking from intellectualist vantage points rather than from the perspective of a specific faith tradition, exhibiting no 'signs of any kind of praxis of faith' in their works.[99] This close link to postmodernism, however, is why Radical Orthodoxy has also been evaluated more positively, as one among many other contemporary ways of criticizing secularism.[100] As such, Radical Orthodoxy is regarded as being committed to pluralism in a way 'that works against the totalizing tendencies of secularism'.[101] In this vein, Radical Orthodoxy is expected to offer a creative alternative vision to all others who strive to overcome the problems associated with secularism.

Putting the question that arises from these contrasting evaluations of Radical Orthodoxy's engagement with postmodernism in theological terms, the question remains about the degree to which postmodern philosophies should be understood as a grace for Christian theology; an issue to which I will return in the next chapter. In sum, while I agree with public theologians that the pluralist context of contemporary West European societies presents to Christian theologians the opportunity of discerning the theological significance of non-Christian positions, and to thus receive the graces mediated by them, this initial discussion of the discrepancies between public and Radical Orthodox theologians has shown already that the issue is more complex. While not many theologians deny that grace is operative also within non-Christian positions, theology's political role in post-Christendom societies is related to one's understanding of the relation between graced nature, graced nature's fulfilment in Christ as well as to sin and Christ's overcoming of sin.[102]

97. Graham, *Between a Rock and a Hard Place*, 135.

98. Hemming, '*Analogia non Entis sed Entitatis*' *International Journal of Systematic Theology*, 119–20, 129; Ford, 'Radical Orthodoxy and the Future of British Theology', *Scottish Journal of Theology*, 394, 397–8; Tanner, review of *Christ and Culture*, *Modern Theology* 23 (2007): 483–4.

99. Graham, *Between a Rock and a Hard Place*, 124; 130; Graeme Richardson, 'Integrity and Realism: Assessing John Milbank's Theology', *New Blackfriars* 84 (2007): 273; Reno, 'The Radical Orthodoxy Project', *First Things* (2000).

100. William A. Barbieri Jr., 'The Post-Secular Problematic', *At the Limits of the Secular*, 142–5.

101. Ibid., 158.

102. In this vein, associating the theological significance of the public with a plurality of 'truth-seeking communities' also might benefit from some further nuancing (Storrar, '2007: A Kairos Moment for Public Theology', 12). It could be assessed how far the non-Christian search for truth is being fulfilled in Christ, and/or in Christian theology. The aspect of sin has been highlighted by some public theologians who refer to Christianity's responsibility of reconciling the world and of bearing witness to God's mercy (Kim, 'Editorial', 3–4). They

Conclusion

In conclusion of this chapter, I agree with public theologians that the current loss of Christianity's unquestioned central place in West European societies provides for a relatively new context for the Christian theological endeavour of enhancing the political life of the whole of society. While I agree that this contemporary context deserves particular theological consideration, I part ways with public theology's problem-centred and apologetic approach. As this chapter has indicated, in so doing, public theologians re-ascribe a privileged position in the societal whole to Christian theology. My hypothesis is that the question about theology's political role in post-Christendom societies can be better approached by way of an increased focus on the public theological incentive to discern the ways in which God's grace is mediated, even in non-Christian positions and insights. In the course of this book, I radicalize this incentive by way of suggesting that also the secularist opposition to Christian theological involvement in public politics should be understood as mediating God's grace, and not primarily as an incentive to retrieve Christianity's apologetic tradition. This approach will help us to re-conceptualize what it means to enhance the political life of post-Christendom societies, beyond the widespread association of enhancement with problem-solving.

I have also begun to introduce schematically the main public theological reservations against Radical Orthodoxy. These concern Radical Orthodoxy's supposed aspirations to reinstall Christendom as the best form of government and the concomitant closure towards non-Christian dialogue partners, which has been associated with erroneous understandings of grace. A more detailed assessment, of both Milbank's and Ward's respective understandings of theology's political role in post-Christendom societies, will include both an examination of the degree to which the public theological reservations against Radical Orthodoxy are justified, and an extrapolation of criticisms that Radical Orthodox theologians could voice towards public theology.

want to raise awareness to those parts of public life which are still in need of redemption. However, they have not yet examined how precisely the public's acceptance of grace and its lack of grace are interconnected.

Chapter 2

RADICAL ORTHODOXY: A CHRISTIAN SOCIAL ORDER AS THE SOLUTION TO THE POLITICAL PROBLEMS OF POST-CHRISTENDOM SOCIETIES

The previous chapter has shown both the existing discrepancies between public theology and Radical Orthodoxy when it comes to the question concerning a faithful Christian response to the contemporary post-Christendom context of West European societies, as well as their underlying, silent agreement that such a response should be problem-centred. Overall, public theologians suspect Radical Orthodoxy of advocating a return to Christian dominance in political matters, even in a post-Christendom context. However, I have raised the concern that this criticism might be turned against public theology itself. This return to Christian dominance has been exposed to be the symptom of the public theological turn to apologetics, at the point when public opposition to theologically motivated political involvement is being interpreted as a problem, in need of an apologetic defence of Christianity as its solution. This chapter is partly meant to exhibit the same move to be at play also in Radical Orthodoxy, thus clarifying the intricate entanglement of a problem-centred understanding of what it means to enhance contemporary democratic life, apologetic defences of particular Christian solutions and the return to Christianity's political dominance.

The exhibition, of how this entanglement characterizes also the Radical Orthodox approach to political theology, proceeds along the lines of the public theological reasoning for why and how Christian theology should be involved in the organization also of post-Christendom societies. I have called the first of such reasonings a secular justification, inasmuch as public theologians justify theological contributions to the surrounding secular societies' conceptions of the common good. In this regard, public theologians criticize Radical Orthodoxy for promoting a countercultural return to Christian dominance, in connection with the movement's firm resistance to any accommodation of Christian theology to secularism. Public theology's second apologetic defence for the public relevance of theological involvement in post-Christendom politics abides by a more explicitly theological reasoning. Public theologians here appeal to the universality of the Christian message, in order to defend the relevance of Christian claims for the whole of society, and they criticize Radical Orthodoxy for misrepresenting this universality, when the movement effectively propagates a dualistic split between Christian theology and non-Christian positions. Apart from these two justifications concerning Christian theology's political relevance for post-Christendom societies, there is also a third justification concerning the endeavour of public theology itself. This justification points in quite a different direction postulating that theology gains the new opportunity of reflecting on the theological significance of non-Christian contributions to public politics in the pluralist cultures that characterize post-Christendom societies. This third justification had been associated with the doctrine of grace, and public theologians criticize Radical Orthodoxy for erroneously regarding non-Christian positions as entirely un-graced and, consequently, irrelevant for Christian theology. In partial defence of Radical Orthodoxy, I have argued that the discussion could be elucidated with the help of a more nuanced examination of the relation between grace and Christian theology, grace and non-Christian positions and the impact of sin upon each.

In this chapter, I present the respective political theologies of John Milbank and Graham Ward in quite some detail, as my own approach relies to a considerable degree on theirs. Accepting the Radical Orthodox distancing from secularism, for reasons explained in Section 2.1, and thus also offering a somewhat countercultural political theology myself, I, nonetheless, do not agree with Radical Orthodoxy's presentation of theology as a solution to the problem posed by secularism. My approach aims at crafting a political theology that can be critical of certain cultural currents, without making the claim that this criticism disqualifies that culture as a whole, and without promising to offer a *better* alternative. In this sense, Section 2.2 serves to distance my approach from Radical Orthodoxy's advocated retrieval of Christianity's lost political dominance, while recovering valuable ideas for a Christian political theology in the contemporary context underneath Radical Orthodoxy's triumphalism. In other words, my work in this part of the chapter is one of disassociating Milbank's and Ward's political suggestions from the Christian triumphalism, in which they are clothed. Section 2.3 will then make clear the theological rationale for my rejection of the Radical Orthodox tendency to promote again Christianity's lost political dominance, by exposing the theology of grace underlying this tendency; a theology of grace, which I dispute for Christological reasons.

2.1 Problematizing the Common Good: Apologetics Beyond Commonality

In the previous chapter, I have explained that public theologians justify the relevance of their discipline partly by arguing that Christian theology can contribute to the common good, as it has been defined by the surrounding society. Charles Mathewes's criticism that this position risks accommodating Christian theology to the mainstream culture has already been briefly mentioned in this context. In what follows, I explain that Radical Orthodoxy does not reject the accommodation of Christian theology to the surrounding culture generally, but that Radical Orthodox authors are wary of very specific threats from a secularist culture, most significantly its concealed perpetuation of Christianity's dominance of bygone times, in a new guise. Pretending to be neutral, in the sense of not being culturally conditioned, secularism now inhabits the central role of organizing the entire society, a role which Christian theology had previously played. Part of the Radical Orthodox project is, thus, to contest secularism's pretended neutrality. In the case of both Milbank and Ward, I begin with an explanation of what they oppose and then introduce what they positively offer as their alternatives. The political implications of Milbank's and Ward's positions will be further developed in Sections 2.2 and 2.3.

a) Milbank's Contestation of Secularism: The Problem of Neutrality

The value of Milbank's thoughts, on the political role of Christian theology in pluralist post-Christendom societies, can only be understood against the background of his disclosure of two contemporarily widespread understandings of reality, both of which tend to perpetuate the problems of Christianity's cultural dominance, inherited from bygone Christendom times.[1] The first, and somewhat primary, ontology contested by Milbank pretends to mirror reality directly in and through its statements and, in so doing, denies being metaphysical.[2] It presents its deliberations as objective truth, thereby concealing that it is but one interpretation of reality among others. I call this ontology modern positivism. The second, namely the postmodern understanding of reality, understands each interpretation of immanent beings as equally disconnected from the truth about reality (if such a truth exists at all), and seeks to overcome metaphysics by way of resisting the temptation to speculate about the interrelation of different immanent beings in the way, Milbank would argue, is done by an overarching ontology. Instead, each particular immanent being is sought out in order to be appreciated in its individual difference from all others.

According to Milbank, both modern positivism and postmodernism deny the culturally specific ontology which they presuppose and upon which their entire endeavour of interpreting reality relies. Noticeably relying on the identification of problematic aspects in other positions, Milbank regards the positivist assumption that 'nature' self-evidently and objectively reveals its own truth to humanity as being

---

1. In sum, Milbank criticizes three philosophies for their disguised perpetuation of Christianity's lost cultural dominance. Besides modern positivism and postmodernism, he also rejects phenomenology. It would, however, exceed the scope of this dissertation to analyze Milbank's opposition to phenomenology in greater detail.

2. Milbank refers to different world views in terms of ontologies by which he means an overarching metaphysical vision of how the particular beings encountered in the immanent world are constituted and interrelated.

politically problematic.[3] This understanding of immanent reality undermines the necessity of metaphysical discussions concerning the truth about the immanent world. Highlighting the political implications of these metaphysical discussions, Milbank laments that, in modernity, people have short-circuited the political path towards truth, by promising to guarantee an access to the truth about nature by way of employing the most adequate scientific method. Metaphysical discussions about the truth are of the greatest political relevance, if the truth about reality is believed to be more multifaceted than modern positivists would allow for. Political decisions are, then, no longer imposed by those who have the power to 'read' nature, but politics depends upon a collective consensus of the human community about the truth revealed in nature. In brief, the problem with positivism's pretended neutrality is that it ascribes the most central role in organizing the whole of society to itself. Metaphysical speculations, as well as cultural biases, are being discarded as politically irrelevant to discussions that take place in the public forum, and modern positivism, in its political variant of secularism, exempts itself from the charge of being culturally biased, which is why it alone is permitted to organize the whole of society.[4]

Milbank understands postmodernism not as overcoming but as perpetuating the problems of modern positivism. Postmodernism, despite its claims to abandon any ontology, still disguisedly adheres to an overarching vision of reality. Milbank interprets postmodernism as yet another metaphysically biased position, which interprets all particular beings as equally cancelling any overarching metaphysical order among beings through their particular existence.[5] The problem with this philosophy is that it generalizes all particular different beings to the same univocal

3. John Milbank, 'Out of the Greenhouse', in *The Word Made Strange: Theology, Language, Culture* (Oxford: Blackwell Publishers, 1997), 258.

4. John Milbank, *Theology and Social Theory: Beyond Secular Reason*, 2nd edn. (Oxford: Blackwell Publishing, 1990, 2006), xvi; John Milbank and Creston Davis, eds, *The Monstrosity of Christ: Paradox or Dialectic?* (Cambridge, MA: MIT Press, 2011), 115–16, 134–5; John Milbank, *Beyond Secular Order: Critique on Modern Ontology* (Oxford: Blackwell Publishing, 2013), 3. Milbank also criticizes Jean-Luc Marion's phenomenology for being less non-foundationalist than he would admit, and exhibits the particular fundamental beliefs about reality that are implicitly assumed by Marion's phenomenology (Milbank, 'Only Theology Overcomes Metaphysics', in *The Word Made Strange*, 36; 42–3). He objects to the phenomenological claim that the truth about reality as a whole *self-evidently* appears in all particular beings as that which remains beyond its manifestation in beings. This claim denies the prior ontology upon which it depends, but relies on a modern positivist epistemology as its foundation (John Milbank, 'The New Divide: Romantic versus Classical Orthodoxy', *Modern Theology* 26 (2010): 32).

5. Milbank, *The Monstrosity of Christ*, 138; John Milbank, 'Truth and Vision', in *Truth in Aquinas*, eds. John Milbank and Catherine Pickstock (Abingdon, Oxon: Routledge, 2001), 25; Milbank, 'A Critique of the Theology of Right', in *The Word Made Strange*, 8.

status of being different.[6] The refusal of an overarching ontology is, therefore, disclosed as a disguised ontology which holds that, in reality, all differences are equal. As such, this interpretation of reality must also be viewed on the same level as any ontology that affirms the political importance of metaphysical speculation concerning (hierarchical) orderings among different particular beings.[7]

This opposition to modern positivism and postmodernism clarifies why Milbank objects to apologetic defences of the relevance of Christian theology in secular terms, where the secular is marked precisely by these two positions. Milbank does not oppose any non-Christian culture, as a matter of principle, but his criticism is directed against the particular cultural context in which he regards himself to be situated. The danger of justifying Christian theology in secular terms consists in agreeing with secularism, as determining the social order of post-Christendom societies, because it is erroneously believed that secularism is less culturally biased and more independent of metaphysical speculation than any faith-based social order could be.

Against the background of this problematization of all positions that claim some neutral access to reality for themselves, one could now expect that Milbank would assume a position which openly confesses its merely subjective and constructed status. Indeed, Milbank upholds the necessity of making the ontology through which reality is accessed explicit.[8] Milbank openly affirms the dependence of his own ontology upon culturally contingent conventions and influences, thus respecting the postmodern intuition that all ontologies are social constructs and are, consequently, alterable.[9] This is why he refuses to provide secure foundations that would account for

---

6. This view is brought to the extreme in what Milbank calls ontologies of violence. These ontologies present all particulars, not as harmoniously ordered, but as violently or indifferently set against each other (Milbank, *Theology and Social Theory*, 4; Milbank, 'The Poverty of Niebuhrianism', in *The Word Made Strange*, 236–7).

7. Milbank, *Theology and Social Theory*, xvi; Milbank, *The Monstrosity of Christ*, 115–16, 134–5; Milbank, *Beyond Secular Order*, 3. Milbank refuses to interpret the constructed status of all ontologies as revelatory of their ultimate arbitrariness. When rendered into *necessary* arbitrariness, the indeterminacy of all human interpretations of reality would be conceived of as something ultimately determined (Milbank, 'The Second Difference', in *The Word Made Strange*, 189).

8. Milbank speaks of a necessary conjecture about the whole in order to perceive any particular being (Milbank, 'Only Theology Overcomes Metaphysics', in *The Word Made Strange*, 42–3).

9. See Gavin Hyman, *The Predicament of Postmodern Theology: Radical Orthodoxy or Nihilist Textualism?* (Louisville, KY: Westminster John Knox Press, 2001), for a critical assessment of the degree to which Milbank accepts postmodern philosophies. Hyman criticizes that Milbank uses postmodern thought only in order to then re-advocate his theological metanarrative, thereby breaking with postmodern sensibilities (30). However, Milbank is also criticized, from the opposite side, for engaging with postmodern thought to the extent that the integrity of the theological concepts he uses is violated (Laurence Paul Hemming,

the correspondence of his own ontology to reality. Instead, Milbank makes the weaker claim that one must 'wager' that his ontology corresponds to reality.[10] At the same time, however, Milbank still maintains that his ontology objectively corresponds to the truth about reality.[11] This characterization of his own ontology, as simultaneously a culturally specific construct *and* objectively truthful, is in line with his opposition to the presumed self-evidence of postmodernism. Milbank accepts the contemporarily widespread belief that ontologies are humanly constructed, but refuses to accept that humanly constructed ontologies self-evidently deviate from reality itself. In other words, he contests the binary opposition between truth and human construction. That ontologies are constructed does not mean that they are necessarily superimposed on the true chaos of reality that can never be accessed by human thought. This conception would disguisedly elevate the observation of human construction onto the ontological level by granting it the last word about the relationship between human thought and reality.[12] As further clarification of the intricate entanglement of a problem-centred approach to political theology and apologetics, I will now show that, on the basis of his identification of certain problems with secular ontologies, Milbank, in a similar move to public theology, also retreats to an apologetic defence of Christian theology, albeit one quite differently shaped, due to Milbank's refusal of secular justifications for the public relevance of Christian theology.

b) Defending Christian Theology: Solving Secularism's Problems

The previous section has shown that, overall, Milbank fundamentally opposes any positivist world view, which would hold that immanent reality could be understood non-metaphysically or without the help of an ontological framework. But where does Milbank's offer of an alternative ontology lead us regarding the question of apologetics? Milbank's ontology has been criticized for displaying traces of fideism and a failure to rationally justify the leap of faith into Christianity he supposedly

'What Catholic Theologians Have to Learn from Radical Orthodoxy: What Radical Orthodoxy Has to Learn from Catholic Theology', *Louvain Studies* 28 (2003): 232–9.

   10. Milbank, 'On Complex Space', in *The Word Made Strange*, 283; John Milbank, 'Culture: The Gospel of Affinity', in *Being Reconciled: Ontology and Pardon* (Oxon: Routledge, 2004), 204–5.

   11. This might be overlooked by those who criticize Milbank for presumably regarding truth as merely a linguistic construction and for privileging a hermeneutic of suspicion over the theological search for truth (Todd Breyfogle, 'Is There Room for Political Philosophy in Postmodern Critical Augustinianism?' in *Deconstructing Radical Orthodoxy: Postmodern Theology, Rhetoric and Truth*, eds Wayne J. Hankey and Douglas Hedley (Aldershot: Ashgate, 2005), 32–3; Jon Marenbon, 'Aquinas, Radical Orthodoxy and the Importance of Truth', in *Deconstructing Radical Orthodoxy: Postmodern Theology, Rhetoric and Truth*, eds Wayne J. Hankey and Douglas Hedley (Aldershot: Ashgate, 2005), 60–1).

   12. Milbank, 'The Second Difference', in *The Word Made Strange*, 189.

demands, due to his appreciation of postmodern non-foundationalism.[13] Milbank's refusal to provide foundations can be partly defended on account of his concern not to pretend to offer a neutral and self-evident access to reality. At the same time, Milbank's equal rejection of the postmodern understanding of constructed ontologies as self-evidently deviating from the truth about reality entails that his ontology cannot demand an entirely arbitrary leap of faith in order to be accepted. For Milbank, an overarching ontology is meant to attune people to perceive *aright* how particular beings in the immanent world reveal knowledge about the nature of reality.[14]

Having identified, as one central problem with secularism, its concealing of the overarching ontology upon which it depends, Milbank defends the public relevance of Christian theology by presenting it as a solution to this problem. Against any pretended neutral access to reality, Milbank openly conjectures that the whole of reality is ordered harmoniously, which is why he refers to his vision as an ontology of peace. By inviting people to perceive reality fundamentally differently than they might have been culturally taught, Milbank seeks to free Western imaginations from any claims to possessing a neutral access to reality. Adopting the postmodern appreciation of particularity, Milbank's understanding of peace does not presuppose or seek out fundamental agreements, but peace is defined as 'the *sociality* of harmonious difference'.[15] According to his ontology of peace, particular beings belong both to a harmoniously ordered whole and exceed the whole in their very particularity.[16] The excess of particulars over the ordered whole means that Milbank's ontology must be continuously growing. As such, it is a cure to all fixed ontologies that undercut people's appreciation of genuine newness or difference.[17] In this way, Milbank apologetically defends his alternative

13. Shakespeare, *Radical Orthodoxy*, 150–2; Marenbon, 'Aquinas, Radical Orthodoxy and the Importance of Truth' in *Deconstructing Radical Orthodoxy*, 62; Lars Albinus, 'Radical Orthodoxy and Post-Structuralism: An Unholy Alliance', *Neue Zeitschrift für Systematische Theologie und Religionsphilosophie* 51: 340–354.

14. Milbank, 'Only Theology Overcomes Metaphysics', in *The Word Made Strange*, 36.

15. Milbank, *Theology and Social Theory*, 5.

16. Ibid.; Milbank, 'A Christological Poetics', in *The Word Made Strange*, 129; Milbank, 'Out of the Greenhouse', in *The Word Made Strange*, 261. In order not to purchase this high estimation of particularity, at the expense of the possibility to make claims about the whole, Milbank's metaphysics builds upon Aristotelian and Neo-Platonist philosophies (Milbank, *Beyond Secular Order*, 24). From Platonism, he retrieves the idea that material beings participate in their ideal perfection. However, Milbank also retrieves the Aristotelian understanding of the immanent world as an integral part of this ideal perfection. Developments in the immanent world expand the ideal forms positively (Milbank, 'A Christological Poetics', in *The Word Made Strange*, 129; Milbank, 'Out of the Greenhouse', in *The Word Made Strange*, 261).

17. Milbank, *Beyond Secular Order*, 24.

ontology by presenting it as being the solution to all of the problems that he associates with secularism.

With regard to the criticism of fideism, Milbank's critics are mistaken when they claim that the only way to see the truth of Milbank's ontology of peace is to be overwhelmed by the whole story that theology would possess as a sort of Gnostic secret knowledge.[18] The mistake made by his critics is to read Milbank's writings about a necessary wager in terms of an idealistic belief in harmony, despite the concrete evidence to the contrary.[19] However, Milbank's argument has shown that we can never reason from conflicting particulars to an overarching ontology. Supposedly conflicting particulars are not *self-evidently* falsifications of an overarching ontology of peace. To counter this perception, Milbank upholds both that reality is truly harmoniously ordered *and* that humanly constructed ontologies participate in this order to various degrees.[20] Refusing the legitimacy to reason from immanent reality to an overarching ontology, Milbank interprets immanent reality through the lens of his ontology of peace and can then indicate where real harmony is already partially realized, even if we are sometimes confronted with conflicting particulars. In this vein, Milbank speaks of a foreshadowing of ontological harmony within the churches, which renders the wager in favour of his ontology more acceptable.[21] People must not arbitrarily accept Milbank's ontology, but they must instead assume for a while that it might be an account that corresponds to reality and then interpret reality through this lens. If the ontology can stand the test, then people might be convinced that it is true. Before I explain in more detail how also Milbank defends his ontology by promising an enhancement of the common good, let me turn to how Graham Ward similarly seeks to disassociate the notion of contributing to a society's common good from collaborating with secularism.

c) Ward's Postmodern Solution: Decentring the Secularist Social Order

While Milbank rejects public theological apologetics in secularist terms, in order to warn against secularism's pretended neutrality, we find in Graham Ward a Radical Orthodox theologian who modifies this rejection. Whereas Milbank's critique is primarily directed against two (related) ontologies, Ward criticizes only the first.[22] Ward joins Milbank in problematizing modern positivism, because it reads

---

18. Shakespeare, *Radical Orthodoxy*, 152–3.

19. Mathewes, *A Theology of Public Life*, 132–3. Perhaps, Mathewes overlooks the Aristotelian influence on Milbank's thought and focuses, one-sidedly, on his Neo-Platonism.

20. Milbank, 'A Critique of the Theology of Right', in *The Word Made Strange*, 12; 28.

21. Milbank, 'Culture', in *Being Reconciled*, 204–5.

22. Ward primarily counters materialism and atomism. See Tonstad, *God and Difference*, 70, for a critique of Ward's criticism of 'ideologies of self-sufficiency', arguing that Ward fails to name those against whom this criticism is voiced and that his theological contribution to contemporary culture is, therefore, 'rather anemic'. For a similar critique

the world through an exclusively immanent frame, and denies that this reading is a culturally conditioned interpretation.[23] Like Milbank, Ward thus objects to modernity's assumed neutrality and concomitantly concealed perpetuation of Christianity's cultural dominance of former times.[24] Ward calls modern positivism a myth in the sense that it naturalizes that which is but a culturally specific social construct.[25] Ward criticizes contemporary culture for being deluded if it believes that the world, as it has been created by the West, is real.[26] Concomitantly, Ward rejects modern secularism as the naturalized ontology that serves as the sole legitimate centre for the social order of many Western societies.[27]

Furthermore, Ward then joins Milbank in the appreciation of the postmodern understanding of every human access to reality as being culturally conditioned.[28] Ward calls this postmodern non-foundationalism a 'weak hermeneutical ontology'.[29] However, while Milbank rejects postmodern non-foundationalism, as perpetuating the positivist myth of neutrality through concealing its foundations, Ward shows a greater belief that the postmodern

of the vacuousness of Ward's criticism of social atomism, see also Insole, 'Against Radical Orthodoxy', *Modern Theology* 20 (2004): 228–9.

23. Graham Ward, *Cities of God* (London: Routledge, 2000), 89. Ward refers to this positivism as reading the world without 'discernment'. See also Graham Ward, *Cultural Transformation* (Cambridge: Cambridge University Press, 2005), 1. Ward still maintains the same line of argumentation in his most recent work *How the Light Gets In*, 64, when he relates Christianity's crusading triumphalism in the early Middle Ages to 'purely intellectualist' modes of reasoning 'that provided seminal means for the procreation of secular reason' and advocates a proper theological combination of intellectual knowledge, liturgical practices and ethical living. He then also explains how theology as prayer shapes people's ability of discernment in greater detail (173–80).

24. Ward, *Cities of God*, 69.

25. Ward, 'The Myth of Secularism', *Telos* 167 (2014): 166; 179. Ward borrows this definition of myth from Roland Barthes, *Mythologies*, trans. Annette Lavers (London: Vintage Books, 2000), cit. by ibid., 177.

26. Graham Ward, *The Politics of Discipleship: Becoming Postmaterial Citizens* (Grand Rapids, MI: Baker Academic, 2009), 99. This contrasts Elaine Graham's claim that, in the wake of secularism, people live in 'a realm in which personal autonomy, reflexivity and freedom of belief are axiomatic', and who wants to incorporate believers into a 'Western cultural imaginary in which the general equilibrium point is 'firmly within immanence' (Graham, 'Unquiet Frontier', *Political Theology*, 38).

27. Ward, 'The Myth of Secularism', *Telos*, 166.

28. Ward, *Cities of God*, 69. This allows him to call secularization a discursive construction (Ward, 'The Myth of Secularism', *Telos*, 176). To indicate that secularization is not a natural development, Ward claims that post-secularity accompanied secularization from the start (168).

29. Ward, *Cities of God*, 20–1.

weak hermeneutical ontology corresponds to reality.[30] In other words, Ward interprets the postmodern ontology not as a perpetuation of, but as the beginning of a solution to the problem identified in modern secularism. He argues that the world has entered a postmodern order and claims that Christian theologians must presuppose a postmodern ontology for their own accounts of the world.[31] While Milbank attempts to invent an alternative ontology, to those implicitly advanced by postmodern philosophies, Ward accepts postmodernism as an overarching vision of reality and tries to show that, if correlated with Christian theology, this ontology would reach its own ends more successfully than if correlated with secularism.[32] In other words, the most crucial distinction between Milbank's and Ward's projects concerns Milbank's rejection of the postmodern ontology, whereas Ward accepts it and seeks to fulfil its aspirations by means of Christian theology.[33] Postmodern philosophies are only regarded as problematic according to the degree to which they still rely on modern metaphysics, a reliance which they themselves, however, aim to overcome.[34] Ward argues that the problem can be best solved

30. At the same time, Ward claims to remain critical of those who understand the postmodern ontology as self-evident natural law or even divine providence (Ward, *Politics of Discipleship*, 83).

31. Ward, *Cities of God*, 62. See also Ward, *Politics of Discipleship*, 76. Ward discusses in *Cultural Transformations and Religious Practices*, 19–60 that even Barth's opposition to apologetics still remains apologetical in the sense of being deeply rooted in the culture from which he spoke. Ward similarly emphasizes the same point of the cultural embeddedness of all Christian theology in *How the Light Gets In* more systematically as conditioning the development of the whole Christian tradition.

32. Ward's claim that postmodern philosophies fail to successfully overcome modernity, and that a postmodern critique of modernity must come 'from the other side of modernity' (Ward, *Cities of God*, 94) should also be understood in a weaker sense than that of Milbank, despite the close affinity they share on the surface.

33. The acceptance of a postmodern ontology implies, for Ward more particularly, that realities are understood as liquid and transmutation is written into the fabric of reality (Graham Ward, 'Transcorporeality: The Ontological Scandal', in *The Radical Orthodoxy Reader*, eds John Milbank and Simon Oliver (London: Routledge, 2009), 294–5; Ward, *Politics of Discipleship*, 83). Privileging, in his ontology, the categories of 'becoming' and 'contingency' over fixed schemes, beings are defined as only contingently stable and identifiable. This is also why Ward accepts that 'our trans-global mind-sets are pluralistic, pragmatic, multicultural, and profoundly hybrid' (Ward, 'The Myth of Secularism', *Telos*, 179). See also Tonstad, *God and Difference*, 65, for the more specific argument that Ward accepts the broader 'cultural-turn to desire, sexuality, and eros' and then 'connects sexuality with God so that Christian theology has a response to dominant, but unsatisfactory, cultural logics of sex and desire'. According to Tonstad, Ward ultimately fails to criticize contemporary culture and instead imports its problems into his understanding of God (59).

34. Ward, *Cities of God*, 94, 169.

through a correlation of postmodern metaphysical assumptions with Christian theology's analogical metaphysics.[35]

Ward's less antagonistic position towards postmodernism can be explained in relation to the way in which he and Milbank each problematize modern positivism. Although both agree that modern positivism is a reductive interpretation of reality, Milbank thinks that this distorted interpretation is connected to an economic and social system which is sufficiently perfect as to continuously cure its own defects.[36] In this sense, the flawed ontology is more powerful than the truth which it continues to undermine. The only way to excavate the truth from underneath the distorted ontology, and to decentre secularism from its position of organizing the societal whole, is to offer an alternative ontology that is as holistic as the currently predominant one. Ward, on the contrary, is more pessimistic about the future viability of the distorted modern positivist ontology when he claims that, without a theological critique, modernity would collapse.[37] In other words, modernity's untruthfulness to reality predetermines modernity to be naturally extinguished at some point, and postmodern non-foundationalism is welcomed as the first sign of modernity's collapse.[38] Postmodernism is already understood as the decentring of secularism, and in this sense as the advent of a solution to a political problem that is intrinsically self-destructive. Where Milbank offers an alternative comprehensive account of reality, as the cure to all the problems he associates with secularism, Ward, thus, joins postmodernity in its own attempt to free Western imaginations from positivism. The solution here offered to the problem of secularism's pretended self-evident interpretation of reality is to open people's eyes to perceive the infinite wealth of meaning contained in the immanent world, once again.

Accepting postmodernism as a new overarching ontology, Ward claims that 'we' live in a 'constant vertigo of semiosis'.[39] Words possess infinite possibilities of meaning. It is uncertain how precisely they relate to reality. Consequently, the Christian world view must replace its truth claims with weaker claims to authenticity.[40] The Christian discourse is, thus, presented as a cultural product

---

35. Ibid., 13. He defines these semiotics by way of five characteristics: The cultural mediation of all knowledge, as well as the excess of meaning of material beings to human interpretations are affirmed, all acts of interpretation are regarded as partly ideological, human beings are defined in economic terms and a 'weak hermeneutical ontology' is presupposed (ibid., 20–1).

36. Milbank, *Theology and Social Theory*, 195.

37. Ward, *Cities of God*, 94.

38. See for example Graham Ward, *Theology and Contemporary Critical Theory*, Second Edition (London: MacMillan Press, 1996, 2000), 160–2; 169–71.

39. Ward, *Cities of God*, 91.

40. Ibid., 71. This is more fully worked out in Ward's *Unbelievable: Why We Believe and Why We Don't* (London and New York: I. B. Tauris, 2014).

on the same level as any other.[41] According to Ward, there is no assurance to be given why one system of beliefs should be better than another, because 'our very believing rests upon a prior believing; reason gives way to persuasion'.[42] At the same time, accepting postmodernity as more truthful to reality than modernity, Ward appreciates persuasion as the dissemination of truth produced by truth itself, while modern scientific reason presumably produces truth.[43] In other words, it is important not to justify the public relevance of Christian faith in secularist terms, because any such justification would produce a truth that deviates from reality. Moreover, it seems as though Ward would defend a more marginal political role for Christian theology, seeing that he wants to position Christianity on the same level with any other faith tradition. It might, however, be the case that Ward would still ascribe to postmodernism a more central role in determining the entire social order than to others, which would then have to be assessed in relation to Milbank's argument that postmodernity itself still perpetuates the tradition of Christianity's cultural dominance. While this issue will be further elucidated throughout the course of this chapter, I now turn to investigate in greater detail how Ward's problematization of secularism is again connected to a particular apologetic defence of Christian theology.

d) Defending Christian Theology: Solving Postmodern Problems

The non-foundationalist repercussions of Ward's theology have invited the criticism that Ward is more influenced by postmodern philosophies than by the Christian theological tradition.[44] Ward is said to escape the theological struggle of determining orthodoxy by merely appreciating the particularity of any religion as such in a postmodern fashion.[45] This renders Ward more vulnerable to the criticism of fideism than Milbank. All particular faith communities are judged as being equally good because they resist the dominance of secular liberalism in contemporary culture.[46] Ward then fails to specify the criteria by which Christianity in particular could be publicly justified. In other words, he simply accepts the framework of Christian doctrines as unproblematic on the basis of the postmodern conviction that the particularity of faith traditions must be maintained against

---

41. Ward, *Cities of God*, 13.

42. Ibid., 73.

43. Ward, 'The Weakness of Believing', *Culture, Theory and Critique* 52 (2011): 243.

44. Tanner, review of *Christ and Culture*, *Modern Theology* 23 (2007): 483; Smith, *Introducing Radical Orthodoxy*, 118–19. Ward has been said to 'more or less "baptize" poststructuralist deconstruction' (Wisse, 'Introduction to the Thinking of Graham Ward', in *Between Philosophy and Theology: Contemporary Interpretations of Christianity*, 68).

45. Smith, *Introducing Radical Orthodoxy*, 118–19.

46. Ward criticizes contemporary culture for being governed too blindly by economic forces (Ward, *Politics of Discipleship*, 116).

the dangers of one monolithic culture.[47] Contrary to these criticisms, I interpret Ward's theology as being driven precisely by the predominant concern to justify the reasonableness of Christianity in postmodern terms. In other words, Ward offers an apologetics of Christianity for what he perceives to be a postmodern mainstream culture.

Overall, Ward justifies Christian theology by presenting it as the solution to problems identified by postmodern philosophers. He argues that Christian theology is better able to attain the postmodern aim of overcoming modern positivism than any atheist postmodern philosophy.[48] Accepting certain postmodern basic assumptions as true, Ward conceives of a space that is opened up through the non-foundationalist suspension of being in possession of the truth.[49] The Christian faith, just like any other belief system, is involved in the politics and metaphysics of organizing this space. On this basis, Ward then, however, problematizes postmodern culture, by arguing that, in its atheistic variants, postmodernism uses its own ontology in a disadvantageous manner.[50] He suspects postmodern culture of rendering non-foundationalism into a new foundation, which should be prevented by Christian theology. Christian theology should use the postmodern non-foundationalist framework in a better way; namely, to confront Christians with the lack of foundations of their faith continuously.[51] As such, he strives to overcome what he conceives as problematic tendency to regard one's own interpretation of reality as being self-evidently true. In other words, Ward's correlation of a postmodern ontology with the Christian analogical world view, far from resolving the instability of meaning, is actually geared to preserve it.[52] Instead of offering an alternative vision of the whole of reality to the prevalent

47. This is also why Ward, like Milbank, has been criticized for refusing to use non-Christian vocabulary that supposedly would be more accessible to a wider public (Graham, *Between a Rock and a Hard Place*, 126; 129–30).

48. Ward criticizes nihilistic renderings of the postmodern ontology inasmuch as they propagate the belief in insurmountable particularity, which might dissolve the world into endless scattered places. At this point, Ward is in agreement with Milbank that some sort of unity, to which all particulars belong, must be believed in (Ward, *Cities of God*, 95).

49. Ibid., 73.

50. Ward, *Politics of Discipleship*, 84. For example, non-foundationalism too easily accommodates arbitrary market mechanisms, insofar as it is advantageous for free market capitalism that people have no strong commitments, as this predisposes them to be constantly persuaded by changing trends.

51. In this sense, Ward wants Christian theology to transcend postmodernism (*Cities of God*, 70).

52. If Ward's Christologically based understanding is being criticized for forgetting that all religion is but a human way of coping with the incomprehensible vastness of the universe (Beverley Clack, 'Radical Orthodoxy and Feminist Philosophy of Religion', in *Interpreting the Postmodern*, 215–29), one might counter that, according to Ward, the Christian faith is rather meant to reflect the incomprehensible vastness of the universe, than to cope with it.

postmodern one, Ward apologetically defends theology's relevance by promising that a continuous theological reinterpretation of the immanent world overcomes the problem of reductive positivist readings of reality.[53]

Ward's claim, that 'nature cannot be natural without the spiritual informing it at every point',[54] must be understood in the context of his opposition to modern positivism. His insistence that 'there is only *one* radical critique of modernity – the critique that denies the existence of the secular as self-subsisting, that immanent self-ordering of the world which ultimately had no need for God. The secular to be secular requires a theological warrant',[55] is not meant to be as exclusivist as it sounds. Instead, anyone who does not regard their own interpretation of the immanent world as the only eternally valid one would participate in the solution of the problem posed by modernity, a solution affirmed by Ward's theology.[56] Against positivism, Ward advocates a more general re-mythologization of materiality with the aim to 'learn to see things otherwise'.[57] His own Christology is then presented as one such way of escaping positivism through a re-mythologization of reality.[58]

At this point, leaving the postmodern level of granting to each faith tradition equal legitimacy, Ward moves to the specificities of the Christian faith. He claims that the solution to contemporary *ills*[59] is to build a culture upon that which is 'true and good and realistic' and not on the 'shifting sands of ephemeral human desires'.[60] In the specific case of Christianity, to build a culture on that which is 'true and good and realistic' means to build a culture around Christ. For Ward, Christ orders reality in the sense that all cultural occurrences exist in Christ.[61] Christian theologians must interpret all beings in terms of their submission to Christ.[62] However, for Ward, this interpretation does not result in some all-encompassing ontology. To the contrary, he claims that understanding particular beings in

53. Ward, 'Spiritual Exercises', in *Christ and Culture*, 234. Christian theology must discern the purpose and appropriate recipient of every particular immanent being that is encountered (Ward, *Cities of God*, 88–9; 91).

54. Ward, *Cities of God*, 88.

55. Ibid., 94 (my emphasis).

56. Ward perceives all human attempts to represent immanent reality to be the ceaseless search for the ground for a legitimate understanding of material reality (Ward, 'Christology and Mimesis', in *Christ and Culture*, FN 22, 41). As a *ceaseless* search for a legitimate interpretation of reality, representation is always in a crisis, which according to Ward must lead to either madness or faith.

57. Ward, 'Spiritual Exercises', in *Christ and Culture*, 219.

58. Ibid., 220.

59. [My emphasis]. Ward names the present crisis of democracy among others.

60. Ward, *Politics of Discipleship*, 74.

61. Wisse, 'Introduction to the Thinking of Graham Ward', in *Between Philosophy and Theology*, 67; Ward, 'Spiritual Exercises', in *Christ and Culture*, 220, Ward, *Cultural Transformation*, 9.

62. Ward, 'The Schizoid Christ', in *Christ and Culture*, 89.

relation to Christ introduces some apophaticism concerning their meaning. Every particular being interpreted in relation to Christ is known only apophatically by a greater unknowing, instead of being unambiguously interpreted as this or that. This does not mean that the meaning of the being becomes entirely uncertain, but that in this very particular being's relation to Christ more than one definite meaning can be perceived.

Overall, when defending Christian theology apologetically for a postmodern audience, Ward is more hesitant than Milbank to pre-empt a wholeness and totality of reality prior to the eschaton. As such, Ward is closer to the position of public theologians such as Jeffrey Stout and Charles Mathewes. They agree that Christian theology affirms reality as one harmonious whole, but they deny that Christian theologians enjoy a privileged standpoint from which they can see how this harmonious whole is concretely constituted. Christian theology, therefore, cannot prescribe the social order for an entire society, because the theological affirmation of an ultimately harmonious reality remains unconvertible into concrete social structures to a considerable degree.

Despite this closeness to Mathewes and Stout, however, Ward's thought could lend itself to ascribe a more central political role to Christian theology in post-Christendom societies. Ward promises to fulfil postmodern aspirations to overcome secularism's imperialism, suggesting that everyone should perceive the infinite wealth of meaning in every particular being and, consequently, should concede that the harmonious order of reality cannot yet be fully captured by any single perspective. In contrast to Milbank's upholding of the Christian ontology as the best overarching vision of the whole of reality, Ward advocates the adherence to particular religious ontologies as an escape route from the domination of secularism's imperialist tendencies. Ward seems to assume that each faith tradition builds its culture on that which is 'true and good and realistic'. This is then vulnerable to Milbank's criticism of postmodernism: Ward assumes the most overarching perspective from which it can be seen that all particularities, except that of atheist secularism, are univocally legitimate. Since Ward moreover argues that Christian theology is better able to fulfil postmodernity's good aspirations, he implicitly advocates Christian theology as the best centre for the organization of the whole of society.

e) *Theological Contributions to the Common Good: Surpassing the Secularist Imaginative*

In sum, John Milbank's and Graham Ward's criticisms of modernity's positivist understanding of reality raise awareness for some problems with these (post) modern ontologies which are related to the question about theology's political role in post-Christendom societies. Milbank and Ward agree with the postmodern critique that secularism is forgetful of its own culturally conditioned status and illegitimately presents its universal claims as being neutral. Secularism, thus, disguisedly perpetuates Christianity's political dominance in times of Christendom, insofar as the notion that secularism should determine the social order, due to its alleged neutrality, is beyond discussion. Milbank then sees this pretended neutrality further perpetuated by postmodern ontologies, while Ward appreciates the postmodern, weak hermeneutical ontology as the first sign of the overcoming of secularism's disguisedly imperialistic assumption of some self-evident neutrality. As solutions to whatever they identify as problematic Milbank, then, constructs an alternative ontology, whereas Ward seeks to fulfil certain postmodern aspirations with the help of Christian theology. This renders Milbank apologetic insofar as he tries to convince people of his ontology by promising them that it is able to cure the problems which he associates with secularism, whereas Ward is engaged in an apologetic defence of Christianity by offering solutions to what certain postmodern philosophers understand as problematic. He shows how, from a postmodern perspective, it would be reasonable to accept Christian contributions to the political endeavour of enhancing post-Christendom societies. Highlighting that both Milbank's and Ward's positions are significantly determined by a problem-centred approach, which again lapses into apologetics at the point at which theological solutions are not publicly accepted, it remains to be examined as to how far this is further connected to an underestimation of the theological significance of a truly pluralist public. First, however, let me speculate how Radical Orthodoxy might criticize public theology, in relation to the latter's justification of the public relevance of political theology in secular terms.

While public theologians criticize the Radical Orthodox approach to political theology for being countercultural in its rejection of secularism as a common ground on which post-Christendom politics can proceed, my exposition of Milbank's and Ward's positions has made clear that they do not oppose secular justifications of Christianity's public relevance due to some general fear of accommodation to the surrounding culture. Instead, Radical Orthodoxy is cautious not to support the particular secularist social order, which imperialistically claims to be neutral. This criticism might apply to public theology insofar as public theologians believe that there is a culturally independent common good to which people from different backgrounds collectively strive. Milbank discloses this very belief as culturally specific,[63] and suggests to us to understand the public, not as a neutral space, but as the realm that is constituted by the encounter of different ontologies.[64] This implies

---

63. Milbank criticizes Habermas's idea of starting from within a tradition and striving towards universal reason by highlighting that there is no way to overcome the culturally specific beginnings from which one starts; even the striving for universal reason remains entirely within the tradition (Milbank, 'Ecclesiology: The Last of the Last', in *Being Reconciled*, 110). Although Elaine Graham finds Habermas's new introduction of religious arguments into an overall secular public sphere similarly unsatisfactory (Graham, 'Unquiet Frontier', *Political Theology*, 37), she nevertheless assumes that all Westerners share a common secularist mindset, an idea which she borrows from Charles Taylor (38).

64. John Milbank, 'The End of Dialogue', in *Christian Uniqueness Reconsidered: The Myth of a Pluralistic Theology of Religions*, ed. Gavin D'Costa (Maryknoll, NY: Orbis Books, 1992), 182.

that Christian theology as well as any other philosophy (religious or secular) must be understood as one particular interpretation of the whole of reality among others.[65] One might say that such a view constitutes a return to Christianity's political dominance only if Christianity is praised to provide the best ontology among this mélange. Moreover, the specific rejection of secularism as one such ontology can only be maintained if one agrees that secularism is a problem in need of a solution, which in this case would be its dissolution. Alternatively, one might, as a Christian theologian, agree with the Radical Orthodox criticism concerning secularism's pretended neutrality, but not agree that this disqualifies secularism altogether. In Chapters 4 and 5 specifically, I will show how a Christian theology that is not primarily concentrated on seeking solutions for existing problems, might be able to respond differently to what is found to be problematic in other people's beliefs and convictions. To clarify the point, at which I part ways with Radical Orthodoxy's cultural criticism, let us reconsider the public theological criticism concerning Radical Orthodoxy's advocated return to Christianity's dominance and its propagation of a, theologically illegitimate, church–world dualism.

2.2 Problematizing Universality: Christian Theology as Dynamic Centre of the Social Order

Although Radical Orthodoxy is in agreement with public theologians who purport that Christian theology is also politically relevant in post-Christendom societies, public theologians think of this relevance in terms of theological contributions to democratic discussions in a secular social order, while Milbank wants theology to offer an alternative understanding of the social order itself.[66] Ward shows how Christian theology can contribute to a public realm that is organized along postmodern sensibilities. This antagonism against secularism is presumably the reason why Radical Orthodoxy has repeatedly been criticized for advocating a return to Christendom.[67] Most particularly, this concerns the Radical Orthodox contention that the whole public would be a better place if it was understood in its relation to God, which leads us to the second public theological justification of theology's public relevance.

As well as arguing that Christian theology can contribute to the common good of an internally pluralist society, public theologians also justify theology's public relevance by way of highlighting the universality of Christian theological insights. This universality presumably implies that the relevance of Christian theological claims surpasses the bounds of the church, insofar as they are meant

65. Milbank, *Theology and Social Theory*, 106.

66. John Milbank, 'The Body by Love Possessed', in *The Future of Love: Essays in Political Theology* (London: SCM Press, 2009), 76.

67. Coles, 'Storied Others', *Modern Theology* 8 (1992): 331–3.

to speak to everybody. In the previous chapter, I have argued that, in relation to this justification, public theologians tend to re-ascribe to Christian theology a central political role. This conflicts with their own best intentions to overcome Christianity's political dominance of former times, in order to craft a political theology suitable to the contemporary post-Christendom context. Unaware of this blind spot in their own approach, public theologians object to the Radical Orthodox interpretation of Christianity's universality, due to its reliance on a dualism between Christian theology and non-Christian positions, resulting in the triumphant elevation of political theology over and above all other political outlooks. They criticize the Radical Orthodox understanding of theology, distinguished by its particular relation to God, as embracing all other positions within its own universal scope, and the presentation of non-Christian positions as depending one-sidedly on Christianity's universal knowledge, when it comes to questions concerning how the whole of society should be politically arranged. In what follows, I will show how Milbank's and Ward's respective attempts of reconceptualizing Christian universality, in terms of Christianity's participation in God, is precisely geared to overcome forms of Christian dominance that are believed to be disguisedly perpetuated by a secularist social order. Again, my task is then to disassociate this altogether valuable reconceptualization of Christian universality from the Christian triumphalism wherein Radical Orthodox authors clothe it, as they present it as the solution to one of secularism's problems.

a) Milbank's Expansive Universality: Participating in God's Ontological Incomprehensibility

While Milbank is being accused by certain public theologians to rely on a church–world dualism when praising his own theo-politics beyond all others, Milbank himself aims at understanding the relation between his own ontology and non-Christian positions much more dynamically. Noticeably, he does not conceive of Christian universal claims, as statically containing the truth about the whole world, and non-Christian claims, as univocally deviating from this truth, and therefore in need of conversion. Instead, Milbank associates theology's universality with the Christian faith in the whole world's participation in God. Non-Christian truth claims also participate in God who is the Truth, albeit it to differing degrees. Underlying this conception of universality is Milbank's understanding of God as superabundant goodness and as the self-reflexive reality in which the immanent world participates.[68] God is at once everything in its absolute fullness as well as its original source. The immanent world participates in God, which means that the harmony of which Milbank's ontology speaks is affirmed to exist primarily in God and by participation in this world.[69] On the one hand, this means that Christian theologians must attend to particular immanent instances of harmony, because

---

68. Milbank, *Theology and Social Theory*, 12.
69. John Milbank, 'History of the One God', *The Heythrop Journal* XXXVIII (1997): 393.

these are revelatory of God, may they occur within or outside of the bounds of the church. On the other hand, Christian theologians must also acknowledge in some way that the harmony in God remains greater than the harmony found in this world. According to Milbank, to affirm God, Christian theologians must affirm a reality which lies beyond their ontological comprehension and into which their ontology can, therefore, advance.[70]

It is important, however, that Milbank interprets God's incomprehensibility not in epistemological but in ontological terms.[71] God's incomprehensibility is said to be an attribute of God's very nature. God is intrinsically superabundant and self-reflexive.[72] Since reality is itself then imagined as being incomprehensible, in terms of expanding through continuously created newness, Christian theology does not aim to possess the *final* grasp of reality. A human ontology cannot eternally capture God in abstract terms that remain the same throughout history, because God continues to reveal something new about Godself through the existence of each new particular being.[73] Consequently, what God is can never be fixed in a universal abstraction or known in advance.[74] Instead, each finite existence, in manifesting God, is an excess to God's very nature and must further refine and expand the human knowledge of God, that is, theology.[75] In sum, the acknowledgement of God allows Milbank's ontology of peace, then, to claim perfect knowledge of the harmonious whole of reality at present,[76] and to maintain that reality is still greater than this perfect knowledge.

---

70. Ibid. This account of participation has been criticized by Nicholas Lash, 'Where Does Holy Teaching Leave Philosophy? Questions on Milbank's Aquinas', *Modern Theology* 15 (1999): 435. For a situating of the argument between Lash and Milbank in the wider theological debates of the 1990s and a demonstration of the degree to which Milbank's understanding of analogy has been shaped in and through his criticism of Lash, see Paul DeHart, 'On Being Heard but Not Seen', *Modern Theology* 26 (2010): 243–77. DeHart sides with Lash against Milbank's reading of analogy in Aquinas. De Hart is particularly critical of Milbank's claim that humankind has direct cognitive access to God through the perception of perfection in created beings (266). DeHart agrees with Lash that using perfection terms in theological speech means that we can affirm more than we can understand (270).

71. Milbank, 'The Force of Identity', in *The Word Made Strange*, 201. Equally, God cannot be a self-subsistent substance because this would imply that there is an outside to God which remains unaffected by God (Milbank, 'The Linguistic Turn as a Theological Turn', in *The Word Made Strange*, 110).

72. Milbank, *Beyond Secular Order*, 25; Milbank, 'Truth and Vision', in *Truth in Aquinas*, 25.

73. Milbank, *Beyond Secular Order*, 25.

74. John Milbank, 'Only Theology Saves Metaphysics: On the Modalities of Terror', in *Belief and Metaphysics*, eds Peter M. Candler Jr. and Conor Cunningham (London: SCM Press, 2007), 452.

75. Milbank, *The Monstrosity of Christ*, 137–8.

76. Milbank, *Beyond Secular Order*, 2.

Milbank cannot uphold his ontology as eternally valid, because he upholds that ontologies have to be constantly revised throughout the course of history in order to remain truthful to reality.[77] Milbank claims that an ontology that is directed towards truth cannot remain within its own hermeneutical circle.[78] From this it follows that Milbank's positioning of his own ontology above others, is not meant to be the best option eternally. Instead, it should be understood as constituting one crucial step on the continuous path into a harmony which is still greater than the present construction. Milbank here conceives of this path towards perfection, just like any hierarchy, as self-cancelling insofar as it is meant to initiate people into the truth.[79] While the stages of this hierarchy are not arbitrary but reasonable constructs, they are admitted to be conventional, to some degree, and in this sense also replaceable.[80] What counts as reasonable convention must stand the test of whether it preserves collective 'standards of excellence'.[81] There must be mutual judgement about how different instances of harmony are to be ranked on the common hierarchy, in the measure of their truth, goodness and beauty. How

---

77. Milbank, 'The Poverty of Niebuhrianism', in *The Word Made Strange*, 250. On the basis that reality is identified as the Good, what is truly real is always registered as pleasure (John Milbank, 'Beauty and the Soul', in *Theological Perspectives on God and Beauty*, eds John Milbank, Graham Ward, and Edith Wyschogrod (London: Trinity Press International, 2003), 24–5). The pleasure is both sensed and abstractly imagined. The abstraction of a sensed pleasure, thus, expands an ontology that is truthful to reality. See also Milbank, 'A Critique of the Theology of Right', in *The Word Made Strange*, 25–6, where Milbank criticizes Jeffrey Stout's position on virtue ethics, and argues against Stout that ontologies do not change arbitrarily, but due to irresistible reasons.

78. Milbank, 'A Critique of the Theology of Right', in *The Word Made Strange*, 28.

79. Milbank, 'Politics: Socialism by Grace', in *Being Reconciled*, 183. Concomitant with his criticism of postmodernity's univocal appreciation of all differences, Milbank laments that postmodern cultures fail to appreciate both 'hierarchical summits' and 'material depth' (Milbank, 'Ecclesiology', in *Being Reconciled*, 107; Milbank, 'On Complex Space', in *The Word Made Strange*, 275). The hierarchy he proposes is, then, meant to value differences in their particularity (Milbank, 'Politics', in *Being Reconciled*, 183). In this vein, it should be mentioned that Milbank opposes any premodern fixed hierarchical order, which he calls ideological insofar as it naturalizes an established hierarchy and fails to admit that any hierarchy is also a social convention (Milbank, 'On Complex Space', in *The Word Made Strange*, 283). In these ideological hierarchies, those at the top get there by chance, sheer power, capital or their ability to seduce the masses (Milbank, 'Politics', in *Being Reconciled*, 183). I, therefore, think that Milbank's self-defence in 'Faith, Reason, and Imagination', in *The Future of Love*, 329), is justified, that those interpreters might be mistaken who criticize him for advocating a conservative return to a premodern understanding of reality in the sense of a 'totally fixed, hierarchical, cosmic, and social order wherein all knew their place'.

80. Milbank, 'Ecclesiology', in *Being Reconciled*, 107. Milbank calls this a 'mythical hierarchy'.

81. Milbank, 'On Complex Space', in *The Word Made Strange*, 279.

a society hierarchizes its order is then not abstractable from some presumably rational principles, but the hierarchical ordering of apparently incommensurable differences must be discussed publicly and continuously. The order discovered is never definite then, but the discussion must be ongoing and the incommensurable individual must always be allowed to exceed the ordered whole.[82] Moreover, it should be acknowledged that, insofar as *all* particularities participate in God's goodness, the hierarchical degrees in which this goodness is mediated should be regarded as equalized on the most fundamental level.[83]

Altogether, Milbank thus presents his ontology of peace as universal precisely because it is not any fixed, abstract interpretative frame, but because it is flexible and dynamic. Milbank claims that Christian theology is the most universal in scope, because it must continue to incorporate all individual particulars, in their very uniqueness, into itself by way of relating their uniquenesses harmoniously to the already existing web of relations between all other unique particulars. Since this relation of unique particulars with each other is also believed to relate them to God, Christian theology must remain open to the future. God is believed to provide ever new unique particulars, which means that the Christian theological task of constructing a harmonious whole is eternally expanding. This also means that, precisely because Milbank affirms his own ontology as universally true, new unique particulars might expand and challenge the whole in such a way that his ontology of peace must be expressed differently in the future. Concerning the criticism that Milbank is advocating the re-establishment of Christendom, it should thus be noted that Milbank does not defend any simplistic return to the past.[84] He does not understand the church, in the sense of a pregiven social structure, to be the solution of all the problems that exist within society at present.[85]

---

82. Ibid., 279–80.

83. Milbank, 'Ecclesiology', in *Being Reconciled*, 107. In this way, Milbank thinks of hierarchy and egalitarianism in non-oppositional terms.

84. Milbank, 'On Complex Space', in *The Word Made Strange*, 285.

85. Milbank has received criticisms for not referring to any concrete church in his ecclesio-central theology, privileging the constant flux of ecclesial identity (Frederick Christian Bauerschmidt, 'The Word Made Speculative? John Milbank's Christological Poetics', *Modern Theology* 15 (1999): 426, 430; Alexander Sider, *To See History Doxologically: History and Holiness in John Howard Yoder's Ecclesiology* (Grand Rapids, MI: Eerdmans, 2014), 190). Milbank responds that he has consciously never talked of a particular church, 'since the Church is not particular, not primarily an institution at all, but a dissemination of love' (Milbank, 'On Theological Transgression', in *The Future of Love*, 166). Milbank argues that the Christian concept of love is intrinsically elusive, and as such resists any institutionalism. Moreover, he claims that Radical Orthodoxy is not meant to give rise to a 'rival church', but that, being ecumenical at its heart, Radical Orthodoxy could be embodied by different denominations (John Milbank, 'Alternative Protestantism: Radical Orthodoxy and the Reformed Tradition', in *Radical Orthodoxy and the Reformed Tradition*, 25–6). This reveals as mistaken all those who associate Milbank's Radical Orthodoxy with the post-liberal understanding of the Christian church

Up to this point, there is no problematic church–world dualism in this account, and Christians could interpret the whole of reality through this hermeneutic lens, without thereby necessarily advocating a return to Christianity's lost political dominance. The latter only results if Christians argued that everyone else must interpret reality through this lens, as well. This happens precisely when Milbank offers his ontology, based on material from the Christian tradition, as opening up a *better* future than contemporary secularism does.[86] In this move, Milbank ascribes to Christian theology the most central political role in post-Christendom societies.

b) Overcoming Secularism's Stagnation: Christianity as the Self-Exceeding Centre of the Social Order

Also at this point, it can be observed that Milbank turns to advocate the return to Christianity's lost dominance, when offering his theological reading of reality as a solution to a problem that he identifies in the current secular social order. In short, Milbank presents his theological ontology as better than secularism with regard to two issues that are also at the heart of public theology. In unison with public theology's attempt to do justice to the internally diversified societies of contemporary Western Europe, and contrary to the public theological suspicion against his work, Milbank argues that his ontology is better able to celebrate plurality in its positivity than secularism.[87] And second, he claims that his ontology is better suited to advancing a society's growth in the truly good at the point at which secularism is focused too one-sidedly at the restriction of damage.

Contrary to those who argue that Milbank's ontology overwrites the reality of pluralism, Milbank shows that, one way or the other, there is an overarching ontology in any case, according to which a plurality of particulars is perceived. Whereas contemporary secularism interprets plurality as the confrontation of fundamentally antagonistic differences, Milbank understands differences as positive mediations of the good.[88] Consequently, instead of understanding all world

as self-contained unity, independent from the wider culture (see, for example, Barbieri, 'The Post-Secular Problematic', in *At the Limits of the Secular*, 129–61; Kathryn Tanner, *Theories of Culture: A New Agenda for Theology* (Minneapolis, MN: Fortress Press, 1997), 97–9). Part of Tanner's misunderstanding seems to be contextual, being insufficiently aware that Milbank speaks from a British context in which, until recently, Christianity has been central to the government of the whole of society.

86. Milbank, *Theology and Social Theory*, xiv. Milbank's church is, then, the emergence of something genuinely new; the church is the double *excess* of theological thinking and practices (Milbank, 'On Complex Space', in *The Word Made Strange*, 285).

87. Milbank, *Theology and Social Theory*, xvi; Milbank, 'The End of Dialogue', in *The Future of Love*, 281. It should also be mentioned here that Mathewes agrees with Milbank on the issue of pluralism (Mathewes, *A Theology of Public Life*, 118, FN21).

88. Milbank, *Theology and Social Theory*, xvi; Milbank, 'The End of Dialogue', in *The Future of Love*, 281.

views that meet in post-Christendom societies as merely arbitrary interpretations of a reality that remains forever unknown, Milbank understands the encounter of different ontologies that constitute the public realm not to be pure chance encounters. Instead, he interprets these encounters as revealing bonds of sympathy between people that are more fundamental than the adherence to any particular world view.[89] The assumption of the existence of these bonds of sympathy at the most fundamental level of reality is no self-evident or supposedly neutral empirical observation. It is rather on the basis of his ontology that Milbank can assume that people are really interrelated by sympathy.[90] In the same vein, Milbank upholds that there is a true good to which all socially constructed ontologies aspire and which, to different degrees, they materialize.[91] Pluralism is, then, not interpreted as chaos to be managed, but as the result of the shared gift of a human nature that is open to develop into different cultural shapes.[92]

This means that Milbank conceives of ontologies on two levels: Every culture possesses an ontology in the sense of an overarching vision of how beings are constituted and interrelated. On a somewhat higher level, there is then his own ontology which embraces all others underneath itself by claiming that other world views make comprehensive sense of the whole of reality, but are unable to see that on a more fundamental level they are related to others.[93] On this more overarching level, Milbank presents his ontology of peace as the solution to the problem posed by its secular counterpart. Whereas the latter supposedly promotes an understanding of the pluralist public as the composition of self-enclosed communities based on equally singular self-subsistent ontologies, his ontology of peace is offered to unify the pluralist public, without thereby diminishing its internal diversity.[94] In this way, Milbank offers his Christian ontology as the solution to the identified lack of commitment to the common good in pluralist societies, and thus parallels public theologians in re-ascribing to Christian theology a more central political role than that of being just one sociocultural group among many others.

Also with regard to the question of a post-Christendom society's orientation to the common good, Milbank identifies as a further problem secularism's failure

---

89. John Milbank, 'Hume *Versus* Kant: Faith, Reason and Feeling', *Modern Theology* 27 (2011): 278.

90. Milbank, 'Culture', in *Being Reconciled*, 204–5.

91. Milbank, 'A Critique of the Theology of Right', in *The Word Made Strange*, 12; 28.

92. Milbank, *Beyond Secular Order*, 2.

93. This distinction is missed by Milbank's critics regularly, critics such as Graeme Smith, 'Pluralism and Justice: A Theological Critique of Red Toryism', *Political Theology* 13 (2012): 330–47 or Larsen, 'The Politics of Desire', *Modern Theology* 29 (2013): 301, who claim that Milbank is unable to appreciate true plurality due to his preference for his own ontological metanarrative.

94. This explanation puts into question the criticism that Milbank could not envision peace between Christians and non-Christians (see, for example, Doak, 'The Politics of Radical Orthodoxy', *Theological Studies* 68 (2007): 377).

to ascribe any substance to what should be regarded as good. He laments that secularism encourages everyone simply to relate to the common good as that which remains forever unknown, and argues that such reluctance to define the common good positively undermines a society's advancement towards a better future.[95] If the common good, as that which is constituted by all social relations within a society (and beyond, if it is understood on a global scale), is believed to remain forever unknown, human beings can only be imagined as being bound together by negative restrictions on their otherwise unlimited freedom.[96] This refusal to define the common good more substantially incurs the danger of being indifferent to the particularity of anyone and anything that occurs as long as it does not interfere with one's own position. Milbank claims that such a conception can only confirm the liberal bourgeois world as it is. There is no possible argument for any substantial change to the social order, for no particular constellation of beings can be regarded as realizing the common good better than any other.[97]

Having identified this problem concerning secularism's insufficiently substantial account of the common good, Milbank then offers his Christian ontology as a solution. According to Milbank, only the affirmation of God, in the sense outlined above, helps a society to advance towards perfection and not to stagnate with the status quo.[98] A politics based on the belief that reality is abundantly good is not one aimed at the mere minimalization of damage.[99] If God is excessive goodness, a politics that affirms its participation in God must aim to constitute an excess to the already realized goodness. Regarding the question of how a society knows what constitutes genuine goodness, Milbank claims that both praxis and political discussions about the common good should not be understood as secondary applications of something which has already been understood abstractly. Instead, praxis and discussions about the good intrinsically belong to the real excess of goodness.[100] And, as something always already partially realized within this world, the notion of the common good is never merely an empty placeholder, but has always already some substantial filling.

95. Milbank, 'A Critique of the Theology of Right', in *The Word Made Strange*, 12.

96. Ibid., 7, 12.

97. Moreover, such an abandonment of ontological claims leaves room for dangerously irrational sects and cults to answer questions about objective truth and goodness (Milbank, 'Only Theology Saves Metaphysics', in *Belief and Metaphysics*, 456).

98. Milbank, 'A Critique of the Theology of Right', in *The Word Made Strange*, 12. This is then also why the criticism that Milbank could better contribute to the existent democracy, if he refrained from using theological vocabulary (Stout, *Democracy and Tradition*, 92–4; 99), misses the point. Stout understands democracy in terms of a struggle to find a publicly acceptable compromise about the truth. Milbank's concern is precisely to offer an alternative to this understanding of democracy.

99. Milbank, 'The Poverty of Niebuhrianism', in *The Word Made Strange*, 236–7.

100. Milbank, *Theology and Social Theory*, 13; Milbank, *Beyond Secular Order*, 29–30.

And since God's goodness itself still expands through each new mediation in the immanent world, the substance of the good is continuously growing. Accordingly, politicians know their own aim of advancing in the common good only through the actual praxis of goodness, for this praxis further expands the substance of goodness.[101] In other words, political agents increasingly come to know more of the substance of the common good precisely in the instantiation of their projects.[102] This conflicts with Stackhouse's understanding of public theology, as the discipline that can indicate the probable direction, which history will take dependent on what fundamental world view is adopted.[103] Stackhouse might have an all too idealistic understanding of world views that cannot account for how world views develop their ideas through attention to historical praxes.

Democratic *discussions* about the common good should manifest a particular society's fiction of the good and ought to be complementary to the political praxis of goodness.[104] Political discussions about the common good are seen not as secondary attempts to describe a good which exists independently; instead, the human discourse about the good co-determines the historical development of goodness, and therefore the particular direction of the excess of the substantial good.[105] Although Milbank calls this a fiction, it should nevertheless be determined as closely as possible by the good itself. To this end, the good must be allowed to act upon the people involved in these democratic discussions. In order for this to occur, one should defend one's own particular understanding of the best project, insofar as this is accompanied by an opening up of oneself to failure and correction by the truly good, which could be better mediated by someone else.[106]

Overall, this shows that Milbank turns to defend theology's central role in a pluralist post-Christendom society, at the point at which he promises that Christian theology is *better* able, than its secular counterpart, to appreciate the positive differences of a plurality of world views, and to organize this plurality along the lines of an ever-expanding, good social order. The contextuality of Milbank's

---

101. Milbank, *Beyond Secular Order*, 29–30; see also Milbank, 'History of the One God', *The Heythrop Journal*, 393; Milbank, *Theology and Social Theory*, 12; 17. Milbank's understanding of metaphysics contrasts Elaine Graham's claim that those who evoke the virtue of metaphysics for the welfare of the whole public remain unhelpfully abstract, which is why she turns to practice (Graham, 'Unquiet Frontier', *Political Theology*, 42). Milbank helps us to see that, while partly depending on a metaphysical framework, every practice expands on this metaphysical framework.

102. Milbank, *Theology and Social Theory*, 13; Milbank, *Beyond Secular Order*, 29–30.

103. Max Stackhouse, 'Introduction', in *Christ and the Dominions of Civilization. God and Globalization: Theological Ethics and the Spheres of Life*, vol. 3, eds Max L. Stackhouse and Diane B. Obenchain (Harrisburg: Trinity Press International, 2002), 56. However, it must be stated, in Stackhouse's defence, that he denies strict predictability of the future.

104. Milbank, 'A Critique of the Theology of Right', in *The Word Made Strange*, 29.

105. Milbank, 'Hume *versus* Kant', *Modern Theology* 27 (2011): 286.

106. Milbank, 'Violence: Double Passivity', in *Being Reconciled*, 39–40.

apologetic defence of Christian theology against secularism appears inasmuch as he advocates the superiority of his own Christian theology over secularism. Whether Christian theology should also be as central in the organization of societies, which are not dominated by secularism, is a matter that would have to be demonstrated separately. One problem with Milbank's apologetic defence concerns his quick conclusion from the observation of the failure of all attempts *to date* to overcome the situation in which one all-encompassing ontology determines the social order for a pluralist society that, therefore, such an overcoming is *in principle* impossible. In this context, Ward's theology can be understood precisely as the attempt to appreciate the critique of one dominating culture more sincerely, and to re-envision a Christian theology which no longer presents itself as the centre of a post-Christendom society. The degree to which Ward succeeds in this endeavour will once again be assessed in relation to how he manages to re-conceptualize Christian universality in a non-dominating manner.

c) Ward's Disruptive Universality: Participating in God's Epistemological Incomprehensibility

In some consonance with public theology and John Milbank, Ward affirms that Christian theology aims for a universal vision on everything.[107] As a comprehensive view about reality, Christian theology must be open and attentive to everything that occurs in the world. As for Milbank so for Ward, the affirmation of God assures that Christian theology is not a closed system, but remains intrinsically open.[108] Whereas Milbank has referred to God's ontological incomprehensibility, however, Ward regards a Christian ontology as being inherently open due to God's *epistemological* incomprehensibility. God is the ultimately unknowable. Ward emphasizes God's unknowability in order to acknowledge the possibility of divine interventions in any Christian understanding of reality.[109] Talk about 'divine interventions' suggests that Christian theological deliberations about reality might not just need to be constantly expanded, as in Milbank's vision, but can also be corrected and revised more substantially. Thus, where Milbank identified secularism's lack of a substantial understanding of the common good as a problem in need of a theological solution, Ward maintains that Christian theology must leave its understanding of God, and thus also of the good, substantially empty, at least to some degree.

Although this might look like a much humbler outlook than Milbank's own, Ward calls his vision of reality 'the truth'.[110] Turning his apophaticism into a positive, universal claim about the nature of reality, Ward generalizes that it is

---

107. Ward, *Politics of Discipleship*, 79.

108. Ward, 'Transcorporeality', in *The Radical Orthodoxy Reader*, 292.

109. Ibid.

110. Graham Ward, 'Radical Orthodoxy and/as Cultural Politics', in *Radical Orthodoxy? – A Catholic Enquiry*, 110.

redemptive to follow one particular faith tradition, without ever aiming in so doing to either grasp or explain God.[111] In other words, Ward still offers his ontology as the solution to what he identifies as problematic, even if the latter differs from Milbank's diagnosis. According to Ward, contemporary culture needs to be redeemed from its striving to control reality.[112] On this basis, he then presents Christian orthodoxy as the solution that can 'deliver the "salvation" promised by God'.[113] Christian theology can redeem the world by counteracting the problems associated with positivist control over reality, through stimulating people to live with the risk intrinsic to the life of faith.[114] Since, according to Ward, there is no assurance that God exists, any faithful surrender to God is bound to remain ambiguous. It is bound to remain uncertain whether the faithful are really attracted by God or whether the desire for God is merely a human projection.[115] For Ward, the act of faith should not resolve this ambiguity. Quite the contrary, Ward evaluates as problematic when Christians claim with too much certainty substantial knowledge about God and the world.

And yet, Ward offers his own Christian reading of reality in relation to God as a solution that should aid society's overcoming of the errors of positivism.[116] Reading reality in relation to God, who remains to a considerable degree substantially unknowable, is being presented as the solution, insofar as such an interpretation of each existing being in its relation to God is meant to allow one to perceive of an infinity of possibilities of what this being truly is. Ward refers to an experience of 'vertigo' if reality is read through the lens of his own Christian theology.[117] While emphatically claiming that he cannot assure that the acknowledged instability of meaning will ultimately lead to fulfilment, and not to dissolution,[118] Ward's entire argument, that embracing this instability is better than denying it by way of some positivist fixation, relies on more insight into the true nature of reality than Ward

---

111. Ward, 'Spiritual Exercises', in *Christ and Culture*, 224–5.

112. This is not a literal following of the biblical texts, but a continuation of the interpretation of reality and God that has been initiated by the Christian scriptures.

113. Graham Ward, 'Receiving the Gift', *Modern Theology* 30 (2014): 85.

114. Indeed, Ward has earned the criticism that his one-sided preference for apophaticism insufficiently acknowledges how the Christian tradition has always also claimed to possess some positive knowledge of God (Ralph Norman, review of *Christ and Culture*, by Graham Ward, *International Journal of Systematic Theology* (2007): 244; Tanner, 'review of *Christ and Culture*', *Modern Theology*, 483).

115. Graham Ward, 'De Certeau and an Enquiry into Believing', in *Between Philosophy and Theology: Contemporary Interpretations of Christianity* (Farnham: Ashgate, 2014), 80.

116. Ward, *Cities of God*, 88. This focus on God, as the power which sustains all objects, is meant to overcome the positive understanding of beings as self-contained entities, and to correspond to the postmodern understanding of beings as most fundamentally contingent and as always involved in a process of becoming (Ibid., 87).

117. Ward, 'Transcorporeality', in *The Radical Orthodoxy Reader*, 294–5.

118. Ibid., 302.

might feel comfortable to admit. If his own theological reading of reality would be on a par with modern positivism, each standing equal chances in leading either to destruction or to fulfilment, Ward could not offer his own ontology as the solution to the problems he associates with positivism.

From his Christian perspective, Ward evaluates positivists as those who must be converted to a more adequate understanding of reality.[119] As a solution to the errors of positivism, Ward advocates a fideistic obedient following of the Christian understanding of God, and reality as narrated in Christ.[120] Simultaneously, Ward appreciates any other (faith) tradition that equally opposes what he regards as being the major contemporary cultural ill.[121] Any faith tradition must be inhabited as a way through which reality is interpreted and engaged.[122] Despite this seemingly extraordinarily humble gesture, I view Ward's position as more disguisedly universalist than Milbank's.[123] Ward appreciates other world views precisely to the

---

119. Burrus, 'Radical Orthodoxy and the Heresiological Habit', in *Interpreting the Postmodern*, 37. Ward is accused of flattening their positions into one reductionist philosophy, one which can then be defeated (43). Milbank has been criticized for the same mistake of generalizing his opponents into one defeatable position (Rowan Williams, 'Saving Time: Thoughts on Practice, Patience and Vision', *New Blackfriars* 73 (2007): 320; Hyman, *The Predicament of Postmodern Theology*, 3).

120. This is not a literal following of the biblical texts, but a continuation of the interpretation of reality and God that has been initiated by the Christian scriptures.

121. Ward, *Politics of Discipleship*, 74. For example, Ward praises green parties and environmentalists, or critical theories originating in the *Frankfurter Schule* (Ward, 'Radical Orthodoxy and/as Cultural Politics', in *Radical Orthodoxy? – A Catholic Enquiry*, 103–4). The criticism that Ward fails to see anything good outside Christian theology and the church (Graham, *Between a Rock and a Hard Place*, 129) should thus be slightly more nuanced. For more examples of what Ward appreciates in contemporary culture see Ward, *Politics of Discipleship*, 218–9.

122. Ward, 'Introduction', in *Christ and Culture*, 18–19. Doctrinal propositions are one integral part of this inhabitation (Ward, 'Allegoria Amoris: A Christian Ethics', in *Christ and Culture*, 217). This means that those critics who claim that Ward (and Milbank) eclipse the church's struggle to incarnate Christ in order to redeem the world by way of equating 'intellectual virtuosity' with redemption, might be mistaken (Reno, 'The Radical Orthodoxy Project', *First Things* (February 2000), cit. by Ford, 'Radical Orthodoxy and the Future of British Theology', *Scottish Journal of Theology* 54 (2001): 394). The Radical Orthodox claim that a correct Christian understanding of reality is integral to the church's task of furthering the world's redemption does not mean that more practical ecclesial tasks have been eclipsed. It is merely stated that the interpretative framework, in which the practice is meant to take shape, is of great relevance.

123. That Ward assumes a universal human nature prior to culture is evident, for example, in his investigation of what makes humans believing beings in *Unbelievable: Why We Believe and Why We Don't*. He assumes that there is a shared human nature, 'an anthropological a priori' disposition to belief (Ward, *How the Light Gets In*, 260), and that the different kind of beliefs humans have are variations of this more fundamental disposition.

extent that they solve the problem he identifies, from his Christian perspective, in contemporary society. At one point, in a text about Christianity, he even claims that 'in fact, "Christian theology" in this text could be replaced with any other cultural practice'.[124] Far from evidencing humility or tolerance, Ward assumes that Christianity's particularity is universal in such a way that it adequately knows what is good about other world views, without attending to their particularities.

Overall, on the one hand, Ward's emphatic denial, of his possessing privileged knowledge of reality on the basis of his adherence to the Christian faith, could be said to lend itself less to the accusation of seeking to revive Christianity's lost cultural dominance of former times than Milbank's. On the other hand, however, Ward presents it as universally true that God is unknowable and that, consequently, the meaning of the whole of reality is unstable, open to change at any moment in accordance with a new divine intervention. The consequences of this understanding of universality for the political role of Christian theology in post-Christendom societies are assessed in the following section.

d) Overcoming Secularism's Fatigue: Christian Theology as Disruptive Centre of the Social Order

Regarding the criticism that Radical Orthodoxy defends a remnant of Christendom, it is important to highlight that Ward calls Christianity 'intrinsically imperialist'.[125] Imperialism has always been a part of the Christian world view, because the territory inhabited by any present church has never been regarded as the whole of reality.[126] Like Milbank, Ward also distinguishes between the role of the church and the role of Christian theology in a pluralist, post-Christendom society. Let me first explain Ward's understanding of the church, and then I will examine, subsequently, Ward's understanding of the role of Christian theology regarding the need to contribute to the entire society's common good and to organize a democracy.

Concomitant with his understanding of God as unknowable, Ward claims that the church needs to be continuously unsettled and displaced by others in order to remain true to itself.[127] At the same time, he refers to displacement in terms of a movement accompanying expansion.[128] The church expands towards

---

124. Ward, *Cultural Transformation*, 8.

125. Ward, *Politics of Discipleship*, 84.

126. Ibid., 90–1.

127. This is why Ward's theology has been appreciated for construing the Christian church as intrinsically open and permeable (Shakespeare, *Radical Orthodoxy*, 142; Doak, 'The Politics of Radical Orthodoxy', *Theological Studies*, 389–90). However, the same ecclesiology has also been criticized for no longer being able to distinguish between being human and being redeemed (Smith, *Introducing Radical Orthodoxy*, 257).

128. Ward, 'Transcorporeality', in *The Radical Orthodoxy Reader*, 299. Ward has been criticized for using the terms 'displacement', 'expansion', 'transformation' and 'cancellation'

its eschatological end through being constantly fractured.[129] Ward does not refer to the church's expansion in triumphant imperialist terms, but in terms of brokenness and woundedness.[130] This view highlights the church's suffering due to its dependence on its surroundings. Ward stresses that the church is constantly relocated, as it lives 'on the edge of both itself and what is other'.[131] Ward, like Milbank, highlights that the incorporation of individuals into the church should not eliminate their unique particularity.[132] Individual differences can be harmoniously blended into one whole, according to Milbank, while they effect an endless fracturing according to Ward. This suggests that, on the level of ecclesiology, Ward resists the charge of perpetuating Christendom imperialism. The integration of other cultures into the church is no longer thought of in terms of adapting the other culture to Christianity primarily, but in terms of unsettling the church through the confrontation with the other culture and, in this sense, in terms of a continuous remodelling of the church. How Ward envisions *theology's* political role in post-Christendom societies remains to be examined.

For Ward, acknowledging God as active governor and regarding Christian theology as participating in this government means, participating in the entire world's perfection, a position not unlike Milbank's.[133] For Ward, however, working towards the world's eschatological perfection does not mean interrelating unique particulars into an ever-expanding harmonious whole. Instead, each particular being is perfected insofar as its identity is continuously displaced. Any stagnation, prior to the attainment of eschatological perfection, must be prevented. Perfection is, thus, understood not in terms of growth, but in terms of dynamism in contrast to fixity. While Milbank understands the perfection of a being in terms of its excess to the expanding whole, Ward's displacement of immanent beings towards their perfection in God means to continuously disrupt the whole.

This emphasis on displacement figures into how Ward envisions a Christian theological contribution to democracy. Whereas Milbank defends a Christian social order by promising to ensure a positive evaluation of pluralism, Ward argues

indiscriminately without specifying the degree to which these terms differently indicate similarity and difference (Tonstad, *God and Difference*, 73).

129. Ward, 'Transcorporeality', in *The Radical Orthodoxy Reader*, 301–2.

130. Ibid., 302; Ward, 'The Body of the Church and its Erotic Politics', in *Christ and Culture*, 108. This emphasis on woundedness and suffering has been criticized for not only following a contemporary cultural trend (Tonstad, *God and Difference*, 70), but also for being symptomatic of an insufficient distinction between finitude and sin in Ward's theology (74–5). I will return to this criticism in my discussion of Ward's understanding of grace.

131. Ward, 'The Body of the Church', in *Christ and Culture*, 107. For example, Ward reads the circumstance that Christians are not only members of the church, but also of other associations as the fracturing of the church and the church's living beyond its boundaries (Ward, *Politics of Discipleship*, 188).

132. Ward, 'The Body of the Church', in *Christ and Culture*, 108.

133. Ward, 'Transcorporeality', in *The Radical Orthodoxy Reader*, 294–5.

that Christian theology can help to achieve true plurality through stirring dispute and contestation.[134] Liberal tolerance should be replaced by dispute, which is why a theologically grounded assertion of one's own position, as well as a clear naming of one's opponent, is needed.[135] In other words, whereas Milbank suggests that Christian theology can enhance democracies through ensuring that discussions are directed towards growth in the truly good, Ward promises to rejuvenate democracies by ensuring that everyone gets to participate in the discussion, and in this way to counter the widespread fatigue with politics. Again, this would, however, re-ascribe a central role to Christian theology in the social order, since it is Ward's Christian conviction that this dispute and contestation would lead to greater harmony and not to warfare.

In sum, Ward's understanding of the political role played by Christian theology in a post-Christendom context must be appreciated for taking into account, more than Milbank does, that the re-establishment of an overarching Christian social order has become problematic.[136] He, thus, shows greater respect to those contemporaries who for various reasons object to any such project. However, Ward's affinity with postmodern philosophies might render him vulnerable to Milbank's criticism of the latter. Ward follows postmodernism in perpetuating an implicit overarching ontology, tending to value world views that are structurally similar to his own over those that are genuinely different. Moreover, Ward's position ends up re-ascribing the most central role in organizing post-Christendom societies to Christian theology. As in the case of public theology, this is connected to Ward's apologetic approach. He defends the political relevance of Christian theology in a postmodern context to the effect that Christian theology is advocated as best able to organize the entire society.

e) Appeals to Christianity's Universality: Surpassing Christian Dominance

Overall, both Milbank and Ward offer ways of understanding Christian universality in dynamic terms that, on the level of ecclesiology, serves to evade the criticism of advocating a return to Christendom. Both Milbank and Ward understand the church to be a community of people that must continuously adapt its organization and structure in accordance with insights derived from surrounding cultures. Nevertheless, both Milbank and Ward remain within the problems of Christendom insofar as they apologetically defend Christian theology as being best able to organize the entire society. Milbank re-envisions a Christian social

---

134. Ward, *Politics of Discipleship*, 180. Similarly, Ward argues that cultural hermeneutics should not orient itself towards the fusion of, but at the critical engagement between, horizons (Ward, *Cultural Transformations and Religious Practice*, 66–7).

135. Ward, *Politics of Discipleship*, 162–3.

136. See for example Ward, *Cultural Transformations and Religious Practice*, 77. See Doak, 'The Politics of Radical Orthodoxy', *Theological Studies*, 368–93, for an argument that Ward succeeds in overcoming the remnant of Christendom that Milbank maintains.

order; Ward holds Christian theology responsible for organizing the encounter between different world views in such a way that the social order of the whole will continue to be disrupted and, in this way, correspond to his own theological vision of reality.

Appreciating Milbank's positive and harmonious evaluation of pluralism, I remain sceptical regarding the question of whether this Christian theological understanding of pluralism should be used apologetically to defend Christian theology's public relevance and to effectively re-ascribe the most central political role in post-Christendom societies to Christian theology. This apologetic defence risks undermining the theological significance of criticisms of Christianity's dominant past and the opposition to theological contributions to public politics. Nonetheless, Christian theologians could use this positive understanding of pluralism as a hermeneutical lens for their interpretation of reality, while not demanding the acceptance of this hermeneutic lens by non-Christians as well.

For now, it can be observed that public theologians are so concerned with not re-establishing a position of Christian hegemony that they tend to co-opt a secularist dismissal of a more positive understanding of pluralism. They say that Christianity must be identifiable as one particular tradition among others in a post-Christendom context.[137] This would, supposedly, be an adequate adaption of Christianity to 'the realities of pluralism'.[138] The discussion above has made clear that there is no neutrally given understanding of the reality of pluralism, but that pluralism must be interpreted from the perspective of some particular ontology.[139] A closer investigation of the public theological understanding of pluralism shows that the sub-discipline tends to operate within a secularist ontology of violence, one which might be too fixed and might inhibit a society's growth towards eschatological perfection.

Many public theologians rely on Max Stackhouse's engagement with pluralism who at first glance seems to be in agreement with Milbank when he claims that a shared framework is necessary for meaningful public debate to take place.[140]

---

137. Thiemann, *Constructing a Public Theology*, 19, cit. by Graham, *Between a Rock and a Hard Place*, 103–4.

138. Graham, *Between a Rock and a Hard Place*, 71; see also 103–4; see also Jeffrey Stout, 'Pragmatism and Democracy: Assessing Jeffrey Stout's *Democracy and Tradition*', *Journal of the American Academy of Religion* 78 (2010), ed. Jason Springs: 441, who equally regards contemporary pluralism as 'a given' that must be considered in political discussions about justice.

139. This also challenges Elaine Graham's claim that it is impossible to disinvent secularism in the sense of no longer being aware that there are a plurality of beliefs and unbeliefs (Graham, 'Unquiet Frontier', *Political Theology*, 38). One could argue that there is not just one perspective on the coexistence of different beliefs, but that the different beliefs inform the way in which this coexistence is viewed.

140. Max Stackhouse, 'Commentary: Public Theology and Democracy's Future', 2004 Templeton Lecture, *The Review of Faith & International Affairs* 7(2) (2009): 50. Stackhouse's

However, for Stackhouse, this shared framework is not an alternative ontology to the prevalent one; he thinks of a normative framework that can guard a society against potential disorder, thus exhibiting an underlying belief in what Milbank calls 'ontologies of violence'. As a theological ethicist, Stackhouse understands faith traditions to be endowed with a restraining function of the spiritual powers which otherwise will lead the world towards chaotic destruction.[141] He speaks of 'globalising powers' in the face of which complex civilizations must be generated, restrained or guided.[142] On this basis, public theology is then presented as being endowed with the task of managing pluralism, which is understood as real chaos without this management. Following Milbank, we could retort that the existence of these antagonistic powers, which need to be restrained by public theology, is far less evident than Stackhouse might assume.

Where Stackhouse wants Christian theology to establish the normative framework for post-Christendom societies, Elaine Graham assumes that there are shared norms regarding intelligibility, truth and reciprocity on the basis of which issues can be publicly analysed.[143] Christian theology should defend its contributions on the basis of these 'publicly intelligible' criteria.[144] The problem with this presupposition is that it uncritically accepts the nation state or the prevalently dominant culture as being able to provide the guidelines for political and civic actions.[145] Both Milbank's and Ward's arguments have made us aware that such a unified vision might not be presupposed in the contemporary context. According to Milbank, these norms might simply be restrictive and, in this way, exhibit the lack of a common vision oriented towards societal growth. According to Ward, these norms might be understood too unambiguously and theology's task would be to reopen people's imaginations to different norms.

---

identification of theology with ontology is also evidenced in his claim that theology must necessarily speak publicly because it is 'an argument regarding the way things are and ought to be' (Max Stackhouse, 'Public Theology and Ethical Judgment', *Theology Today* 54 (2006 [sic.]): 165, cit. by Graham, *Between a Rock and a Hard Place*, xxiii).

141. Stackhouse, 'Introduction', in *Christ and the Dominions of Civilization*, 36. See also Stackhouse, *Globalization and Grace*, 152, in which he presents the Christian interpretation of the world as fallen as being self-evident.

142. Stackhouse, 'Introduction', in *Christ and the Dominions of Civilization*, 18.

143. Graham, *Between a Rock and a Hard Place*, 98. Stout negates the existence of these shared commitments of a whole society, but argues that, nonetheless, theologians can contribute their insights to the public forum, in the hope of attaining mutual understanding (Stout, *Democracy and Tradition*, 112–13). Mathewes also contends that Christian theology must hope that reality forms a harmonious whole without being able to indicate what this means concretely (*A Theology of Public Life*, 74–5; 132–3).

144. Graham, *Between a Rock and a Hard Place*, 110. Graham builds here upon David Tracy's work.

145. Elaine Graham, for example, refers to a 'shared purpose' that is related to some 'common citizenship' (Graham, 'Unquiet Frontier', *Political Theology*, 45).

Overall, the problem with the public theological interpretation of pluralism is first that it (unconsciously) accepts the supposedly neutral overarching understanding of difference, as antagonistic, and in this way returns to an implicitly imperialistic positioning of all particular differences underneath its own overarching gaze.[146] And second, this understanding of pluralism is politically problematic as it tends to subscribe to the regulative power of the nation state as necessary means by which to restrict the otherwise antagonistic plurality of world views. Once any assumption about pluralism has been dismantled as being culturally specific, Milbank's understanding of pluralism, as intrinsically harmonious, offers itself as a better alternative Christian theological understanding of plurality in the post-Christendom context. However, what remains problematic is Milbank's unconcessional advocacy of a privileged position for Christian theology.

Thus far, it has only been argued that Milbank and Ward both fail to envision a less central political role being played by Christian theology in post-Christendom societies than it used to play in previous eras. However, I have not yet argued why such an advocacy of Christian theology, as being central to the social order, should be objected to. Since my hypothesis is that the objection should come from the perspective of Christian theology itself, it is now time to analyse the theological underpinnings of Milbank's and Ward's respective arguments. Whereas it has already been made apparent that the central role played by Christian theology is associated with the theological task of relating all of reality to God for both Milbank and Ward, how they envision all of reality as participating in God must be examined more closely. In terms of Christian doctrine, this issue can be elucidated by analysing Milbank's and Ward's respective understandings of grace, sin and redemption. The question concerns the degree to which they regard non-Christian positions and insights as mediating the world's graced relation to God, in how far they regard them as sinfully rejecting their relation to God and in how far Christian theology is believed to participate actively in the world's redemption through also relating non-Christian insights to God.

2.3 Problematizing Common Grace: Fulfilling the Theological Significance of the Public

As mentioned in the previous chapter, Milbank has been repeatedly criticized for prematurely discarding the theological significance of non-Christian interlocutors,[147] while Ward is most frequently applauded for being the Radical

---

146. This universality is also apparent when Graham, drawing upon Charles Taylor, refers to certain commonalities 'we' moderns supposedly all share (Graham, 'Unquiet Frontier', *Political Theology*, 34). It might be questioned who this 'we' is.

147. Lewis Ayres, review of *Theology and Social Theory: Beyond Secular Reason*, by John Milbank, *Scottish Journal of Theology* 45 (1992): 125–6; David J. Dunn, 'Radical Sophiology:

Orthodox author who displays the most amicable stance towards non-Christian dialogue partners.[148] Milbank's critics say that he is bound to overlook the theological significance of other world views, given that he simply overwrites everything else with his Christian ontology.[149] Instead of seeing how they might contribute to the harmony he advocates, dissonant voices are simply being excluded.[150] Ward, on the contrary, is said to acknowledge that theological sensibilities resurface in late-modern culture and that the sacred reappears within the post-Christendom context.[151] Nevertheless, Ward has been criticized for stopping halfway in his respect for the theological significance of non-Christian insights. Ward's theology, not unlike Milbank's, is also primarily aimed at the transformation of contemporary culture by an apologetic 'defense of the Christian faith' against the dominant cultural currents.[152] In this vein, he allegedly does not sufficiently allow Christian theology to be informed and corrected by insights drawn from the surrounding context.[153] The continuous negotiation between Christian theology and its surrounding context is one-sidedly presented in terms of a theological address to the cultural 'malaise', more than it is in terms of a reciprocal exchange between world views.[154]

Fr. Sergej Bulgakov and John Milbank on Augustine', *Studies in East European Thought* 64 (2012): 227–49; Shakespeare, *Radical Orthodoxy*, 176; Roberts Skerrett, 'Desire and Anathema', *Journal of the American Academy of Religion* 71 (2003): 800–2.

148. Ford, 'Radical Orthodoxy and the Future of British Theology', *Scottish Journal of Theology*, 389; Grumett, 'Radical Orthodoxy', *The Expository Times* 122(6) (2011): 264; Newell, 'Communities of Faith, Desire, and Resistance', in *The Poverty of Radical Orthodoxy*, 181; Wisse, 'Introduction to the Thinking of Graham Ward' in *Between Philosophy and Theology*, 65–6.

149. Larsen, 'The Politics of Desire', *Modern Theology*, 301–2.

150. Roberts Skerrett, 'Desire and Anathema', *Journal of the American Academy of Religion*, 800–2. She claims that this would contradict the peacefulness that Milbank advocates. Some critics appreciate the content, but reject the rhetoric of Milbank's argument as formally exclusivist (Coles, 'Storied Others', *Modern Theology*, 333; McDowell, 'Theology as Conversational Event', *Modern Theology* 19 (2003): 483–509; Davies, 'Revelation and the Politics of Culture', in *Radical Orthodoxy? – A Catholic Enquiry*, 116).

151. Graham, *Between a Rock and a Hard Place*, 124.

152. Ward, 'Introduction', in *Christ and Culture*, 18.

153. Graham, *Between a Rock and a Hard Place*, 108. Burrus observes that Ward presupposes the authority of traditional Christian orthodoxy despite contemporary cultural currents (such as feminism) that put certain doctrines into question (Burrus, 'Radical Orthodoxy and the Heresiological Habit', in *Interpreting the Postmodern*, 38, FN 5). Although Ward argues that theological discourse must be critically assessed by cultural studies, since it is in a way one cultural phenomenon among others (Ward, 'Radical Orthodoxy and/ as Cultural Politics', in *Radical Orthodoxy? – A Catholic Enquiry*, 102), I agree with Burrus's criticism to a large extent.

154. Graham, *Between a Rock and a Hard Place*, 128.

These criticisms have been connected to Milbank's and Ward's supposedly erroneous understandings of grace. They presumably associate grace with Christian theology one-sidedly and, thus, overlook how grace is also mediated by non-Christian positions.[155] Overall, I argue that Milbank's and Ward's understandings of grace are more nuanced than their critics admit. The first part of my respective expositions of Milbank's and Ward's theologies of grace consists of explaining how each understands non-Christian positions as aspirations for grace. For Milbank, these are already good and can be perfected by Christian theology, whereas non-Christian aspirations for grace are neutrally open, according to Ward, and can be completed through Christian theology. In the second part of my exposition of Milbank's and Ward's respective understandings of grace, I turn again to their advocacy of theology's central political role in post-Christendom societies. One might suspect that their relatively positive understanding of non-Christian positions, as aspirations for grace, might allow one of these positions to take centre stage without leading to societal disaster. This is why I examine Milbank's and Ward's respective understanding of sin, showing how their promise to overcome secularism by way of Christian theology depicts secularism as being sinful primarily. I conclude my discussion by way of criticizing the way in which both of their respective positions are marked themselves by that which they define as being sinful and their shared failure to differentiate sufficiently between Christ's fulfilment of nature's aspiration for grace and Christian theology's sinful, and thus often failed, furthering or completion of Christ's redemption.

a) Milbank's Self-Excessive Grace: Perfecting Non-Christian Goods

Milbank understands grace in terms of a gratuitous excess. Grace always effects more than the filling of a lack.[156] Grace is the structure of 'outcome exceeding occasion'.[157] This structure applies to both the grace of creation and the grace of Christ: The occasion for creation was to create another to God, but the outcome was creatures who were open to deification. The occasion for Christ's Incarnation was to redeem humankind from sin, but instead of merely reinstating the original state of creation, human nature now became united with God.[158] Highlighting the consistent structure of grace, Milbank focuses primarily upon the continuity of all that which Christian theologians understand as grace.[159] At the same time, however, and in line with the aforementioned explanation of Milbank's understanding of the excessive goodness of reality, grace is not to be understood in terms of an abstract,

---

155. Neil Ormerod, 'The Grace-Nature Distinction and the Construction of a Systematic Theology', *Theological Studies* 75 (2014): 516, n.3.

156. Milbank, 'Incarnation', in *Being Reconciled*, 67.

157. Milbank, 'The Programme of Radical Orthodoxy', in *Radical Orthodoxy? – A Catholic Enquiry*, 44; Milbank, 'Incarnation', in *Being Reconciled*, 69.

158. Milbank, 'Incarnation', in *Being Reconciled*, 66–70.

159. Ibid., 66.

general principle but in terms of the very specific gift or talent which individuals receive from God.[160] Consequently, Milbank stresses explicitly that the content of grace cannot be circumscribed by theology because grace can be mediated by the yet unknown stranger.[161] This allows for unknown variations of the content of grace, which defeats the accusation that Milbank cannot conceive of how non-Christians are moved genuinely differently by God's grace than Christians.

To the contrary, Milbank applies his understanding of grace in terms of 'outcome exceeding occasion' to the encounter between Christians and non-Christians. Reconciliation between two, presumably conflicting, positions does not mean settling for a compromise, but involves searching for a new disclosure which is more extreme than both positions.[162] This would mean that if Christian theologians seek to renew their tradition, through receiving non-Christian insights, then these insights can never be directly applied, but the renewal must be found in the excess to both positions once they are harmoniously blended.

Accordingly, Milbank argues that his ontology is not a wishful return to some prior age, but that he renews traditional Christian understandings of reality by incorporating all which is good and valuable in those criticisms voiced by modern secularists.[163] In other words, Milbank acknowledges that even those positions, which he dismisses, contain some truth which must expand his own vision of the harmonious whole. In line with an understanding of grace's fulfilling of the natural desire for grace, Milbank does not advocate any wholesale dismissal of secularist ontologies, but aims to show how the secularist discourse remains less perfect without the help of Christian theology.[164] The embrace by Christian theology does not destroy non-Christian positions, but must manifest the arrival of grace to them.[165] When Milbank claims that, from the perspective of his Christian

---

160. Milbank, 'Can Morality Be Christian?' in *The Word Made Strange*, 227. Milbank refers to a non-identical repetition of God's grace in each individual gift.

161. Milbank, 'Politics', in *Being Reconciled*, 171.

162. Milbank, 'The Programme of Radical Orthodoxy', in *Radical Orthodoxy? – A Catholic Enquiry* 44.

163. Milbank, *Beyond Secular Order*, 4.

164. Milbank, 'The Programme of Radical Orthodoxy', in *Radical Orthodoxy? – A Catholic Enquiry*, 37.

165. Milbank explicitly understands this disintegration of other ontologies not as violent invasions, but as a gift of grace to them (Milbank, 'Can Morality be Christian?' in *The Word Made Strange*, 221). He argues that all apparent violence must be judged on whether it strengthens or weakens humanity. Milbank's ontology is, thus, aimed at beneficially invading other world views, which is why Milbank seeks to persuade rhetorically by positive attraction and not by coercion. Interpreted from the perspective of Milbank's theology of grace, the criticism, that Milbank has been too greatly influenced by the arguments he seeks to combat, somewhat loses its sting (DeHart, 'On Being Heard but Not Seen', *Modern Theology*, 248–9; 271). He is said to be so determined to negate his opponents' positions that his position is predominantly the negative image of their own. On the basis of Milbank's

ontology, any secular realism is unable to 'understand the world aright',[166] this does not mean that they are entirely erroneous, but that they remain partial. When his critics suggest that Milbank should not interpret his opponents as rejecting, but as distorting the truth,[167] Milbank is likely to agree.

From the perspective of Milbank's theology of grace, it only follows that other positions are not treated as integral wholes which need to be preserved. Instead, how they blend with Milbank's own account of reality into something new must be examined. However, his understanding of grace leaves us with the question as to why Milbank seeks to replace the secularist social order with his theological alternative. The way in which he discards secularism suggests that, on this more overarching level, Milbank does not focus primarily on all that is good in secularism, but on the problems with secularism that need to be overcome by Christian theology. This approach would better chime with an understanding of grace as filling a lack than with grace in terms of the excessive fulfilling of an already good nature. The issue can be clarified through a closer analysis of the way in which Milbank understands how grace overcomes sin.

b) Overcoming the Sin of Pride: The Grace of Christian Theology as Solution to Political Problems

According to Milbank, the Fall originated in the human refusal of God's immeasurable grace and love.[168] More precisely, Milbank associates this refusal with humankind's prideful mistrust in the overall goodness of God and reality. Due to the abundance of grace, there is an uncertainty concerning what precise grace one will receive and what precise grace one will pass on in every encounter with others.[169] Sin, then, involves mistrusting the goodness of reality insofar as people refuse the risk involved in the gift exchange of unknown goods. It is sinful to read the unknown 'as source of threat ... rather than potential or gift'.[170]

Regarding the effects of sin, Milbank upholds that sin has no effect on God. The real superabundance of goodness exists perfectly in God, despite the Fall.[171] God continues to relate to all of reality. Rejecting any ontologization of evil, evil

understanding of grace, however, the defeated position and his own must constitute an excess, one which resembles but surpasses both.

166. Milbank, 'The Poverty of Niebuhrianism', in *The Word Made Strange*, 244.

167. Mathewes, *A Theology of Public Life*, 125.

168. Milbank, 'Forgiveness', in *Being Reconciled*, 46–7; Milbank, 'Postmodern Critical Augustinianism', in *The Future of Love*, 344.

169. Milbank, 'Grace', in *Being Reconciled*, 150.

170. Ibid. This also explains why Milbank agrees with Luther that the Augustinian understanding of original sin as pride should be buttressed by interpreting this pride as originating in an even more fundamental fear (Milbank, 'Can Morality be Christian?' in *The Word Made Strange*, 230).

171. Milbank, 'The Second Difference', in *The Word Made Strange*, 182–3.

is not regarded as a necessary part of reality, but as a contingent occurrence in the world.[172] However, the Fall has an effect on human nature and, consequently, upon reality's relation to God. Milbank associates sin with the distortion of the human desire for God.[173] Subsequent to the Fall, people no longer mediate only the superabundance of goodness, which is why there are now 'impossible interval[s]' in nature which do not participate in God's grace.[174] Evil is a real intrusion into graced reality.[175] Nature, in the sense of immanent history, is an apocalyptic mixture of grace and evil.[176] Evil is the opposing force that continues to distract the harmonious whole.

Grace, then, overcomes sin by restoring the distorted desire for God. This is mediated whenever people are moved by the superabundant goodness of reality, despite all of their inhibitions and incapacities.[177] So, in order to overcome evil, people need to take the hopeful risk that the harmony, and not the opposing force, will ultimately win.[178] Human policies based on grace need to continuously determine the precise evil that inhibits a fuller realization of the Good. Every evil must be traceable in terms of a lack of integration into the harmonious whole. More fundamentally, however, Milbank stresses that Christian politics are *primarily* oriented not towards the elimination of evil, but towards a society's advancement in the truly good.[179] Consequently, a Christian interpretation of reality must commence with redemption and not with evil.[180] In other words, Christian theologians must take the risk of reading world history always through the interpretative lens that, ultimately, all reality is graced and, thus, harmonious. Historical occurrences of evil or of suffering cannot be understood as falsifications of the ultimate goodness of reality. Disregarding what happens, Christians cannot

172. Milbank, *Theology and Social Theory*, xviii. Milbank claims that only the doctrine of the Fall allows him to maintain the claim that reality is good and harmonious and to acknowledge, this notwithstanding, the reality of evil (Milbank, 'Out of the Greenhouse', in *The Word Made Strange*, 263; Milbank, 'Grace', in *Being Reconciled*, 149).

173. Milbank, 'Evil', in *Being Reconciled*, 10.

174. Milbank, 'The Second Difference', in *The Word Made Strange*, 182. Milbank situates these impossible intervals between the economic and the immanent Trinity. The logic seems to be that the economic Trinity is different from the immanent Trinity, because the former is the manifestation of the latter in a sinful world.

175. Milbank, 'The Poverty of Niebuhrianism', in *The Word Made Strange*, 244.

176. Milbank, 'Ecclesiology', in *Being Reconciled*, 133; Milbank, 'Violence', in *Being Reconciled*, 42–3.

177. Milbank, 'Evil', in *Being Reconciled*, 10.

178. Milbank, 'Ecclesiology', in *Being Reconciled*, 133; Milbank, 'Violence', in *Being Reconciled*, 42–3.

179. The political reasons for this opposition to any ontologization of evil is best summarized in Milbank, 'Can Morality Be Christian?' in *The Word Made Strange*, 219–32.

180. Milbank, 'Introduction', in *Being Reconciled*, xii.

deny that God relates to the world, as this most overarching outlook is not just one more fact which could be verified or falsified by empirical evidence.

Concerning the question of how Milbank's understanding of grace and sin influences his understanding of the relation between Christian theology and non-Christian positions, it must first be stressed that it is precisely his understanding of grace in terms of self-excess that allows Milbank to advocate Christian theology as centre of a not-exclusively Christian society. Milbank argues that even though non-Christians and Christians rely equally upon, and participate in, God's grace, this participation in redemptive grace does not oblige people to become Christian.[181] Instead, those who become Christians constitute an excess to the ongoing work of redemption. Analogously to grace's relation to sin, Christianity must be more than the filling of a lack. This means that Christians and non-Christians could likewise participate in the social order that corresponds to Milbank's theology of grace.

At the same time, however, concerning the fallen world, Milbank highlights that God did not redeem humankind from sin by way of any supernatural intervention, but by tracing a way towards redemption in Christ.[182] Apart from Christ, people might not see that they are related to God, and even if they do see this, they might not be able to respond to God's grace in their actions.[183] This does not imply that all non-Christians only intrude sinfully into the graced harmony, but it means that only those who read reality in relation to Christ, that is, Christian theologians, possess the restored vision of how true harmony will be achieved. This claim constitutes the first theological reason for Milbank to advocate a theological social order for post-Christendom societies.

Secondly, his apologetic defence of a Christian social order, against the strict secularist opposition to theological involvement in politics, can be related to Milbank's interpretation of secularism as being primarily sinful and Christian theology as being primarily graced. In correspondence with his understanding of grace and sin, Milbank calls sinful any ontology that posits good and evil as being on the same ontological level.[184] This is an understanding that denies the human dependence on grace.[185] Humans are imagined as being able to choose freely between good and evil, which means that the goodness of the world would depend on human choice. This is precisely the way in which secularism organizes a society, focusing primarily on people's freedom, not on people's dependence. At this point, Milbank's theology of grace is not so much the excess to the secularist conception as it is its overcoming.

181. Milbank, 'Incarnation', in *Being Reconciled*, 68.

182. Ibid., 65.

183. Milbank, 'Foreword', in *Introducing Radical Orthodoxy*, 17–18.

184. Milbank, 'Evil', in *Being Reconciled*, 8. For Milbank's rejection of those readings that interpret the Fall as a divinely granted free choice for evil see ibid., 15–16; Milbank, 'Can Morality be Christian?' in *The Word Made Strange*, 224.

185. Milbank, 'Evil', in *Being Reconciled*, 8.

The first theological problem with Milbank's theological rationale for a Christian social order concerns Milbank's failure to see that, in apologetically defending Christian theology against the secularist opposition to theologically informed political involvement, he perpetuates his own understanding of sin in terms of 'proud mistrust'.[186] Milbank presents his Christian theology as being the cure for all problems with secularism, instead of taking the hopeful risk that, despite its many shortcomings, this secularist opposition to Christian theology still mediates God's grace. In other words, his defensive apologetics prevents Milbank from perceiving the grace that might be mediated by the vehement opposition to Christian theological contributions to politics in post-Christendom societies. Milbank's persistent focus on the failure of secularism could, then, be read as Milbank's proud attempt to save the world by his own efforts.[187]

This problem can be related to a more fundamental theological problem with Milbank's position, namely that he insufficiently distinguishes between Christ's redemption, including the restoration of the human vision, and the Christian theological *sinful* participation in this redemption. He fails to acknowledge that, as sinners, Christian theologians still fail to see clearly the way towards redemption that has been traced in Christ. Kathryn Tanner will be introduced in Chapter 3 and Edward Schillebeeckx in Chapter 4 as two theologians who are more sensitive to the continuous failure of Christian theological attempts of seeing how Christ's redemptive work can be further realized on earth.

c) Ward's Kenotic Grace: Completing Non-Christian Goods

The greatest theological difference between Ward's and Milbank's understandings of grace is that while Milbank understands grace in terms of self-excess, Ward understands grace in terms of a simultaneous double-movement of kenosis and completion. This once more appertains to the grace of creation as well as to the grace of the Incarnation.

---

186. For a similar criticism that Milbank's solution 'imitates the errors of that which it attempts to replace' see Insole, 'Against Radical Orthodoxy', *Modern Theology*, 224. However, Insole associates the problem with Milbank's imitation of postmodern constructivism, which Insole then suggests could be overcome by focusing on empirical reality to a higher degree (227–8). I, to the contrary, follow Milbank in asserting that any access to empirical reality depends upon one's ontology, but argue that precisely if reality is assessed through the lens of a Christian ontology of peace, then theologians would have to trust in secularism's goodness to a higher degree than Milbank does. Furthermore, Insole then advocates a certain form of political liberalism, in its supposed neutrality, as being the best form of government (237), whereas I follow Milbank in questioning such neutrality.

187. A similar criticism concerns Milbank's inability to appreciate 'theologically significant inactivity' as for example in practices of lament (Kevin Derksen, 'Milbank and Violence: Against a Derridean Pacifism', in *The Gift of Difference: Radical Orthodoxy, Radical Reformation,* eds. Chris H. Huebner and Tripp York (Winnipeg, Manitoba: CMU Press, 2010), 38, FN 33).

After a brief exposition of both graces, I will consider the implications for the way Ward can appreciate the theological significance of non-Christian positions and then move on to an examination of the way in which this influences his apologetic defence of theology's central political role in post-Christendom societies (section d).

While Milbank understands creation as excessive surplus to God, Ward understands creation as the kenotic self-emptying of God, which is 'extravagant and costly'.[188] God created a void to be filled. Although Ward denies the existence of a void as such, because the movement of kenosis is immediately accompanied by a movement of completion,[189] the understanding of creation in terms of God's kenosis still allows Ward to conceive of there being a 'place for suffering as a passion written in creation'.[190] There is a risk of suffering, even prior to the Fall.[191] The risk is not only a risk for humankind, but it is even a risk for God. This indicates that Ward gives more room to thinking about some positive lack than Milbank does. For Ward, the lack *is* in order to be completed. For Milbank, to the contrary, the nothingness which comes into existence with creation is really nowhere. Ward refers to the movement of kenosis and completion in terms of a suffering (the opening up to the other) which at the same time glorifies (the completion).[192] Milbank criticizes these kenotic theologies that account for suffering and evil in reference to God's providential creation because by presenting evil as part of a greater good the gravity of evil is diminished.[193]

188. Ward, 'Suffering and Incarnation: A Christian Politics', in *Christ and Culture*, 255. Ward not only speaks of a risk that God took vis-à-vis creation, but also of a risk within the Trinity; he understands the Trinity as infinite self-exposition to the Other (261).

189. Ward, 'Suffering and Incarnation', in *Christ and Culture*, 261. Only insofar as God's goodness is identified with God's kenotic self-emptying can Ward then also uphold that 'creation itself, while not God, is an expression of the ... goodness ... of the Godhead' (Ward, *Cultural Transformation*, 58).

190. Ward, 'Suffering and Incarnation', in *Christ and Culture*, 254.

191. Ibid., 255.

192. Ibid., 261.

193. Milbank, 'Critique of the Theology of Right', in *The Word Made Strange*, 23. (Tonstad makes the same claim in reference to Ward's theology, and argues that Ward theologically justifies suffering (Tonstad, *God and Difference*, 81)). In Milbank's ontology, there would be no place and no time for this suffering to occur in the original order of creation. For him, creation ex nihilo does not mean that creation originates in 'Nothing'. Prior to creation there is only God's plenitudinous goodness and no 'Nothing' (Milbank, 'Forgiveness', in *Being Reconciled*, 55). Creation ex nihilo means that created reality is suspended between nothing and infinity (Milbank, 'Postmodern Critical Augustinianism', in *The Future of Love*, 339). The finitude of creatures is ceaselessly cancelled out, because it is continuously constituted by God's infinity (Milbank, 'Incarnation', in *Being Reconciled*, 74). It is also in this sense that creation, at the same time, reveals and conceals the absent God: God is the infinite passing away of the finitude and, thus, is not finitely identifiable as anything in creation (Milbank, 'Logos: Pleonasm, Speech and Writing', in *The Word Made Strange*, 78). Because

In a similar vein to his kenotic understanding of creation, Ward understands the Incarnation in Christ as incomplete, and therefore as in need of further completion by the church. In his argument, Ward differentiates between the divine *Logos* and the *Logos* as it is incarnated in the life of Jesus Christ. The divine *Logos* is the perfected and completed human nature that exists in God.[194] This perfect human nature is incarnated in Jesus only initially, and must still be brought to its completion through the continuous integration of all other human beings into itself.[195] The Incarnation is not fully accomplished before all of humankind has reached its perfection.[196] The church's continuous imitation of Jesus Christ, for the further completion of the Incarnation, must be an interplay between subjection to Christ and interpretative freedom.[197] This means that Ward does not regard the church as one-sidedly depending on God's offer of redemption, but as actively and creatively completing the redemption once begun in Christ.[198] He argues that 'something of what it is to be God ... comes about by an identification with what is human'.[199]

Overall, Ward conceptualizes grace differently than Milbank. Milbank understands grace in terms of excess, while Ward thinks of grace in terms of self-emptying completion. For Ward, God is already the completion of all goodness in Godself which God, however, abandoned for the creation of the world. Whereas the fullness of goodness is with God, the world is merely the secondary appearance

finitude is nothing of itself, the movement of finite beings through time means that the finality of each moment is cancelled out by the next (Milbank, 'Postmodern Critical Augustinianism', in *The Future of Love*, 339). In this sense, finitude continuously becomes nothing, while infinity draws all creatures into itself, and nothing has no being. Similar to Milbank's understanding, Ward also interprets the continuous cancelling of finitude as 'the mark of God within creation' (Ward, 'Allegoria Amoris', in *Christ and Culture*, 188). However, Ward reads this cancelling out in terms of dispossession and self-denial. Whereas for Milbank there is nothing that is left behind, there *is* something of which God is continuously dispossessed for Ward. This is related to Ward's understanding of the Cross about which he argues that here grace has integrated that which is other into itself (Ward, 'The Displaced Body of Jesus Christ', in *Radical Orthodoxy: A New Theology*, 170–1). Christ's patient endurance of evil is now a new grace (Ward, 'Allegoria Amoris', in *Christ and Culture*, 188).

194. Ward, 'The Body of the Church', in *Christ and Culture*, 106.

195. Milbank, to the contrary, would affirm Jesus as the complete Incarnation of the *Logos* and all further human imitations as the excess to this Incarnation.

196. Ward, 'The Body of the Church', in *Christ and Culture*, 106.

197. Ward, *Politics of Discipleship*, 186–7. In *How the Light Gets In*, 199, Ward connects the church's interpretative freedom to God's providential economy.

198. This is connected to Ward's understanding of the Incarnation as revelatory of God's participation in human life on the one hand, but also of the participation of human life in God on the other (Ward, 'The Body of the Church', in *Christ and Culture*, 105–6; 'The Schizoid Christ', in *Christ and Culture*, 75; Ward, *Politics of Discipleship*, 186–7).

199. Ward, 'The Body of the Church', in *Christ and Culture*, 105–6.

of this goodness.[200] Whatever is good in the world does not coincide with what is good in God, but the worldly goodness must be made to coincide with God's goodness through the world's return to God. That creation was a risk for both God and creation means that the return of creation to God is a completion for both God and creation. Whereas Milbank conceives of the return in terms of an excess for both God and creation, Ward refers to the return in terms of self-identification within difference.[201] God is further differentiated within, but not positively expanded upon, in the sense that Milbank imagines.

This conception of grace, in terms of God's kenotic self-emptying, would entail that non-Christian positions must be regarded as the grace of equally 'empty' material, which can be taken up by Christian theology in order to complete the world's redemption. Ward, thus, argues that 'the secular age, ..., is neither good nor bad in and of itself. Rather, it is just the time *we* have been given to redeem.'[202] Non-Christian positions are not regarded as evil or sinful, but as incomplete. Likewise, God and the Incarnation of the *Logos* are incomplete, which seems to position Christian theology even more centre stage than it was in Milbank's theology of grace. Christian theologians are responsible for the redemption of the world as well as for the completion of God.[203]

Whereas this conception of grace explains Ward's treatment of postmodernism, in the sense of an aspiration for grace which is completed by Christian theology, it does not explain why Ward opposes a secularist social order for a post-Christendom society. In the following section, I argue that Ward does not present Christian theology as the completion of secularism, but as its overcoming, which again can be elucidated through an investigation of Ward's understanding of sin and grace's overcoming of sin.

d) Overcoming the Sin of Domination: The Disruptive Grace of Christian Theology as a Solution to Political Problems

For Milbank, sin was the mistrust in the fundamental goodness of reality and the proud belief that the goodness of reality depends upon humankind, instead of acknowledging humankind's own dependence on God's grace. If, according to Ward, creation itself is ambiguous, mistrust in the goodness of reality cannot be sinful. If worldly reality is a mixture of emptiness and completion, then a certain mistrust regarding that which one will receive by opening oneself up to the world,

---

200. Ward, 'Allegoria Amoris', in *Christ and Culture*, 187.

201. Ibid.

202. Graham Ward, 'History, Belief and Imagination in Charles Taylor's *A Secular Age*', *Modern Theology* 26 (2010): 348.

203. That it is indeed primarily Christian theology, and not the church, is suggested by Ward's argument that the world is further redeemed through the re-narration of the Christian narrative that has begun with the writing of the Gospels (Ward, 'Christology and Mimosis', in *Christ and Culture*, 42–4).

should be legitimate. For Ward, then, sin is 'the lust to dominate'.[204] The attempt to dominate and control reality is disobedient to God, because God created reality in a manner that is ambiguous and uncontrollable.

Ward depicts the overcoming of the lust to dominate in terms of an unconditional opening up of oneself to the reception of grace, in whatever shape it is given. Ward associates the Fall with a situation of being lost, in which we still live, and theology's redemptive task is to begin with losing oneself in this fallen world.[205] Affirming Christ in some way as the objective redeemer of the world, Ward argues that the suffering of immersion into the world can only be born 'insofar as Christ as the pioneer of our faith has borne all things and brought all things in submission to him'.[206] At the same time, however, Ward immediately emphasizes that the human recognition of Christ is integral to Christ's work of redemption.[207] If Milbank places a strong emphasis on the active theological effort to redeem the world from sin, Ward places an even stronger emphasis on the same point. According to Ward, humanity's sinful lust to dominate reality must be reoriented through following Christ's privileging of grace over security and stability.[208] That this is more a duty than a gift is apparent in Ward's suggestion that Christ's suffering is redemptive. Christ's suffering manifests the redemptive freedom of living without precisely knowing what is going on.[209] Whereas Milbank has claimed that Christians *can* open themselves up to the historical mixture of grace and sin, because they know that grace will annihilate sin eventually, Ward claims that people *must* open themselves up to the mixture of good and evil in history, because *they* will redeem the world from sin in this way. Instead of speaking of an inherent attraction to grace, Ward refers to a conversion to grace, which can only occur if one is already transformable.[210] In other words, human beings must be of a certain kind (namely transformable) before they can receive grace.

Ward then continues to equate this human transformability with vulnerability. Vulnerability is associated with exposing oneself to the exterior world. One's own boundaries must be transgressed towards the not-yet-fully-known. Since reality is understood as being most fundamentally ambiguous, participation in the movement of grace demands a continuous self-abandonment as contrasted to self-protection, fear or narcissism.[211] In other words, people must sacrifice certain dispositions in order to receive grace.[212] The sacrificial self-abandonment

---

204. Ward, 'Suffering and Incarnation', in *Christ and Culture*, 255.

205. Ward, *How the Light Gets In*, 149–55.

206. Graham Ward, 'Affect: Towards a Theology of Experience', *Radical Orthodoxy: Theology, Philosophy, Politics* Vol. 1 (2012): 73.

207. Ward, 'The Schizoid Christ', in *Christ and Culture*, 87.

208. Ward, 'Suffering and Incarnation', in *Christ and Culture*, 255.

209. Ward, 'Christology and Mimesis', in *Christ and Culture*, 57–8.

210. Ward, 'Affect', *Radical Orthodoxy: Theology, Philosophy, Politics*, 69.

211. Ward, 'The Schizoid Christ', in *Christ and Culture*, 82–3.

212. Ward, 'Suffering and Incarnation', in *Christ and Culture*, 262.

simultaneously bestows grace onto others, insofar as one draws their suffering into oneself.

Regarding the question of how the above exposition impacts upon the way in which Ward ascribes a central political role to Christian theology, it is important to highlight that Ward does not view non-Christians as entirely un-graced. He explicitly argues that only God can see who rightly imitates Christ and who truly belongs to the ecclesial community of the saved.[213] Moreover, non-Christians could be acknowledged to be moved genuinely differently by God's grace, depending on what the ambiguous world offers. The only people who can be definitively called un-graced are those who prevent the open reception, that is, modern positivists with their firm definitions that are being presented as self-evident, and political secularists who likewise present their own political order as being best due to its supposed independence from specific cultural influences.

Ward's apologetic defence of theology's political relevance for post-Christendom societies then takes a different route to that of Milbank. Milbank's positive understanding of grace stressed a prior dependence upon God's offer of grace for any active human completion of God's redemptive work. Ward's emphasis on the 'continual self-abandonment'[214] for human participation in grace, on the contrary, downplays any sense of theology's joyful reception of non-Christian insights. Instead, Ward defines faithfulness as that which remains when nothing appears to be given and when one solely lives for a future that others can enter into.[215] Ward argues that in order to receive grace, there must be a lack and a sense of dissatisfaction with what one has.[216] Theologians should 'scream into the darkness "Save me"'.[217] Accordingly, Ward evaluates the present situation in terms of us 'all' being able to 'see that the world is fucked up' and us 'all still hoping for something that can stop it from being so fucked up'.[218] In other words, Ward's interpretation of the current state of the world, as remarkably un-graced, helps his apologetic defence of theology's task to complete the world's redemption once begun in Christ.[219] Ward's universalizing 'we' at this point of interpreting the contemporary situation as particularly problematic is remarkable.

---

213. Ward, *Politics of Discipleship*, 202. The whole community of those who continue to respond to God's offer of grace then moves towards salvation (Ward, 'The Schizoid Christ', in *Christ and Culture*, 82–3).

214. Ward, 'The Schizoid Christ', in *Christ and Culture*, 82.

215. Ibid., 80.

216. Ward, *Politics of Discipleship*, 266.

217. Ward, *How the Light Gets In*, 165.

218. Ian Warlick, 'Post-Secularity, Hegel and Friendship: An Interview with Graham Ward', *Radical Orthodoxy: Theology, Philosophy, Politics*, 337.

219. Tonstad has also claimed that Ward's strong emphasis on necessary suffering undermines an adequate conceptualization of the gratuity of grace (Tonstad, *God and Difference*, 81–2).

On this basis, Ward then explains how situating oneself within the Christian narrative can help people to develop a habit of opening themselves up to the ambiguous reality for the further redemption of the world.[220] To 'speak of, through and by revealedness' redeems people from the sinful lust to dominate.[221] Events in the contemporary context must be related to the Christian narrative in order to 'open up a space between what we think we know and what is true'.[222] The narrative must be followed faithfully and imaginatively without there being any final understanding.[223] The Christian narrative, thus, serves to dislodge fixed and settled understandings of the world in order to let the superabundance of the truth shine forth.[224] Adhering to the Christian narrative forges a way for people through the world that prevents them from providing final explanations or definitions.[225] Conversely, also, cultural references to Christ from non-ecclesial contexts, perhaps uttered by non-Christians, are theologically significant for Ward.[226] There is, then, no final explanation or reason as to why the specific Christian narrative should be followed, but Ward shows how the Christian narrative can be followed as one possible way of preventing any domination and control over reality.[227] Theologically systematizing thought is also not meant to finally render the Christian tradition manageable, but to form disciples of the 'Unsearchable' God whose works are 'incomprehensible'.[228]

At the same time, however, Christian theology is defended as being best able to see how the secularist social order ought to be overcome and would, as such, replace secularism's central position. Here, it is not clear how Ward's account of how people can live in the world, without dominating reality through their explanations, would escape becoming the dominating explanation of how to

---

220. Ward, 'Christology and Mimesis', in *Christ and Culture*, 42. See Ward, 'The Schizoid Christ', in *Christ and Culture*, 84.

221. Ward, 'Spiritual Exercises', in *Christ and Culture*, 246.

222. Ibid.

223. Ward, 'Christology and Mimesis', in *Christ and Culture*, 56–7.

224. Ibid., 30–1; 56–7.

225. The constant flux of orthodoxy must be acknowledged, instead of replacing one reified understanding of God with another (Ward, 'Receiving the Gift', *Modern Theology*, 84). This is why Ward has been criticized for evading the problem of identifying what constitutes a true revelation according to the Christian tradition (Smith, *Introducing Radical Orthodoxy*, 109–113, FN73).

226. Ward, *How the Light Gets In*, 130–1.

227. Besides this situating of oneself within the Christian narrative, Ward also names prayer as a way to learn to open oneself up to the ambiguities of history (Ward, *Cultural Transformation*, 59–60; Ward, 'Affect', *Radical Orthodoxy Radical Orthodoxy: Theology, Philosophy, Politics*, 74–5). Ward is quick to point out that 'prayer is not a safe place, in the sense that it is not a stable place. Prayer requires a surrender of control' (Ward, *Cultural Transformation*, 60).

228. Ward, *How the Light Gets In*, 32; 3–34.

best live in the world. Like Milbank, Ward risks perpetuating the sin he wants to overcome on the most overarching level, because he is so concerned with defending theology's political relevance for post-Christendom societies apologetically, which he strongly associates with theology's ability to solve societal problems.

Moreover, Ward also fails to differentiate between Christ and theology's sinful completion of Christ's work. Overall, Ward's theology leaves the impression that we live in a fallen reality and that Christianity is endowed with the task of redeeming the world from its sinfulness. On the basis of Ward's understanding of Christ as only the incomplete Incarnation of the divine *Logos*, it becomes impossible to indicate where and how Christians fail in completing the redemption initiated by Christ. If Ward suggests that Christian theology should scandalize people in a Christ-like manner,[229] Ward does not account for how not only the Christ-likeness but also the sinfulness of Christian theologians might cause their deliberations to be scandalous. Even when Ward admits that theological language can be impacted by sin, he exempts liturgical acts and language from this sinfulness, claiming that in the celebration of the Eucharist theological language is being 'made to appear pure, innocent, and free from ideology'.[230] The confession that theological language is impaired by sin is then nearly undone when he continues to deny any strict distinction between the church's liturgy and theological reflection upon this liturgy, arguing that both are indissolubly interwoven.[231] Ward's strong focus on the Christian duty to suffer for the world's complete redemption, and his presentation of vulnerability and fracturedness as something which Christians have to attain heroically in order to redeem the world, leads to the question of whether Christians should not instead acknowledge to always already be vulnerable and fractured because they are sinful. Should the argument not rather go this way: Christians should open themselves up to grace, because only in this way can they receive the gift which cures them of their sin?

If I argue that Ward depicts the world too one-sidedly as being fallen, or that he associates Christian theology too one-sidedly with the promise of the whole world's redemption, it must be acknowledged that Ward also seeks to distance his own theology from any nostalgic reproaches that might be voiced against Milbank's project due to the latter's focus on the lapse from Christian orthodoxy in the late Middle Ages.[232] Ward still claims to interpret history, despite this lapse, in terms of 'an ongoing adventus' of Christ's salvation, not as the advance towards history's apocalyptic end.[233] At this point, Ward distinguishes between Christ and the church, arguing that, however much the church has failed, it cannot quench the Christian hope for the entire world's salvation. Importantly for this discussion,

229. Ward, 'Introduction', in *Christ and Culture*, 19.

230. Ward, *How the Light Gets In*, 34.

231. Ibid., 122–3.

232. Ward states his uncertainty about the extent to which these are justified in reference to Milbank's work (Ibid., 71).

233. Ibid., 72.

Ward here refers to Schillebeeckx's trust in the reality of salvation outside of the church[234], as well as to Schillebeeckx's call on theologians to actualize the universality of Jesus's message in changing situations.[235] Ward, at this point, weaves Schillebeeckx's position into his own theology, interpreting this actualization of Jesus's message in terms of a call upon theologians to relate the contemporary situation to the biblical narrative of Jesus. Together, Ward's argument suggests, then, that the church's past failure can be redeemed by the hope of contemporary Christian theologians who believe in the world's salvation nonetheless. In this way, Ward fails to acknowledge the way in which the church's past failures also impair the vision of what contemporary Christians should rightly hope for.[236] In this respect, Ward's position does not constitute an alternative to Milbank's who similarly does not advocate a return to some idealist past, but who instead focuses on problems in the past and present in order to voice his theological promise of a better future. The difference merely appertains to their respective promises.

My exposition of Schillebeeckx's theology, in Chapter 4, will provide a more distinct alternative. I will interpret the passages in his work referred to by Ward as suggesting that Christ's universal salvation, despite the church, is a reality here and now, that Christian theologians must attend to in order to gain new hope. The task of Christian theologians is then not to promise a better future, but to discern how the contemporary situation mediates the reality of redemption, and to name this redemption in reference to the life of Jesus of Nazareth.

If the emphasis was not so much laid on the Christian theological ability to redeem the world, and more upon the Christian theological dependence on the redemption which has already been offered, then Ward's theology of grace would still provide some helpful insights. It can be learnt from Ward that in their opening up to grace, theologians might also receive the sin and suffering of a fallen world with the concomitant risk of being drawn right into it. Contrary to Ward, it should then be emphasized that this is not something which theologians *must* do, but something which they *can* dare to do precisely because they can trust that grace will raise them up again eventually. On this basis, then, Ward's repeatedly criticized and strong reliance upon postmodern philosophies should be applauded. Trusting in the superior power of grace, Christian theologians do not have to be afraid of the shortcomings of atheistic

---

234. Edward Schillebeeckx, *Jesus in Our Western Culture: Mysticism, Ethics and Politics* (London: SCM Press, 1986), 7, cit. by Ward, *How the Light Gets In*, 72.

235. Schillebeeckx, *Jesus in Our Western Culture*, 40, cit. by Ward, *How the Light Gets In*, 130–1.

236. Ward does acknowledge Christian theology's partiality and its liability to errors. However, he clearly associates these errors with fear as 'the affective heart of sin', and the perpetuation of the 'violences of denominationalism and sectarianism' (Ward, *How the Light Gets In*, 117; 143–4), indicating that Ward is not sensitive to the way in which the entanglement in sin might also impair his own vision of the exact problem which needs to be overcome.

postmodernism, but should be concerned primarily with receiving aright the grace that postmodern thought can offer. This would also be a cure for both Milbank's and Ward's anxiety with overcoming all of the world's sinfulness by way of Christian theology. Instead of pointing to other's failures, and to the way in which Christian theology can repair them, a focus on grace might allow Christian theologians to be with others in their failures.

e) Concretizing Grace: Surpassing Christian Dominance with a Political Christology

In light of the discussion above, it is now time to assess the roles attributed to grace and Christ in contemporary public theological literature. Public theologians have referred to Christology, thus far, mainly in reference to questions concerning ontology and apologetics.[237] Ontological references concern the claim that the revelation in Christ leads to a greater insight into the workings of the world, whereas apologetic references appeal to the church's mission to publicly confess Christ.

As the most prominent representative of the ontological public theological interpretation of Christ, Max Stackhouse abstracts universal knowledge from the revelation in Christ. The existence of a divinely established order of the world is presupposed and it has been claimed that society must mirror this order as perfectly as possible in order to flourish.[238] It has been abstracted from Old Testament revelation that covenantal relationships are the essential basis of any democracy.[239] Christ is, then, interpreted as revealing that love is the inner spirit of covenantal relationships. Public theology's apologetic references to Christ are closely connected to this ontological interpretation of Christ's public relevance. The public theological claim that witnessing to Christ in secular democracies should take the form of witnessing to universally intelligible core values that promote the common good is a concern closely connected to the claim that the revelation in Christ provides universal knowledge.[240] A more explicit witness to Christ is dismissed as this is associated with Christianity's search for a privileged place in society. Instead of advocating that the social order should be explicitly

---

237. Dirkie Smit distinguishes between theistic, Christological and pneumatological justifications of the relevance of public theology ('Notions of the Public and Doing Theology', *International Journal of Public Theology*, 450–1).

238. Deirdre Hainsworth and Scott R. Paeth, 'Introduction', in *Public Theology for a Global Society: Essays in Honor of Max L. Stackhouse*, x.

239. Stackhouse, 'Public Theology and Democracy's Future', *The Review of Faith & International Affairs*, 54.

240. De Gruchy, 'Public Theology as Christian Witness', *International Journal of Public Theology* 1 (2007), 26. De Gruchy explicitly opposes the aspiration to convert people to Christianity through one's witnessing to Christ; presumably because he associates such aspiration with Christendom.

Christ-centred, public theologians argue, on the basis of the biblical identification of Christ with truth, that they seek to recognize Christ wherever truths are spoken in the democratic forum.[241] 'It would … be arrogant to assume that one knows in advance which human voices are speaking truly.'[242] Similarly, Graham argues that the Incarnation has revealed that 'the practical – the human – discloses, embodies and shows forth the theological.'[243] God's grace is primarily revealed in activities of healing and caring for others.[244] Christ is here interpreted as the transformer of culture who urges Christians to cooperate constructively in an incarnational manner for the sake of the world's redemption.[245] 'The primary expression of public theology, then, will be in practical demonstrations that authentic faith leads to transformation, as a matter not just of interpreting the world but changing it.'[246] This argument is meant to present doctrinal expressions only as secondary additions to this primary theological language of practice.[247]

The problem with these understandings of Christ is that, contrary to public theology's intentions, they do not overcome Christendom imperialism. The public theological account suggests that the positions of non-Christians are still being evaluated according to that which Christian theologians abstract from the revelation in Christ.[248] It is not at all clear how Christian theologians would further the world's redemption and transform the world to what they believe is good if they were confronted with non-Christians who understand the terms 'good' or 'a healed human nature' differently. If these apologetic defences of Christian involvement in public politics can indeed convince non-Christians, because the word 'Christ' is being avoided, seems to depend, to a large extent, upon the similarity between what Christians and non-Christians understand to be 'core values'.

At this point, public theologians might highlight the importance of conversation between conflicting positions. Jürgen Habermas argues that, in secularized pluralist societies, a plurality of groups should each transcend their own particular

---

241. Stout, *Democracy and Tradition*, 110.

242. Ibid., 111–12.

243. Elaine Graham, 'Health, Wealth or Wisdom? Religion and the Paradox of Prosperity', *International Journal of Public Theology* 3 (2009): 20.

244. Ibid., 23. Mathewes also understands the churches' public task primarily as one of witnessing in the sense of repeating the pattern of Christ's life and death (Mathewes, *A Theology of Public Life*, 138). Christian engagement in politics then becomes primarily a resistance to the imperialistic domination of any power structures, and a search for God who remains greater than all of them (159–61).

245. Graham, *Between a Rock and a Hard Place*, 174.

246. Ibid., 215.

247. Graham, 'Health, Wealth or Wisdom?' *International Journal of Public Theology*, 23.

248. For an argument that Stackhouse's references to God depict God as extraordinarily passive and as always substitutable by something else, see Philip Ziegler, 'God and Some Recent Public Theologies', *International Journal of Systematic Theology* 4 (2002): 137–55.

perspective in order to arrive at a more expanded common vision.[249] However, this whole agenda remains entirely within the bounds of one particular interpretation of the Christian tradition as is evidenced in the public theological elaboration that all religions are undergirded by something deeper than themselves.[250] 'Religions' are seen as organizing the immanent world, including their own societies, according to what they perceive as being the ideal laws of reality.[251] On this basis, it is then argued that there are abstract universals, such as integrity, justice and truth, which can function as objective measures against which each particular religion could be assessed.[252] Overall, this argument favours abstraction over unique particulars in exactly the same way in which the abstraction of core values was favoured over the unique particularity of Christ. The logic of the argument, thus, remains entirely within the logic of one particular Christology. If Christ is interpreted in an abstract way, then Christian theology can once again be placed at the centre for the organization of a not-exclusively Christian society. That other faith traditions might see the world and the relation between concrete reality and abstract universals radically differently is something that is ignored by this position. Instead of appreciating the theological significance of non-Christian positions, this public theological Christology tends to have everyone conform to its own theological position in disguise.

Conclusion

Overall, Milbank's and Ward's theologies are of great value for the discussion about theology's political role in post-Christendom societies because they challenge the self-proclaimed neutrality of secularism. This suggests that public theology might want to be slightly more countercultural, precisely in order not to promote or perpetuate Christianity's lost political dominance in a new guise. Challenging secularism's fixed understanding of universality, which tends to evaluate all cultures according to some univocal standard, Milbank offers an alternative Christian social order. His reading of reality as fundamentally harmonious could allow for a positive evaluation of all non-Christian world views, and thus advance the project of finding a less central political role for Christian theology in a post-Christendom context. However, Milbank advocates a return to Christianity's political dominance of bygone ages when seeking to replace the secularist social order by his Christian

---

249. Jürgen Habermas, 'Dialogue: Jürgen Habermas and Charles Taylor', in *The Power of Religion in the Public Sphere*, eds Eduardo Mendieta and Jonathan Vanantwerpen (New York and Chichester, West Sussex: Columbia University Press, 2011), 66.

250. Stackhouse, 'Introduction', in *Christ and the Dominions of Civilization*, 16.

251. Ibid., 17.

252. Ibid., 20; De Gruchy, 'Public Theology as Christian Witness', *International Journal of Public Theology*, 26.

alternative. Altogether, he presents secularism less as mediating grace, to some degree, than as sinful problem in need of theological redemption. On the most overarching level, concerning who should determine the social order, he presents Christian theology not as a perfection of what is already good in secularism, but as its overcoming and replacement. I disagree with this conception of the relation between Christian theology and secularism for Christological reasons. With this move, Milbank undermines that human sinfulness also impacts upon the theological vision of redemption, thereby effectively conflating Christ, in his unique perfection, and Christian theology.[253] An alternative theological approach to post-Christendom politics could acknowledge to a greater degree that the Christian theological vision is impaired by sin, which should render less ambitious any promises that a Christian social order would solve all contemporary political problems.

Ward's political theology might be regarded as less ambitious, as he understands (atheist) postmodernism as already breaking with the secularist imaginary, which he equally aims to overcome. Nevertheless, by seeking to complete postmodern aspirations with the help of Christian theology, Ward can be seen as effectively presenting Christian theology as the best solution to all remaining problems associated with secularism and its postmodern overcoming. Whereas Ward respects, more than Milbank, the criticism that Christianity's political dominance of former times should be more effectively overcome, he partly fails in his endeavour, insofar as he repeats and perpetuates postmodernity's concealed universalism, measuring any other world view in accordance with the standard set by his own. I have argued that this is again connected to Ward's problem-centred, apologetic defence of Christian theology against secularism, directed towards a postmodern audience. The displacement of the secularist social order becomes a replacement of secularism by Christian theology as the new centre, one which organizes how different cultures can live most harmoniously in one shared society. Ward's account could also be helped through acknowledging the impacts of sin onto the theological vision, particularly regarding any ability to see how the work of redemption once begun in Christ will be completed.

The theological weakness of Milbank's and Ward's positions concerns their insufficient differentiation between Christ and Christian theology. They reason too quickly from Christ's redemptive work to theology's active furthering of that work. Christian theology's central political role in post-Christendom societies is, then, too one-sidedly defended in connection to the promise of solving the entire society's political problems. On the one hand, this paints the contemporary

---

253. However, I am less concerned with Milbank's supposed failure to read 'the history of the church [... as] a history of redeemed failures' (Kevin L. Hughes, 'The Ratio Dei and the Ambiguities of History', *Modern Theology* 21 (2005): 659), as I interpret Milbank's theology as presenting the history of the church as one big failure. Instead, I contest Milbank's presentation of Christian theology, which he believes to be able of overseeing all at once how this failure can be redeemed at present.

situation very bleakly, thereby downplaying the Christian focus on thankfulness and joy for the redemption that has already been won by Christ. On the other hand, Milbank and Ward risk downplaying the traditional importance of confessing theology's own deep involvement in sin and our continuous reliance upon Christ's forgiving grace. In other words, Milbank and Ward both lack a more substantial theology of failure and, for this reason, all too triumphantly present Christian theology as the faith tradition endowed with the task of universal redemption.

If we search for how political theology could take on a less central role, in the contemporary West European context, it is important to assess the third alternative way of answering the question concerning an adequate theological response to post-Christendom societies, briefly mentioned in Chapter 1. Besides public theology, and Radical Orthodoxy, there are post-liberal Protestant theologians, who argue that Christian theology's whole endeavour of organizing the political life of the entire society, beyond the bounds of the church, has been mistaken, and that it is now time, to restrict political theology, once again, to internal ecclesial matters. In other words, these thinkers provide reasons as to why theology's political contributions should *never* be central in a non-exclusively Christian social order. Public theologians have distanced themselves from this strand of political theology, because they claim that a more nuanced understanding of grace would allow and compel Christian theologians to also address directly political issues beyond the confines of the church. An assessment of the theology of grace underlying the post-liberal Protestant rejection of any remnant of Christendom will thus aid a better understanding of what political theology in a post-Christendom context could look like. My concerns regarding the theological necessity of a sufficiently clear differentiation between Christ and Christianity, recognizable in the confession of Christianity's liability to sin and continuous dependence on Christ's unique perfection, will be key in this assessment.

Chapter 3

POST-LIBERAL CHRISTOCENTRISMS: A NON-DOMINATING CHRISTIANITY AS PRINCIPLED SOLUTION TO THE PROBLEM OF CHRISTENDOM

If this chapter turns to theologians who argue that 'any remnant of Christendom' must be overcome,[1] it should be conceded that the post-Christendom context, as such, does not present us with one new social order, but that the establishment of a truly pluralist social order still demands much discussion. Milbank discloses how atheist alternatives are now perpetuating Christianity's lost cultural and political dominance, insofar as their own position's cultural contingency is denied and an unjustifiable neutrality is pretended. Much of secularist thought's concealed dominance, as criticized by Radical Orthodoxy, has been discovered to also be operative in a great deal of public theological literature that frequently accords a central role in the politics of post-Christendom societies to Christian theology – Max Stackhouse's influential thought being one eminent example. In this sense, both Radical Orthodoxy *and* a great deal of public theology can be criticized for insufficiently overcoming a remnant of Christendom. However, the possibility that Christian theology would play the most central political role also in contemporary West European societies cannot simply be discarded on the grounds that we now live in a post-Christendom context.

Questioning the undifferentiated equation of Christendom with something evil, Milbank argues that the evaluation of Christendom, as something either good or bad, depends on how Christian theology uses its power and that any power used for the sake of love should be welcomed.[2] Contrary to the criticism

---

1. Tripp York, 'The Ballad of John and Anneken', in *The Gift of Difference: Radical Orthodoxy, Radical Reformation,* eds Chris H. Huebner and Tripp York (Winnipeg, Manitoba: Carnegie Mellon University Press, 2010), 51; see also Doak, 'The Politics of Radical Orthodoxy', *Theological Studies* 68 (2007): 369; 376. Others have labelled Milbank's ontology a form of 'Neo-Constantinianism' (Smith, 'Pluralism and Justice', *Political Theology* 13 (2012): 346).

2. John Milbank, 'Foreword', in *The Gift of Difference: Radical Orthodoxy, Radical Reformation*, eds Chris H. Huebner and Tripp York (Winnipeg, Manitoba: Carnegie Mellon University Press, 2010), xiv–xv. Milbank here justifies coercion whenever it is directed to peace

of Radical Orthodoxy's alleged return to Christendom, it must be noted that Radical Orthodoxy is not concerned with a nostalgic return to premodern times, but seeks instead to envision a better social order than the currently prevalent secularist one. Consequently, Milbank presents his Christian ontology of peace as solution to what he identifies as particularly problematic in contemporary politics, promising to establish with this ontology a more peaceful social order than any of its secularist counterparts. Ward, in contrast, conceives of postmodern positions as already initiating a successful overcoming of secularism's disguised dominance and reconfigures his theology accordingly as a fulfilment of this endeavour. These Radical Orthodox proposals should, at least, be heard as one valid option among others, when the political future of post-Christendom societies is being discussed.

I think, however, that there are Christological reasons as for why such a remnant of Christendom, found in public theological and Radical Orthodox responses to the post-Christendom context, should be overcome. This turn to Christology might be welcomed by contemporary followers of John Howard Yoder, who has convinced many that, on Christological grounds, Christian theology cannot determine the social order for a non-exclusively Christian society.[3] My assessment of Yoder's Christology, in this chapter, will elucidate that I disagree rather fundamentally with Yoder's particular Christocentric reasoning as for why Christianity's political dominance should be overcome.[4] I then turn to Kathryn Tanner, as she has already bridged the discrepancy between post-liberal Protestantism and public theology in an original manner. In common with public theologians and Radical Orthodoxy, Tanner advocates her Christian theology as a contribution to the wider society's search for solutions to contemporary political problems. However, her emphasis on the church's sinfulness and liability to failure allows Tanner to attribute to political theology a less central political role in an inherently pluralist society.[5] The degree to which Tanner

---

in the sense in which he understands it (xvi). For a criticism of this justification of the 'tragic necessity of violent practices' or of coercion in the name of peace, see York, 'The Ballad of John and Anneken' in *The Gift of Difference*, 57–60; Chris K. Huebner, 'Radical Orthodoxy, Radical Reformation: What Might Milbank and Mennonites Learn from Each Other?', in *The Gift of Difference: Radical Orthodoxy, Radical Reformation*, eds Chris H. Huebner and Tripp York (Winnipeg, Manitoba: CMU Press, 2010), 214.

3. Others have argued that one of the main differences between Yoder and Milbank consists of the latter's advocacy of a Constantinian church (Sider, *To See History Doxologically*, 183; Harry J. Huebner, 'Participation, Peace, and Forgiveness: Milbank and Yoder in Dialogue', in *The Gift of Difference: Radical Orthodoxy, Radical Reformation*, eds Chris H. Huebner and Tripp York (Winnipeg, Manitoba: CMU Press, 2010), 203).

4. My assessment is based primarily on John Howard Yoder, *The Politics of Jesus* (Grand Rapids, Michigan: Eerdmans, 1972, 1994).

5. Tanner explains that she distanced herself from her post-liberal roots precisely because she believes that the churches must be challenged by developments in the public spheres instead of simply demonizing the extra-ecclesial public in a sectarian manner (Kathryn Tanner, 'How My Mind Has Changed: Christian Claims', *The Christian Century*

successfully combines a problem-centred approach to politics with a non-dominating political theology remains to be examined.

3.1 Problematizing Theology's Public Relevance: Yoder's Rejection of Theological Promises

John Howard Yoder provides some considerable Christological reasons that challenge the very idea that Christian theology could defend its public relevance by providing solutions for the political problems of a post-Christendom society. As one of the most renowned *theological* critics of Christendom, Yoder offers arguments that mitigate public theology's and Radical Orthodoxy's promised contributions to the whole society's common good, as well as their different appeals to Christianity's universality, in order to defend apologetically a central political role for Christian theology in the contemporary West European context. Put briefly, Yoder conceives of a conflict between obeying the rule of the unpredictable God revealed in Jesus Christ, and any promises concerning positive contributions to a not-exclusively Christian society's common good. Furthermore, Yoder conceives of a conflict between translating Christianity's universality into terms of public relevance, and Christianity's due respect for human freedom. While appreciating the way in which this offers first glimpses into what a less problem-centred theological contribution to the politics of a post-Christendom society could look like, I will distance myself from the particular Christocentric rationale underlying Yoder's rejection of these two types of public theological apologetics. As will be further elucidated in my assessment of how this third, post-liberal Protestant, understanding of political theology in a post-Christendom context conceives of the theological significance of non-Christian positions, Yoder still understands Christian theology as a solution to political problems in the surrounding society. He only differs from public theology and Radical Orthodoxy insofar as he neither expects the non-Christian public to agree with his theological assessment of what is problematic nor with his proposed solution. It remains to discern what to embrace of Yoder's political Christology, and what to abandon, when crafting my fourth alternative to the three most prominent theological responses to the post-Christendom context.

a) Problematizing the Common Good: Christianity's Commitment to God's Unpredictable Rule

In stark contrast to public theology, and also to my nuanced assessment of Radical Orthodoxy, Yoder rejects any political theology that defends its own relevance

---

(2010): 44–5). For a more extended discussion of post-liberal ecclesiologies, see Tanner, *Theories of Culture*, 104–10. Tanner argues here that post-liberal theologians, following the lead of George Lindbeck, acknowledge non-Christian cultural influences on Christianity, while simultaneously upholding a distinct and self-contained Christian identity.

by promising to contribute to the common good of a not-exclusively Christian society. Similar to Mathewes's criticism of public theology, in this regard, Yoder also seeks to maintain a distance to non-Christian conceptions of the common good. He argues that, if theologians promise to contribute to the wider society's common good, they risk replacing Christianity's proper orientation towards its eschatological goal, with secular concerns.[6] This conviction, that committing oneself, as Christian theologians, to contribute to a not-exclusively Christian society's common good might compromise one's faithfulness to the proper Christian goal, set by God, is undergirded by a certain type of Christocentrism.

It is Yoder's conception of God's freedom, in the sense of God's unpredictability,[7] and his understanding of a Christian life in terms of perfectly following Christ's obedience to God's incalculable rule, which account for his reservations concerning any Christian commitment to the wider society's common good. Interpreting the Incarnation in kenotic terms, Yoder suggests that Jesus in his humanity, and not God in God's divinity, should be exemplary for any Christian politics.[8] Yoder draws from the Old Testament command to 'Be Holy as I am Holy' (Lev. 19:2) in order to argue that knowledge of God is only necessary insofar as it aids the human ethical imitation of God.[9] Believing that people attempted to follow this command, he conceives of a whole Jewish tradition of imitating God which culminates in Jesus who perfectly imitates God to the effect that God is most adequately known in Jesus.[10] In the aftermath of the Incarnation, imitating God means to be a follower of Christ.[11] A Christian politic should thus be distinguished by its severe attempt to imitate Jesus Christ.[12]

Read in light of Yoder's kenotic understanding of the Incarnation, and the stark split he makes between humanity and divinity, the imitation of the human Jesus prevents any idolatrous imagining of God's rule over the world that remains free from human expectations. The human Jesus is the one who rightly subjects to the divine rule, precisely by renouncing divine dominion over the world.[13] By already promising to achieve a certain goal in the immanent world, Christian theologians would compromise their faithfulness to God's surprising rule. Due to

---

6. Yoder, *Politics*, 230; 238.

7. Ibid., 238–9.

8. Yoder's interpretation of the doctrine of kenosis has been interpreted as an undoing of Adam's prideful longing for God-likeness (Travis Kroker, 'Is a Messianic Political Ethic Possible? Recent Work by and about John Howard Yoder', *Journal of Religious Ethics* 33 (2005): 149). However, regarding Yoder's argument concerning the human calling to imitate God, one might just as well say that Adams' sin is to imagine God according to human likeness, and that Christ revealed that people should long to be like the true God.

9. Yoder, *Politics*, 114.

10. Ibid., 99.

11. Ibid., 113–14.

12. Ibid., 10; 99.

13. Ibid., 234–6.

God's freedom, the goal to which Christians aspire might be less foreseeable than a promise of contributing to the achievement of the wider society's goals would demand.[14] A secular understanding of the common good might be too fixed, as for Christians to contribute to it. As followers of Christ, Christian theologians should not be as concerned as public theologians presuppose they are about their desire to 'make things move into the right direction'.[15] Such desire always bears the risk of moving things according to one's own imaginings, instead of following the God-willed course of history.

When assessing the particularities of Jesus's life, as the good to be imitated by a Christian politic, Yoder highlights even more that the good to which a Christian politic should be oriented is most drastically distinct from non-Christian conceptions of the good, insofar as Christians are called to continuously reshape their understanding of the good, in accordance with the effects of God's unpredictable rule in this world. Since Yoder postulates that Christ's obedience to God's rule reached its height at the crucifixion, he infers that any Christian understanding of the good must be fundamentally cruciform. According to Yoder, the Cross was not only paving the way to redemption, but it was redemption itself: 'The cross is not a detour or a hurdle on the way to the kingdom, nor is it even the way to the kingdom; it is the kingdom come.'[16] In other words, the true goal which Christians should aspire might radically differ from anyone's expectations.[17] Whereas people had expected that God would save the world, no one had expected that salvation would manifest itself at the Cross. Only those believing in Christ's Resurrection can dare to trust in the ultimate victory of what others might conceive as powerless failings.[18] Christians, thus, cannot promise to contribute to the wider society's common good, because what Christians and non-Christians evaluate as positive, or as success, differs radically. For want of a sufficiently positive image of its goal, Christian theology solely possesses positive knowledge of the means, namely following God's rule, by which the world is believed to reach its proper eschatological goal. The effectiveness of this particularly Christian political stance cannot be verified apart from appeals to the Resurrection, and this undermines the possibility of any apologetic defence of theology's public relevance, in reference to theological contributions to the common good.

14. Ibid., 238.

15. Ibid., 228; 238.

16. Ibid., 51.

17. Ibid., 86.

18. It has been argued by others that Yoder emphasizes this understanding of the Resurrection as a presupposition for the continuation of the story that has begun in Jesus Christ more in several other of his writings than he does in *The Politics of Jesus* (Craig A. Carter, *The Politics of the Cross: The Theology and Social Ethics of John Howard Yoder* (Grand Rapids, MI: Brazos Press, 2001), 100–5).

b) Problematizing the Imposition of Christian Universality: Suffering Under
Humanity's Free Disobedience of God's Rule

When public and Radical Orthodox theologians have furthermore appealed to Christianity's universality in order to defend theology's public relevance, one could interfere with Yoder's claim that, despite the universal exemplary nature of Jesus's humanity, people must follow this example *voluntarily*.[19] Although he believes that obeying God's rule is universally the best orientation for any human society, Yoder did not antecede Radical Orthodoxy in advocating a return to Christianity's political dominance. Yoder argues that embodying God's eschatological rule of peace already in this world, meant precisely to renounce any goal of establishing a peaceful society here and now, whenever such endeavour would necessitate that one violently subjects all those who still disagree.[20] Yoder understands it as principally violent to impose one's own conception of what is good onto others, even if one believes that this is meant to better their lives.[21] Advocating Yoder's Christian politics of obedience to God's rule as solution to political problems of a not-exclusively Christian society would undermine the necessarily free assent to the Christian faith.[22] This leaves us to wonder why Christians should understand this free assent, and consequently also the human freedom to disobey God's rule, as itself a good that is worthy of protection.

It is again a look at the particularities of Jesus's life, as that which needs to be imitated by Christian politics, which accounts for Yoder's claim that God's rule can only be obeyed voluntarily, and thus cannot be implemented in a not-exclusively Christian society, even if Christians believe it to be universally the best. According to Yoder, Christian theology cannot provide political guidance to non-Christians because, a Christian politics must first and foremost conform to the call to complete

---

19. Yoder, *Politics*, 130–1.

20. Ibid., 237. The biblical reference for this political stance concerns Jesus giving himself and his mission over to Roman rule instead of ensuring the attainment of his goal within the immanent world, when peace could not be established by peaceful means. Milbank agrees that the practice of peace must at the same time be the way to the end and the end itself (Milbank, 'Foreword' in *The Gift of Difference*, xvii). However, he has been criticized, from the Radical Reformist angle, for justifying coercion in the name of peace (Huebner, 'Radical Orthodoxy, Radical Reformation', in *The Gift of Difference*, 214).

21. Others have criticized Yoder for inferring from the historical failure of Constantinianism that Christendom principally conflicts with the core of Christian faith (Doerksen, *Beyond Suspicion*, 144–5). Consequently, he is said to erroneously undermine any reading of Christendom as a positive template for the church's mission in society (148).

22. Milbank's advocacy to reinstall a Christian social order has been criticized precisely for undermining the religious freedom of non-Christians, who would be bound to live within Christian social structures despite their non-belief in Christ (Doak, 'The Politics of Radical Orthodoxy', *Theological Studies*, 376).

in one's body 'that which was lacking in the suffering of Christ' (Col. 1:24).[23] Identifying that which was lacking in Christ's suffering with further suffering, Yoder associates Christian politics with suffering for the further redemption of the world.[24] This, however, can only be demanded of Christians, because they freely and explicitly assent to follow in the footsteps of Christ. Christians are called to obey amid suffering and to trust God that a not yet discernible victory is yet to come.[25] Since this makes sense only to those who believe that Jesus Christ is the self-revelation of God, obedience to God's universal rule can only be demanded of those who choose to follow Christ.[26] In other words, it is precisely Jesus's *free* acceptance of his suffering and death which must be imitated by the rest of humankind.[27]

This suffering is most poignantly embodied in Christianity's stance of non-violent subordination to the surrounding society's policies. Even if the surrounding society sinfully disobeys the divine rule when dominantly imposing its policies onto everyone, the Cross reveals the inefficiency of any counter-imposition of peace.[28] The Cross reveals that history is not restored to ontological peacefulness through imposing the Christian ontological vision onto the entire society.[29] Although the Cross already establishes the eschatological kingdom ontologically, the sinful rejection of the divine rule dominates in history, because God's rule is not imposing itself powerfully. Since God's ontological reign of peace does

23. Yoder, *Politics*, 237. See Ted Grimsrud, 'Jesus to Paul', in *John Howard Yoder: Radical Theologian*, ed. J. Denny Weaver (Eugene, OR: Cascade Books, 2014), 187–206 for an argument of how Yoder regards Paul as supporting and extending the politics that has been inaugurated by Jesus Christ.

24. Yoder, *Politics*, 237.

25. Ibid., 125.

26. Yoder understands faith as an assurance of the hoped for and a conviction that the unseen exists (Yoder, *Politics*, 125, FN 31. See also John Howard Yoder, *The Priestly Kingdom: Social Ethics as Gospel* (Notre Dame: University of Notre Dame Press, 1984), 137). At this point, Yoder distinguishes between a more general human ethics and the specific Christian ethics. The former demands of everyone a minimum degree of justice (Earl Zimmerman, 'Oscar Cullmann and Radical Discipleship', in *John Howard Yoder: Radical Theologian*, ed. J. Denny Weaver (Eugene, Oregon: Cascade Books, 2014), 155–7). The two are connected in that there are hidden implications within this more general ethics and God's providential ordering of the world, which are explicated in Christ alone (John Howard Yoder, 'Jesus – A Model of Radical Political Action', in *Faith and Freedom: Christian Ethics in a Pluralistic Culture*, eds David Neville and Philip Matthews (Hindmarsh SA: ATF Press, 2003), 163–4). This resembles the Radical Orthodox differentiation between the extra-ecclesial public as aspiration for grace and the churches as the fulfilment of this aspiration.

27. Yoder, *Politics*, 95; 131. Yoder claims that this is the only consistent New Testament definition of a faithful imitation of Christ.

28. Ibid., 239.

29. Ibid., 86.

not yet effect the transformation of the social order into one harmonious whole, Christians must patiently suffer under the dominion of existing social orders.[30] God's non-violent rule will only reach its final eschatological consumption once all of the old order has been overcome by non-violent subordination.

Yoder's Christology, thus, poses two main challenges to both public theology's and Radical Orthodoxy's propagation of Christian theological solutions for wider societal problems: the integrity of Christianity's orientation to God's rule might be undermined, and the freedom of non-Christians might be violated, when demanding of them a suffering for peace which can only be accepted voluntarily. As an alternative, Yoder claims that the Christian faith demands the non-violent subordination to the ruling social order, not the establishment of a Christian social order or the apologetic defence of theological contributions to the existing social order.[31]

c) The Church as a Solution to Society's Political Problems

But how does this position Yoder in respect to my criticism of problem-centred political theologies? Yoder's concern with Christian integrity, claiming that 'the very existence of the church is its primary task',[32] might be viewed with suspicion by public theologians, precisely due to a seeming reluctance to solve wider societal problems. Public theologians are convinced that, in a post-Christendom context, 'the salvation of the world, and not the survival of the Church, is and should be the guiding principle of public theology'.[33] However, Yoder's stance cannot be as easily connected to the withdrawal from political engagement as the public theological criticism might suggest. Quite the contrary, most contemporary scholars reject sectarian readings of Yoder's theology and appreciate the contemporary political relevance of Yoder's Christology.[34]

---

30. Ibid., 51.
31. Ibid., 209.
32. Ibid., 150.
33. Graham, *Between a Rock and a Hard Place*, 223.
34. Richard Bourne, 'Witness, Democracy and Civil Society: Reflections on John Howard Yoder's Exilic Ecclesiology', *Ecclesiology* 3(2) (2007): 196–7; Carter, *The Politics of the Cross*, 26; Doerksen, *Beyond Suspicion*, 42; 50; 67; 212–16; Thomas Heilke, 'Yoder's idea of Constantinianism: An Analytic Framework Toward Conversation', in *A Mind Patient and Untamed: Assessing John Howard Yoder's Contributions to Theology, Ethics, and Peacemaking*, eds Ben C. Ollenburger and Gayle Gerber Koontz (Telford, PA: Cascadia Publishing House, 2004), 89–125; Kroker, 'Is a Messianic Political Ethic Possible?', *Journal of Religious Ethics*, 142; Philip N. LaFountain, 'Theology and Social Psychology: Pluralism and "Evangel" in the Thought of Peter Berger and John Howard Yoder', *Theology Today* 69 (2012): 31; John C. Nugent, 'The Politics of YHWH: John Howard Yoder's Old Testament Narration and Its Implications for Social Ethics', *Journal of Religious Ethics* 39 (2011): 92; Elizabeth Phillips, 'We've Read the End of the Book: An Engagement with Contemporary Christian

For Yoder, being preoccupied with the integrity of the church is not a form of sectarian self-centredness, but the church's integrity is meant to complete the whole world's redemption. According to Yoder, God does not redeem the world by a purely supernatural intervention, but the church must continue to redeem history in the imitation of Christ.[35] My investigation of the theological rationale of Milbank's and Ward's problem-centred political theologies, providing solutions for political problems in a post-Christendom society, showed a connection of this approach to the ways in which they attributed to Christian theology the responsibility of perpetuating or completing Christ's victory over sin, in the contemporary context. For Milbank, sin is overcome through trusting in the ontological priority of grace, and he promises that a better future will be realized if a social order was built on that trust. According to Ward, sin is overcome through an obedient following of particular faith traditions, which would lead to an eventual absolution of the current political dominance of the secular social order, and thus of the sin of controlling reality. Yoder, similarly, associates sin with the idolization of existing social structures, to the extent that obedience to God's unpredictable rule over the cosmos is prevented.[36] At the Cross, Jesus overcame sin insofar as he obeyed God alone, and not the Roman social structures of the time.[37] By not conforming to these social structures, Jesus revealed their true contingency, thus reversing their false idolization.[38] If clinging to existing social structures is identified as a political problem, its solution is revealed at Christ's Crucifixion. Nevertheless, Yoder refrains from promoting this as a solution for the political problems of a not-exclusively Christian society, because of the way in which Yoder conceives of the Christian commitment to non-violent love.

Central to Yoder's understanding of redemption is that Christ overcame sin by allowing people to remain sinful. Yoder, here seems to suggest that, directly or indirectly, forbidding people to sin is necessarily violent, and as such conflicts with God's rule of love, to which Jesus freely conformed.[39] Obedience to this love implied that, in spite of his knowledge of the sinfulness of the surrounding social order, Jesus did not aspire to replace it violently by some revolutionary enforcement of a new social order. Quite the contrary, Jesus's single-hearted directedness towards

---

Zionism Through the Eschatology of John Howard Yoder', *Studies in Christian Ethics* 21 (2008): 342–61; Glen H. Stassen, 'A Nonviolent Public Ethic', in *John Howard Yoder*, 251; J. Denny Weaver, 'Introduction', in *John Howard Yoder*, 21. There are ongoing discussions about the extent to which Yoder's Christology has been informed by the Bible and/or by doctrinal developments. However, an engagement in these debates would exceed the scope of my argument.

35. Yoder, *Politics*, 222–3.
36. Ibid., 141–2.
37. Ibid., 234.
38. Ibid., 145.
39. Ibid., 234.

God's love put him at the mercy of his neighbours.[40] That God did not intervene at the Cross reveals that God does not rule over humankind by sovereign power, and, consequently, leaving the ordering of the cosmos to God means, at the same time, leaving the ordering of history to sinful humankind. In this sense, God's non-violent rule respects people's freedom not to obey to this rule.

Yoder's understanding of how Christ has overcome sin, and thus also of theology's political responsibility to further Christ's work of redemption in the contemporary context, is closer to that of Ward than to that of Milbank. However, where Ward tended to repeat secularism's problem, associated with the sin of controlling reality, at the point at which his argument implicitly suggested that secularism's political dominance must be replaced, Yoder might be viewed to envision more coherently a truly non-controlling Christian politics. Yoder emphasizes Christ's primary role in this redemptive work, which is important regarding my criticism of Milbank and Ward for conflating Christ and church. Christ is the one who actively defeats all that which remains sinful, while Christians need only to distance themselves from sin.[41] They can trust that God will protect and save them in such a way that they would not violently have to defend themselves against their contesters.[42]

Noticeably, however, Yoder shares with public theology and Radical Orthodoxy a common starting point for political theology's endeavours, namely the identification of a problem, a lack of redemption. Yoder refers to a lack even in Christ's suffering, which must be completed by Christianity. Beginning with the identified lack of redemption in this world, Yoder equally envisions theological solutions for the whole society's political problems. Yoder differs from Radical Orthodoxy only inasmuch as he does not expect non-Christians to agree with him on what he identifies as problematic. By way of directing theological reflection at the church's integrity, Christian theology indirectly contributes to the solution also of the wider society's political problems – indirectly in the sense that, due to their different convictions, non-Christians might not recognize this as comprising a positive contribution or a real solution. But, this hesitancy to impose his solution onto non-Christians is precisely part of Yoder's solution to what he conceives as problematic in his surroundings. In this sense, Yoder presents theology's political relevance in terms of its replacement of a goal-oriented politics with a rule-oriented one.[43] Adhering to the church's political rule is meant to complete the whole society's redemption, and, as such, to overcome eventually all that which

---

40. Ibid., 236.

41. Ibid., 149. This is why it has been argued that Yoder stresses the priority of grace and emphasizes that the church's task is not so much to build the Kingdom as it is to meet it and to respond to Christ's prior work of redemption (Alain Epp Weaver, 'After Politics: John Howard Yoder, Body Politics, And the Witnessing Church', *The Review of Politics* 61 (1999): 659).

42. Yoder, *Politics*, 80–5.

43. Yoder argues that Christendom did not simply modify Christianity but directed it towards a different goal altogether (Yoder, *The Priestly Kingdom*, 138–9).

is still problematic in this world. Yoder refrains from making any substantial promise concerning where his political solution would lead to, which poses an obstacle to associating his political approach with claims to theology's public relevance in relation to the whole society's common good. According to Yoder, Christians must take it on faith that his political theology does indeed lead to the entire world's further redemption, and, in this sense, resolve the political problems of contemporary societies.

Being convinced, however, that domination over others is always violent, and thus poses to political theology a problem in need of a redemptive solution, Yoder's Christology presents us with a *principled* rejection of a central role of political theology in any not-exclusively Christian context. Political theologians ought to motivate Christians to participate patiently in Christ's redemptive suffering under the present, sinful social order until it has been non-violently subverted. This is always the case, irrespective of the particular circumstances in any specific society, given that the society falls under the broad category of not being exclusively Christian, and thus being allowed to remain in sinful disobedience to God's rule. All this might evoke the question of whether Yoder's theological vision might undermine a sufficient acknowledgement of the workings of God's grace in unexpected places, which would confirm one of public theology's reservations against post-liberal theologies. Perhaps, one might wonder, a greater recognition of the grace mediated by the non-Christian public might present to Christian theology a somewhat different understanding of what counts as problematic and what counts as a solution, in contemporary post-Christendom societies, than Yoder would have us believe.

3.2 *The Theological Insignificance of the Post-Christendom Context: Yoder's Kenotic Grace as Principled Solution to All Political Problems*

While Yoder has provided considerable reasons as for why political theology should be more hesitant regarding its promised contributions to a not-exclusively Christian society's common good, and more aware concerning the dangers of imposing its own universal claims on those who explicitly refuse to follow Christ, it is now time to examine the strong separation between Christians and non-Christians, underlying Yoder's argumentation. Yoder's strict distinction between Christian theology, whose ethic is determined by a commitment to Jesus Christ, and the wider society whom Christian theologians must call to faith in Christ[44] is as vulnerable as Radical Orthodoxy to the public theological criticism of downplaying the importance of non-Christian mediations of God's grace.[45] The Christian

---

44. John Howard Yoder, 'Three Unfinished Pilgrimages', in *Faith and Freedom*, 134–5.

45. Graham, *Between a Rock and a Hard Place*, 102; 113; 223; Storrar, 'A Kairos Moment for Public Theology', *International Journal of Public Theology* 5 (2011): 8–9, 11; Reynolds, 'A Closed Marketplace', *International Journal of Public Theology* 8 (2014): 204.

churches, as exemplary communities of restored humanity, and the Christian theologians who work within their bounds might be arrogantly presented as superior to anyone else, and would as such be immunized from any non-Christian criticism.[46] In stark contrast to this suspicion, however, Yoder's theology has been characterized as particularly open to self-criticism.[47] This discrepancy necessitates a closer assessment of the degree to which the public theological objection is justified, that Yoder's separation between the Christian community that follows Christ on the one hand, and the rebellious world which disobeys God's rule on the other, might insufficiently acknowledge the theological significance of the non-Christian public. An examination of the implicit understanding of grace in Yoder's Christology will clarify the extent to which Yoder's Christology allows for some genuine Christian theological learning from non-Christians.

a) Overlooking Extra-Ecclesial Grace: The Principled Integrity of Yoder's Theological Vision

Against the suspicion that his strict separation between the church and the non-ecclesial public could underestimate the import of common grace, Yoder claims to respect both, the integral otherness of non-Christian communities as well as their theological significance.[48] Despite his Christocentrism, Yoder does not deny that God's grace is also mediated outside the bounds of the church. He affirms that God's continuous creative grace also acts through established social structures.[49] God's grace is not only mediated by the church, but also by the structures that order society in a good way.[50] Even sin does not prevent God from still creatively

---

46. Due to the post-liberal Protestant emphasis on ethics, the churches' superiority is associated with their 'radically Christocentric *rule* of life' (Graham, *Between a Rock and a Hard Place*, 116) (my emphasis).

47. Huebner, 'Radical Orthodoxy, Radical Reformation', in *The Gift of Difference*, 213.

48. John Howard Yoder, 'Meaning after Babble: With Jeffrey Stout beyond Relativism', *Journal of Religious Ethics* 24 (1996): 132–3. He rejects the post-liberal theological assumption that different communities in a pluralist public are fundamentally incommensurable and insists instead that it is possible to transcend the particularities of different discourses. However, this is not due to some universal perspective and language.

49. Yoder, *Politics*, 140–1. Instead of grace Yoder speaks of power as he lends this imagery from Hendrikus Berkhof's interpretation of the Pauline letters (Hendrikus Berkhof, *Christ and the Powers* (Scottdale, PA: Herald, 1962).

50. Yoder has been criticized, however, for predefining the state as sinful and always as a distorted image of the true politics of the church, because the state as Yoder defines it necessarily follows an ethics of dominion (Dorothea Bertschmann, 'The Rule of Christ and Human Politics – Two Proposals: A Comparison of the Political Theology of Oliver O'Donovan and John Howard Yoder', *The Heythrop Journal* LVI (2015): 430; 434–5). Others, however, argue that Yoder provides a theologically grounded conception of the state which might serve public theology's engagement in and with governmental structures (James King,

acting through these structures and from affecting new order.[51] Contrary to the suspicion that the churches' social structures are set up as perfect examples that always mediate God's grace, Yoder acknowledges that the extra-ecclesial public can sometimes mediate God's grace more truthfully than the church and can, consequently, demand the revision of ecclesial structures.[52] For example, grace might be mediated in all instances in which people are defended from adversaries without using any violence. This indirect defence could be mediated by the churches and non-Christian groups alike.

Thus, contrary to the public theological suspicions of post-liberal theologies, Yoder does not appreciate contemporary pluralism as the occasion that finally allows Christian theologians to concentrate on the life of the church alone as one self-sufficient community among others. To the contrary, Yoder appreciates the pluralist context because he believes that by penetrating other world views, Christian theologians may see something about the gospel which had previously been invisible.[53] Yoder explains that Christian theologians should enter into other world views, deeply enough to utter their own message in the words and concepts of the other.[54] One purpose of this endeavour might be to discern whether certain non-Christian practices and rules should also be obeyed by Christians or if they should be non-violently endured.[55]

'Theologizing the State: What Hauerwas Could Have Learned From Yoder', *International Journal of Public Theology* 8 (2014): 313–29. Somewhat more in support of the first interpretation, Yoder restrains from ratifying the state as such and refers merely to God's providence as sometimes using state government for good purposes (Yoder, *Politics*, 198).

51. Yoder, *Politics*, 141–2. This resembles Milbank's claim that God's plenitudinous goodness is unaffected by human sin (Milbank, 'Foreword', in *Introducing Radical Orthodoxy*, 17; Milbank, *Theology and Social Theory*, xviii).

52. Nathan Hershberger, 'Patience as Hermeneutical Practice: Christ, Church and Scripture in John Howard Yoder and Hans Frei', *Modern Theology* (2015): 5–6.

53. Yoder, 'Meaning after Babble', *Journal of Religious Ethics*, 135.

54. Ibid., 132–3.

55. This is why Yoder has been applauded for delivering a much more concrete and contextualized theology than either Karl Barth or John Milbank (Chris K. Huebner, 'Can a Gift Be Commanded? Theological Ethics Without Theory by Way of Barth, Milbank, and Yoder', *Scottish Journal of Theology* 53 (2010): 474; Harry J. Huebner, 'The Christian Life as Gift and Patience: Why Yoder Has Trouble with Method', in *A Mind Patient and Untamed*, 26–7; C. Rosalee Velloso Ewell, 'The Word Made Silent: Reflections on Christian Identity and Scripture', in *The Gift of Difference*, 77; Gerald J. Mast, 'Deconstructing Karl Barth', in *John Howard Yoder*, 170; Nugent, 'The Politics of YHWH', *Journal of Religious Ethics*, 91). For a more specific comparison between Milbank's supposedly more abstract and Yoder's more concrete ecclesiology see Sider, *To See History Doxologically*, 183–94. In relation to my argument in the previous chapter, however, I do not interpret Milbank's theology as one-sidedly abstract as his critics often contend.

Despite this acknowledgement of possible ecclesial failures and the theological significance of non-Christian world views, however, Yoder's kind of Christocentrism places his own theology on a level above both the church and the pluralist society in which it exists. Although Yoder assumes that the complete understanding of God's revelation in Christ is extended over time, he ascribes to theologians the responsibility of ensuring that the extended understanding is truthful to the original revelation.[56] At this point, Yoder must distinguish between some theological insight into the original measure of Christ-likeness, and the practical following, as well as the further explication of this insight. In some way, Christian theology must read reality through what it deems to be the most truthful lens and then judge everyone accordingly.[57] Although this reading is partly aimed at the self-critique of current ecclesial structures and practices, Yoder fails to account for the possibility that grace could ever be mediated in a way that would demand the critical revision of his theological assumption that a rule of non-violent love redeems in any circumstance that which is still sinful and problematic in the world.

Seeking to free people from sinfully following social structures, in order to enable them to follow God's unpredictable rule, Yoder now presents us with God's supposedly eternal non-violent rule.[58] Is this not equally limiting any appropriate acknowledgement of God's unpredictable freedom? While Yoder might allow for the critical revision of ecclesial structures, and the addition of further nuances to his theology, he could not admit any new and surprising act of God in history that would demand a more substantial revision of his supposedly eternal rule of non-violent love.[59] For example, while Milbank has us question whether having

56. Grimsrud, 'Jesus to Paul', in *John Howard Yoder*, 188.

57. Yoder, *Politics*, 140–1; 155.

58. Even Christ did not change these rules, but instead fulfilled them and explicated all of their implications (Yoder, 'Jesus – A Model of Radical Political Action' in *Faith and Freedom*, 164).

59. At this point, it should be mentioned that Yoder is often described as being a Biblical realist (Gayle Gerber Koontz, 'Confessional Theology in a Pluralistic Context: A Study of the Theological Ethics of H. Richard Niebuhr and John H. Yoder' (unpublished doctoral dissertation, Boston University, 1985), 173, cit. by Carter, *Politics of the Cross*, 56; 63–4; Nugent, 'The Politics of YHWH', *Journal of Religious Ethics*, 74, 87; Earl Zimmermann, 'Sixteenth-Century Anabaptist Roots', in *John Howard Yoder*, 100; Branson L. Parler, *Things Hold Together: John Howard Yoder's Trinitarian Theology of Culture* (Harrisonburg: Herald Press, 2012), 86, 89; Joel Zimbelman, 'The Contribution of John Howard Yoder To Recent Discussions in Christian Social Ethics', *Scottish Journal of Theology* 45 (1992): 376–8). Yoder supposedly acknowledges Jesus Christ as the climax of reality, and seeks to measure everything else against the biblical witness to Jesus Christ (Carter, *Politics of the Cross*, 74). Instead of understanding the gospel accounts of Jesus Christ literally, Yoder is aware that this biblical witness also stems from a particular context. If an interpretation of the Scriptures is questioned by new scientific insights, however, it is never the reality to which the

more political power than others is necessarily violent in any context, Yoder assumes that dominant power necessarily and eternally equates violence.[60] This is particularly pertinent insofar as Yoder has been criticized for downplaying the importance of all biblical events that do not confirm his own Christology.[61] It might well be that God's acts in history are far more mysterious than Yoder has us believe. For example, could not also a society's orientation towards a set goal, in accordance with its particular understanding of the common good, challenge Christian theologians to discern God's unpredictable rule to be operative also within this human orientation? Perhaps, Yoder's assumption of a contrast between the stability of human plans and projects, and God's dynamic rule is itself all too fixed and predictable. On this level, there is a strict distinction between Yoder's graced insight that non-violence is the most powerful and only legitimate option for ecclesial politics, and all alternative understandings of divine or human governance as lacking grace.

b) Denying Gratuity: Focusing on the Church's Duty

Yoder's fixation of God's offer of grace into the scheme of a strict rule of non-violence already defies one side of grace's utter gratuity. Yoder's God is not free to bestow grace in any other way than the one predicted by Yoder's rule of non-violence. If we now look at the human side, Yoder has equally been criticized for downplaying the gratuity of grace. In particular, Yoder's strong stress on the *ethical duty* to align oneself with God's grace has been criticized for defying any conception of grace as a gratuitous gift, offered primarily to be enjoyed by its recipients.[62] It

Bible refers, and always the interpretation of that reality which must be regarded as faulty and revisable. Yoder's aim is then to read the Bible in such a way that the reality itself, to which the Scriptures bear witness, comes to speak, without being unnecessarily limited by the contemporary understanding of the world (Carter, *Politics of the Cross*, 101). Yoder's focus on the church as the community that reads the Bible most adequately has been called 'ecclesial epistemology' (Doerksen, *Beyond Suspicion*, 64).

60. I, thus, align myself with those who criticize that Yoder, despite his own best intentions, is insufficiently Christocentric. Although some characterize Yoder as being an intentionally unsystematic theologian, in order to respond to Christ's free rule, the extent to which Yoder has successfully escaped the danger of over-determining his Biblical interpretations by his particular lens, remains debatable (Doerksen, *Beyond Suspicion*, 24–5; 27–8). Concerning his interpretation of history, it is said that it is precisely because of his rejection of systematizing thought that Yoder prefers 'sweeping statements' in support of his overall argument over detailed historical analysis (28).

61. Hershberger, 'Patience as Hermeneutical Practice', *Modern Theology*, 6; 14. Yoder is criticized for reducing the New Testament to its ethical and political implications (Doerksen, *Beyond Suspicion*, 89).

62. Colin Gunton has criticized Yoder for minimizing the doctrine of justification by grace alone in his ethical Christology (Colin Gunton, '"Until He Comes": Towards an Eschatology

might be countered that Yoder conceives of grace as God reigning *for* humankind, and, in this sense, of freeing humankind from the burden of planning their future. Grace allows people to simply follow the unpredictable God to wherever they are being led. The gratuitous character of this grace is undermined, however, when Yoder speaks of an ethical practice of grace that is rewarded with grace.[63] Effectively rendering God's offer of grace into the reward for a human merit, Yoder argues that 'only one who practices grace can receive grace'.[64] This binds God once again to the principle of non-violence, not allowing God to bestow grace onto the violent, and thus refusing to understand God's rule in terms of forgiveness.[65] Accordingly, Yoder's theology has been found to be lacking an adequate account of human limitations in the ongoing work of redemption.[66] He is said to verge on the presentation of the church as 'superhuman'.[67] An understanding of grace in terms of God's forgiveness might allow Christian theologians to discern new mediations of grace more dialectically, even in instances that deviate from their predefined understandings of grace, as will be shown in the remaining chapters.

This downplaying of the gratuity of grace is connected precisely to the starting point of Yoder's political Christology, namely a lack of redemption in need of a theological solution. Instead of suggesting that there is an inherent attractiveness of the grace abiding in one's own context, knowledge of the revelation of God's redemptive grace at Christ's Resurrection becomes necessary, to enable people to follow God's rule freely and thus redeem the present lack of grace. Since their own context is characterized primarily by its lack of grace, people first have to be rationally convinced that redemptive grace is really in their greatest interest (eschatologically), before they can align themselves with this grace, and before they will be rewarded with further grace. Altogether, this, and particularly Yoder's assumption that people must suffer for the world's redemption, in order to receive further grace, negatively affects Yoder's otherwise high appreciation of human freedom. Once suffering is presented as a duty for the further redemption of the world, it becomes questionable to what degree this suffering can be freely accepted. To what extent does Yoder not simply present us with a new rule, which might bind the freedom of church members and close their eyes to God's true rule, which might unpredictably direct them elsewhere? It could become impossible for those educated by Yoder ever to refuse the non-violent suffering which is demanded of them for the sake of the world's redemption.[68]

---

of Church Membership', *International Journal of Systematic Theology* 3 (2002): 189).

63. Yoder, *Politics*, 62–3.

64. Ibid., 63.

65. Ibid., 62–3.

66. Gunton, '"Until He Comes"', *International Journal of Systematic Theology*, 189.

67. Brad East, 'An Undefensive Presence: The Mission and Identity of the Church in Kathryn Tanner and John Howard Yoder', *Scottish Journal of Theology* 68 (2015): 342.

68. An examination of whether Yoder's abuse of probably more than 100 women is itself a symptom of his theology of grace would surpass the scope of this dissertation (Rachel

c) Reconsidering Yoder's Principled Rejection of Christendom

In order to conclude my discussion of the value of Yoder's Christology to answering the question concerning theology's political role in post-Christendom societies, it can first be said that, in contrast to public theology and Radical Orthodoxy, Yoder questions the very possibility of defending the Christian theological involvement in secular politics apologetically. His most interesting objection to these apologetic endeavours, in reference to the present discussion, concerns Yoder's claim that Christian theologians lack the positive vision of the goal towards which they strive. The promise of contributing towards the attainment of a set goal risks compromising Christianity's faithful imitation of Christ by the greater concern about the effectiveness in moving towards this goal.[69] Yoder reminds us that Christians who are primarily called to follow God's rule might not be as concerned with the desire to 'make things move into the right direction'[70] as most advocates of a central role for political theology in post-Christendom societies might be. According to Yoder, the effects of God's rule are less predictable, because God rules through non-violent powerlessness, rather than through the imposition of a set social order onto others.[71] This argument might question both public theology as well as Radical Orthodoxy insofar as their promises of a better societal future are indicative of a positive vision and a desire to move society towards it.

In a sense, I agree that theological promises concerning the attainment of a better future via a specific path are liable to overlook the possibility that God might set a different goal than those envisioned by Christian theologians. However, I distance myself from Yoder's stress on some supposedly necessary obedience to God's rule, and on the ethical duties that would ensue. When substantiating this

Waltner Goossen, 'The Failure to Bind and Loose: Responses to Yoder's Sexual Abuse', *The Mennonite* (1 December, 2015), https://themennonite.org/feature/failure-bind-loose-responses-john-howard-yoders-sexual-abuse/ (accessed 15 July, 2016)).

69. Yoder, *Politics*, 230.

70. Ibid., 228; 238.

71. This understanding of God as free from human expectations associates Yoder more closely with public theologians like Mathewes and Stout as well as with Graham Ward than with John Milbank. Having recently received positive attention from the side of postmodern philosophers for presumably according with an ontology that prioritizes particularity over determinative laws and rules (Daniel Barber, 'The Particularity of Jesus and the Time of the Kingdom: Philosophy and Theology in Yoder', *Modern Theology* 23 (2007): 63–89; Nathan Kerr, 'Transcendence and Apocalyptic: A Reply to Barber', *Political Theology* 10 (2009): 143–52), Yoder's understanding of Christianity's non-violent rule could be closely related to Ward's weak hermeneutical ontology by the help of which Ward seeks not to dominate any aspect of reality. Also Yoder's rejection of foundationalism is strikingly postmodern: Yoder rejects foundationalism because it downplays that *every* world view demands people's free assent (Yoder, 'Meaning after Babble', *Journal of Religious Ethics*, 134–5) (my emphasis).

emphasis, Yoder assumes too much positive knowledge concerning the precise path towards the set goal of eschatological peace. I would like to suggest inferring more unpredictability into what precise political trajectory is advisable in a particular context – not in reference to God's unpredictable rule which Christian politics are called to obey, but in reference to God's unpredictable offer of grace, which Christian politics are invited ever anew to receive and to embrace. Christian theologians might then be advised to refrain from presenting their own insights as solution to the problems of the surrounding society's political problems, not because it would have to be assumed with Yoder that a not-exclusively Christian society is, by definition, unwilling to follow Christ's rule, but because Christian theologians would have to assume that much more of the solution, than they might have dared to imagine, is already present within their surrounding society.

3.3 Extrinsic Universality: Tanner's Non-Dominating Solutions to Political Problems

We have now seen the value and possible shortcomings of three major strands of theological responses to the post-Christendom context. Despite the different ways in which they have elaborated on it, all authors discussed thus far share a strong emphasis of theology's redemptive role in relation to the surrounding society, and all have run the risk of conflating God's offer of redemption in Christ with political theology. In the case of both public theologians and Radical Orthodoxy, theology's vision of the world's redemption in Christ was associated with the theological ability to offer solutions to contemporary societal problems, whereas Yoder offered his vision of God's rule of the world as a blueprint for Christian political action, irrespective of the question of whether these actions solve societal problems in any way society would deem as being effective. By starting with a lack or a problem in need of a solution, all have stressed theology's (ethical) task of completing redemption, and, as a consequence, all have tended to overlook the possibility that also what they predefine as problematic might be theologically significant, mediating one of God's abundant gifts of grace.

Broadly speaking, Kathryn Tanner also shares a fundamentally problem-centred approach to political theology, when seeking to attend to 'the most pressing problems and issues of contemporary life'.[72] Tanner justifies her problem-centred approach as explicitly as public theologians in reference to the need of apologetically defending theology's public relevance. Not unlike Graham Ward, Tanner situates contemporary apologetics within a postmodern context, in

---

72. Tanner, 'How my Mind has Changed', *The Christian Century* 127 (2010): 40. Her *Economy of Grace* is precisely such an attempt to construct a comprehensive Christian the-ological understanding of economics (Kathryn Tanner, *Economy of Grace* (Minneapolis: Fortress Press, 2005), 2–6).

which Christian theological inputs are being evaluated as one legitimate form of tradition-based arguments among others.[73] According to Tanner, this situatedness within a postmodern context implies that Christian theology no longer needs to justify its public relevance by way of adhering to secular procedural norms of dialogue, but, instead, by way of offering solutions to wider societal problems, the quality of which is appreciated by all.[74] Tanner wants to solve contemporary political problems, by way of drawing upon the Christian tradition, and then interpreting the whole contemporary situation 'in a Christian light'.[75] In so doing, Tanner, despite her overall positive evaluation of the contemporary postmodern climate, moves on to problematize the entire present cultural context, and offers her theology as a solution.

Not unlike Milbank and Ward, Tanner refers to a 'narrowness of a contemporary sense of the realistic', and she parallels them in looking at the past, not for any nostalgic reasons, but for a solution that promises a more viable future.[76] In striking agreement with Radical Orthodoxy, Tanner draws upon the Christian tradition in order to 'shock and startle' in the sense of offering 'an escape from

---

73. Like Radical Orthodox authors, Tanner is also aware that a postmodern understanding of reality is not theologically neutral. More like Ward than like Milbank, however, Tanner evaluates postmodernity as a more beneficial context than modernity for Christian theology (Tanner, *Theories of Culture*, 61).

74. Tanner, 'How my Mind has Changed', *The Christian Century*, 40–1. For example, in times when the governing system of society fails, such as the failure of market capitalism in the recent financial crisis, 'religion' can play the crucial role of reminding everyone that markets are meant to serve the welfare of the entire society. By holding the highest standards of universal well-being, religions can put markets under the pressure to work for the best of all (Kathryn Tanner, 'Is Capitalism a Belief System?' *Anglican Theological Review* 92(4) (2010): 632–3).

75. Tanner, 'How my Mind has Changed', *The Christian Century*, 45. Tanner parallels Milbank in his desire to attain 'the broadest possible ecumenical vision' (42). Similarly concerned with constructing an all-encompassing world view, Tanner highlights that faith in Christ influences one's whole understanding of the world (Tanner, *Theories of Culture*, 113; 123). Tanner also speaks explicitly of a 'theological vision of reality' in Kathryn Tanner, 'Shifts in Theology over the Last Quarter Century', *Modern Theology* 26 (2010): 39. This is why Tanner's systematic theology has been described as a search for the totality in order to render the core of Christianity easily accessible to her readers (Christine Helmer, 'A Systematic Theological Theory of Truth in Kathryn Tanner's *Jesus, Humanity and the Trinity*', *Scottish Journal of Theology* 57 (2004): 206–7).

76. Tanner, 'How my Mind has Changed', *The Christian Century*, 42. Whereas Hackett deems ultimately failed Tanner's 'laudable attempt of retrieving traditional Christological debates in order to refresh our contemporary thinking' (Chris Hackett, 'Review Essay: What's the Use of a Skeleton Key for Christian Theology?: A Report on an Essential Problematic in Kathryn Tanner's *Christ the Key*', *Radical Orthodoxy: Theology, Philosophy, Politics* 2 (2014): 192), I do not investigate the accurateness of Tanner's historical work.

the taken-for-granted certainties of life by referring them to something that remained ever beyond them'.[77] Whereas some have criticized Tanner, saying that her approach presupposes the impeccability of the Christian tradition,[78] Tanner conceives of this correlation of Christian theology with contemporary problems as both at once a solution to these problems and a (correcting) renewal of the Christian tradition.[79] Changing contexts and practices must continuously renew one's understanding of the whole Christian theological system as well as of particular doctrines.[80]

Overall, Tanner offers a valuable alternative to the approaches already discussed, insofar as she combines a problem-centred approach with a Christocentric approach to political theology.[81] I have criticized that public and Radical Orthodox theologians, in their eagerness to solve contemporary political problems, re-ascribe to political theology the most central political role also in a post-Christendom society. The theologically disputable point of this move consists in their conflation of Christ's unique redemptive role, and theology's participation therein, the result of which is an underestimation of the theological significance of non-Christian dialogue partners. Noticeably, Tanner explicitly states that, when interpreting non-Christian positions through a theological lens, 'Christianity does

---

77. Tanner, 'How my mind has changed', *The Christian Century*, 43. This is also why Tanner does not explain Christian claims in secular terms, but seeks to transpose the secular grounds of arguments (*Theories of Culture*, 117).

78. Charles Hefling, 'Review Article Christologies and Philosophies', *Anglican Theological Review* 93(4) (2011): 693–4; James J. Buckley, review of *Christ the Key*, by Kathryn Tanner, *Modern Theology* 27 (2011): 701. These criticisms seem, however, to overlook the very nuanced way in which Tanner reflects, for example, upon the shortcomings of theological understandings of atonement and sacrifice (Kathryn Tanner, 'Incarnation, Cross, and Sacrifice: A Feminist-Inspired Reappraisal', *Anglican Theological Review* 86(1) (2004): 35–56).

79. Tanner, 'How my Mind has Changed', *The Christian Century*, 40. Tanner positions herself within a wider trend of theologians presently characterized by this approach in Tanner, 'Shifts in Theology', *Modern Theology*, 40.

80. Tanner, *Theories of Culture*, 78.

81. Tanner calls the Incarnation 'the center of [her] theology in a most thoroughgoing way' (Kathryn Tanner, 'The Church and Action for the World: A Response to Amy Pauw', *Scottish Journal of Theology* 57 (2004): 232). However, it is striking that Tanner expressed the theme of the non-competition between God and creation already before her venture into Christology, and that it has been criticized precisely for not sufficiently considering the doctrine of the Incarnation (David A. Ford, review of God and Creation in Christian Theology. Tyranny or Empowerment?, by Kathryn Tanner, *Religious Studies* 26 (1990): 552), and that her *Christ the Key* has been described as being 'not really about christology so much as' it applies 'a Christological Denkfigur to other theological loci' (Steffen Lösel, 'Book Forum', *Theology Today* 68 (2011): 330). Rather than invalidating Tanner's Christocentrism, I simply understand these criticisms as indication that Tanner does not contrast accessing the truth about Christ with relying upon human interpretative frameworks.

not need to keep the upper hand ...; the Word does'.[82] This suggests that, also when offering theological solutions to wider societal problems, Tanner seeks ultimately to let Christ solve the problem. Remembering the insights we gained from Yoder's Christocentrism, this might mean that Tanner consciously abstains from ever imposing her solutions onto those who disagree. Her Christocentrism might allow her to escape the charge of advocating any ecclesial superiority, removed from public criticism and correction, over non-Christian positions.[83] But, let me further disentangle Tanner's position, in order to understand more precisely how her theological approach to public politics differs from that of the already discussed authors.

a) *Theological Reception of the Common Good: God's Egalitarian Bestowal of Grace*

If we ask again the question concerning theology's contributions to the common good in a post-Christendom society, Tanner, without explicitly distancing herself from non-Christian understandings, offers a particularly theocentric understanding of the common good. Calling God the self-subsistent fullness who 'provides to the world ... its non-divine existence, and all that it includes: life, truth, beauty, goodness in their finite forms',[84] Tanner understands God as the source of all goodness as well as the immediate source of every particular being's goodness.[85] Tanner thus understands the whole world as equally graced

---

82. Tanner, *Theories of Culture*, 147 (see also p. 114).

83. See Tanner, 'The Church and Action for the World', *Scottish Journal of Theology*, 228–9. Concerning the question of the degree to which Tanner's ecclesiology is sufficiently contextual to fulfil this promise, opinions differ from criticizing Tanner's ecclesiology for a lack of concreteness (Hackett, 'What's the Use of a Skeleton Key for Christian Theology?', *Radical Orthodoxy: Theology, Philosophy, Politics*, 191–2) to praising her work for reflecting the Wittgensteinian conviction that the church is a particular community of practices and language games which need to be critically analysed in light of contemporary challenges (Nicholas M. Healy, 'Practices and the New Ecclesiology: Misplaced Concreteness?' *International Journal of Systematic Theology* 5 (2003): 287; 290–1).

84. Tanner, *Jesus, Humanity and the Trinity*, 42.

85. Tanner, *God and Creation in Christian Theology*, 44. Whereas Milbank thought of the creaturely mediation of God's immediate presence in a hierarchical way, Tanner stresses that God is the immediate source of all creatures in the same way (46). At this point, Tanner has been criticized from a Radical Orthodox perspective, for upholding this fundamental egalitarianism, not for any convincing Christological, but for liberal secular reasons (Hackett, 'What's the Use of a Skeleton Key?' *Radical Orthodoxy: Theology, Philosophy, Politics*, 197). However, the criticism could be reversed and it might be evaluated as positive given that Tanner, in contrast to Radical Orthodoxy, does not presuppose liberalism as Christianity's unquestionable enemy.

by God's goodness, constituting a graced environment for human existence.[86] Human nature in itself, on the contrary, is merely the empty vessel which can receive God's good gifts.[87] Human nature is particularly malleable and open in order to become good eventually.[88] Being more malleable than other creatures means that anything that impresses itself upon humans becomes an element of their constitution. All this suggests that a society orients itself to the common good by entering a relationship with God, the source of all goodness, and by receiving the graces God offers.[89]

One first important question is whether Tanner associates this understanding of the common good with a societal problem in need of a solution. A look at Tanner's understanding of sin indeed reveals that she views as problematic the

---

86. Kathryn Tanner, *Christ the Key* (Cambridge: Cambridge University Press, 2010), 129. The concept of grace has been called the centre around which the rest of Tanner's argument in *Christ the Key* and *Jesus, Humanity, and the Trinity* gravitates (Hefling, 'Christologies and Philosophies', *Anglican Theological Review*, 695; Amy Plantinga Pauw, 'Ecclesiological Reflections on Kathryn Tanner's Jesus, Humanity and the Trinity', *Scottish Journal of Theology* 57 (2004): 222; Helmer, 'A Systematic Theological Theory of Truth in Kathryn Tanner's *Jesus, Humanity and the Trinity*', *Scottish Journal of Theology*, 203, 212–3).

87. Kathryn Tanner is said to attempt in *Christ the Key* to construe 'a truly non-anthropocentric interpretation of the *imago Dei*' (Hilda Koster, 'Book Forum', *Theology Today*, 317). Some have criticized Tanner for undermining any more substantial understanding of human interiority and the human self (Paul DeHart, 'f (S) I/s: The Instance of Pattern, or Kathryn Tanner's Trinitarianism', in *The Gift of Theology: The Contribution of Kathryn Tanner*, eds Rosemary P. Carbine and Hilda P. Koster (Minneapolis: Fortress Press, 2016), 29–55), or for not sufficiently explaining the metaphysics underlying her Christological anthropology (Hefling, 'Christologies and Philosophies', *Anglican Theological Review*, 696–7, 704; William Wood, review of *Christ the Key. Current Issues in Theology*, by Kathryn Tanner, *Scottish Journal of Theology* 66 (2013): 266). There are divergent views on whether Tanner thinks of the Incarnation as Christ's assumption of a general human essence in which all human beings participate or whether only the particular humanity of Jesus of Nazareth is assumed and sanctified (Oliver Crisp, *Revisioning Christology: Theology in the Reformed Tradition* (Farnham: Ashgate, 2011), 124). Hefling tends to read Tanner as presupposing a generic human essence which is assumed by Christ, whereas Helmer argues that Tanner refers to Christ's assumption of an individuated nature, following the tradition of medieval and seventeenth-century Orthodox Protestantism (Helmer, 'A Systematic Theological Theory of Truth in Kathryn Tanner's *Jesus, Humanity and the Trinity*', *Scottish Journal of Theology*, 216). My own argument suggests that, in Tanner's Christology, Christ's assumption of the particular human nature of Jesus effects a change in a generic human essence, which must be individually accepted in order to be effective.

88. Tanner, *Christ the Key*, 28, 37, 44–6, 137–8.

89. This would be a political rendering of Tanner's claim that humans are not by nature united or even similar to God, but they are naturally made *for* a relationship with God (ibid., 2).

denial of the world's continuous dependence upon God as the transcendent source of its goodness. Not unlike Milbank, Tanner also understands sin in terms of humankind's mistaken view that people are good due to their own achievements, instead of duly acknowledging that any such goodness is given to them from their graced environment.[90] What concerns the effects of sin, Tanner argues that a graced life now exists 'in competition with another potentially all-embracing … pattern of existence marked by futility and hopelessness'.[91] The more people imagine themselves as the authors of their own good, the less open they are to the reception of new gifts of grace from God.[92] The same original empty human nature, when sinful, is filled up with 'the wrong inputs' to the effect that human beings are less capable of receiving God's grace.[93] In this way, a human being becomes ever more estranged from his/her fully graced eschatological ideal. The same could be said of a society if the problem is translated from the individual onto the social level. As such, the logic of Tanner's argument implies that those positions that understand the common good in terms of combining all good human efforts, each contributing their intrinsic best to a common project, should be rejected as problematic – for these conceptions would inhibit a society's receptiveness of the truly good, which comes from outside its own resources.

Or, could this argument also imply that Christian theologians would have to receive as external good also those positions that present the common good in terms of human efforts? For an answer to this question, we should look at the way in which Tanner conceives of Christianity's universality. Differently phrased, the question is whether Tanner thinks that her theological understanding of the common good should be universally adopted, or whether it suffices if Christians adopt it, thus contributing their part to resolving that which Tanner diagnoses as problematic in the whole of society.

b) Problematizing the Imposition of Christian Universality: Acknowledging Christ's Uniqueness

Tanner can be more hesitant in expecting everyone to adopt her theological understanding of a society's orientation to the common good, because of the way in which she stresses not only Christ's universal exemplarity, but also Christ's unique redemptive work.[94] Not unlike Yoder, Tanner understands Christ in terms of setting a

---

90. Ibid., 34–5.

91. Tanner, *Jesus, Humanity and the Trinity*, 112.

92. Tanner, *Christ the Key*, 70.

93. Ibid., 67; 70.

94. Tanner's theology has been repeatedly criticized for insufficiently explaining the mechanism of Christ's redemptive work (Hackett, 'What's the Use of a Skeleton Key?', *Radical Orthodoxy: Theology, Philosophy, Politics*, 206–7; Lösel, 'Book Forum', *Theology Today*, 334–335; Crisp, *Revisioning Christology*, 114–115; 127; Anthony D. Baker, 'Convenient Redemption: A Participatory Account of the Atonement', *Modern Theology* 30 (2014): 99–100, 102; William Wood,

perfect example for the rest of humankind.[95] However, rejecting kenotic interpretations of the Incarnation, Tanner understands God's redemptive power to be fully present throughout Jesus's fully human life.[96] Her conception of God in terms of self-subsistent goodness allows Tanner to understand Jesus's divinity in terms of Jesus's continuous

review of *Christ the Key.* Current Issues in Theology, by Kathryn Tanner. *Scottish Journal of Theology*, 366; Helmer, 'A Ssystematic Ttheological Ttheory of Ttruth in Kathryn Tanner's *Jesus, Humanity and the Trinity*', *Scottish Journal of Theology*, 217); Carl S. Hughes, '"Tehomic" Christology? Tanner, Keller, and Kierkegaard on Writing Christ', *Modern Theology* (2015): 10; David P. Henreckson, 'Poessessing Heaven in Our Head: A Reformed Reading of Incarnational Ascent in Kathryn Tanner', *Journal of Reformed Theology* 4 (2010): 178, which is why I attempt to clarify the issue in this section.

95. Kathryn Tanner, *Jesus, Humanity and the Trinity: A Brief Systematic Theology* (Minneapolis: Fortress Press, 2001), 9; 17.

96. Kathryn Tanner, 'Article Review: David Brown's Divine Humanity', *Scottish Journal of Theology* 68 (2015): 112. This corresponds to Tanner's non-contrastive account of the relation between God and creation, which is meant to uphold both God's radical transcendence to and intimate involvement in the world (Kathryn Tanner, *God and Creation in Christian Theology: Tyranny or Empowerment?* (Minneapolis, MN: Fortress Press, 1988), 45.) Tanner understands God's transcendence in the sense of God not being directly mediated by any creature (Tanner, *Jesus, Humanity and the Trinity*, 43–4). Faith in this God implies that the world depends upon an extrinsic transcendent source that holds the world in existence and perfects it without revealing anything about Godself in so doing (1; 44; 67). This is why Tanner has been criticized for undermining the traditional importance of positive revelations of God's nature (Hackett, 'What's the Use of a Skeleton Key?', *Radical Orthodoxy: Theology, Philosophy, Politics*, 198; Sarah Coakley, 'Why Gift? Gift, gender and Trinitarian relations in Milbank and Tanner', *Scottish Journal of Theology* 61 (2008): 232–3; Crisp, *Revisioning Christology*, 131; Helmer, 'A Systematic Theological Theory of Truth in Kathryn Tanner's *Jesus, Humanity and the Trinity*', *Scottish Journal of Theology*, 217; Henreckson, 'Poessessing Heaven in Our Head', *Journal of Reformed Theology*, 179). For a positive reception of Tanner's understanding of God's radical transcendence in relation to discussions in eco-theology see Hilda P. Koster, 'Questioning Eco-Theological *Panentheisms*: The Promise of Kathryn Tanner's Theology of God's Radical Transcendence for Ecological Theology', *Scriptura* 111 (2012:3): 385–94. For arguments that Tanner's entire theological oeuvre is unified by the theme of the non-competition between God and creation see Hefling, 'Review Article Christologies and Philosophies', *Anglican Theological Review*, 695; Michael Root, 'The Wrong Key: A Review of *Christ the Key* by Kathryn Tanner', *First Things* (December 2010), http://www.firstthings.com/article/2010/12/the-wrong-key (accessed 28 January, 2014); Hughes, '"Tehomic" Christology?', *Modern Theology* (2015): 4. Hughes relates Tanner's non-contrastive understanding of God and creation to the Barthian influence on her thought (5). Others have observed that Tanner's Barthian approach does not prevent her theology from bearing many similarities to that of Schillebeeckx (John R. Sachs, 'Responses to Tanner's Jesus, Humanity and the Trinity', cit. by Jean Donovan, *CTSA Proceedings: Anthropology Group* 58/ 2003: 157). See Martin Poulsom, *The Dialectics of Creation: Creation and the Creator in Edward*

drawing on God's fully present redemptive power, which gradually perfected Jesus's humanity for the world's redemption.[97] Christ's fully human life is God's own insofar as it is lived in strict union with God.[98] And, Christ is an example to the rest of humankind in the way in which he receives his goodness from God.

Tanner, hence, understands the Incarnation not in terms of some immediate redemption of creation, but as redeeming the world through the course of Jesus's life.[99] All effects of sin, from which the world needs to be redeemed, are overcome precisely at the point at which Jesus is subjected to them, because Christ's relationship to God reworks the situation.[100] Christ receives the grace which God bestows onto the world and weaves it into the situation, so to speak. Jesus redeemed his own humanity and that of everyone else from the tendency to store up sinful inputs in one's own constitution.[101] This human tendency was redeemed precisely at the point when Jesus was exposed to the violent death of the crucifixion.[102] Here, Jesus's relationship to God, the transcendent source of all grace, helped him to endure the harm he had to suffer. Jesus, thus, remained open to God's grace and did not integrate the harm done to him into his constitution. Concretely, this could mean that Jesus did not become harmful himself and did not close himself off to the full receptivity of God's grace. If this pattern was to be imitated by contemporary political theology, those positions that are interpreted as obstacles to a society's orientation to the common good, as something always arriving from outside, would not have to be defeated. Theology's task would rather be to remain open to God's offer of grace and to introduce this grace into the problematic position.

Tanner highlights that, whereas this openness to grace in a fallen world was to some extent risky for Christ, as there was no assurance that sin would not win

---

Schillebeeckx and David Burell (London: Bloomsbury, 2014), for a comparison of Tanner's non-contrastive view of God and creation with Schillebeeckx's theology of creation.

97. Tanner, 'David Brown's Divine Humanity', *Scottish Journal of Theology*, 111.

98. This rejection of kenotic understandings of Christ reveals Chris Hackett's claim that Tanner presents humanity and divinity 'in Christ in irreducible opposition' to be insufficiently nuanced (Hackett, 'What's the Use of a Skeleton Key?', *Radical Orthodoxy: Theology, Philosophy, Politics*, 198).

99. Tanner, *Christ the Key*, 260–2.

100. Ibid., 262.

101. Ibid., 257–8.

102. Ibid., 257–7. Importantly, Tanner rejects the idea that Christ revealed a cruciform pattern of redemption (Tanner, 'The Church and Action for the World', *Scottish Journal of Theology*, 231–2). Instead, Jesus's human death was redeemed by Christ, in union with God, at the point of the crucifixion (Tanner, *Christ the Key*, 269). This means that Tanner agrees with feminist theologies – and, I wish to add, with Schillebeeckx – that salvation has been achieved despite the Cross, not thanks to it (251). In sharp contrast to Yoder, and also to Ward to some extent, Tanner rejects any positive view of suffering (Tanner, *Jesus, Humanity and the Trinity*, 76).

the upper hand at the Cross, such risk has been definitely overcome. Tanner here strictly distinguishes between Christ and the rest of humankind, inasmuch as Christ, due to his divinity, uniquely redeemed the whole world.[103] She argues that the whole point of Christ's Crucifixion was to redeem humankind in our stead, to the extent that no one has to suffer for redemption any longer.[104] It is in this sense that we should understand the effects of Christ's salvific deeds to be universal. Humankind's environment will always be filled with God's grace.[105] People's sinful stocking up of themselves with sinful inputs can be undone by the grace of redemption, and will not stop God from offering ever more grace.

103. Tanner's identification of Jesus specifically with the Word has been criticized for an eisegesis of 'the christological dogma into the account of Jesus' life, rather than deducing it from the latter' (Lösel, 'Book Forum', *Theology Today*, 335–6); for a similar criticism concerning Tanner's drawing upon Chalcedonian doctrine, rather than on the biblical narratives, see Mary Catherine Hilkert, 'Responses to Tanner's Jesus, Humanity and the Trinity', cit. by Jean Donovan, *CTSA Proceedings: Anthropology Group* 58/ 2003: 157; Buckley, review of *Christ the Key*, *Modern Theology* 27 (2011): 700. Tanner presumably draws an entirely abstract picture of Jesus Christ's humanity, loosened from its 'narrative context below' (Hackett, 'What's the Use of a Skeleton Key?', *Radical Orthodoxy: Theology, Philosophy, Politics*, 204). Tanner has been criticized for one-sidedly stressing Christ's divinity (Helmer, 'A Systematic Theological Theory of Truth in Kathryn Tanner's *Jesus, Humanity and the Trinity*', *Scottish Journal of Theology*, 215). Supposedly, the coherence of Tanner's theology downplays the particularities of the Bible, the theological tradition, and the experience of actual Christian communities (Hughes, '"Tehomic" Christology?', *Modern Theology* (2015): 8). This resonates with the broader critique that Tanner's theology displays an overall lack of contextuality and an unjustifiable abstractness (Ford, review of God and Creation in Christian Theology, *Religious Studies*, 552; Kimlyn J. Bender, 'Christ, Creation and the Drama of Redemption: "The Play's the Thing"', *Scottish Journal of Theology* 62 (2009): 153, FN 14). Sarah Coakley also expresses doubts concerning Tanner's supposed optimism regarding 'the power of theological *ideas* to change political or economic structures' (Coakley, 'Why Gift?', *Scottish Journal of Theology*, 228–9).

104. Tanner, *Jesus, Humanity and the Trinity*, 74–6.

105. Tanner, *Christ the Key*, 270–1. This has earned Tanner the criticism that she illegitimately protects humankind from the 'messiness of life' (Hackett, 'What's the Use of a Skeleton Key?', *Radical Orthodoxy: Theology, Philosophy, Politics*, 206–8). At the same time, Tanner has been criticized, from the opposite angle, of being inconsistent inasmuch as she denies that the Word itself suffers and dies on the Cross, whereas all other aspects of Jesus's life are assumed into the Trinity (Lösel, 'Book Forum', *Theology Today*, 334–5). In contrast to both critics, Tanner's argument that no human being has to suffer for the world's redemption does not imply any promise that human beings will not suffer in a fallen world. The human being Jesus also had to suffer, but it was not his human suffering which effected God's graciousness. God's graciousness took up this suffering and redeemed it. Consequently, this suffering does not enter the Trinity but transpires into nothingness, which is why it is right to say that the Word does not suffer.

This focus on Christ's unique and eternally effective work of redemption sheds new light on the discussion concerning problem-centred approaches to politics, inasmuch as Tanner provides a theological rationale for not beginning one's political reflections with the identification of some lack. This disassociates Tanner's position from those who drew upon Christianity's duty to complete the world's redemption in order to promise positive contributions to the entire society's political organization. Tanner's theological approach might allow her to appreciate the theological significance of non-Christian positions to a higher degree, inasmuch as everyone is most fundamentally regarded as a beneficiary of the redemption uniquely won by Christ. In order to analyse the way in which Tanner strikes the balance between the church's call to imitate Christ and its dependence and receptivity of a redemption that has been uniquely won by Christ in greater detail, I now turn to the way in which Tanner describes the church's participation in Christ's redemptive work.

c) *The Church's Dependence on God's Grace as Solution to Society's Problems*

According to Tanner, Christ's redemptive work not only assures God's continuous offer of grace onto the world,[106] it also prevents any further loss of the world's receptivity of this grace, such that there could not be a second Fall from grace. Tanner argues that Christ has effected 'a new relationship of God to creatures that renders the gift of divine power to human beings more efficacious and secure than before'.[107] Christ not only reveals the dependency of created reality upon God, and of humans on their graced environment, but he also effected a change within human nature. Since Christ is the human being who, by nature, is in a right relation to God, he cannot lose this relationship. A person's attachment to Christ affects the same insoluble union with God, which means that grace can now also become a part of a human being's own constitution.[108] Following the Incarnation, people are no longer either empty or filled up with sin; they can also be filled with grace. Those people who are attached to Christ participate in Christ's divinity in such a way that they no longer one-sidedly depend upon the grace given to them from outside.

Through their attachment to the Word, once grace is received, Christians now possess this grace as their own in Christ. Similar to Milbank's understanding of Christians as positively exceeding Christ, Tanner also argues that 'Christ's life is extended in new directions as it incorporates our lives within it'.[109] Christ's relationship to God is imitated by the rest of humankind whenever a human being is assumed by Christ, the incarnated Word, in order to live in closest union with

---

106. Tanner, *Jesus, Humanity and the Trinity*, 22.
107. Kathryn Tanner, 'Book Forum', *Theology Today*, 346.
108. Tanner, *Christ the Key*, 14.
109. Tanner, *Jesus, Humanity and the Trinity*, 74.

God.[110] However, this being filled with grace should not be imagined primarily as some storing up of grace, perfecting the human individual in terms of some inner growth. Instead, being filled with grace translates into becoming an active distributor of grace.[111] The filling up with sinful inputs is prevented through one's primary occupation of sharing with others that which one has received. All remaining sin will be overcome once everyone bestows their received goods onto others.[112]

This argument explains why, despite her affirmation of the church's participation in Christ's divinity, Tanner can maintain that the church is different from non-Christian groups not due to any intrinsic quality, but only due to the free grace of God in Christ, which remains extrinsic to the church.[113] The church is different from non-Christian groupings insofar as it is witness to something outside itself. Everyone, Christians and non-Christians, must be viewed as someone in need of Christ's grace most fundamentally. Active participation in Christ's ongoing redemptive work primarily means sharing with others the grace one continues to receive from outside. This suggests that, when faced with positions that seem to block a society's orientation to the common good, Christian theologians should not be concerned with defending their theological understanding of the common good apologetically, but they should motivate the church to continue distributing the grace God bestows onto the world to the wider society. Only when those who are still sinful open themselves up to receive the graces that are bestowed upon them from outside, could they eventually be converted to becoming ever more receptive channels of a societal gift exchange.

It could be questioned, however, why Tanner focuses on contemporary *problems* in the first place if her argument is that Christians should primarily recognize the *grace* that surrounds them. Those positions that present the common good in terms of combined human efforts are still being evaluated as problems in need of a theological solution, even if Tanner successfully refrains from imposing her theological solution onto them. At this point, Tanner's position exhibits parallels with that of Yoder. Both suggest that Christ, and following him, Christianity, redeem the world from its present sinfulness, by allowing the world to remain sinful, rather than by imposing onto the world a theological social order geared to orient a whole society away from sin, towards the good. The logic of Tanner's position, however, might suggest that she hesitates to impose her own theological vision on those whom she conceives as sinful, because she expects them to be already receptive mediators of graces that she has not yet been able to appreciate from her perspective. Yet, Tanner leans more towards a 'Yoderian' model of recognizing a sinful situation and of distributing the graces that Christian theology has already stored up in its tradition. Importantly, despite her otherwise convincing focus on

110. Ibid., 9.
111. Tanner, *Christ the Key*, 37.
112. Ibid., 90.
113. Tanner, *Theories of Culture*, 101–2; 113.

the church's dependence and reception of redemption, Tanner turns this reception into an ethical task. Tanner draws upon Edward Schillebeeckx's theology in order to argue that Christians *must* follow Jesus in living in union with God through their own situations.[114] If Christians are not responsible for the world's redemption, but are primarily joyous beneficiaries of this redemption, we might wonder where this 'must' comes from. As I will argue in Chapter 4, Schillebeeckx does not understand the Christian calling to imitate Christ primarily in terms of an ethical duty. The issue of whether this imitation is interpreted in the sense of imposing an ethical duty onto the church or not will prove to be decisive for the question concerning the political role of Christian theology in post-Christendom societies.

3.4 The Non-Competitive Significance of the Post-Christendom Context: Tanner's Extrinsic Grace to Overcome Christian Dominance

This returns us once again to the question of the degree to which non-Christian positions are being interpreted as theologically significant. The more non-Christian positions are acknowledged to mediate God's grace, the more marginal becomes the political role that could be ascribed to Christian theology. The more the emphasis is on theology's unique insight into how the world is being redeemed by Christ, the more responsible Christian theology would see itself for providing the solutions for the entire society's problems. Having already argued how Tanner understands the church as called to participate in Christ's redemptive work, and as such bearing the promise of contributing positively to the whole society's orientation to the common good, I will now explain that most fundamentally, however, she positions Christians on the same level as any other human being, namely at the level of being sinners in need of God's bestowal of grace, which remains extrinsic to everyone. This introduces an additional dynamic into the discourse about theological responses to the post-Christendom context, a dynamic that I like to embrace, in view of my criticisms of previous approaches.

a) Acknowledging Extra-Ecclesial Grace: Non-Competitive Completion of the Theological Vision

The discussion above suggests that Tanner's theology presents reality as being primordially graced, because the God on whom it depends is thought of in terms of plenitudinous positivity. She stresses that God bestows grace freely upon all creatures, Christians and non-Christians alike, and she is in agreement with Elaine Graham that this grace might find non-Christians in ways unknown to Christians.[115] Because God's creative grace is also active outside of the church,

---

114. Tanner, *Jesus, Humanity and the Trinity*, 74 (my emphasis).
115. Tanner, *Theories of Culture*, 101.

Tanner understands a pluralist society as being good in its own right, and not only as an aspiration for a grace that needs to be perfected by the church.[116] Her understanding of Christ's unique and definite realization of redemption, thus, allows Tanner to acknowledge that God might bestow graces in ways entirely different from any pre-established theological vision of reality. Consequently, her overarching theological vision of how the world is graced would have to be modified through attendance to the concrete graces mediated by non-Christian positions. Tanner's understanding of grace in terms of extrinsic gifts translates in Tanner's explanation that Christian theologians and non-Christians share the same material, which they then use differently.[117] Calling Christianity 'essentially parasitic', Tanner understands Christianity as ever only becoming a comprehensive way of life where theologians receive and modify the practices and beliefs of others.[118]

Regarding the modification of this extrinsic grace, Tanner, like Radical Orthodox theologians, contends that Christian theology participates in Christ's redemption of the world through relating non-Christian material to God. Contrary to Milbank and Ward, however, who laud themselves for being able to make *more* sense of reality than secularism through relating reality to God, Tanner seeks to propose a less triumphant perfection of non-Christian material by Christian theology. According to her, theology's orientation to God implies that non-Christian material must be modified with the aim of correcting existing shortcomings in both the extra-ecclesial public as well as in the church.[119] It is noteworthy, however, that in associating this relation of non-Christian material to God with theology's imitation of the way in which Christ redeemed the world, Tanner again implicitly promises to contribute positively to society as a Christian theologian. As in the case of Yoder, the concrete positive outcome of this redemptive activity might not be foreseeable, since it is left to the unpredictable God, but theologians should be convinced that they do something good.

Tanner's non-competitive theology, although harmonizing not unlike that of Milbank, then promises to achieve a more peaceful pluralist society in a slightly different way. Tanner uses her ontological framework of non-competition not in order to defend the superiority of Christian theology over alternative world views

---

116. Ibid. Tanner claims that God's grace is active in non-Christian acts whenever they exhibit the same purifying and loving effects as Christian acts (Tanner, *Jesus, Humanity and the Trinity*, 64). At another point, however, Tanner talks of a non-Christian culture's 'openness to grace' rather than its mediation of grace. For a detailed and nuanced examination of aspects within capitalism that could be understood as mediating grace see Tanner, 'Is Capitalism a Belief System?', *Anglican Theological Review*, 617–35.

117. Tanner, *Theories of Culture*, 112. (This is partly to differentiate her ecclesiology from post-liberals who understand Christianity in terms of a self-contained and independent society, 111).

118. Ibid., 113.

119. Ibid., 114.

apologetically, but in order to approach others in such a way that any apparent conflict between the two world views is overcome.[120] At this point, Tanner's non-contrastive conception of God translates into a 'non-competitive' conception of Christianity's relation to non-Christians.[121] The goal of any conversation between Christians and non-Christians is not agreement, but mutual understanding.[122] For such a peaceful encounter, God's grace must be imagined to be bestowed equally upon everyone, even if this materializes in different shapes. However, this way of approaching each other should not be defended triumphantly as the best solution to all conflicts in society. The point is rather that, where Christians are interpreting reality through the lens of Tanner's theology, they would not strive to impose their own understanding of a peaceful conversation onto everyone, but they would only assume this hermeneutics because they see themselves as already equally privileged with all other recipients of grace.[123] Tanner thus promises to achieve a more peaceful society not by way of installing a new social order or new ethical guidelines for everyone, but by way of ensuring that Christians contribute their best share to a peaceful coexistence.

Whatever Christian theologians understand about the non-Christian position, through and after this conversation, can then be integrated into the Christian tradition.[124] The systematic whole of Christian theology is not meant to exclude, per definition, all those particulars which do not fit into this whole.[125] Tanner would rather prefer these particulars to modify the theological vision.

---

120. The same hermeneutic also applies to an understanding of seemingly conflicting Christian doctrines. Tanner's systematization has been said to be driven by her desire to provide the necessary conceptual ground on which the otherwise rather confusing uncertainty of Christianity's primary sources can stand (Hughes, '"Tehomic" Christology?', *Modern Theology* (2015): 3–4).

121. Tanner, *Economy of Grace*, 22–9. Tanner here relates economics to questions of societal organization by critically building on Pierre Bourdieu's understanding of societies as fundamentally economic. Whereas he understands this in the sense of societies being organized along the competition over privileged positions, Tanner claims that if Christians organize the distributions of goods according to the concept of grace this would constitute a fundamental critique of such competitive social orders.

122. Kathryn Tanner, 'Respect for Other Religions: A Christian Antidote to Colonialist Discourse', *Modern Theology* 9 (1993): 5.

123. For the way in which Tanner imagines such a Christian approach to conversation to proceed in practice see ibid., 1–3; 13.

124. Tanner, *Theories of Culture*, 98. Although Tanner contrasts her approach with that of Milbank, Tanner similarly claims that Christian theology only emerges through the continuous integration of material from outside into itself. That Tanner misunderstands Milbank's position as exemplifying the post-liberal Protestant approach to culture has been mentioned in Chapter 2.

125. Tanner, *Theories of Culture*, 76. Tanner associates such an understanding of Christianity as self-contained unity with a modern understanding of culture (95).

On this basis, we can then understand Tanner's integration of secular non-anthropocentric philosophies or liberal positions into her theology. Whereas some have criticized this as simplistic accommodation of Christian theology to some secular trends, this criticism in turn fails to recognize the grace that is mediated by non-anthropocentric or liberal philosophies. Due to Tanner's positive understanding of grace, the integration of new contextual insights into Christian theology should be internally diversifying.[126] Tanner's nuanced integration of non-anthropocentric thought into Christian theology is not based on the assumption that this secular philosophy was neutral; its culturally specific status is fully acknowledged. Refraining from universalizing non-anthropocentrism as the only adequate interpretation of reality, Western Christian theologians can receive non-anthropocentric philosophies as a welcome incentive to confessing Christianity's centuries-long history of sinfully measuring everything according to the standard set by oneself.[127]

Overall, Tanner's understanding of approaching non-Christians in conversation thus corresponds to her writings about how Christ redeems the world from sin. Christ reveals the world's continuous dependence upon the reception of goods from beyond its own stores, and that humankind is healed from sin through distributing the goods one receives with others equally. In this sense, faith in Christ can be associated with the promise that every human being will be healed from sin if all occurrences are, once again, read in their relation to God as their transcendent source.[128] Consequently, the different gifts of grace mediated by Christianity's conversation partners should be appreciated in their unique positivity, rather than being merged into something else. For the same reason, Christian theology should receive non-Christian contributions through understanding the other position as much as possible, without demanding the conversion to Christianity of those who made these contributions. In this way, Tanner upholds Christian theology's all-encompassing vision of how the world is being redeemed in Christ

126. Ibid., 158. Tanner, in this vein, understands Christianity's universality in terms of a breaking open of narrow cultural bonds (146). In terms of church membership, Christianity is not one more social group among others, but it is the overarching group which blurs the distinction between all others because anyone can join the Christian church (100).

127. Tanner claims that Christian theologians should not be too quick to universalize their arguments about dialogical openness, because Christianity, more than any other faith tradition, has violated this dialogical openness in the past (Tanner, 'Respect for Other Religions', *Modern Theology*, 4). At the same time, Tanner tends to universalize Christian particularity to general religion in Tanner, 'Is Capitalism a Belief System?', *Anglican Theological Review*, 617–35, in which she examines the relation between 'religion' and market capitalism. Her claim that 'religions' expect the most universal well-being of all of humankind might need further nuancing, because not every 'religion' expresses its beliefs in this way, and what is understood as universal well-being might differ greatly, to the effect that other faith traditions might not be as compatible with the mechanisms of market capitalism as Christianity.

128. Tanner, 'Book Forum', *Theology Today*, 343.

and, nevertheless, couples this with a rejection of placing Christian theology at the centre of the social order. The centre must remain Christ, whose superabundant offer of grace surpasses that which Christian theology could adequately mediate. However, how exactly Tanner acknowledges the impact of sin on non-Christian positions, as well as on the Christian theological vision has not yet been fully explained. It remains to be assessed how Tanner conceives of sin's impact on the way in which the church is related to the non-Christian public in terms of both what the church can receive from outside as well as what it can offer.

b) Appreciating Gratuity: Acknowledging the Church's Sinfulness

Despite Tanner's paralleling of Milbank's understanding of Christians as positive excess to Christ, they part ways at the point when this becomes central to Milbank, and it becomes much less central for Tanner. Whereas Milbank focuses on the church's excess to God's goodness, Tanner focuses primarily on the restoration of created goodness, and regards the question of what God might 'gain' to be only of a secondary importance.[129] She stresses more that received grace is not primarily returned to God, but is passed on to other creatures.[130] This is not to say that a human return of grace to God, and thus an excess of divine goodness, is impossible.[131] However, Tanner stresses that such a return is not the norm, but that it is the surprising and exceptional excess of the already good healing of sinful human nature. At this point, Tanner distinguishes between Christ's perfect humanity and the sinful humanity of Christians. 'Ever struggling against our own sinful impulses, we never exhibit Christ's own perfect humanity.'[132] Consequently,

129. Tanner, *Economy of Grace*, 68–9; 71.

130. Ibid., 70.

131. Ibid., 71–2.

132. Tanner, *Jesus, Humanity and the Trinity*, 97. This nuances the criticism that Tanner unduly underestimates the sinfulness and shortcomings of humankind in her conception of how human beings can participate in God's bestowal of grace onto others (Plantinga Pauw, 'Ecclesiological Reflections on Kathryn Tanner's Jesus, Humanity and the Trinity', *Scottish Journal of Theology*, 225–6; Helmer, 'A Systematic Theological Theory of Truth in Kathryn Tanner's *Jesus, Humanity and the Trinity*', *Scottish Journal of Theology*, 217; Bender, 'Christ, Creation and the Drama of Redemption', *Scottish Journal of Theology*, 152, FN 12; Hackett, 'What's the Use of a Skeleton Key?', *Radical Orthodoxy: Theology, Philosophy, Politics*, 209). That Tanner would derive too easily an unproblematic notion of human gift exchange from God's unconditional giving is a common criticism against her. She is said to thereby downplay the risks and costs that are involved in any such unconditional giving on the human level. While sufficiently highlighting the continuous human failure to adequately mediate the Trinitarian gift exchange, Tanner explains that she does not focus on sin and finitude in her theology, because this might compromise the call on Christians to participate unconditionally in God's gift exchange (Tanner, 'The Church and Action for the World', *Scottish Journal of Theology*, 232).

the Christian bestowal of goods onto others is, in most cases, defective. The church's participation in Christ's redemptive work does not always constitute an excess to the goodness of the gift received, but the gift is usually distorted.[133] 'We are always giving back in a lesser form what God gave to us: the goods are always damaged to some degree or other by fallible and sinful creatures.'[134] In this vein, Tanner confesses that 'the history of Christian thought comprises indeed one of the most comprehensive and detailed accounts of human failing ever assembled'.[135]

In contrast to all the other theologians introduced thus far, Tanner argues that due to sin, Christians are 'as much outsiders as insiders to a life in Christ'.[136] 'Christians remain threatened by sin despite their acceptance of salvation in Christ; they have reason to continue to pray for God's forgiveness.'[137] This means that Christians cannot promise to perfect the extra-ecclesial public in any direct way by their own good works, but that they can only participate in the redemption of the world as 'graced sinners'.[138] God's action must always purify and surpass Christian action. This acknowledgement of humankind's liability to sin translates, for Tanner, in the church's relation to the non-Christian public inasmuch as such relation is meant to accord with God's merciful justice. According to Tanner's theology of grace, gifts are not to be distributed according to some supposedly just measure of what the recipients deserve on the basis of their active contribution to the common good, but gifts should be bestowed in accordance with someone's need, irrespective of what they may return.[139] Tanner stresses that no human failure can ever alter one's standing in the covenant with God in Christ, who intercedes for them and continues to justify them despite themselves. God bestows 'merciful gift[s] of what is undeserved' and expects nothing in return.[140] The proper human response to this offer is to participate in this merciful gift-giving onto the world.[141] This means that Tanner's understanding of the extra-ecclesial public, as good in its own right, does not disacknowledge the extra-ecclesial public's sinfulness. It is, rather, in accordance with Tanner's understanding of God's mercy that she can mercifully focus on the extra-ecclesial public's goodness, rather than on its shortcomings. No sinfulness would ever undo the fact that the extra-ecclesial public is primarily an expression of God's faithful bestowal of grace.

Moreover, Tanner's acknowledgement of humankind's liability to sin translates into a high degree of appreciation of the beneficial purpose of social structures.

---

133. Tanner, *Economy of Grace*, 66–7.

134. Ibid., 68.

135. Tanner, 'Is Capitalism a Belief System?' *Anglican Theological Review*, 628.

136. Tanner, *Theories of Culture*, 101.

137. Ibid., 100 (see also p. 110).

138. Tanner, *Jesus, Humanity and the Trinity*, 63.

139. Kathryn Tanner, 'Justification and Justice in a Theology of Grace', *Theology Today* 55(510) (1999): 522–3.

140. Ibid., 5165–518.

141. Ibid., 519.

Economic and social structures that channel human self-interest into a mutually beneficial way are necessary presuppositions to realizing Christianity's hope for a universal community of love.[142] Tanner, thus, favours an economic system which is structured in such a way that individual benevolence becomes virtually unnecessary.[143] At this point, Tanner seems to associate sin more with shortcomings concerning human actions than with an impairment of people's visions. It is, in some ways, easier to envision beneficial social structures than to move individuals to good actions. This should make us question the degree to which Tanner confesses her own theological vision to be affected by sin, and the extent to which she presents it as redemptive means for an otherwise fallen world. This issue will prove to be decisive for the question concerning Christian theology's political role in post-Christendom societies.

c) Reconsidering Tanner's Theological Solutions for Societal Problems

Importantly, Tanner seeks to focus, in her theology, primarily on God, and not on human ideas about God.[144] She is wary not to elevate anything human onto God's position and wants that Christians obey God alone. Similar to Ward and Yoder, Tanner conceives of God's freedom from theological ideas about God in terms of God's unpredictability.[145] The consistence of God's free grace can only be determined in retrospect, not in advance.[146] However, also in retrospect, God's guidance of the Christian tradition is not identifiable with any concrete aspect of Christian history.[147] Again, the argument seems to distinguish the theological tradition of ideas, symbols and practices from Christ who won the world's redemption. The Christian tradition, just as the rest of the world, depends entirely upon Christ's redemption.[148]

Yet, at the same time, Tanner maintains that in any historical period, Christian theologians must make judgements and openness to God's correction means that Christians must acknowledge the possibility that God might nevertheless move in a different direction in the future.[149] On this basis, Tanner parallels Milbank's work in constructing an all-encompassing systematic vision, against the background of which all particulars can be assessed.[150] She views it as being every Christian's

---

142. Tanner, 'Is Capitalism a Belief System?', *Anglican Theological Review*, 625.

143. Ibid., 626–7.

144. Tanner, *Theories of Culture*, 126.

145. Tanner refers to Christ's Cross and Resurrection as reversing human expectations.

146. Tanner, *Theories of Culture*, 138.

147. Ibid., 136.

148. Tanner, *Jesus, Humanity and the Trinity*, 63.

149. Tanner, *Theories of Culture*, 155.

150. Tanner, *Jesus, Humanity and the Trinity*, xiii–xix. Tanner argues that attempting to build the theological openness to God into the theological system risks pointing more to the human activity of being open than to God (Tanner, *Theories of Culture*, 151).

responsibility to engage in such an endeavour to the effect that Christianity should be *a genuine community of argument* characterized by its common openness to correction and edification by others, and its shared hope to be faithful disciples of Christ.[151] The rule of this community must be humility. Tanner attempts to leave God entirely outside of her own theological system, as an external judge. Her acknowledgement of theology's entanglement in sin implies that, for Tanner, 'being genuinely open to the Word[,] always involves opening oneself to the risk of failure'.[152]

In this context, Tanner argues that, acknowledging their sinfulness, Christian theologians must be willing to submit to the judgements of others.[153] It is precisely the seriousness of sin on all sides of a debate which renders the prospect of mutual correction a salutary gift.[154] This understanding of the Christian contribution to public politics, as potentially wrong or at least incomplete, allows Christian theologians to receive insights from non-Christians as enrichments or corrections.[155] This need for correction from non-Christians is then also why Tanner opposes the idea of an entirely Christian culture.[156] At the same time, Christian theologians are called to criticize the wider society, and transform it primarily for society's sake, not in order to convert people to Christianity. This returns us to the issue concerning whether God could ever offer a new grace that breaks with Tanner's own theological vision. Acknowledging the human liability to sin, Tanner cannot present her extrinsic view of grace as being the definite and eternal truth about reality.

Tanner insufficiently engages with the problem that theology's entanglement in sin might distort the theological vision to such an extent that theologians might not even know what exactly should be evaluated as being problematic in their own, as well as in non-Christian, positions. Her primary focus on societal and ecclesial problems in need of a solution, and not on the graces which are already being received, is indicative of Tanner's confidence that Christian theology is able to know and point out sin. This confidence contrasts my own hypothesis that non-Christian positions might reveal problems to Christian theology, which Christian theologians could not have seen from their own distorted perspective. For example, Tanner understands closing oneself off from the reception of grace to be sinful, and identifies this as a problem in need of a theological solution. What, however, if this trust in human efforts and closing oneself off from external gifts

---

151. Tanner, *Theories of Culture*, 123–4.

152. Ibid., 151.

153. Ibid., 125–6. For an appreciation of Tanner's emphasis on the church's continuous need for reform in faithfulness to its own tradition and in dialogue with the surrounding culture, which is also influenced by Christ's redemptive work, see Healy, 'Practices and the New Ecclesiology?' *International Journal of Systematic Theology*, 291.

154. Tanner, *Theories of Culture*, 154–5.

155. Tanner, 'Respect for Other Religions', *Modern Theology*, 3.

156. Tanner, *Theories of Culture*, 102–3.

bore itself the seeds of a solution to a political problem that Tanner cannot see from her own perspective?

Conclusion

The discussion, found in the first two chapters of this book, has pointed in the direction of ascribing a less central political role in contemporary post-Christendom societies to Christian theology than those apologetically defended by public theologians on the one hand, and by Radical Orthodoxy on the other. Moreover, I have argued that both public as well as Radical Orthodox theologians, with their problem-centred approaches to politics, have tended to conflate Christ's redemption with the theological task of completing this redemption, over and against which I have expressed my preference for a more Christocentric position. Thus, in this chapter, I have introduced two different Christocentric approaches to the question concerning the political role of Christian theology in post-Christendom societies; in so doing I have related to public theology's conscious distinction of their own discipline from post-liberal Protestant responses to the question. Public theologians reject the post-liberal Protestant stance where it entails any sectarian withdrawal from political engagement in post-Christendom societies, and where it exhibits an illegitimate belief in Christian integrity to the detriment of acknowledging the theological significance of non-Christian outlooks.

It should have become clear that Christocentric responses to the post-Christendom context, and the ascription of a humbler political role to Christian theology, do not necessarily imply a sectarian withdrawal from the political arena. Yet, I have distanced myself from Yoder's specific Christocentrism, by way of rejecting his principled opposition to both apologetics as well as to Christendom. I prefer a Christocentric approach to the question of theology's political role in post-Christendom societies not in order to safeguard Christianity's integrity, but, following Tanner in this respect, in order to acknowledge the way in which the Christian theological vision of redemption is impaired by sin. Yoder's doubts that Christian theologians might not possess a positive vision of a political goal, on the basis of which they could promise to contribute positively to the society's common good, is helpful for my own approach, but according to different reasons than those advanced by Yoder. According to Yoder, Christian theologians positively know that the principle of non-violent love will guide them towards their true, but unknown, eschatological goal. Against this, I maintain that, impaired by sin, Christian theologians might want to acknowledge that they also lack the positive vision of how to reach their goal. This renders any theological promise of contributing positively to the completion of the world's redemption to be even more questionable than it is in Yoder's theology.

Tanner's Christology headed already more into the direction of crafting a fourth theological approach to the post-Christendom context. She acknowledges the difference between Christ's unique realization of redemption and the sinful furthering of Christ's redemptive work by the church and Christian theology to a greater extent than the others. We part ways, however, at the point at which Tanner still offers Christian solutions to greater societal problems. By taking the acknowledgement of the impacts of sin onto the theological vision one step further, I would like to suggest that at this particular moment in time, in a post-Christendom context, Christian theologians might be better advised to refrain from offering their solutions to problems of the greater societal whole. To this end, I would like to take Tanner's stress on theology's reliability on God's continuous offer of external graces one step further, suggesting that this theological perspective might allow for a less problem-centred approach to politics than hers. Even if Christian theologians think they identify something as problematic in their societal surroundings, they might first want to look at the graces mediated by this supposed problem, before they begin inventing a solution. Such an approach might help theologians to see more clearly where Christian theology itself poses a problem to society, in need of a solution. In the following chapter, I present Edward Schillebeeckx as a theologian who is not so much concerned with identifying problems in order to offer theological solutions as apologetic defence of theology's positive impact on society as he is concerned with continuously receiving the graces discernible in non-Christian positions. The direction thus set by my interpretation of Schillebeeckx's thought will serve as most significant signpost for crafting a theological approach to the post-Christendom context that constitutes a new alternative to the most prominent existing positions in the debate.

Chapter 4

EDWARD SCHILLEBEECKX'S CHRISTOLOGY OF REDEMPTION: A REALISTIC GRACE OPTIMISM DESPITE POLITICAL PROBLEMS

I have argued throughout this work that, regarding the question of appreciating the theological significance of non-Christian positions, all theologians introduced thus far fail to understand the way in which what they identify as problematic in their surrounding societies might still mediate God's grace, thus being theologically significant. In the case of public theology and Radical Orthodoxy, their problem-centred approaches to the political situation in post-Christendom context tends to re-ascribe to Christian theology a central role in the political arena. The loss of Christianity's political dominance is, thus, not acknowledged as something good, but sought to be rehabilitated in a new guise. I have related this upholding of a remnant of Christendom, by both public theology and Radical Orthodoxy, to their respective Christologies, and critiqued that an insufficient differentiation existed between Christ's offer of redemption and the Christian theological ability to mediate this offer. A more Christocentric theology might welcome to a greater extent the idea that Christianity no longer dominates the politics of a not-exclusively Christian society.

On this basis, John Howard Yoder and Kathryn Tanner were presented as two post-liberal Protestant theologians who both reject Christendom as a matter of principle, due to their Christocentric outlooks. Criticizing Yoder's specific Christocentrism for its assumption of an integrity on the part of Christian theology, which predisposes him not to recognize the *specific* theological significance of his surroundings, I welcomed Kathryn Tanner's Christocentrism insofar as it allows her to acknowledge the impacts of sin upon her own theological vision, to a greater extent. Due to this sinfulness, also criticisms raised by non-Christians must be received as a welcome gift for Christianity. At the same time, Tanner still approaches political questions primarily by seeking theological solutions for what she identifies as problematic, thereby refusing to interpret these problematic aspects themselves primarily as theologically significant.

The challenge of this chapter is not only to offer an interpretation of Schillebeeckx's approach to the post-Christendom context, as one that is particularly distinct through its reluctance to focus primarily on political problems in need of a theological solution. The major part of this chapter is dedicated to defending such an approach against the accusation of constituting an overly naive capitulation to the secular mainstream. To this end, I will present Schillebeeckx's Christology as offering a way for political theology to acknowledge political problems while not using them as its starting point for the endeavour of defending theology's public relevance through offering solutions.

4.1 De-Problematizing Church Decline: The Theological Significance of Atheism

Let me begin my introduction of Edward Schillebeeckx's Christology as a contribution to this discussion about theology's political role in post-Christendom societies, by first presenting Schillebeeckx's extraordinarily positive reception of what others might have primarily perceived as problematic, namely the rise of atheism throughout his career. This sets Schillebeeckx apart from all of the above-mentioned theologians, as he does not engage with atheism by way of apologetically defending Christianity against those who have turned their back to it. Instead, he is concerned from the outset with understanding the grace that is mediated by the arguments of those who have left the church. On this basis, I can then turn to the objections that have been voiced against Schillebeeckx's positive stance towards atheism; namely, the charges of being naively optimistic and of naturalizing grace. Schillebeeckx's 'grace optimism' is said to assume too easily that atheists still follow the guidance of God's grace, thereby neglecting the way in which they also sinfully reject God's grace. In other words, Schillebeeckx is reproached for insufficiently criticizing atheism's shortcomings. Against this criticism, I will argue that far from being naively optimistic, Schillebeeckx interpreted atheism through a hermeneutic that combined a grace optimism with a pessimistic anthropology. The rest of this chapter explains how this hermeneutic is related to Schillebeeckx's Christology, centring on Christ's Resurrection. In the same vein, I contest the most widespread interpretations of Schillebeeckx's work, which associate his understanding of grace with creation. I contend that Schillebeeckx's primary focus on the grace of redemption means that he does not neglect the world's fallenness, but that he has a certain soteriological understanding of how grace overcomes sin, which is also manifest in his engagement with atheism and which distinguishes him from Milbank, Ward, Yoder and Tanner.

a) Early Career: Atheism's and Christianity's Entanglement in Structural Sin

By 1945, Schillebeeckx's reflections on atheism were already very nuanced. At this point, he conceived of atheism and Christianity as two equally intelligible interpretations of the social context at the time. More precisely, Schillebeeckx associated atheism with a pessimistic outlook and Christianity with an optimistic outlook.[1] His overall positive approach to atheism is especially evidenced in the late 1950s when Schillebeeckx welcomes the new situation, in which Catholicism began to lose its cultural hegemony, as a possible opportunity for Catholicism to receive anew God's grace.[2] Relating this positive evaluation of Catholicism's more marginal role in Flemish society to his understanding of grace, Schillebeeckx distinguishes between an atheist search for God's absence, which might lead people to God, and a theological search for God's presence which might distance people from God.[3] The reverse side of this optimism, regarding the future to which atheism could lead, is Schillebeeckx's rather bleak interpretation of the current state of the church.

Schillebeeckx argues that many contemporaries discard Christianity because Christians fail to visibly bear witness to the grace they proclaim with their words.[4] He claims that for Christianity to be convincing, people must encounter someone whose life confronts them with the plausibility that life can be transformed into something more beautiful.[5] In other words, rather than searching in the surrounding society for a problem that led people to abandon Christianity, Schillebeeckx presents the church's own imperfections as an occasion for people's embracing of atheism.

A few years later, Schillebeeckx presents the relation between ecclesial and atheist sinfulness on a structural level. He then argues that while previously people were socially pressured to practice Christianity, this has now turned into the social pressure not to practice Christianity.[6] Schillebeeckx refuses to associate the de-Christianization of a majority of his surrounding culture with personal

---

1. Edward Schillebeeckx, 'Christelijke Situatie III. – Naar een oplossing: Bovennatuurlijk Exclusivisme', *Kultuurleven* (1945): 601–2. Schillebeeckx positively judges atheism to be one possible, but not necessary, result of his surrounding culture's development towards conscious criticism and self-reflection.

2. Edward Schillebeeckx, 'Op zoek naar Gods afwezigheid: Ontkerstening of een historische genadekans', *Kultuurleven* 24 (1957): 282.

3. Schillebeeckx, 'Op zoek naar Gods afwezigheid', *Kultuurleven*, 278. Importantly, Schillebeeckx associates the finding of God at the end of the atheistic search primarily with God's active revelation, which subverts the human denial of God (282).

4. Edward Schillebeeckx, *Christ the Sacrament of the Encounter with God*, trans. Paul Barret, N. D. Smith, *CW* vol. I (London: Bloomsbury T&T Clark, 2014), 152 [259–61]. In all references to the *Collected Works*, I also refer in brackets to the page numbers of the original English translations.

5. Schillebeeckx here refers to the biblical account of the murderer dying next to Christ on the Cross who was converted by looking into Christ's eyes, discovering in them a depth to which his own heart was capable.

6. Edward Schillebeeckx, 'Theologische reflexie op godsdienstsociologische duidingen in verband met het hedendaagse ongeloof', *Tijdschrift voor Theologie* 2 (1962): 69–70. This association of atheism with social coercion had already been present in Schillebeeckx, 'Op zoek naar Gods afwezigheid', *Kultuurleven*, 283.

sinful rejections of God.[7] Arguing that God alone will judge the extent of sin of each individual atheist, he asks Christian theologians to trust in God's mercy with regard to atheists' entry into heaven.[8] At the same time, Schillebeeckx calls on his fellow Christians not to cease striving to be holy as their heavenly Father is holy. He understands the church not as a community of the perfect, but as the institution in which people can strive towards perfection, a perfection which is achieved according to the measure that people accept the real church.[9] This move is indicative of Schillebeeckx's reception of atheism as a challenge to the church. The church's sinfulness, which led to atheism, can be healed if the church can understand the atheist criticism aright and directs itself accordingly.

Two particular aspects of Schillebeeckx's early thoughts about atheism are remarkable in relation to the discussion advanced in previous chapters. First, he understands atheism and the church to be involved in the same structural sin of coercion, and secondly, he acknowledges that God's grace moves both Christians and atheists despite this structural sin. Consequently, the theological significance of the path pursued by atheists in their rejection of Christianity cannot simply be discarded on the grounds that their overall outlook is damaged by sin. Schillebeeckx does not yet reflect, however, on the implications of his interpretation of atheism for theology's political role in post-Christendom societies.

b) The 1960s: Interpreting Atheism through a Hermeneutic of a Realistic Grace Optimism

Throughout the 1960s, Schillebeeckx further developed his reflections on the theological significance of atheism.[10] Schillebeeckx's engagement with atheism in this

---

7. Schillebeeckx, 'Op zoek naar Gods afwezigheid', *Kultuurleven*, 283. In the early 1960s, Schillebeeckx further elaborates that sociology can help theology understand the conditions of human freedom in a society, which is theologically important in relation to the necessarily free acceptance of the gospel (Schillebeeckx, 'Theologische reflexie op godsdienstsociologische duidingen in verband met het hedendaagse ongeloof', *Tijdschrift voor Theologie*, 70; 75).

8. Schillebeeckx, 'Op zoek naar Gods afwezigheid', *Kultuurleven*, 283.

9. Ibid.

10. Ibid., 276–91; Edward Schillebeeckx, 'De betekenis van het niet-godsdienstige humanisme voor het hedendaagse katholicisme', in *Modern nietgodsdienstig humanisme*, ed. W. Engelen (Nijmegen, Utrecht 1961), 74–112; Edward Schillebeeckx, 'Herinterpretatie van het geloof in het licht van de seculariteit. Honest to Robinson', *Tijdschrift voor Theologie* 4 (1964): 109–50; Edward Schillebeeckx, 'De ascese van het zoeken naar God', *Tijdschrift voor Geestelijk Leven* 20 (1964): 149–58; Edward Schillebeeckx, 'Het leed der ervaring van Gods verborgenheid', *Vox Theologica* 36 (1966): 92–104; Edward Schillebeeckx, 'Christelijk geloof en aardse toekomstverwachtingen', in *De kerk in de wereld van deze tijd. Schema dertien. Tekst en commentaar* (Vaticanum II, 2) (Hilversum, Antwerpen 1967), 78–109; Edward Schillebeeckx, 'Het nieuwe Godsbeeld, secularisatie en politiek', *Tijdschrift voor Theologie* 8 (1968): 44–65; Edward

period can be explained with reference to his statement that, in the 1960s, Christianity underwent a greater crisis than ever before.[11] While speaking of a crisis, Schillebeeckx, however, refrains from one-sidedly focusing on problems in need of a solution. He explicitly rejects any alarmism and argues that, although society will not automatically move in the right direction, theologians should *trust* that throughout the ages, some theologians have fallen prey to a crisis of faith, whereas others guided the Christian faith safely through it. Schillebeeckx then calls on Christian theologians to embrace a 'realistic grace optimism'.[12] Reiterating his previous argument, Schillebeeckx still contends that Christians should trust that those who have left the church in order to follow an integral humanism may not find God, but that God will always find them. He argues that atheist reactions against Christianity can be remedies for the Christian faith if Christians continue to listen to God's revelation in the Bible and in contemporary reality. His approach to atheism in subsequent years can thus be understood as Schillebeeckx's attempt to guide the church through its present crisis with the help of a realistic grace optimism.

In 1962, discussing the theological significance of sociology, Schillebeeckx argues that what sociologists term 'church decline' can be theologically understood as a cleansing of the church.[13] The church is now presented with the opportunity to appear less as an institution of dominating power and more as an attractive place in the midst of this world.[14] At the same time, Schillebeeckx interprets church decline as being indicative of his culture's maturing to a greater trust in the universal immanence of God's grace.[15] Combining both aspects, Schillebeeckx interprets contemporary church decline as the negative preparation for a renewed sacramental appearance of the church. Again this is indicative of an optimism regarding the future, and a rather bleak assessment of the church's present state. Noticeably, the solution to the identified crisis of Christianity is sought more within the atheist reaction to the church than within the resources of the Christian tradition.

Schillebeeckx then reiterates his earlier contention that those who leave the church should not be regarded as sinful. Now he even argues that, to the contrary, Christians are sinful if they fail to change their apostleship and pastoral care in faithfulness to God and in accordance to the new economic and social

Schillebeeckx, 'Het Evangelie als appél in onze geseculariseerde wereld (1)', in *Het Evangelie als appél* [Groepsgesprek van de religieuzen; 28] (Mechelen (1969)), 5–17. His volume *God and Man* was praised at the time for providing an 'enlightening view … to the problems of secularity' (R. R. Masterson, review of *God and Man*, by Edward Schillebeeckx, *The Thomist: A Speculative Quarterly Review* 34(1) (1970): 133).

11. Edward Schillebeeckx, 'Leven in God en Leven in de Wereld', in *God en Mens* (Bilthoven (Holland): Uitgeverij H. Nelissen, 1965), 72.

12. Schillebeeckx, 'Leven in God en Leven in de Wereld', in *God en Mens*, 115.

13. Schillebeeckx, 'Theologische reflexie op godsdienstsociologische duidingen in verband met het hedendaagse ongeloof', *Tijdschrift voor Theologie*, 70.

14. Ibid., 75–6.

15. Ibid., 70.

situation.[16] He interprets the contemporary situation as one in which people have discovered their full humanity. And yet, Schillebeeckx refrains from affirming atheism on the whole, but instead retains a critical distance therefrom. He argues that contemporary atheists, for a certain time, erroneously think that God is not greater than humanity and, therefore, assume that human beings can be satisfied within the immanent sphere. He understands this attitude as being marked by a sinful weakness. Nevertheless, he is quick to highlight that this sinful weakness is not able to undo the grace which is operative in the world as an unconscious desire prior to the reception of the sacraments.[17] In other words, Schillebeeckx here succeeds in criticizing a position without at the same time problematizing it.

Still seeking to learn from atheism, Schillebeeckx argues that Christians should acknowledge the mundane world from within their relationship with God. He explains that this means to respect nature as developing according to its own rules, and to take up nature into one's dialogue with God.[18] Schillebeeckx stresses that, in being lifted up towards God, nature remains integral. Immanent values, such as humanization are evaluated as good, and Christians are called to collaborate with non-Christians for the further realization of these values.[19] Overall, this suggests that Schillebeeckx is convinced that allowing atheism to develop its full potential would help to overcome both the shortcomings of atheism and the sinfulness of the present church.

In 1965, in this vein, Schillebeeckx understands the Anglican bishop John A. Robinson's (a)theology as an incentive to renew Christian theology.[20] He regards atheism as revelatory of a partial truth, which had remained hidden in Christendom.[21] Schillebeeckx then reconnects this partial truth to the affirmation of God in order to render it more dynamic.[22] At this time, Schillebeeckx conceives

---

16. Ibid., 65.

17. Ibid., 69.

18. Schillebeeckx, 'Dialoog met God en Christelijke Seculariteit', in *God en Mens*, 160. For example, Schillebeeckx welcomes the secularist intuition that sins against other creatures must be healed through reconciliation with the respective creature. Understanding this readiness to repentance as already being a grace from God, he also understands the reconciling approach towards the other as an undoing of the sin with respect to God. And yet, Schillebeeckx claims that the sinner's communion with God is only fully restored in the explicit personal encounter with Christ in the church (Schillebeeckx, 'Leven in God en Leven in de Wereld', in *God en Mens*, 147–9).

19. Schillebeeckx, 'Dialoog met God en Christelijke Seculariteit', in *God en Mens*, 161.

20. Schillebeeckx published two articles in response to Robinson's (a)theology (Schillebeeckx, 'Leven in God en Leven in de Wereld', in *God en Mens*, 66–149; Schillebeeckx, 'Dialoog met God en Christelijke Seculariteit', in *God en Mens*, 150–66).

21. This partial truth is that love lies at the deepest level of reality (Schillebeeckx, 'Leven in God en Leven in de Wereld', in *God en Mens*, 84; 149).

22. Ibid., 72–3; 79–80. Schillebeeckx argues that the atheist understanding of the world, as a closed horizon, is officially regarded as a heresy because profane reality is loosened

of the relation between atheism and Christianity in terms of the former as providing positive images of God, and the latter as correctly directing these images towards God.[23] The structure is still that of Christian theology perfecting atheism's already good aspiration for grace. Schillebeeckx could be interpreted, at this point, however, as seeking primarily how atheism is able to restore the sinful theological vision, and not as seeking to repair the problems in atheism with the help of theology.

It must be conceded, nevertheless, that, around the same time, Schillebeeckx more negatively judges some variants of atheism as ideological interpretations of secularization.[24] To counter this ideology, Schillebeeckx seeks to show that secularization could also be understood from within Christianity. Taking the atheist interpretation of the world seriously, Schillebeeckx claims that Christian theologians must show that the secular existence itself contains elements that point to an absolute mystery. Developing this thought a bit further, in 1969, Schillebeeckx wants to present Christian theology as a humanly meaningful interpretation of reality.[25] The way in which Schillebeeckx seeks to counter ideological variants of atheism, then, still reflects his early distinction between atheism and Christianity along the lines of pessimism and optimism. He argues that, as much as Christians can be with atheists in this world, Christians cannot accept the latter's interpretation of the world as unredeemed and their understanding of life as directed towards death.[26] In contrast to this interpretation, Christian life must always be a saving presence in and with the living God. This does not undo the misery which gave rise to the atheistic pessimism, but it shows that pessimism is not the only self-evident conclusion to be drawn from this misery.[27] Thus, while identifying a certain ideological variant of atheism as problematic, Schillebeeckx's solution is not to convert all atheists back to Christianity, but simply to move them to a point from which they can, at least, acknowledge that their own interpretation of reality is not the only one possible.

Overall, and throughout the 1960s, Schillebeeckx's interpretation of atheism still followed the structure of detecting atheism's aspiration for grace and theology's

---

from the greater whole to which it belongs. Like Radical Orthodoxy later, Schillebeeckx here also understands atheism as a consequence of the fideist absolute separation of God from the world, which makes a godless world possible (147).

23. Ibid., 79–80; Schillebeeckx, 'Dialoog met God en Christelijke Seculariteit', in *God en Mens*, 161–2.

24. Edward Schillebeeckx, 'Zwijgen en spreken over God in een geseculariseerde wereld', *Tijdschrift voor Theologie* 7 (1967): 346–7. Schillebeeckx here refers to the atheism that confuses an erroneous God of the gaps with the real living God.

25. Edward Schillebeeckx, 'Enkele hermeneutische beschouwingen over de eschatologie', *Concilium* 5 (1969): 50.

26. Schillebeeckx, 'Dialoog met God en Christelijke Seculariteit', in *God en Mens*, 165.

27. Ibid., 166. Schillebeeckx speaks of worldly fiascos entering the mystery of salvation that is wrought by Christ alone.

completion of this aspiration. It is striking, however, that for Schillebeeckx, interpreting atheism as aspiration does not lead him to focus primarily upon that which atheism is lacking, but on that which is already good. Even in treating atheism as one ideological whole, Schillebeeckx argues that each element within atheism can be redeemed from this ideology by taking it up into the church's lived communion with God. This communion with God is not to replace that which it has taken up, but to appreciate it in its integrity. This reception of atheism, then, still accords with Schillebeeckx's early distinction between atheists being entangled in sinful social structures that restrict their freedom, and God's grace as being stronger than these sinful social structures in the sense that grace can still move individual atheists in a good direction. In accordance with this distinction, atheists could not be converted to Christianity by subverting the ideological understanding of reality at once, because this move would neglect the grace which is mediated in this understanding despite its errors. Instead, Schillebeeckx suggests that Christian theologians ought to discern how the individual elements of existence in this reductive ontology still mediate God's grace. Moreover, theologians have to attend to atheism's good aspiration for grace in order to restore the shortcomings of their own theological vision.

c) Late Career: The Political Relevance of Theology's Realistic Grace Optimism

Reflections about the relation between Christianity, secularization and atheism remain of great concern for Schillebeeckx, also in the 1970s.[28] During this time, Schillebeeckx begins to engage with atheist ideology critiques,[29] and thinks increasingly about Christianity's political engagement in society.[30] At the same

---

28. Edward Schillebeeckx, 'Crisis van de geloofstaal als hermeneutisch probleem', *Concilium* 9 (1973): 33–47; Edward Schillebeeckx, 'Godsdienst van en voor mensen. Naar een criteriologie voor godsdienst en religie', *Tijdschrift voor Theologie* 17 (1977): 353–70; Edward Schillebeeckx, 'God, Society and Human Salvation', in *Faith and Society. Acta Congressus Internationalis Theologici Lovaniensis* 1976 (Bibliotheca Ephemeridum Theologicarum Lovaniensium XLVII) (Gembloux 1978), 87–99; Edward Schillebeeckx, 'Openbaringsdichtheid van menselijke ervaringen en moderne geloofsmogelijkheden', *Verbum* 46 (1979): 14–29; Edward Schillebeeckx, 'Wezen en grenzen van het christendom', *De Vrij-Katholiek* 54 (1979): 8–9.

29. Edward Schillebeeckx, 'Kritische theorie en theologische hermeneutiek: confrontatie', *Tijdschrift voor Theologie* 11 (1971): 113–39; Edward Schillebeeckx, 'Naar een verruiming van de hermeneutiek: de "nieuwe kritische theorie"', *Tijdschrift voor Theologie* 11 (1971): 30–50; Edward Schillebeeckx, 'Kritische theorieën en politiek engagement van de christelijke gemeente', *Concilium* 9 (1973): 47–61.

30. Edward Schillebeeckx, 'The Christian and Political Engagement', *Doctrine and Life* 22 (1972): 118–27; Edward Schillebeeckx, 'Stilte, gevuld met parables', in *Politiek of Mystiek? Peilingen naar de verhouding tussen religieuze ervaring en sociale inzet* ((Utrecht, Brugge)

time, Schillebeeckx devotes focused attention to Christology.[31] It is in this period that Schillebeeckx commences to acknowledge the impairment of his own theological vision due to sin.

In the 1970s, Schillebeeckx relates his earlier insight that atheism reveals to Christian theology a heightened trust in the immanence of God's grace to the domain of politics.[32] He interprets this atheist insight as a stimulus for an increased ecclesial sociopolitical engagement for the well-being of all of humankind now and in the future. Important for our discussion here, concerning theology's political role in post-Christendom societies, Schillebeeckx argues that theology is no longer the queen of the sciences, but that, by acknowledging the autonomy of the natural sciences, theology has become a political science.[33] Other sciences must inform the theological understanding of the Christian faith and, thus, be regarded as sources of theology. Conversely, theology must be critical regarding any scientific reductive understanding of reality. Since the immanent world is regarded as being the constitutive symbol of God's real presence, the political engagement for the wholeness of the world is at once a mediation of grace and an advance of realized salvation.[34] In disagreement with the atheist denial of God, Schillebeeckx then argues for a combination of prayer and politics.[35] The prayerful acknowledgement of God's excessive gift of grace, which cannot be exhausted by the human response, should help Christians to begin always anew, despite any human failures.[36] It seems that, at this later stage of his career, Schillebeeckx still relies on his early distinction between atheism as a pessimistic and Christianity as an optimistic understanding

1972), 69–81; Edward Schillebeeckx, 'Mysterie van ongerechtigheid en mysterie van erbarmen', *Tijdschrift voor Theologie* 15 (1975): 3–24.

31. Edward Schillebeeckx, 'Ons heil: Jezus' leven of Christus de verrezene', *Tijdschrift voor Theologie* 13 (1973): 145–65; Edward Schillebeeckx, 'De vrije mens Jezus en zijn conflict', *TGL* 29 (1973): 145–55; Edward Schillebeeckx, *Jezus, Het verhaal van een levende* (1974), Edward Schillebeeckx, 'De "God van Jezus" en de "Jezus van God"', *Concilium* 10 (1974): 100–15; Edward Schillebeeckx, 'De vraag naar de universaliteit van Jezus', in *De vraag naar de universaliteit van Jezus*. Openingswoord en inleidingen gehouden voor het congres van de Werkgroep voor Moderne Theologie op 20 oktober 1975 te Utrecht (Utrecht 1975), 15–26; Edward Schillebeeckx, 'Jezus en de menselijke levensmislukking', *Concilium* 12 (1976): 86–96; Edward Schillebeeckx, *Gerechtigheid en liefde : genade en bevrijding* (1977); Edward Schillebeeckx, 'Waarom Jezus de Christus?', *TGL* 33 (1977): 338–53; Edward Schillebeeckx, 'Op weg naar een christologie', *Tijdschrift voor Theologie* 18 (1978): 131–56; Edward Schillebeeckx, 'Jezus voor wie vandaag gelooft', *Kultuurleven* 46 (1979): 887–901.

32. Schillebeeckx, 'Stilte, gevuld met parables', in *Politiek of Mystiek*, 71–2.

33. Schillebeeckx, 'The Critical Status of Theology', *World Congress 'The Future of the Church'*, Brussels 12–17 September 1970.

34. Schillebeeckx, 'Stilte, gevuld met parables', in *Politiek of Mystiek*, 72; 75.

35. Ibid., 72.

36. Ibid., 74; 78.

of reality; he is still presenting Christianity's political role in terms of a continuous motivator for further political engagement, also in the face of failure.

How Schillebeeckx's move, to position theology as one science among others, is related to what he identifies as problematic, is further clarified in 1973 when he distinguishes between a crisis of the language of faith and a crisis of faith. He asserts that there is a crisis of the contemporary language of faith, which he evaluates positively.[37] This crisis has been initiated through theology's forgetfulness that scientific and religious language both refer to the same reality of the coming of God's Kingdom.[38] According to Schillebeeckx, this crisis of the language of faith is not to be regarded primarily as a problem, but it should be welcomed as an occasion to vitalize the Christian faith, through remembering again that the difficulty in finding the right language to express the reality of Christ is not itself problematic, but rather constitutive of the Christian faith. Schillebeeckx stresses that there is no guarantee that Christian theology will succeed in experimenting with this difficulty.[39] And yet, also this risk of possible failure is not a problem, but it can be taken in faithful trust in the Holy Spirit's guidance of the church, which allows theologians to be mistaken at times.[40]

Schillebeeckx assumes that there is an evocative surplus in the language of the surrounding culture, and the language of faith is meant to express that which remains implicit in all other languages.[41] In this way, Christian theology is but one science among others, but it is also holistic, given that it assembles what all the other sciences express about the arrival of God's Kingdom. It is noteworthy that, at this point, Schillebeeckx introduces a distinction between theology's confession of Christ, as fulfilment of all cultural expectations, and theology's inability to mediate this fulfilment. Theology names the surrounding society's aspiration for grace in such a way that the fulfilment by Christ remains extrinsic to theology's own utterance.[42]

Also throughout the 1980s, Schillebeeckx devoted a great deal of thought to the relation between Christianity and the surrounding society.[43] Elaborating further

---

37. Schillebeeckx, 'Crisis van de Geloofstaal als hermeneutisch probleem', *Concilium*, 36. In the extreme case of Protestant dialectic theology, the crisis of the language of faith has led to a crisis of faith, because if all language of faith has become obsolete, there cannot be any living faith (41).

38. Ibid., 39–40.

39. Ibid., 46.

40. Ibid., 38–9.

41. Ibid., 40.

42. Ibid., 45.

43. Edward Schillebeeckx, 'Het theologisch zoeken naar katholieke identiteit in de twintig-ste eeuw', in *De identiteit van katholieke wetenschapsmensen* (Annalen van het Thijmgenootsc-hap 68/II) (Baarn 1980), 175–89; Edward Schillebeeckx, 'Wereldlijke kritiek op de chris-telijke gehoorzaamheid en christelijke reactie daarop', *Concilium* 16 (1980): 17–29; Edward Schillebeeckx, 'Ingekeerd of naar de wereld toegewend?', *TGL* 37 (1981): 652–68; Edward

on his earlier understanding of history as the medium of God's dialogue with humankind, Schillebeeckx now develops his earlier apophatic emphasis on God's hiddenness.[44] Schillebeeckx now argues that, in order to fulfil theology's prophetic task, Christian theologians must listen to the foreign prophecy with which the world confronts it.[45] Combining this with an apophatic stress of God's hiddenness, Schillebeeckx claims that this foreign prophecy must partly be discerned not in positive images, but in negative contrast experiences. In these, people experience the absence of what should be, followed by a multitude of different, equally legitimate positive projects that are all aimed at overcoming the negative contrast.[46] The theological task is, then, to discern *with* society the best project in each particular situation.[47]

This already sets the path for Schillebeeckx's most explicit discussion of the question about theology's political role in post-Christendom societies in 1986, when he rejects any Christian exclusivism or imperialism as antithetical to the gospel.[48] Although he maintains that theology's support of people's lived experience with God belongs to the most ultimate inspirations of humanism, Schillebeeckx refrains from advocating a central role for Christian theology in the determination of the social order.[49] At this point in his career, Schillebeeckx interprets the true humanity of Jesus Christ to be both revealing and concealing

---

Schillebeeckx, 'Christelijke identiteit en menselijke integriteit', *Concilium* 18 (1982): 34–42; Edward Schillebeeckx, 'Vanzelfsprekendheid van een eigentijds geloof', in *Zijn de Middeleeuwen nu echt voorbij? Over verschuivingen in een katholiek paradigma* (Nijmegen 1987), 39–44. Schillebeeckx still confesses that Christians must be concerned with both the humanization of the world and with the relation between God and humanity (Edward Schillebeeckx, 'Spreken over God in een context van bevrijding', *TGL* 40 (1984): 7–24; Edward Schillebeeckx, 'Christelijke spiritualiteit als ziel en bevrijding van de ethiek', *TGL* 41 (1985): 407–18.

44. Edward Schillebeeckx, '"Gij zijt een verborgen God". Jesaja 45,15. Een vastenmeditatie', *TGL* 43 (1987): 27–30; Edward Schillebeeckx, 'Christelijke identiteit, uitdagend en uitgedaagd: Over de rakelingse nabijheid van de onervaarbare God', in *Ons rakelings nabij: Gedaanteveranderingen van God en geloof. Ter ere van Edward Schillebeeckx*, ed. M. Kalsky e.a. (Nijmegen/Zoetermeer, 2005), 13–32.

45. Edward Schillebeeckx, 'Op zoek naar de heilswaarde van politieke vredespraxis', *Tijdschrift voor Theologie* 21 (1981): 238, 239.

46. Ibid., 239.

47. Ibid., 243. This explains why Schillebeeckx argues at the same time that Roman Catholic bishops should be engaged in political discussions, even in a society which is no longer predominantly Roman Catholic, and that he advocates a continuous reform of the church (Ibid., 240–1; 243). He explains the need for continuous reform as a precondition for the church, to remain grounded in God's gratuitous justifying grace in Christ, which is not gained by any merit.

48. Edward Schillebeeckx, *Als politiek niet alles is. Jezus in onze westerse cultuur*. Abraham Kuyper-lezingen 1986 (Baarn: Ten Have, 1986), 9–10.

49. Ibid., 9–10.

God, which is why Christians cannot claim that Christ is the only path to God.[50] Schillebeeckx fears that interpreting Christ as the sole path to God would conflict with his observation of atheists who are engaged in the struggle for a more humane future.[51] Consequently, Christians can no longer claim that it is solely their faith in God's self-revelation in Christ that would endow them with the privileged knowledge indicating the way to a better future.

Altogether, this brief outline of the development of Schillebeeckx's interpretation of atheism throughout his career shows that he has continued to focus on the grace that is mediated by atheist positions, despite what he, at times, calls atheism's overall reductive understanding of reality. This is connected to the 'realistic grace optimism' that is characteristic of his entire oeuvre, and his understanding of atheism as an equally legitimate pessimistic interpretation of reality. Until the 1970s, Schillebeeckx still presented Christian theology as the fulfilment of atheism's aspiration for grace, with a focus on that which is good about this aspiration, not on the lack it expresses. Nevertheless, Schillebeeckx stated explicitly that atheist solutions to societal problems are to be seen as being on the same level as theological ones only at the end of his career.[52] He explicitly refrained from presenting Christian theology as a solution to societal problems, and advocated Christian theology as one conversation partner among others in common political projects of positively overcoming evil and suffering. He now wanted theology to express society's aspiration for grace, while distancing himself from promising that theology itself could fulfil these aspirations. From one side, this can still be interpreted as being in line with Schillebeeckx's grace optimism: God's offer of grace is too abundant to be expressed by Christian theology alone. From the other side, however, I argue in both this chapter and the next that the *particular* grace mediated in Schillebeeckx's increasingly atheist context revealed to him the impairment of the theological vision through sin; an impairment which should be acknowledged by Christian theologians in order to guide Christian theology safely through its crisis and to restore the theological vision eventually. This is why, towards the end of his career, Schillebeeckx wrote that Christian theology must express the divine reality, but in a 'stammering' way.[53]

50. Ibid., 10; 22. Schillebeeckx has previously expressed this view with regard to the true historicity of Christ in *Church: The Human Story of God*, trans. John Bowden, *CW* vol. 10 (London: Bloomsbury T&T Clark, 2014), 163 [164–5]. He explains that a historical, contingent human being cannot represent the fullness of God exhaustively. Roger Haight calls this a shift from Christocentrism to a theocentrism that is mediated through Christ in Schillebeeckx's thought (Roger Haight, 'Engagement met de wereld als zaak van God: Christologie & Postmoderniteit', *Tijdschrift voor Theologie* 50 (2010): 92).

51. Schillebeeckx, *Als politiek niet alles is*, 11.

52. Schillebeeckx, *Church*, 79 [81–2].

53. Ibid., 75 [77–8].

4.2 A Naively Optimistic Interpretation of Atheism?

In order to advance my argument that Schillebeeckx's theology of grace is valuable for contemporary public theology, it should first be mentioned that Schillebeeckx's reconciliatory stance towards atheism has been criticized for not only being naively optimistic, and insufficiently critical, but also for exhibiting an erroneous understanding of grace.[54] Contrary to this criticism, this chapter's purpose is to argue that Schillebeeckx's attitude towards atheism was undergirded by one consistent understanding of grace, in terms of God's merciful forgiveness, an understanding of grace which, I claim, should be revitalized for answering the question concerning contemporary theology's contributions to political discussions in post-Christendom societies.

a) Objection to Schillebeeckx's Naive Optimism: Problematizing Theology's Accommodation to Secular Society

Schillebeeckx's interpretation of atheism must be understood as being broadly situated within the context of discussions about the risks of naturalizing grace that surrounded the Second Vatican Council. This is of particular interest insofar as John Milbank, building upon Henri de Lubac's theology, accuses more liberal[55] theologians of naturalizing the supernatural.[56] Naturalizing the supernatural means that Christianity, including its faith in God, can be exhaustively explained in secular terms. This idea of a natural order as already containing the supernatural within it is regarded not only as being unorthodox, but also as objectionable for political reasons.[57] If such an integral natural order is affirmed, then atheism is legitimized as the most coherent understanding of immanent reality to which Christianity is merely a superfluous addition.[58] This would mean accepting the secularist world view as a neutral fundament upon which Christian theology can be built, and the Christian faith could no longer be legitimately appealed to as a critical corrective to secular politics. De Lubac consequently upholds that nature's aspiration for grace cannot be fulfilled without the help of Christian theology.[59] The non-Christian

---

54. Schillebeeckx has been criticized for displaying 'an almost naive neglect of the problem of sin here' (Robert C. Ware, review of *God and Man*, by Edward Schillebeeckx, *Theological Studies* 31(2) (1970): 351).

55. By liberal, in this context I mean those theologians associated with the theological journal *Concilium* after Vatican II.

56. Milbank, *Theology and Social Theory*, 207; 222. The accusation is primarily aimed at Karl Rahner.

57. Henri De Lubac, 'The Total Meaning of Man and the World', *Communio* 35 (2008): 619–20.

58. Ibid., 622.

59. Paul McPartlan, *The Eucharist Makes The Church: Henry de Lubac and John Zizioulas in Dialogue* (Edinburgh: T&T Clark, 1993), 12; 22–3.

world is understood only as 'receptive readiness' to be fulfilled in Christ.[60] This means that Christian theology must attend to extra-ecclesial developments, but the focus of this attention is never on the world in its own right. Instead, it must be detected how precisely the world prepares itself for the reception of its fulfilment in Christ.[61] It is noteworthy that, in the Radical Orthodox elaborations of this position at least, the perfection of nature by grace is equated with the perfection of non-Christian philosophies and politics by Christian theology.[62]

In striking resemblance to the post-liberal criticism of public theology's supposed accommodation to the surrounding culture, Schillebeeckx has also been criticized for erroneously naturalizing the Christian faith.[63] Objections have been raised regarding Schillebeeckx's assumption that the secular realm is sanctified by divine grace without the help of the church, and that Christian theologians merely have to point to this extra-ecclesial grace.[64] Schillebeeckx is accused of being too optimistic regarding developments in the extra-ecclesial public.[65] However, this criticism is reductive insofar as Schillebeeckx's optimism, concerning the

---

60. Nicholas J. Healy, 'Henri de Lubac on Nature and Grace: A Note on Some Recent Contributions', *Communio* 35 (2008): 564.

61. Aidan Nichols, 'Henri de Lubac: Panorama and Proposal', *New Blackfriars* 93 (2012): 18; Francesca A. Murphy, 'De Lubac, Grace, Politics and Paradox', *Studies in Christian Ethics* 23 (2010): 429–30. Milbank summarizes de Lubac's position in the following: 'Christianity is a humanism, else it is misunderstood. On the other hand, secular humanism is the absolute antithesis of the Gospel' (John Milbank, *The Suspended Middle: Henri de Lubac and the Debate Concerning the Supernatural* (London: SCM Press, 2005), 9).

62. Murphy, 'De Lubac, Grace, Politics and Paradox', *Studies in Christian Ethics* 23 (2010): 416.

63. Henri de Lubac, *A Brief Catechesis on Nature and Grace* (San Francisco: Ignatius Press,1984), 200; 219; 228; a more philosophical argument that Schillebeeckx accommodates the Christian tradition to secular culture can be found in Louis Dupré, 'Experience and Interpretation: A Philosophical Reflection on Schillebeeckx' *Jesus* and *Christ*', *Theological Studies* 43.1 (1982): 49–50. Robert Schreiter argues that this criticism concerning Schillebeeckx's erroneous secularization of the Christian faith is shared by many (Robert Schreiter, 'Indicators of the Future of Theology in the Works of Edward Schillebeeckx', in *Edward Schillebeeckx: Impulse für Theologien im 21. Jahrhundert – Impetus Towards Theologies in the 21st Century*, ed. Thomas Eggensperger, Ulrich Engel and Angel F. Méndez Montoya (Ostfildern: Matthias Grünewaldverlag, 2008), 27).

64. De Lubac, *A Brief Catechesis on Nature and Grace*, 193–4. Much later, Schillebeeckx explains that his statement *Extra mundum nulla salus* has often been erroneously criticized because the critics laid the whole stress on *mundum*, whereas his own emphasis lies on *salus* (Edward Schillebeeckx, 'Letter from Edward Schillebeeckx', in *Edward Schillebeeckx and Contemporary Theology*, eds. Lieven Boeve, Frederiek Depoortere, and Stephan van Erp (London: T&T Clark, 2010), xiv–xv).

65. De Lubac, *A Brief Catechesis on Nature and Grace*, 196. See also George H. Tavard, review of *Interim Report on the Books Jesus and Christ*, by Edward Schillebeeckx, *Journal*

all-pervading presence of grace in the extra-ecclesial realm, is not discussed *theologically*. Instead, Schillebeeckx's acknowledgement of non-Christian mediations of grace is simply being discarded as 'inclusive formula[s] ..., simple cliché[s] or ... a program of secularistic ideology'.[66]

Schillebeeckx's position can be defended against his critics, by way of explaining in more detail the relation between his theology of grace and his optimism regarding atheism. My argument follows more observant critics whose research suggests that Schillebeeckx is as adamant in interpreting nature only in its relation to grace as de Lubac is.[67] On this basis, it appears that Schillebeeckx's critics misidentify the point of disagreement between their own and Schillebeeckx's understandings of the relation between Christian theology and non-Christian understandings of the world. The disagreement does not concern the relation between nature and grace so much as it concerns the role of Christian theology in fulfilling nature's aspiration for grace. Not unlike de Lubac, Schillebeeckx also characterizes nature most fundamentally as an aspiration for grace, as has already become apparent in my above exposition of Schillebeeckx's interpretation of atheism.[68] However, Schillebeeckx is more hesitant to claim that the balance between fulfilling and postponing this fundamental human aspiration for grace is best struck by Christian theology. Most fundamentally, Christian theology must also be regarded as an aspiration for grace, on the same level with non-Christian outlooks.[69]

---

of Theological Studies 32 (1981): 574, who similarly calls Schillebeeckx's understanding of secularism naive.

66. De Lubac, *A Brief Catechesis on Nature and Grace*, 200. Moreover, de Lubac calls Schillebeeckx's grace optimism pagan and a biased reading of the New Testament (215–16).

67. Erik Borgman, *Edward Schillebeeckx: A Theologian in His History*, trans. J. Bowden (London: Bloomsbury T&T Clark, 2006), 57; Philip Kennedy, *Schillebeeckx* (London: Geoffrey Chapman, 1993), 135; Stephan Van Erp, 'The Sacrament of the World: Thinking God's Presence Beyond Public Theology', *ET Studies* 6/1 (2015): 128.

68. Borgman, *Edward Schillebeeckx*, 51. It is this craving for grace that is named by Christian theology. Also, Schreiter understands Schillebeeckx as examining the world's expectations in order to understand Christian salvation in a contemporary context, while also highlighting that it is not the worldly expectations, but God who ultimately defines salvation (Schreiter, 'Indicators of the Future of Theology in the Works of Edward Schillebeeckx', in *Edward Schillebeeckx: Impulse für Theologien im 21. Jahrhundert*, 34). See Edward Schillebeeckx, 'Arabisch-Neoplatoonse Achtergrond van Thomas' Opvatting over de Ontvangelijkheid van de Mens voor de Genade', *Bijdragen* 35 (1974): 298–308, where Schillebeeckx explains that humans are most fundamentally a desire for God, which cannot be fulfilled by human strength but only by God's grace. At another point, Schillebeeckx refers to an implicit directedness of all humankind towards Christ by virtue of their creation (Edward Schillebeeckx, 'Kerk en mensdom', *Concilium* 1 (1965): 77).

69. This can be related to Schillebeeckx's suspicion of authoritative power, which, from early on in his career, led him to reject the view that submission to the Roman Catholic Church was necessary to receive grace (Borgman, *Edward Schillebeeckx*, 50).

This criticism concerning Schillebeeckx's supposedly naive assessment of atheist thought would, however, be justified if those interpretations that link Schillebeeckx's understanding of grace to his theology of creation were believed to be adequate. To date, there is indeed nearly unanimous scholarly agreement that Schillebeeckx's positive attitude to non-Christian positions is related to his theology of creation, in the sense that God's creative grace can be trusted to be present throughout the entire society. This link would indeed render Schillebeeckx's theology unjustifiably optimistic at the expense of duly acknowledging atheism's sinful imperfections. Contrary to both, Schillebeeckx's critics as well as those who appreciate his theology of creation, I contend that Schillebeeckx's theology of *redemption* undergirds both his understanding of grace as well as his positive attitude towards atheism. The difference being that, grounded in a theology of redemption, Schillebeeckx does not neglect the sinfulness of humankind, including atheists. Instead, he operates with a particular understanding of how the world's sinfulness is overcome in Christ. The Christian Resurrection faith, in the superior power of God's forgiveness over human sin, also determines Schillebeeckx's understanding of how societal problems are being solved.

b) De-problematizing Schillebeeckx's Cultural Accommodation: Appreciating Secular Society's Participation in Redemption

At first glance, my claim that Schillebeeckx's assessment of atheism is based on his theology of grace accords with the observation that 'the strong accent on grace – the presence and power among us – has characterized Schillebeeckx's theological project from its beginning. The creator God "bent towards humanity" has promised to be with us always – even to the end of the world'.[70] In this vein, it has been suggested that Schillebeeckx's treatment of creation and grace could be taken up by future scholars in order to further contemporary discussions about a faithful collaboration between Christianity and secular culture.[71]

Further nuancing this suggestion, however, instead of stressing the influence of Schillebeeckx's theology of creation on his engagement with non-Christian positions, I argue that his theology of redemption is more decisive for his optimism

---

70. Mary Catherine Hilkert, "Grace-Optimism': The Spirituality at the Heart of Schillebeeckx's Theology', *Spirituality Today* 43 (1991): 220–39, http://www.spiritualitytoday.org/spir2day/91433hilkert.html (accessed: 13.12.2013).

71. Schreiter, 'Indicators of the Future of Theology in the Works of Edward Schillebeeckx', in *Edward Schillebeeckx: Impulse für Theologien im 21. Jahrhundert*, 34. It has been argued repeatedly that Schillebeeckx's entire theological oeuvre is based on his theology of creation (A. R. Van de Walle, 'Theologie over de werkelijkheid: Een betekenis van het werk van Edward Schillebeeckx', *Tijdschrift voor Theologie* 14 (1974): 461–90; Frans Maas, 'Stem & Stilte: Waarheid en openbaring bij Schillebeeckx', *Tijdschrift voor Theologie* (2010): 61; Haight, 'Engagement met de wereld als zaak van God', *Tijdschrift voor Theologie*, 76).

concerning atheist mediations of grace.[72] Highlighting the import of redemption, rather than creation, on his theology of grace is crucial because it means that Schillebeeckx's optimism concerning non-Christian positions is not based on an overestimation of human nature. Instead, considering the Fall and human sinfulness, Schillebeeckx works with a particularly pessimistic anthropology.[73] By pessimistic anthropology I mean that Schillebeeckx has little trust in the success of human efforts, and continues to acknowledge the probable failure of *all* human projects. Yet, at the same time, he maintains the 'realistic grace optimism' alluded to in the above historical outline of Schillebeeckx's interpretation of atheism. Combining his grace optimism and his pessimistic anthropology, Schillebeeckx's theological reception of non-Christian insights reflects his conviction that 'it is precisely this sinful world which is an object of God's mercy',[74] and in order to overcome contemporary societal, as well as ecclesial problems, Schillebeeckx searches for mediations of this mercy in his context.

That Schillebeeckx calls his grace optimism realistic can be explained with reference to his emphasis on the mediated character of grace. He stresses throughout that grace can be known from human experience in the world, in this way countering idealistic understandings of grace. Schillebeeckx calls grace an experience of the totality of reality that cannot be entirely conceptualized.[75] 'In our human experiences we can *experience* something that transcends our experience and proclaims itself in that experience as unexpected grace.'[76] Schillebeeckx defines grace as the surplus of reality, the abundant positivity of reality.[77] Grace is the all-

---

72. Philip Kennedy most explicitly states that Schillebeeckx does not engage with creation from the vantage point of redemption (Philip Kennedy, 'God and Creation', in *The Praxis of the Reign of God*, eds. Mary Catherine Hilkert and Robert J. Schreiter (New York: Fordham University Press, 2002), 39–40). However, Kennedy himself previously claimed that Schillebeeckx's entire theology is a soteriology 'cocooned in' a theology of creation (Philip Kennedy, 'Continuity underlying Discontinuity: Schillebeeckx's Philosophical Background', *New Blackfriars* 70 (1989): 275). My interpretation, then, accords more with Borgman's, who argued that Schillebeeckx's theology is driven by the question of what it means to be redeemed (Erik Borgman, 'Retrieving God's Contemporary Presence: The Future of Edward Schillebeeckx's Theology of Culture', in *Edward Schillebeeckx and Contemporary Theology*, 244).

73. Schillebeeckx understands grace not primarily as a perfection of nature but as an overcoming of sin (Schillebeeckx, *Christ: The Christian Experience in the Modern World*, trans. John Bowden, *CW* vol. 7 (London: Bloomsbury T&T Clark, 2014), 76–7; 518–19; 626–7 [87; 530; 637]). This has been rightly observed by Louis Dupré in 'Experience and Interpretation', *Theological Studies* 43.1 (1982): 32.

74. Schillebeeckx, *Christ*, 547 [557].

75. Ibid., 519 [531].

76. Ibid., 66 [78].

77. Schillebeeckx, 'Towards a Catholic Use of Hermeneutics', *God the Future of Man*, trans. N.D. Smith, *CW* vol. 3 (London: Bloomsbury T&T Clark, 2014), 23–4 [34–6]; Schillebeeckx, *Christ*, 83–4 [95].

encompassing reality in which all natural positivity participates. However, grace cannot be reduced to the sum total of all natural positivity. Instead, grace can be identified at the point at which all natural positivity merges into mystery.[78] In other words, the positivity of nature itself suggests that there is more than this natural positivity. This affirmation of more than natural positivity is what Christians call grace. In this sense, it can be known from human experiences of nature that grace transcends nature. In my subsequent presentation of Schillebeeckx's Christology, I will clarify that this experience of reality, which Christians call grace, is a post-Resurrection experience of the world as redeemed.[79] It is not the only self-evident experience of nature, but once nature is interpreted through a hermeneutic of redemption, Christian theologians can explain how nature is experienced as being graced. And precisely this interpretative experience of reality allows Christian theologians not to focus primarily on problems, as will be further elaborated in the course of this chapter.

c) *Grace Optimism and Pessimistic Anthropology: Schillebeeckx's Realistic Theology of Redemption*

Schillebeeckx's trust in the grace of redemption is not naive, insofar as he works with a particularly pessimistic anthropology. Towards the end of his study of the biblical understandings of grace, Schillebeeckx summarizes that all gospels 'testify at the same time both to the depth of human failure in a world of finite and sinful men [*sic*], and to the depth of the triumphant mercy of God in a world which in the last resort is experienced as "God's world"'.[80] Schillebeeckx even interprets the only unforgiveable sin against the Holy Spirit as the deliberate rejection of 'the principle of God's mercy in Jesus'.[81] In a similar vein, Schillebeeckx repeatedly stresses the

---

78. Edward Schillebeeckx, 'The Development of the Apostolic Faith into the Dogma of the Church', *Revelation and Theology*, trans. N.D. Smith, *CW* vol. 2 (London: Bloomsbury T&T Clark, 2014), 54 [80–2].

79. Lieven Boeve, 'Experience According to Edward Schillebeeckx: The Driving Force of Faith and Theology', in *Divinising Experience: Essays in the History of Religious Experience from Origen to Riceour*, ed. Lieven Boeve and Laurence P. Hemming (Leuven: Peeters, 2004), 207–8.

80. Schillebeeckx, *Christ*, 826 [830]. Schillebeeckx highlights that due to human sinfulness, the Old Testament term *hesed* acquires the connotation of mercy and forgiveness (84 [96]).

81. Ibid., 626 [637]. In another place, Schillebeeckx explains that reality is always already graced and redeemed, and sin is the human rejection of their dependence on that reality (547 [555–6]). See also Edward Schillebeeckx, 'Vergebung als Modell menschlicher Autonomie und die Gnade Gottes', in *Die Widerspenstige Religion: Orientierung für eine Kultur der Autonomie?*, ed. Toine van den Hoogen, Hans Küng and Jean-Pierre Wils (Kampen: Pharos, 1997), 141, where Schillebeeckx defines sin as the refusal of God's forgiving love.

fundamentally undeserved character of grace.[82] A Christian understanding of grace always already includes God's forgiveness of human sin.[83] This indicates that, similar to Kathryn Tanner, Schillebeeckx understands grace not primarily as a reality within human nature but as the natural environment in which humankind always already exists.[84] Schillebeeckx affirms a grace optimism inasmuch as God's faithful bestowal of grace can be trusted, as well as a pessimistic anthropology insofar as this grace is unmerited by humans. This grace optimism is ontological, given that the superior power of all goodness and justice over all evil and injustice is acknowledged.[85] Schillebeeckx calls this grace optimism 'the mother of all

82. Schillebeeckx, *Church*, 115 [116–17]; Edward Schillebeeckx, *Interim Report on the Books Jesus and Christ*, trans. John Bowden, *CW* vol. 8 (London: Bloomsbury T&T Clark, 2014), 45; 112 [52–3; 128–9]; Schillebeeckx, *Christ*, 84; 519; 627 [95–6; 530–1; 637].

83. Schillebeeckx, *Christ*, 76–7; 84; 627 [87–8; 96; 637].

84. Schillebeeckx, 'The Non-Conceptual Intellectual Element in the Act of Faith: A Reaction', *Revelation and Theology*, 259–60 [61–4]. Indicating that, similar to Tanner, Schillebeeckx understands grace primarily as God's continuous bestowal of gifts onto the world, he argues that attachment to earthly possessions might inhibit a person's appreciation of God's trustworthiness (Edward Schillebeeckx, *Jesus: An Experiment in Christology*, trans. John Bowden, *CW* vol. 6 (London: Bloomsbury T&T Clark, 2014), 122–3 [142–4]).

85. Schillebeeckx argues that 'in Christ, God assures that everything will ultimately be good for those who love him' (Schillebeeckx, *Christ the Sacrament*, 156 [266–8]); he speaks of 'the superiority of all justice and goodness to injustice' as 'the experience of the absolute presence of God's pure positivity in the historical mixture of meaning and meaninglessness' (Schillebeeckx, *Church*, 94–5 [96–8]), of an 'eternal difference between good and evil' (136 [138]), of ascribing 'pure positiveness [sic] to God', and refers to God's essence in terms of 'a promoter of the good and an opponent of all evil, injustice and suffering' (Schillebeeckx, *Interim Report*, 105 [119–20]); he speaks of God's refusal 'to acknowledge the superior strength of evil and so with his own divine being stand[ing] surety for the defeat of evil in all its forms' (Schillebeeckx, *Jesus*, 155 [178]); explaining the Old Testament term *hesed*, Schillebeeckx explains God's relation to humankind as one not only of good will but of 'generosity, overwhelming, unexpected kindness which is forgetful of itself, completely open and ready for "the other"' (Schillebeeckx, *Christ*, 83 [94]); with regard to belief in the anti-Christ, Schillebeeckx explains that Christians must acknowledge evil as a power while affirming that the power of grace in Christ has the last word (570–1 [579–80]); he explains the Christian understanding of election as based on the conviction that 'life is directed by God in freedom and goodness', and that God's love 'turns all things to good for those who love God'. Christians affirm the 'fundamental goodness of God's purposes with man [sic]' and 'the ultimate meaning of human life' (625 [635]); he furthermore explains that this promise 'enables, allows and obliges us to give wellbeing and goodness the final say in a way that is grounded in Jesus, because the Father is greater than all suffering and greater than our inability to experience ultimate reality as a trustworthy gift' (Schillebeeckx, *Jesus*, 586 [625]); he explains that this hope for the future is based upon God's faithfulness who provides 'certainty about the goodness of the plan of creation which is both the beginning

Christianity'.[86] By a pessimistic anthropology, I mean that, in accordance with an Augustinian understanding of evil as privation, Schillebeeckx distinguishes between all goodness as deriving from God and as, therefore, ultimately lasting and all evil as deriving from human sin.[87] Human sin is the reason why history is a mixture of good and evil. As a combination of both an optimistic theology and a pessimistic anthropology, the superior power of grace is identified as God's *mercy* at the heart of reality.[88]

Explaining Schillebeeckx's aforementioned trust that, despite their entanglement in sinful social structures, individuals can be moved by God's grace, Schillebeeckx's pessimistic anthropology does not prevent him from being optimistic regarding the human ability to continuously respond to God's grace. He still regards every human being as being intrinsically inclined towards grace.[89] However, this is not so much due to any optimism concerning human nature, but is rather to do with Schillebeeckx's understanding of grace in terms of mercy. Due to God's merciful grace, human beings participate in God irrespective of their sinfulness.[90] That God's grace is most fundamental means that it is always at people's disposal, even despite any human rejection of this grace.[91] God's merciful acceptance of people, despite their sinfulness, means that reality is not only good in terms of an unaffected stability. Schillebeeckx not only refers to the superior power of the good over evil, but he also claims that from a Christian perspective the whole of reality is *concerned* with human salvation.[92] 'Wherever we turn, God's grace is always there ahead of us. His face *confronts* us in everything.'[93] In other words,

and the eschaton. ... It is "very good" (Gen. 1:31)' (Schillebeeckx, 'The Interpretation of the Future', *The Understanding of Faith: Interpretation and Criticism*, trans. N.D. Smith, *CW* vol. 5 (London: Bloomsbury T&T Clark, 2014), 7 [7–8]).

86. Schillebeeckx, *Interim Report*, 61 [71–2]. Schillebeeckx calls the *Parousia* Christology the mother of all Christianity insofar as it affirms that despite all appearances to the contrary, the Kingdom of God is still coming. See also Schillebeeckx, *Jesus*, 602 [640] where Schillebeeckx explains that the core of Christianity is that 'human history – with its successes, fiascos, illusions and disillusions – is transcended by the living God'.

87. Schillebeeckx, 'The Interpretation of the Future', *The Understanding of Faith*, 7 [7–8]. Schillebeeckx understands evil as incomprehensible and inexplicable (Schillebeeckx, *Christ*, 720 [727]). For a discussion of the Thomist roots of Schillebeeckx's understanding of evil as privation see Kathleen McManus, 'Suffering in the Theology of Edward Schillebeeckx', *Theological Studies* 60 (1999): 481–2.

88. Schillebeeckx, *Church*, 6; 97 [6–7; 99–100]; Schillebeeckx, *Jesus*, 4 [20–1].

89. Schillebeeckx, 'The Non-Conceptual Intellectual Element', *Revelation and Theology*, 246 [40–2]; Schillebeeckx, *Christ*, 773–4 [776].

90. Schillebeeckx, *Church*, 125 [126–7].

91. Ibid., 88 [90–1].

92. Schillebeeckx, *Christ*, 742 [747–8].

93. Schillebeeckx, 'The Non-Conceptual Intellectual Element', *Revelation and Theology*, 265 [70–2] (my emphasis).

to attribute the origin of goodness to the merciful God means that there is an active relating of graced reality towards humanity. God as pure positivity[94] actively bends towards humankind and, in this way, draws humankind into the goodness of reality. It is this emphasis on God's mercy which allows Schillebeeckx, despite his pessimistic anthropology, to conceive of a fundamental human readiness to respond to the graced reality which surrounds them.[95] The boundary between God and humankind is entirely on the human side.[96] 'The rejection of the merciful love of God is the only barrier which can be thrown up against mercy.'[97]

Some of the most prominent interpreters of Schillebeeckx's theology relate his optimism regarding atheism to his understanding of creation. Christians must attend to the secular world because the creator God is salvifically present in all of history.[98] However, I want to suggest in this chapter that Schillebeeckx's optimism concerning atheism can be best disassociated from naivet if the focus is shifted towards God the Redeemer, emphasizing his particular understanding of how human sinfulness is overcome by Christ.

4.3 Christ's Definite Overcoming of Evil: Grace as Solution to the Humanly Irresolvable Problem of Sin

An examination of Schillebeeckx's Christology will not only further clarify the theological underpinnings of his grace optimism and his pessimistic anthropology, but also expose how Schillebeeckx's specific Christocentrism values particularly the mediated character of grace, thus distancing his position from the principled rejection of Christendom advanced by post-liberal Protestants. Finally, it can be explained how Schillebeeckx's Christology allows for responding to the post-Christendom context in a way that is both less problem-centred and less apologetic than the public theological and the Radical Orthodox approaches. Substantiating these claims, I show in the following how Schillebeeckx's interpretation of the Cross is the basis for his pessimistic anthropology, and how his grace optimism is

---

94. Schillebeeckx, *Church*, 73; 94 [75; 96–7]; Schillebeeckx, *Christ*, 88–9 [100]. In Christ it has been revealed that God is universal love for all (Schillebeeckx, *Church*, 175 [176–7]; Schillebeeckx, *Interim Report*, 19 [22–3]).

95. Schillebeeckx, 'The Non-Conceptual Intellectual Element', *Revelation and Theology*, 258 [59–61]. This also explains why Schillebeeckx claims that Christianity is more a matter of being chosen than one of human choice (Edward Schillebeeckx, 'Godsdienst van en voor mensen', *Tijdschrift voor Theologie*, 366).

96. Schillebeeckx, *Interim Report*, 101 [115–16]; Schillebeeckx, *Jesus*, 591 [628–9].

97. Schillebeeckx, *Christ*, 626 [637].

98. Lieven Boeve, 'Introduction: The Enduring Significance and Relevance of Edward Schillebeeckx? Introducing the State of the Question in Medias Res', in *Edward Schillebeeckx and Contemporary Theology*, 10.

related to Christ's Resurrection. In my exposition of Schillebeeckx's Christology, I follow his claim that faith in the Resurrection entails three affirmations: First, that of a new creation in which evil is definitely overcome; second, the approval of Jesus as a concrete and unique person and third, that the church has been founded by Christ.[99]

a) Cross: Human Sin against God's Grace

Although Schillebeeckx is adamant in his claim that the Cross itself is not redemptive, it nevertheless plays an important part in his theology of redemption. While associating redemption primarily with the Resurrection as 'God's overwhelming power over evil',[100] Schillebeeckx argues that the significance of the Resurrection can only be recognized in the light of the seriousness of Christ's death.[101]

Elucidating what I mean by a pessimistic anthropology, Schillebeeckx understands the crucifixion as definitive rupture between sinful humankind and God's grace.[102] Understanding God as pure positivity, Schillebeeckx ascribes full responsibility for Jesus's violent death to humankind.[103] Importantly, Schillebeeckx does not exempt the church from humankind's sinful rejection of Christ, but

---

99. Schillebeeckx, *Jesus*, 609 [648–9]. My explanation of the first implication serves to elucidate further the Christological underpinnings of Schillebeeckx's realistic grace optimism, the second implication is related to Schillebeeckx's emphasis on the mediated character of grace and the third implication is important regarding the question of problem-centred approaches to politics.

100. Schillebeeckx, *Church*, 126 [127–8]; see also Schillebeeckx, 'The New Image of God, Secularization and Man's Future on Earth', *God the Future of Man*, 112 [184–6]; Edward Schillebeeckx, 'The Church and Mankind', *World and Church*, trans. N.D. Smith, *CW* vol. 4 (London: Bloomsbury T&T Clark, 2014), 95 [123–4]; Schillebeeckx, *Jesus*, 91–2; 304–5; 603 [111–13; 334–6; 641–2]; Schillebeeckx, *Christ*, 545–6; 722; 795 [555; 729; 799].

101. Edward Schillebeeckx, 'Kerk en mensdom', *Concilium* 1 (1965): 71.

102. Schillebeeckx, 'The Church and Mankind', *World and Church*, 95 [123–4]; Schillebeeckx, *Jesus*, 263; 273; 612 [294–5; 305–6; 652–3]; Schillebeeckx, *Christ*, 722 [729].

103. Schillebeeckx, 'Kerk en mensdom', *Concilium* 1 (1965): 71. This explains why Schillebeeckx opposes any interpretation of Jesus's death as salvific in itself (Edward Schillebeeckx, *Theologisch geloofsverstaan anno 1983*. Afscheidscollege gegeven op vrijdag 11 februari 1983 door Mag. dr. Edward Schillebeeckx o.p. hoogleraar Systematische Theologie en Geschiedenis van de Theologie, Nijmegen (januari 1958 tot 1 september 1982) (Baarn: Nelissen, 1983), 7; Schillebeeckx, *Jesus*, 250; 260; 274; 278; 612 [281–2; 306–7; 310–11; 652–3]). In this context, Schillebeeckx has been criticized for being insufficiently aware of traditional, more positive interpretations of the salvific value of the Cross (Helen F. Bergin, 'The Death of Jesus and its Impact on God – Jürgen Moltmann and Edward Schillebeeckx', *The Irish Theological Quarterly* 52 (1986): 201; John P. Galvin, 'The Death of Jesus in the Theology of Edward Schillebeeckx', *The Irish Theological Quarterly* (1983): 169; 177; Peter Phillips, 'Schillebeeckx's Soteriological Agnosticism', *New Blackfriars* 78 (1997): 76–84).

instead interprets Peter's denial of Jesus as the future church's abandonment of Christ at the Cross.[104] Consequently, at Jesus's crucifixion there is a real break between all of humankind and God. At the crucifixion, there is a real lack of grace in humanity, elucidating Schillebeeckx's pessimistic anthropology. At the moment of the crucifixion, the only human who sides with God's grace is Jesus, who is at this point entirely isolated from the rest of humankind. In other words, Schillebeeckx relates Christ's uniqueness not so much to the Incarnation as to the Cross.

As has been stressed repeatedly, it is central to Schillebeeckx's thought that Jesus had not been abandoned by God on the Cross.[105] The crucifixion reveals that 'God is also present in human life where he is absent from human view'.[106] Schillebeeckx interprets God's silence at the Cross as indicative of the way in which love endures all evil.[107] Obedience to the silent God means that Jesus continued to love his fellow humans, leaving it to the reality of love to decide upon the future.[108] In this sense, Jesus's 'solidarity with God in an anti-divine situation brought us salvation'.[109] Jesus was not primarily concerned with the consequences for his own life, because of his single-hearted trust in God. Jesus's death revealed that his life and message were unconditional.[110] At the same time, and in sharp contrast to Yoder, Schillebeeckx regards the Cross not as a victory, but as a failure, and claims that it is a mystery that this historical failure did not erase Jesus's faith in God.[111] 'Ultimately Jesus' death is a question to God – the God whom Jesus proclaimed.'[112] This is why Schillebeeckx refrains from setting Jesus's crucifixion as an ethical example to be followed by all Christians.

Phillips mainly criticizes Schillebeeckx's supposedly incorrect understanding of the biblical meaning of sacrifice.

104. Schillebeeckx, 'Kerk en mensdom', *Concilium* 1 (1965): 71. Of course, one could counter that the Church patiently endured Christ's crucifixion if one associates the Church with Mary, rather than with Peter.

105. Galvin, 'The Death of Jesus in the Theology of Edward Schillebeeckx', *The Irish Theological Quarterly* (1983): 174; Bergin, 'The Death of Jesus and its Impact on God', *The Irish Theological Quarterly* 52 (1986): 196; Robin Ryan, 'Holding on to the Hand of God: Edward Schillebeeckx on the Mystery of Suffering', *New Blackfriars* 89 (2007): 120–1; Edward Krasevac, 'Salvation 'Thanks to' or 'In Spite of' the Cross?', *New Blackfriars* 93 (2011): 572–9. For Schillebeeckx's own explanation of this point see Schillebeeckx, 'Jezus en de menselijke levensmislukking', *Consilium* 12 (1976): 88–9.

106. Schillebeeckx, *Church*, 124 [125–6]; Schillebeeckx, *Interim Report,* 117 [134–5].

107. Schillebeeckx, *Jesus*, 284 [317–18].

108. Ibid., 277 [309–10] ; Schillebeeckx, *Christ*, 789–90; 818–19; 825–6 [793–4; 823; 830].

109. Schillebeeckx, *Jesus*, 612 [652–3].

110. Schillebeeckx, *Als politiek niet alles is*, 28.

111. Schillebeeckx, *Jesus*, 277 [309–10].

112. Ibid., 286 [319].

Consequently, the seriousness of Christ's crucifixion means that the whole of creation could have evaporated into the nothingness from whence it came. The death of the only human who consistently aligned himself with God's grace puts God's continuous offer of grace more into question than anything else ever could.[113]

b) Resurrection: God's Ontological Forgiveness

In the aftermath of the crucifixion there is, then, an absolute separation between humankind and God, with the sole exception of Jesus who is reconciled to God.[114] Consequently, humankind's real lack of grace following the crucifixion can only be healed by Christ. At this point, Schillebeeckx's emphasis on divine forgiveness moves to the forefront. Schillebeeckx understands the Resurrection as God's sole initiative of mercy over the entire absurdity and meaninglessness of Christ's death.[115] In the Resurrection, humankind has been redeemed by Christ because Christ here forgives sinful humankind.[116] At this moment, the whole of humankind has found mercy before God.[117] Only in this sense of Christ's forgiveness is it then appropriate to say that, in Christ, humanity has already risen through Christ's suffering to glory with the Father.[118] This does not lead Schillebeeckx to affirm some mysterious transformation of human nature in any abstract sense. It means that God continues to bestow grace onto the world despite human sin, which indicates that Schillebeeckx understands God's mercy as a reality external to humankind, meeting human beings from outside of themselves.[119]

113. Edward Schillebeeckx, 'Leven ondanks de dood in heden en toekomst', _Tijdschrift voor Theologie_ 10 (1970): 437.

114. Schillebeeckx, 'Kerk en mensdom', _Concilium_ 1 (1965): 71-2.

115. Schillebeeckx, 'Leven ondanks de dood in heden en toekomst', _Tijdschrift voor Theologie_, 437.

116. Schillebeeckx, 'Kerk en mensdom', _Concilium_ 1 (1965): 71; Schillebeeckx, 'De zin van het mens-zijn van Jezus, de Christus', _Tijdschrift voor Theologie_ 2 (1962): 145. Schillebeeckx admits that this representative nature of Christ cannot be anthropologically explained (145-6).

117. Schillebeeckx, 'Kerk en mensdom', _Concilium_ 1 (1965): 67-8. This is Schillebeeckx's interpretation of God the Father's appointment of the humiliated Christ at His right hand.

118. Schillebeeckx, 'The Church and Mankind', _World and Church_, 91 [117-18].

119. That Schillebeeckx understands God's bestowal of grace primarily as a reality external to humankind, and in this sense humankind as always living within the supernatural order, is overlooked by Stephen J. Duffy, _The Graced Horizon: Nature and Grace in Modern Catholic Thought_ (Collegeville, Minnesota: The Liturgical Press, 1992), 162, which invalidates Duffy's criticism that Schillebeeckx cannot account for how an infant, incapable of choice, could be called graced (165). Duffy erroneously turns Schillebeeckx's claim that people always already live in the reality of God's grace, either in the mode of acceptance or in the mode of sinful rejection, around and suggests that this would imply that being graced depends on the human choice for grace. Quite the contrary, Schillebeeckx's argument sug-

The Resurrection is, thus, not so much the revelation of God's creative grace as it is the revelation of God's mercy over the sinful world.[120] Yet, at the same time, the Resurrection is not a reaction against evil, but it reveals the persistence of goodness despite all evil.[121] There is, thus, a continuity of grace in both creation and redemption, but the point is that this continuity is no automatism, but that the continuity has been effected by Christ's gratuitous forgiveness of humankind in the Resurrection.

Elucidating what I mean by pessimistic anthropology, Schillebeeckx calls Christ's forgiveness of humankind in the Resurrection a pure act of God's grace.[122] The Resurrection is a revelation that comes from God alone.[123] It is the event of God being God.[124] Not even Jesus Christ's humanity is active at this point.[125] The human passivity at the Resurrection, stressed by Schillebeeckx, is precisely why the Resurrection has the greatest ontological impact.[126] One could say that the Resurrection was the only occurrence in history, not at all affected by human sin.[127] The Resurrection is not one event in history among many, but the most all-encompassing reality.[128] The Resurrection is the greatest turning point in history

gests, seeing that people always already live in a graced environment, they are most likely to accept grace unconsciously.

120. Schillebeeckx, *Christ*, 547–8; 763–4 [557; 766].

121. Schillebeeckx, *Church*, 127 [128–9]; Schillebeeckx, *Christ the Sacrament*, 156 [266–8]; Schillebeeckx, 'The Interpretation of the Future', *The Understanding of Faith*, 10 [11–12]; Schillebeeckx, *Interim Report*, 97 [110–11].

122. Schillebeeckx, 'Kerk en mensdom', *Concilium* 1 (1965): 71. See also Schillebeeckx, *Jesus*, 328; 484; 603; 608; 610 [359–60; 525; 641–2; 647–8; 649–0]. Whereas Milbank focuses on those biblical passages that refer to Christ's self-raising from the dead, Schillebeeckx claims that the earlier Christian tradition understood the Resurrection of Christ to be a pure act of God (Schillebeeckx, *Jesus*, 484; 603 [525; 641–2]).

123. Schillebeeckx, *Jesus*, 610 [649–50]. In the Resurrection, God offers an unmerited abundance of meaning (Schillebeeckx, 'Leven ondanks de dood in heden en toekomst', *Tijdschrift voor Theologie*, 434).

124. Schillebeeckx, 'Leven ondanks de dood in heden en toekomst', *Tijdschrift voor Theologie*, 434.

125. Schillebeeckx, 'Kerk en mensdom', *Concilium* 1 (1965): 71.

126. Schillebeeckx speaks of the Resurrection as a non-empirical event because it is transhistorical (Schillebeeckx, *Interim Report*, 64 [74–5]; Schillebeeckx, 'The Interpretation of the Future', *The Understanding of Faith*, 10 [11–12]; Schillebeeckx, *Jesus*, 306; 348; 491 [336–7; 380–1; 532]).

127. The Incarnation, in comparison, is somewhat entangled with the history of human sinfulness, as Herodes's murder of the firstborns, as well as Jesus's birth in a stable due to the innkeepers refusal of hospitality illustrate.

128. I, hence, disagree with those who argue that Schillebeeckx's 'functional Christology' fails to maintain that in Christ God has acted decisively for the salvation of all of

and, as such, inaugurates an entirely new situation of the world.[129] The situation is entirely new, insofar as all suffering and evil has definitely been overcome.[130] And yet, Jesus Christ is the only point in which history is already eschatologically completed.[131] This means that all history can only be understood adequately in the light of Jesus Christ.[132]

The implications of such a Christocentric interpretation of history are twofold. On the one hand, because of God's mercy, the whole world has already received the *promise* of its final appraisal in Jesus Christ.[133] This is why Christians can trust in an ultimately good end of history, despite all remaining evil.[134] In this sense, the whole of history is already completed in Christ.[135] On the other hand, a Christocentric interpretation of history also means that history carries its own judgement within it: It has already been decided that all goodness will persist and that all evil will vanish.[136] However, the concrete shape of this goodness has not yet been determined definitively and is open to historical developments.[137] In other words, history 'continues as usual', but the overall reality in which it takes place has changed.[138] That the concrete shape of the eschaton is still open to developments is related to Schillebeeckx's emphasis of the mediated character of grace, which will be clarified in the subsequent section regarding Schillebeeckx's interpretation of Jesus's life as anticipation of the Resurrection, as well as in Section 2.4 regarding Schillebeeckx's understanding of the Resurrection as God's affirmation of the unique person, Jesus.

humankind (Kenneth Surin, 'Atonement and Christology', *Neue Zeitschrift für Systematische Theologie und Religionsphilosophie* 24 (1982): 132).

129. Schillebeeckx, 'Kerk en mensdom', Concilium 1 (1965): 72; Schillebeeckx, *Jesus*, 357; 490 [390; 531–2].

130. Schillebeeckx, 'Mysterie van ongerechtigheid en msyerie van erbarmen', *Tijdschrift voor Theologie* 15 (1979): 17.

131. Schillebeeckx, 'The Church and Mankind', *World and Church*, 92 [119–20].

132. Ibid.; Schillebeeckx, *Jesus*, 502 [541–3].

133. Schillebeeckx, 'The Church and Mankind', *World and Church*, 91–2 [118–20].

134. Schillebeeckx, *Jesus*, 122–3 [142–4].

135. Schillebeeckx, 'The Church and Mankind', *World and Church*, 92 [119–20]; Schillebeeckx, *Jesus*, 160 [182–4].

136. Schillebeeckx, 'The Interpretation of the Future', *The Understanding of Faith*, 10 [11–12]; Schillebeeckx, 'Revelation, Scripture, Tradition and Teaching Authority', *Revelation and Theology*, 10 [14–16]; Schillebeeckx, *Jesus*, 306; 603 [336–7; 641–2]; Schillebeeckx, *Christ*, 773–3 [776]; Schillebeeckx, *Church*, 128 [129–30].

137. Schillebeeckx, 'Revelation, Scripture, Tradition and Teaching Authority', *Revelation and Theology*, 10 [14–16].

138. Schillebeeckx, *Jesus*, 491 [532].

c) Incarnation: Overcoming Sin through Pure Positivity

My argument, that Schillebeeckx's understanding of grace is related to redemption rather than creation, could be questioned by his often-cited presentation of Christ as 'concentrated creation'.[139] Despite this focus on the Incarnation's continuity with creation, I will expose how Schillebeeckx's understanding of the Incarnation is connected to the Resurrection and, thus, focuses on Christ's overcoming of the sin of fallen creation.[140] Further clarifying what is meant by the transhistorical nature of the Resurrection, Schillebeeckx explains that, in retrospect, Jesus's whole life can be understood as an anticipation of the Resurrection.[141] Interpreted through Schillebeeckx's theology of redemption, Jesus's actions are, at the same time, saving actions in this world and eschatological acts that overcome all evil definitely.[142] They are, as such, already the initiation of a new world. In this sense, the Resurrection is no superaddition onto Jesus's earthly life, but the Resurrection is this concrete earthly life itself insofar as its positivity persists despite and beyond Jesus's death.[143] Jesus's whole life anticipates the Resurrection in which only grace persists, and his death is only part of this life because some still reject this grace.[144]

This means that Schillebeeckx's grace optimism is realistic in the sense of being connected to the concrete shape of Jesus's life. Schillebeeckx argues that traces in Jesus's life must account for any Christian grace optimism.[145] God must be

---

139. Schillebeeckx, *Interim Report*, 110–12 [126–8]; Philip Kennedy, 'God and Creation', in *The Praxis of the Reign of God*, 53; Roger Haight, *The Future of Christology* (New York, London: Bloomsbury, 2005), 191; Poulsom, *The Dialectics of Creation,*188, n.50; Daniel P. Thomson, 'Schillebeeckx on the Development of Doctrine', *Theological Studies* 62 (2001): 306; Mary Catherine Hilkert, 'The Threatened Humanum as Imago Dei: Anthropology and Christian Ethics', in *Edward Schillebeeckx and Contemporary Theology*, 135; Dennis Rochford, 'The Theological Hermeneutics of Edward Schillebeeckx', *Theological Studies* 63 (2002): 252–3.

140. As such, my argument qualifies Stephan van Erp's suggestion that the fundamental role of the Incarnation in Schillebeeckx's theology needs further exploration (Stephan van Erp, 'Incessant Incarnation as the Future of Humanity: The Promise of Schillebeeckx's Sacramental Theology', in *Sacramentalizing Human History: In Honour of Edward Schillebeeckx (1914-2009)*, eds. Erik Borgman, Paul D. Murray, and Andrés Torres Queiruga (London: SCM Press, Concilium, 2012), 92–105.

141. Schillebeeckx, *Church*, 125–6; 128 [126–8; 129–30]; Schillebeeckx, *Interim Report*, 117 [134–5].

142. Schillebeeckx, *Jesus*, 121.

143. Schillebeeckx, 'Leven ondanks de dood in heden en toekomst', *Tijdschrift voor Theologie*, 433.

144. Schillebeeckx, *Church*, 126 [127–8].

145. Schillebeeckx, *Jesus*, 35; 229 [52–3; 258–9]; Schillebeeckx, *Christ*, 547–8 [557].

recognized in the concrete humanity of Jesus.[146] In this context, Schillebeeckx understands Jesus's life as revelatory of God's being, as pure positivity, insofar as Jesus was never against anything but most fundamentally in support of positive causes.[147] Schillebeeckx explains his grace optimism in relation to Jesus who did nothing but good.[148] Jesus was positively oriented towards God's saving love, and only secondarily did this imply that he opposed everything that inhibited this loving grace from flourishing.[149] Whereas the eschatological scheme of his day sought to transform people's ethical behaviour through proclaiming God's final judgement, Jesus transformed people's lives through the proclamation of God's unconditional love.[150] In this way, Jesus's concrete life reveals God as giver of grace towards humanity.[151] Situated in a fallen world, Jesus's life reveals that the grace of redemption overcomes sin, not through confrontation or direct accusation, but through mercy.

Interpreting Jesus's life through the perspective of the Resurrection, Schillebeeckx holds that the salvific value of the crucifixion also only emerges when Jesus's death is read in the context of his whole life and Resurrection. God, as pure positivity, has been revealed in Jesus's stance towards his approaching crucifixion insofar as he overcame oppression and suffering by remaining good.[152] Schillebeeckx, not unlike Yoder, claims that Jesus was killed due to his non-violent subordination to the ruling powers.[153] Schillebeeckx also argues that Jesus freely accepted his death, due to his obedience to God.[154] However, whereas Yoder presents Jesus as faithfully obeying the ethical principle of non-violence, despite any fatal consequences, Schillebeeckx explains Jesus's obedience to God at the Cross in terms of Jesus's participation in the ontological reality of love. This is important because it explains why Schillebeeckx refrains from attributing any redemptive significance to suffering and from postulating any ethical duty of furthering Christ's work of redemption. There is no duty for Christians to obey

146. Schillebeeckx, 'Persoonlijke Openbaringsgestalte van de Vader', *Tijdschrift voor Theologie* 6 (1966): 278–9. Jesus is the concrete manifestation of the Godhead in the world (Schillebeeckx, *Jesus*, 121 [141–2]).

147. Schillebeeckx, *Jesus*, 123–4 [143–5].

148. Ibid., 161; 169–70 [183–4;192–4].

149. Ibid., 123–4; 154–5 [143–5; 177–8]. Schillebeeckx argues that Jesus's acts of goodness were not restrained by any mundane law (215 [242–3]; Schillebeeckx, *Christ*, 584 [591–2]).

150. Schillebeeckx, *Jesus*, 116; 122 [135–6; 142–3].

151. Schillebeeckx, *Theologisch geloofsverstaan anno 1983*, 6. Schillebeeckx also calls Jesus a 'prophet of salvation' in contrast to prophets of doom (Schillebeeckx, *Jesus*, 119–20 [138–40]).

152. Schillebeeckx, *Church*, 126 [127–8].

153. Schillebeeckx, *Jesus*, 282 [315–16].

154. Ibid., 277 [309–10]; Schillebeeckx, *Theologisch geloofsverstaan anno 1983*, 7.

any principle of non-violence, but Christians might be so attracted and supported by the reality of God's love, that they are enabled to endure unjust suffering.

Due to the cruciformity of grace's triumph over evil, the Christian faith in redemption is neither obvious nor self-evident.[155] Far from postulating any naturally self-evident interpretation of Christ as grace for the world, Schillebeeckx is concerned with showing how Christ can be understood as grace for the world if his life is understood through a hermeneutic of the Resurrection. The Cross reveals that redemption cannot only be seen where good triumphs over evil, but also where an alignment with evil is voluntarily refused.[156] 'Christology is God's presence in this world, but under the sign of weakness.'[157] Consequently, the understanding of Jesus's life as mediation of divine grace can only be accepted on the basis of 'a vote of confidence'.[158] In other words, the Christian faith that grace is mediated in creation does not mean that interpreting reality as graced would be the sole self-evident interpretation of reality. This explains why Schillebeeckx can interpret atheism as an equally legitimate, but more pessimistic interpretation of reality.

Overall, it has now become clearer why Schillebeeckx's grace optimism is not naïve. He is realistic, regarding human sinfulness and works with a particular understanding of how God's forgiving grace overcomes this sin. Due to the Cross, Christians must acknowledge their own as well as other people's sinfulness, but due to the Resurrection, Christians can trust in God's forgiveness. Schillebeeckx does not present this understanding of reality as a self-evident implication of Jesus's earthly life, but he shows how Jesus's earthly life can be understood on the basis of this hermeneutical framework.

4.4 God's Eternal Approval of Jesus as a Unique Person: Contextual Mediations of Grace

The above discussion indicates that, with respect to the Christian faith in the reality of redemption, the Resurrection can be understood as God's eternal act

---

155. Schillebeeckx, *Jesus*, 132, 248; 284 [152–3; 279; 317–18]; Schillebeeckx, *Christ*, 777; Schillebeeckx, *Church*, 124; 180 [125–6; 181–2]. Schillebeeckx emphasizes that on the Cross, Jesus was not consoled by God's presence and that he remained silent about the mystery that sustained him. Hilkert consequently argues that Schillebeeckx's understanding of grace is dialectical. Due to evil, God can only be experienced indirectly as the compassionate heart of reality despite all evil (Mary Catherine Hilkert, 'Experience and Revelation', in *The Praxis of the Reign of God*, 60–1).

156. Schillebeeckx, *Church*, 124 [125–6]; Schillebeeckx, *Interim Report*, 116 [133–4]; Schillebeeckx, *Jesus*, 243; 266–9; 278 [273–4; 297–301; 310–11].

157. Schillebeeckx, *Christ*, 533 [542].

158. Schillebeeckx, *Jesus*, 264 [295–6].

of creative grace on the one hand, and as God's new forgiveness of human sin on the other. Whereas it could seem as though Schillebeeckx draws on the biblical Jesus in order to confirm his already established hermeneutical framework, I will now turn to the way in which Schillebeeckx also reversely emphasizes the way in which any predefined understanding of grace must be modified in accordance with the concrete life of Jesus of Nazareth.[159] Schillebeeckx adamantly insists that the Christian world view is not laid out in ideals, but in the concrete person of Jesus.[160] Thus, the mediated character of grace plays a crucial role in Schillebeeckx's theology.

a) Jesus's Full Divinity: The Non-triumphant Shape of Grace

His claim that any predefined understanding of grace must be modified in accordance with the concrete life of Jesus Christ is connected to Schillebeeckx's second understanding of the Resurrection as an event that was entirely new, regarding the unique person, Jesus.[161] Christian Resurrection faith implies that, instead of vanishing at his death, Jesus was taken up into the persistent reality of redemption.[162] Again, Schillebeeckx stresses that Jesus did not include himself in God's own life at the Resurrection, but that this inclusion was God's sole initiative.[163] Jesus's outward orientation was 'rewarded' by God's legitimatization of Jesus at the Resurrection.

That God was fully incarnate in the concrete man Jesus means that Christian knowledge of God must be Christ-shaped.[164] Jesus's concrete life determines the Christian understanding of God.[165] Even in the inadequacy of Jesus's humanity to reveal God's transcendent being and in thus obscuring the immanent Trinity to

159. This is important, especially regarding those who criticize Schillebeeckx for an eisegesis of his theory into the Biblical texts (Joyce A. Little, review of *The Church with a Human Face*, by Edward Schillebeeckx, *The Thomist: A Speculative Quarterly* 52(1) (1988): 163).

160. Schillebeeckx, *Christ*, 628 [639].

161. Schillebeeckx, *Church*, 127 [128–9]; Schillebeeckx, *Christ*, 514–15 [526].

162. Only at the Resurrection of Jesus did it become apparent that the historical Jesus is fully divine (Schillebeeckx, *Interim Report*, 67 [78–9]; Schillebeeckx, *Jesus*, 353 [385–6]). This proves erroneous Surin's claim that Schillebeeckx would present Jesus only as remarkably unique person, but would fail to account for the full divinity of Christ (Surin, 'Atonement and Christology', *Neue Zeitschrift für Systematische Theologie und Religionsphilosophie*, 146–7).

163. Schillebeeckx, *Jesus*, 465 [505–6]. Schillebeeckx refers to Jesus' refusal to legitimate himself at the crucifixion (464 [504–5]).

164. Schillebeeckx, 'De zin van het mens-zijn van Jezus', *Tijdschrift voor Theologie*, 149–50; Schillebeeckx, 'Salvation History as the Basis of Theology: *Theologia* or *Oikonomia*?', *Revelation and Theology*, 281 [94–5].

165. Schillebeeckx, *Jesus*, 510; 617 [548–9; 658–9]; Schillebeeckx, *Christ*, 774–5; 823–4 [777; 828]; Schillebeeckx, 'The New Trends in Present-Day Dogmatic Theology', *Revelation and Theology*, 300 [123–4].

some extent, Jesus reveals the precise measure between God's transcendence and all immanent mediations of grace.[166] This measure will never be surpassed until the eschaton.[167] God's bestowal of grace continues to be Christ-shaped.[168] In this way, the Incarnation can be interpreted as God becoming God *for* humankind in the concrete person of Jesus of Nazareth.[169] Jesus's life revealed that God is gracious towards humankind by nature. Acknowledging God's changelessness, Schillebeeckx then contends that creation is also primarily God's sharing of God's goodness with others.[170] In this way, the redemption, effected by Jesus, proceeds from God.[171] However, this redemption then also returns to the glory of God, which means that Schillebeeckx conceives of a reciprocal exchange of grace between God and Jesus.[172] In other words, although grace always proceeds from God, the way in which grace is mediated in this world shapes God's own life.

This view's implications can best be seen in reference to the crucifixion. Schillebeeckx contends that, at the Cross, it has been revealed that grace

---

166. Schillebeeckx, *Jesus*, 618–19 [659–61]; Schillebeeckx, *Christ*, 624–5 [635].

167. Schillebeeckx, 'Revelation, Scripture, Tradition and Teaching Authority', *Revelation and Theology*, 13 [19–20].

168. Schillebeeckx, 'Theologia or Oikonomia?', *Revelation and Theology*, 278 [89–91]; Schillebeeckx, 'The Church and Mankind', *World and Church*, 95 [123–4]; Schillebeeckx, *Jesus*, 482; 503; 603 [523–4; 543–4; 641–2]; Schillebeeckx, *Christ*, 3–4 [19–20]; Schillebeeckx, *Interim Report*, 67; 117–18 [78–9; 134–7]; Schillebeeckx, *Church*, 128 [129–30]. This is also why Schillebeeckx regards the historical-critical method as important (Schillebeeckx, *Jesus*, 60 [80]). In this sense, Schillebeeckx responded to Vatican II's search for a new Christology by offering an entirely new framework for Christology (Philip Kennedy, 'Human Beings as the Story of God: Schillebeeckx's Third Christology', *New Blackfriars* 71 (1990): 126–7). Schillebeeckx widened the scope of Christology by way of relating the results of historical-critical biblical studies to classical Christology in his books *Jesus* and *Christ* (Fergus Kerr, *Twentieth-Century Catholic Theologians* (Oxford: Blackwell Publishing, 2007), 55). In 'De Toegang tot Jezus van Nazaret', *Tijdschrift voor Theologie* 12 (1972): 28–60, Schillebeeckx explains that he uses the historical-critical method, not as a supposedly neutral access point to Jesus Christ, but because his contemporaries asked the sort of questions about Jesus that could best be answered by historical-critical research (28–32). He stresses that the offer of grace in Christ is, however, definitely not the same in biblical times as it is now (56), which means that the results of the historical-critical method cannot simply be understood literally as answers to contemporary Christological questions.

169. Schillebeeckx, 'Persoonlijke Openbaringsgestalte van de Vader', *Tijdschrift voor Theologie*, 276; 285; Schillebeeckx, 'De zin van het mens-zijn van Jezus', *Tijdschrift voor Theologie*, 128; This is also why Schillebeeckx understands Christ's humanity as the Father's gift to the Son (141–3).

170. Schillebeeckx, 'De zin van het mens-zijn van Jezus', *Tijdschrift voor Theologie*, 134; 138.

171. Schillebeeckx, *Jesus*, 519 [556–7].

172. Ibid.

overcomes evil through defencelessness.[173] Jesus's death reveals the superior power of defencelessness, which disarms evil.[174] In a similar vein, Schillebeeckx also interprets the beatitudes as affirming the ultimate power of powerlessness.[175] Far from rendering this as an ethical principle, however, Schillebeeckx's pessimistic anthropology comes to the fore when he stresses that God alone can deliver the world from all remaining suffering and evil.[176] The point of believing in the superior power of defencelessness is, then, not to seek to redeem the world through non-violence, but to trust in the world's redemption despite all the remaining evil.[177] Altogether, both beatitudes and crucifixion suggest that understanding the world through Schillebeeckx's realistic grace optimism does not imply that one would have to ignore the realities of unjust suffering and death.[178] Instead, the way in which unjust evil and suffering has been overcome by Christ is revelatory of what Christians should understand by the term grace. Grace is not primarily associated with triumphant and glorious bliss, but more with the gently reticent environment that embeds all earthly events, and breaks forth in its full splendour only very rarely if ever, because it would not sidestep all remaining evil. And yet, Schillebeeckx spends much effort to discern how this-worldly mediations of grace reveal more about grace's eternal, blissful face.

b) Understanding the Reality of Redemption: The Theological Significance of Contemporary Society

In accordance with the transhistorical significance of the Resurrection, Schillebeeckx not only understands Jesus's earthly life, but also all other human acts of genuine goodness, as eternally significant anticipations of the Resurrection.[179] This is why the concrete shape of the eschaton has not been defined at the moment of Christ's Resurrection, but remains open to further developments. Consequently, whereas all other theologians introduced thus far have provided theological solutions to contemporary political problems, because they held themselves responsible to further Christ's work of redemption, Schillebeeckx turns the issue around. He looks at the contemporary context for mediations of grace, in order to refine his understanding of redemption.

Stressing the mediated character of grace, and opposing any idealistic understandings of redemption, Schillebeeckx claims that Christian theologians

---

173. Schillebeeckx, *Interim Report*, 117 [134–5]; Schillebeeckx, *Church*, 127 [128–9].

174. Schillebeeckx, *Jesus*, 603 [641–2]; Schillebeeckx, *Interim Report*, 117 [134–5]; Schillebeeckx, *Church*, 126 [127–8].

175. Schillebeeckx, *Jesus*, 154 [177–8].

176. Ibid.

177. Schillebeeckx, *Church*, 180–1 [181–3].

178. Schillebeeckx, *Jesus*, 629–31[669–73].

179. Ibid., 162 [184–5]. Analogous to Jesus, God also integrates the dead into God's own life (Schillebeeckx, *Interim Report*, 119–20 [137–9]).

are called to express what it means to say that all of reality participates in Christ's redemption in ever new situations.[180] Any contemporary articulation of faith in Jesus Christ must be co-determined by people's relation to the ever renewing reality of redemption.[181] The history of salvation must enter into the Christian definition of God.[182] This means that theologians should 'collate, seriously and responsibly, elements in history which may lead to a new, authentic "disclosure" or source of experience', thereby exposing the 'unfathomable depths' in historical events.[183] Later interpretations of redemption, thus, widen theology's understanding of the historical Jesus.[184] In short, the way in which Christ redeems the world right now cannot be known merely through studying Christological texts from the past, because God's new offer of grace, as it is mediated in the contemporary context, further shapes the Christian understanding of redemption.[185]

Whereas all other theologians discussed thus far have placed the focus on how Christian theology can actively complete the world's redemption, Schillebeeckx is the first one to say that without first recognizing redemption in the contemporary context, Christian theologians cannot adequately know what they should be completing. Nevertheless highlighting the importance of naming this reality of redemption theologically, Schillebeeckx distinguishes between salvation as liberating grace, and revelation as the explicit naming of this grace in reference to God.[186] Salvation is the whole of history, insofar as it derives from God, that is, insofar as it is graced.[187] God's salvation is then primarily a reality in history, and only secondarily a conscious experience and recognition by the faithful.[188] Yet, at the same time, Schillebeeckx argues that since salvation is the all-encompassing

---

180. Schillebeeckx, *Jesus*, 39; 43; 400–1 [56–7; 61–2; 436–8].

181. Ibid., 537.

182. Schillebeeckx, 'Theologia or Oikonomia?', *Revelation and Theology*, 280 [92–4]; Schillebeeckx, *Jesus*, 519 [556–7].

183. Schillebeeckx, *Jesus*, 533 [571].

184. Ibid., 42; 192; 358–9; 434 [60–1; 217–18; 391–3; 471–2].

185. Ibid., 38 [55–6]; Schillebeeckx, *Christ*, 551 [561].

186. Schillebeeckx, 'Revelation, Scripture, Tradition and Teaching Authority', *Revelation and Theology*, 5–6 [6–9]; Schillebeeckx, *Jesus*, 39 [56–7]; Schillebeeckx, *Church*, 7 [7]. In this sense, Schillebeeckx refuses the notion of 'anonymous Christians', given that the whole point of Christianity is to name that which is already good in the world and to thus perfect this goodness through the naming. For an argument that Schillebeeckx understands even the Christian naming of reality as still a divine, and not as a human, initiative, see Bernadette Schwarz-Boennecke, 'Die Widerständigkeit der Wirklichkeit als erstes Moment des Erfahrens', in *Edward Schillebeeckx: Impulse für Theologien im 21. Jahrhundert*, 94–109.

187. Schillebeeckx, *Jesus*, 595 [633–4]. Schillebeeckx here distinguishes himself from conceiving of God's salvific acts in terms of sporadic interventions into an otherwise neutral course of history.

188. Schillebeeckx, 'Linguistic Criteria', *The Understanding of Faith*, 33 [36–7]; Schillebeeckx, *Church*, 12 [12–13].

reality in which the whole world participates, salvation is never not interpreted.[189] Schillebeeckx argues that Christ's interpretation of God's offer of salvation is uniquely original and adequate, which is expressive of his Christocentrism and indicates a somewhat humbler role for Christian theology.[190]

Metaphysically, Schillebeeckx is able to appreciate God's offer of grace in reality as a reality that surpasses human interpretation, with the help of the notion of the implicit intuition.[191] This notion helps Schillebeeckx to differentiate between a noetic and a conceptual knowledge of the immanent world.[192] Noetic knowledge concerns the personal contact of the knower with the reality that is known.[193] Conceptual knowledge merely participates in this noetic knowledge. This means that Schillebeeckx seeks mediations of redemption within the exterior world.[194] There is a mysterious depth in this world, a depth which can be discovered and celebrated by Christian theology.[195] Theologians' environment contains a surplus in which their interpretations can truly participate. In other words, the notion of the implicit intuition helps Schillebeeckx to posit the reality of grace in the material world and only by participation in theological interpretations. Human interpretations of the world can really participate in grace, but they are bound to fall short of capturing the entire positivity that resides in the reality of redemption that surrounds humankind.[196]

---

189. Schillebeeckx, 'Revelation, Scripture, Tradition and Teaching Authority', *Revelation and Theology*, 6 [8–9]; Schillebeeckx, *Church*, 10 [10–11].

190. Schillebeeckx, 'Theological Criteria', *The Understanding of Faith*, 43 [47–8]; Schillebeeckx, 'Revelation, Scripture, Tradition and Teaching Authority', *Revelation and Theology*, 7 [9–11].

191. Schillebeeckx has adopted this notion from the Thomist phenomenologist Dominique De Petter (Borgman, *Edward Schillebeeckx*, 42). According to Philip Kennedy, De Petter had the 'single most important and enduring influence' on Schillebeeckx's work (Kennedy, 'Continuity underlying Discontinuity', *New Blackfriars* 70 (1989): 266).

192. Schillebeeckx, 'Towards a Catholic Use of Hermeneutics', *God the Future of Man*, 88 [147–8]; Schillebeeckx, 'The Non-Conceptual Intellectual Dimension in our Knowledge of God According to Aquinas', *Revelation and Theology*, 213; 220; 235 [166–7; 177–8; 201–2].

193. Schillebeeckx, 'Towards a Catholic Use of Hermeneutics', *God the Future of Man*, 8 [12–13]; Schillebeeckx, 'What is Theology?', *Revelation and Theology*, 88 [132–4]; Schillebeeckx, 'The Non-Conceptual Intellectual Dimension', *Revelation and Theology*, 220 [177–8].

194. Schillebeeckx, 'The Concept of "Truth"', *Revelation and Theology*, 198 [18–20]; Schillebeeckx, 'The Non-Conceptual Intellectual Dimension', *Revelation and Theology*, 210; 218; 231; 238 [161–2; 174–5; 194–6; 205–6]; Schillebeeckx, *Church*, 27 [27–8].

195. Schillebeeckx, 'The Non-Conceptual Intellectual Dimension', *Revelation and Theology*, 212 [164–6].

196. Schillebeeckx, 'The Concept of "Truth"', *Revelation and Theology*, 198 [18–20]; Schillebeeckx, 'The Non-Conceptual Intellectual Dimension', *Revelation and Theology*, 213; 216; 218; 231 [166–7; 170–2; 174–5; 194–6]; Schillebeeckx, 'Theologia or Oikonomia?', *Revelation*

This means that Schillebeeckx rejects the view that all conceptual expressions equally deviate from some supposedly inexpressible reality to which they point.[197] The inexpressible reality of redemption really does give a definite content to theological concepts. There is, thus, a plurality, not a vague infinity, of truthful interpretations of the grace mediated in the world.[198] However, for Schillebeeckx, it is important that reality itself, not the human conceptual grasp thereof, determines the Christian understanding of redemption.[199] The grace mediated in the contemporary context is best expressed if theologians are aware that their interpretations fall short of the fullness of redemption experienced in their noetic contact with their environment.[200] In other words, Schillebeeckx claims that theological interpretations should somehow reflect that they remain partial expressions of the way in which nature mediates grace.

This is not to present theological interpretations of the reality of redemption as merely decorative adornment, but Schillebeeckx understands the unity of the objective reality of salvation, and its interpretation in revelation, as redemptive. 'God's eschatological presence in Jesus and man's [sic] ultimate understanding of reality are correlative'[201] in such a way that 'the objective *being* of the content of faith, and thus its intelligibility, is its saving value.'[202] In other words, God's salvation in history is only completed if its significance is theologically recognized. For it is only in the light of revelation that a human life can be led in personal communion with God. 'The whole purpose of the history of salvation is to be an *epiphaneia* of God.'[203] The function of revelation is to glorify God through the faithful acceptance of God's way of salvation.[204] In this way, Schillebeeckx defines

---

and Theology, 285 [100–2]; Schillebeeckx, 'Theological Criteria', *The Understanding of Faith*, 54; 56 [60–1; 62–3].

197. Schillebeeckx, 'Towards a Catholic Use of Hermeneutics', *God the Future of Man*, 26–8 [38–43]; Schillebeeckx, 'What is Theology?', *Revelation and Theology*, 88 [132–4]; Schillebeeckx, 'The Non-Conceptual Intellectual Dimension', *Revelation and Theology*, 216; 220 [170–2; 177–8]; Schillebeeckx, 'Theological Criteria', *The Understanding of Faith*, 56 [62–3].

198. Schillebeeckx, 'Towards a Catholic Use of Hermeneutics', *God the Future of Man*, 27 [40–1]; Schillebeeckx, 'The New Trends in Present-Day Dogmatic Theology', *Revelation and Theology*, 292 [110–12].

199. Schillebeeckx, 'Towards a Catholic Use of Hermeneutics', *God the Future of Man*, 28 [41–2]; Schillebeeckx, *Church*, 43 [43–4].

200. Schillebeeckx, 'The Concept of "Truth"', *Revelation and Theology*, 198 [18–20]; Schillebeeckx, 'The Non-Conceptual Intellectual Dimension', *Revelation and Theology*, 213 [166–7]; Schillebeeckx, 'The New Trends in Present-Day Dogmatic Theology', *Revelation and Theology*, 292 [110–12].

201. Schillebeeckx, *Jesus*, 596 [634–5].

202. Schillebeeckx, 'What is Theology?', *Revelation and Theology*, 110 [169–70].

203. Schillebeeckx, 'Theologia or Oikonomia?', *Revelation and Theology*, 282 [95–7].

204. Ibid., 283 [97–9].

revelation as that saving event in which the reality of God visibly 'touches' human reality.[205] However, this argument cannot be turned around, to the effect that a lack of redemption would be affirmed in those who live their lives not in personal communion with God. The whole point of the argument is that living one's life in personal communion with God is the best and most beautiful, and in this sense, the only fully redeemed human life, because such a life tops all purely inner-worldly goodness and beauty.

Schillebeeckx's appeal to Christian theologians to recognize contemporary mediations of redemption, through a noetic contact with the immanent world, a contact which surpasses that which can be conceptually expressed,[206] is important for an understanding of how Schillebeeckx's conceives of the relation between Christian theology and non-Christian outlooks. For Schillebeeckx, faith in the Christian God demands attentiveness to concrete mediations of God's bestowal of grace.[207] Christian theologians understand their own faith only through interpreting the way in which God's grace is manifest in the contemporary lives of people.[208] This is why he claims that 'an intense presence-in-the-world is a necessary condition for theology'.[209] At the same time, Schillebeeckx's emphasis on the superabundant positivity that permeates the exterior world leads him to deny the human ability to have an exhaustive total vision of redemption.[210]

And yet, admitting that only Christ perfectly interprets God's offer of salvation, whereas Christian theologians could fail to do so adequately, means that Jesus Christ is posited as a unique standard of what Christian theologians should assess as redemption when they examine their context for mediations of grace. For Christians to be oriented towards God, as pure positivity, means assembling around Christ.[211] The ways in which Jesus's uniquely adequate interpretation of grace restrains the interpretative openness of theological interpretations of the reality of redemption, as it is mediated in the contemporary context, needs further elucidation.

c) *The Variety of Theological Interpretations of Redemption: Jesus Christ as Centre of Unity*

Since the theological interpretation of the reality of redemption in each context is integral to Schillebeeckx's understanding of grace, each generation's

205. Ibid., 279 [91–2].

206. Schillebeeckx, 'The Non-Conceptual Intellectual Dimension', *Revelation and Theology*, 215; 219 [169–70; 175–7].

207. Schillebeeckx, *Theologisch geloofsverstaan anno 1983*, 11.

208. Schillebeeckx, *Church*, 110 [111–12]. Schillebeeckx talks more specifically of God's liberating love as discernible in people's life as true mediation of God's Kingdom.

209. Schillebeeckx, 'What is Theology?', *Revelation and Theology*, 107 [165].

210. Schillebeeckx, *Jesus*, 577–8 [614–16].

211. Schillebeeckx, 'The Church and Mankind', *World and Church*, 91 [117–18].

expectations of salvation, its aspiration for grace, must be responded to with a contemporary interpretation of the world's redemption in Christ.[212] At the same time, Schillebeeckx is quick to highlight that a Christian understanding of Christ should never be predetermined by the contemporarily prevalent world view or by contemporary expectations, but that the prevalent world view and its expectations must be corrected with reference to the concrete person of Jesus of Nazareth.[213] This again highlights Schillebeeckx's acknowledgement of the sinfulness of humankind. What people call redemption might not coincide with God's concrete offer. What is important for this discussion is the role Schillebeeckx ascribes to Christian theology in naming the concrete offer of redemption in a certain context correctly, and what this implies with regard to theology's ability to complete the world's redemption.

Schillebeeckx affirms that there is no access to the earthly Jesus apart from the Christological testimony of the early church.[214] However, Schillebeeckx emphasizes that this community of first Christians reflected what Jesus himself was and did. The new life they sensed in themselves was interpreted in remembrance of the earthly Jesus.[215] The community of the church is not founded upon or bound together by an abstract value, but by the concrete person of Jesus Christ.[216] The decisive factor in interpreting new offers of redemption is that the interpretation remains truthful to the concrete reality of Jesus Christ.[217] Consequently, God's contemporary offer of salvation in Christ can only be understood through continuous engagement with the biblical reports about the primary response to this offer.[218] It should be borne in mind that the early church stood under the sole norm of the concrete historical Jesus, who must be the abiding interpretative norm for Christianity.[219] All new Christian interpretations must, consequently, allow Jesus Christ to have a determinate influence on them.[220] Given that Schillebeeckx opposes a mere

---

212. Schillebeeckx, *Jesus*, 42–3 [60–2].

213. Ibid., 46; 92–3; 437 [64–5; 112–14; 475–6]. For an explanation of the reshaping of an Aristotelian world view with reference to Jesus Christ, see ibid. 525–7 [563–4].

214. Ibid., 28 [44–5].

215. Ibid., 28 [44–5]. Schillebeeckx also interprets the empty tomb tradition as a way to state the identity between the crucified Jesus and the risen Christ (303 [333–4]), and as a symbol for the community of Christian believers (305 [335–6]). Similarly, Schillebeeckx does not interpret the stories about appearances of the risen Christ as proofs of the Resurrection, but as the early church's missionary mandate (323 [354]).

216. Schillebeeckx, 'The Church and Mankind', *World and Church*, 90 [116–17].

217. Schillebeeckx, *Jesus*, 537 [575–6]. Likewise, Schillebeeckx denies that there is an essential core of religious experiences in general that could be unequivocally conceptualized (551 [589–90]).

218. Ibid., 40 [58–9]; Schillebeeckx, *Christ*, 56; 632–3 [70; 644]; Schillebeeckx, 'Persoonlijke Openbaringsgestalte van de Vader', *Tijdschrift voor Theologie*, 279.

219. Schillebeeckx, *Jesus*, 437 [475–6]; Schillebeeckx, *Christ*, 7–8; 51–2 [24; 65–6].

220. Schillebeeckx, *Christ*, 56 [70].

conceptual development of the ideas about Jesus, all interpretations must be constantly corrected with reference to the concrete reality of Jesus.[221] Schillebeeckx contends that there is room for the human imagination, but that this imagination must always be subdued under the concrete reality of Jesus for correction.[222]

Schillebeeckx, thus, differentiates between the concrete reality of Jesus and theological interpretations of this reality. He argues that the historical reality of Jesus contains a gratuitousness which cannot be directly conceptualized.[223] In other words, Schillebeeckx posits the abundance of redemption in the concrete life of Jesus Christ and not in the Christian interpretation thereof.[224] In this way, the concrete Jesus of Nazareth is the only norm for Christian faith, even if this reality is always mediated by the conceptual pre-understandings of a certain time.[225] It is this concrete reality of Christ that motivates Christians to ponder about the implications.[226] And, since the fullness of meaning resides in the historical Jesus, later explications of that meaning must have already been implicitly present in the concrete life of Jesus of Nazareth. In this way, Schillebeeckx stresses that Christ is the only proper index for any analogical knowledge of God gained through new experiences of redemption.[227]

Schillebeeckx then refrains from any triumphant presentation of theology's naming of the reality of redemption, in its relation to Christ, and argues that Christian theologians must highlight that it is Christ himself and not the Christian interpretation which is redemptive, claiming that there is always some disharmony between people's experience of redemption in Christ and the conceptualization of that reality.[228] Schillebeeckx highlights that the Christian conception of salvation and grace must continuously be measured against the concrete offer of redemption in Jesus Christ.[229] This is why Christian theology must sometimes distance itself from its older interpretations, which are no longer necessary for a contemporary experience of Christ.[230]

Consequently, for Schillebeeckx, Christian orthodoxy is not primarily marked by its philosophical coherence, but by the adequate remembrance of the reality of Jesus Christ.[231] On the conceptual level, different Christologies cannot be

---

221. Schillebeeckx, *Jesus*, 446 [485–6].

222. Ibid., 46 [64–5]; Schillebeeckx, *Christ*, 623 [633].

223. Ibid., 29 [45–6].

224. Ibid., 569; 571 [606–7; 609–10].

225. Ibid., 445 [484–5].

226. Ibid., 521 [559–60].

227. Schillebeeckx, 'What is Theology?', *Revelation and Theology*, 93 [141–2].

228. Schillebeeckx, *Jesus*, 32 [49–50].

229. Ibid., 6–7; 92 [22–4; 112–13].

230. Schillebeeckx, 'Persoonlijke Openbaringsgestalte van de Vader', *Tijdschrift voor Theologie*, 281.

231. Schillebeeckx, *Jesus*, 42 [60–1]. Schillebeeckx also explains faith in the true divinity of Jesus not as the logical conclusion of the early church's Greek ontology, but because

unified, and it is impossible to specify some definite conceptual criteria for a truthful Christology.[232] The only unifying factor is the experience of redemption in Jesus Christ that is bound to remain pluriform in its expressions.[233] No single interpretation is identical with the essence of Christian faith, which is the reality of Jesus Christ itself.[234] The pluriformity is then limited by the reality itself in which the interpretations all participate.[235] All Christological confessions must always remember the unique life of Jesus Christ.[236] In other words, the experience of redeemed reality in Christ must be primary, and the conceptualization of that reality secondary.[237]

Overall, the centrality of contemporary mediations of grace to Schillebeeckx's theology distinguishes him from all other theologians that have been discussed in previous chapters. Whereas certain public theologians, as well as John Howard Yoder, have been criticized for an understanding of grace that is insufficiently dynamic and modifiable in accordance with new mediations, Radical Orthodoxy tries to envision a more dynamic understanding of grace. However, both Milbank and Ward introduce this dynamic by way of focusing on the contribution made by the theological interpretation to the understanding of grace in every new historical context. With this move, they tend to undervalue the way in which the abundance of grace is mediated in their contemporary context prior to theological interpretations, in favour of elevating their theological interpretation of reality onto the level of constituting the most promising solution for current political problems. While Tanner is closest to Schillebeeckx's position, when claiming that grace is abundantly and equally distributed in our environment, she nevertheless starts her political thinking with building not on the already existent grace, but on the identified problems in need of a solution. This poses an obstacle to a discernment of grace also in those political outlooks that have already been prejudged as most problematic. Schillebeeckx's understanding of the way in which

it had been discovered in the church's prayer. Although the ecclesial liturgy only knew of prayers in Jesus directed to the Father, many of the faithful had started to pray directly to Jesus (528 [566–7]).

232. Schillebeeckx, 'The Context and Value of Faith-Talk', *The Understanding of Faith*, 16–17 [17–19]; Schillebeeckx, *Jesus*, 35; 612 [52–3; 652–3]; Schillebeeckx, *Christ*, 623 [633–4]. At the same time, Schillebeeckx maintains that there must be an ecumenical striving for a unified conceptualization of that reality (*Jesus*, 41 [59–60]). At certain junctions one interpretative route must be pursued, even if there are legitimate alternatives (533 [571]). Only if the path taken leads to *aporias* is it necessary to investigate if and how the choice at the decisive church council was one-sided.

233. Schillebeeckx, *Jesus*, 4; 38; 404; 537 [20–1; 55–6; 440; 575–6]; Schillebeeckx, *Christ*, 4; 69–70; 623 [20; 83–4; 634].

234. Schillebeeckx, *Jesus*, 537 [575–6].

235. Ibid., 41–2; 437 [59–61; 475–6].

236. Ibid., 30; 201 [46–7; 226–8].

237. Ibid., 29 [45–6].

grace is primarily mediated in the contemporary reality of the world's redemption in Christ and only by participation in non-Christian and Christian interpretations of that reality, promises to offer a way in which the theological significance even of that which is most commonly understood as problematic can be appreciated, the fruits of which will be shown in Chapter 5.

4.5 Humankind's Reliance on God's Forgiveness: The Church as Problem for Society

Not only interpreting the Resurrection as revelation of the superior power of grace over evil and of Jesus's constitutive part in the reality of redemption as a unique person, Schillebeeckx also calls Christ's Resurrection the abiding foundation of the church.[238] Schillebeeckx's emphases of God's sole act in the Resurrection, the superior power of grace over evil and the abiding inclusion of Jesus's unique person in this grace are also discernible in his deliberations about the church. Whereas I have already explained how Schillebeeckx's focus on the Resurrection relates to his simultaneous upholding of a grace optimism and a pessimistic anthropology, as well as to his appreciation of the mediated character of grace, this final part of my interpretation of Schillebeeckx's Christology returns more explicitly to the discussion of Christian theological contributions to secular politics, and particularly to apologetic defences of theology's positive impact upon post-Christendom societies in connection to its unique ability to solve certain political problems.

a) Acknowledging the Church's Sinfulness: Against Promises of Positive Contributions to Society

Overall, Schillebeeckx argues that the church exists because God converts people to Christianity.[239] The church is founded on the Resurrection insofar as it is the gathering of those people who experienced the forgiveness of their sin of rejecting Jesus Christ.[240] The church, thus, lives on the strength of the renewal of the lives of

---

238. Ibid., 324 [355–6].

239. Ibid., 298; 314–15; 320; 350–3; 468; 482; 503; 603 [329; 344–6; 350–1; 508–9; 523–4; 543–4; 641–2]; Schillebeeckx, *Christ*, 792–3; 798 [796: 802]; Schillebeeckx, *Interim Report*, 65; 67 [75–6; 78–9]; Schillebeeckx, 'Jezus' leven of Christus de verrezene', *Tijdschrift voor Theologie* 13 (1973): 154. Schillebeeckx argues that the same structure in which the disciples were converted to Christianity after the Resurrection also applies to contemporary Christians (Schillebeeckx, *Jesus*, 289; 296; 315 [320–1; 326–7; 345–6]).

240. Schillebeeckx, 'De Toegang tot Jezus van Nazaret', *Tijdschrift voor Theologie*, 36. This re-assembling of the disciples is the sole verification of the Resurrection. They re-assemble because the Resurrection objectively happened, not in order to invent it (Schil-

its members.[241] Primarily, this means that the church regards its own foundation as gratuitous: No human being, apart from the risen Jesus himself, causes people to assemble in one community.[242] Christians interpret their own lives as part of the Christian story, which begins with a personal experience of God that is interpreted as being initiated by Jesus Christ.[243] The reception of divine forgiveness is, thus, the only condition for becoming a Christian, and initiates a conversion.[244]

According to Schillebeeckx, the conversion to the Christian faith is marked by the structure of an initial bewildering disintegration of one's original world view, and a completing reintegration of that bewildering experience into a new world view.[245] Jesus's disciples already underwent such a conversion when they met the earthly Jesus. Their bewilderment concerned the unconditional faith in God, to which they had been invited through their contact with Jesus.[246] In this contact, Jesus freed them from any anxious self-concern, which allowed them to abandon everything and commit themselves freely to God.[247] Importantly, Schillebeeckx conceives of this free surrender to following Christ not primarily in terms of a duty, but as a gift. Jesus's life enabled his disciples to trust in God's absolutely faithful goodness towards humankind.[248] This trust was shattered at the crucifixion, for

lebeeckx, 'Leven ondanks de dood in heden en toekomst', *Tijdschrift voor Theologie*, 436). Schillebeeckx, thus, takes a middle position between Bultmann's subjectivism and the objectivism of those who understand the Resurrection to have been an empirically verifiable event (Kerr, *Twentieth-Century Catholic Theologians*, 63).

241. Schillebeeckx, *Jesus*, 507 [545–6].

242. Ibid., 356 [389–90]. For an explanation of how Schillebeeckx's understanding of the Resurrection decisively differs from that of Bultmann, see Erik Borgman, 'Edward Schillebeeckx's Reflections on the Sacraments and the Future of Catholic Theology', in *Sacramentalizing Human History: In Honour of Edward Schillebeeckx (1914-2009)*, eds. Erik Borgman, Paul D. Murray, and Andrés Torres Queiruga (London: SCM Press, Concilium, 2012), 16–18, and Erik Borgman, 'als het ware een sacrament – Naar een theologische visie op de reëel bestaande kerk', in *Trouw an Gods toekomst – De blijvende betekenis van Edward Schillebeeckx*, ed. Stephan van Erp (Tijdschrift voor Theologie, 2010), 135–8. In these articles, Borgman criticizes Schillebeeckx for inconsistently giving up his project of writing a new ecclesiology, because he despaired over the Roman Catholic Church's malfunctioning, in the aftermath of Vatican II. Borgman, correctly, in my view, highlights that it would have been more consistent to argue that the sinfulness of the church, instead of being seen as an obstacle to the project of formulating an ecclesiology, should be acknowledged as an undeniable element of a contemporary ecclesiology.

243. Schillebeeckx, *Jesus*, 321 [351–2].

244. Ibid., 345; 349 [378–9; 381–2].

245. Schillebeeckx, 'Godsdienst van en voor mensen', *Tijdschrift voor Theologie*, 359; 369.

246. Schillebeeckx, *Jesus*, 175; 196 [199–200; 221–2].

247. Ibid., 176; 197 [200–1; 222–3].

248. Ibid., 122–3 [142–4].

here it seemed as if human sinfulness had gained the upper hand.[249] In this way, the disciples experience Christ's death again as the disintegration of their previous world view. This disintegration, and the frailty of their faith in the abundance of God's grace, is positive insofar as it enables the disciples to understand the *full* implication of Jesus's life.[250] Only at the Resurrection did it become apparent that God's grace overcomes all human evil, that no human failure has the last word and that God's grace is entirely undeserved by humankind.[251]

It is impossible to demonstrate the reasonableness of Christianity from the perspective of any other world view conclusively, because God's forgiveness, breaking with the logic of human calculations, is not the conclusion of any existing premises.[252] In this sense, the Resurrection as revealing the reality of God's merciful forgiveness demands faith. Instead of apologetically defending their faith, by offering solutions to contemporary political problems, Christians are called to confess that they are only justified by God's unconditional mercy.[253] As a community of sinners who are all equally called into the ecclesial assembly by God's unconditional offer of grace despite human sin, the church cannot promise to contribute to the wider society's common good.[254] For, any such promise is mitigated by the Christian acknowledgement that the church is bound to fail to meet its own standards, namely those set by the concrete life of Jesus.[255] This should relativize all promises concerning the achievement of a better future through theological efforts to solve the whole society's political problems.

Instead, by accepting God's forgiveness, converted people are reconciled with their past in a way that gives them new confidence in the future.[256] Converted

---

249. Ibid., 122-3 [142-4]. In contradistinction to Ward, Schillebeeckx does not interpret the disciples' frailty of faith after Jesus's death to be a total lapse of faith (193; 354 [218-19; 386-7]). He claims that only Mark's gospel presents this frailty as a total lapse. See also Schillebeeckx, 'Ons heil: Jezus' leven of Christus de verrezene', *Tijdschrift voor Theologie*, 152).

250. Schillebeeckx, 'Godsdienst van en voor mensen', *Tijdschrift voor Theologie*, 370.

251. Schillebeeckx, *Jesus*, 289; 603 [320-1; 641-2]; Schillebeeckx, *Christ*, 626; 825-6 [636-7; 830]; Schillebeeckx, *Interim Report*, 66 [76-7]. Moreover, the importance of the mediated character of grace also became only apparent at the Resurrection, insofar as, prior to the Resurrection, the disciples could have recognized that God was active in Jesus, but they could not have called the entire person of Jesus divine (Schillebeeckx, 'Jezus' leven of Christus de verrezene', *Tijdschrift voor Theologie*, 150-1; Schillebeeckx, *Jesus*, 296; 321; 348-9; 353; 490; 607-8 [326-7; 351-2; 380-2; 385-6; 531-2; 646-8]; Schillebeeckx, *Christ*, 795; 823-4 [799; 828]; Schillebeeckx, 'De Toegang tot Jezus van Nazaret', *Tijdschrift voor Theologie*, 52).

252. Schillebeeckx, *Jesus*, 358-9 [391-3].

253. Ibid., 350 [382-3].

254. Ibid., 182; 632 [207-8; 673-4].

255. Ibid., 632 [673-4].

256. Ibid., 631 [671-3].

people's confidence concerns the approaching of God's Kingdom despite human failures.²⁵⁷ Christians are reconciled with 'God's way of doing things'²⁵⁸, which means that their overall outlook is based upon the faith that all that which is truly good will persist and all that is evil will vanish. The church's conversion enables it to dedicate itself to the further realization of redemption on earth even if the effects are not immediately seen.²⁵⁹ On the basis of their faith in the crucified and risen Christ, Christians can learn to see grace, as it is mediated in this world beyond apparent evil and suffering. 'By persevering in grace, the believer personally accepts God's grace in Christ as a reality which is consistently affirmed, which becomes the basis of hope for resurrection ... and eschatological consummation.'²⁶⁰ This 'eschatological hope makes the commitment to the temporal order *radical* and, by the same token, declares any existing temporal order to be only relative'.²⁶¹

However, this incessant striving towards the further realization of God's Kingdom on earth, cannot be used as an argument to defend the church's political relevance apologetically, when faced with public opposition, because this would reverse the proper directionality of the church's witness. Coupled with Schillebeeckx's acknowledgement of the church's sinfulness, the church's incessant alignment with the reality of redemption that surrounds it could only serve as a witness to God's unceasing offer of forgiveness.²⁶² Others have argued that, according to Schillebeeckx, the triumph of grace must be visible in the church in order to be believable.²⁶³ My argument further refines this claim by highlighting that Schillebeeckx's theology is most distinctly important for contemporary theology insofar as he imagines the church to be a visible community of *merciful* grace. The church, for Schillebeeckx, must not be a perfect community of the sinless.²⁶⁴ God's triumphant grace in the church's weakness, not in the church's glory, manifests the reality of God in this world.²⁶⁵ People must be enabled to see that grace is effective in everyone who sincerely tries to do their best, and the reality of redemption

257. Ibid., 133 [153–4]; Schillebeeckx, *Christ*, 519–20 [531].

258. Schillebeeckx, *Jesus*, 631 [671–3]; Schillebeeckx, *Christ*, 804 [808].

259. Schillebeeckx, *Christ*, 501 [514].

260. Ibid., 520 [532]. At this point, my interpretation of Schillebeeckx diverts from that of Ward (Ward, *How the Light Gets In*, 72–3), as mentioned in chapter 2.

261. Schillebeeckx, 'Church, Magisterium and Politics', *God the Future of Man*, 97 [160–1].

262. Schillebeeckx, *Church*, 181–2 [182–4].

263. Hilkert, 'Grace-Optimism', *Spirituality Today*, 220–39.

264. Schillebeeckx, *Christ the Sacrament*, 147–8 [250–3].

265. Ibid., 149 [254–5]; Schillebeeckx, 'The Church and Mankind', *World and Church*, 92 [119–20]; Schillebeeckx, *Jesus*, 13 [30–1]; Schillebeeckx, *Interim Report*, 91 [103–4]. Erik Borgman explains that Schillebeeckx's conviction that Christians mediate God's power not only in their strength but also dialectically in their weakness distances Schillebeeckx's 'humble humanism' from Maritain's 'heroic humanism'. Consequently, Schillebeeckx claims that Christians must always keep a distance towards their own culture (Borgman, *Edward Schillebeeckx*, 96–7).

must be recognizable in the utter generosity and gratuity that underlies this effort, despite its failings.[266] The church's continuous penitence is then a crucial element of the church's witness to God's forgiveness of all human failures.[267] The church's most fundamental role in society is to show in its life and praxis that the world has been redeemed by Christ, enabling people to put their trust not in human, but in divine strength.[268] Thus, if the church's political engagement meets public opposition, theologians should not apologetically defend this engagement, but rather discern how this opposition itself shows forth signs of redemption, for the redirection of the church's political praxis.

Understanding the church as an assembly of forgiven sinners, grounded in God's mercy, Schillebeeckx understands Christianity essentially not as a human cultural project, but as humans giving themselves over to divine deeds.[269] The conversion to Christ 'means to act and think like Jesus ..., who, by emptying himself ... made others rich.'[270] Since Christ's redemption is mediated in the contemporary context, their readiness to receive forgiveness entails that Christians pursue their own thoughts less and become more open to learning from the grace that surrounds them. Regarding the question concerning theology's political role in post-Christendom societies, this foregrounds the difference in reading Schillebeeckx's understanding of grace in terms of redemption, rather than in terms of creation. Associating Schillebeeckx's understanding of grace with creation, commentators claim that he would argue that Christianity is the guarantor of the humanization and liberation of the whole world.[271] My interpretation, in contrast, suggests that Christ alone is the guarantor and that Christians, as much as non-Christians, benefit from this undeserved divine gift. This explains also why, instead of apologetically defending how Christian theology can positively contribute to the whole society's common good, Schillebeeckx's theology is more directed to correcting the sinful church. In contrast to post-liberal theologies, which turn to the church because of the sinful world's inability to understand Christ, Schillebeeckx turns to the church as theology's primary addressee, because he acknowledges the church's sinfulness. He seeks to understand how non-Christian outlooks mediate the reality of redemption in order to strengthen, renew or correct the church's dedication to the further manifestation of this reality.

266. Schillebeeckx, *Christ the Sacrament*, 160–1 [270–3].

267. Schillebeeckx, 'The Context and Value of Faith-Talk', *The Understanding of Faith*, 17 [18–19].

268. Schillebeeckx, *Christ the Sacrament*, 156 [266–8].

269. Schillebeeckx, 'Leven in God en Leven in de Wereld', in *God en Mens*, 131.

270. Schillebeeckx, *Christ*, 520 [532].

271. Haight, 'Engagement met de wereld als zaak van God', *Tijdschrift voor Theologie*, 79–80.

b) Imitating Christ: Against Promises of Completing the World's Redemption

It could be objected that this stress on the church's sinfulness downplays the Christian calling to imitate Christ, and that this calling allows or even obliges theologians to promise that the church will complete or exceed the world's redemption. However, contrary to the theologians introduced thus far who all, in their different ways, draw on this call to imitate Christ in order to apologetically defend the church as a positive influence on society, Schillebeeckx understands the church's imitation of Christ primarily as a gift to be enjoyed and only secondarily as a duty on the basis of which a promise could be made. Instead of focusing on any duty to imitate Christ for the further redemption of the world, the focus should be on the fact that the church *can* imitate Christ. According to Schillebeeckx, Christians are primarily invited to imitate Christ's relationship to God.[272] Jesus's calling God 'Abba' is indicative of a uniquely familiar and simple relationship that demands no medium between God and humankind.[273] The church follows Christ by responding to God in a similar way as Jesus did, addressing God as Father.[274] Once more, Schillebeeckx interprets this address as primarily revelatory of the trustworthiness of God's benevolence towards humankind, but also of the expectation that humankind is willing to align itself with this benevolent reality.[275] Schillebeeckx calls this address the heart of Christianity.[276]

At this point, Schillebeeckx affirms the true reciprocity between Christians and God that is not only a one-sided dependence.[277] Understanding the historical Jesus as a truly divine being means that God was really influenced by Jesus's contemporaries. To encounter the earthly Jesus meant to encounter God.[278] In this way, the Incarnation enabled people to enter into a personal relationship with God.[279] This relationship with God is central to the Christian faith and can be

272. Schillebeeckx derives this claim from the Biblical miracle stories. People were healed, independent of either their belief or disbelief in Jesus, but only those who were redeemed accepted this healing as invitation into an interpersonal relationship with God (Schillebeeckx, *Jesus*, 171; 238 [194–5; 267–9]).

273. Ibid., 142; 217; 228–31; 236; 507 [163–4; 245–6; 257–61; 265–6; 545–6]. Also, the Ten Commandments are not meant to restore people's relationship to God, but they command that every ethical action should originate in people's relationship with God (225–6 [253–5]).

274. Ibid., 232–4 [261–4]; Schillebeeckx, *Christ*, 529; 630 [539; 641].

275. Schillebeeckx, *Jesus*, 233–4; 238; 458 [262–4, 267–8; 498].

276. Ibid., 236; 507 [265–6; 545–6].

277. Schillebeeckx, 'De zin van het mens-zijn van Jezus', *Tijdschrift voor Theologie*, 133–4.

278. Schillebeeckx, 'Leven in God en Leven in de Wereld', in *God en Mens*, 139; Schillebeeckx, 'Persoonlijke Openbaringsgestalte van de Vader', *Tijdschrift voor Theologie*, 280.

279. Schillebeeckx, 'De zin van het mens-zijn van Jezus', *Tijdschrift voor Theologie*, 139.

repeated by every new generation.[280] This means that Christian theologians should not present God's absoluteness in terms of a fixed stability, but they should stress that God really reacts to humans and answers their prayers.[281] That this imitation of Christ's relationship to God is not primarily to be translated into a duty imposed on Christians for the further redemption of the world is again related to Schillebeeckx's Resurrection Christology, given that it is accompanied by an emphasis on joy as the primary focus of Christian life.[282]

'Jesus' whole life was a celebration of God's reign, as well as an orthopraxis in accord with that kingdom.'[283] 'Jesus is the man who delights in God himself.'[284] Jesus was so enthralled by God that his whole life became a celebration of God and, as such, a model for Christian orthopraxis.[285] Schillebeeckx argues that 'joy is a fundamental ingredient in Christian ethical action. For Christian ethics is more something that is graciously *allowed* than something that is firmly compelled.'[286] This joy consists in God and humankind being each other's happiness.[287] Christians experience that reality is gracious towards them and return this grace in a joyful celebration to God.[288]

In this sense, the church is not a 'holy remnant', but the firstborn of a new creation who already celebrates eschatological redemption.[289] Christians are distinguished from non-Christians primarily inasmuch as they experience the final consummation of reality's redemption already now, as they live already in a personal relationship with God.[290] Christians should not understand themselves to be more ethically apt than non-Christians, but as particularly hopeful due to their experience of the reality of redemption.[291] The point of liturgical celebration is, thus, primarily to praise God, to recall the reason for this praise through remembrance of Jesus Christ and to bid to God in prayer to be faithful to this promise of grace also in the future.[292] Accordingly, Schillebeeckx claims that Jesus did not primarily pass on certain sayings but the church, as a liberation movement,

---

280. Schillebeeckx, 'Persoonlijke Openbaringsgestalte van de Vader', *Tijdschrift voor Theologie*, 279–80.

281. Schillebeeckx, 'De zin van het mens-zijn van Jezus', *Tijdschrift voor Theologie*, 133–4.

282. Schillebeeckx, *Jesus*, 178; 190 [202–3; 215–16]; Schillebeeckx, *Christ*, 91–2 [102].

283. Schillebeeckx, *Jesus*, 237 [266–7].

284. Ibid., 122 [142–3].

285. Ibid., 122 [142–3].

286. Schillebeeckx, *Christ*, 580 [587].

287. Schillebeeckx, *Jesus*, 122 [142–3].

288. Schillebeeckx, *Christ*, 625–6 [636].

289. Schillebeeckx, *Church*, 153 [154–5].

290. Schillebeeckx, *Jesus*, 179 [203–4].

291. Schillebeeckx, *Christ*, 548–9; 551 [558; 561].

292. Schillebeeckx, 'Revelation-in-Reality and Revelation-in-Word', *Revelation and Theology*, 38 [56–8].

characterized by its thankful relationship to God.[293] The church is a liberation movement insofar as the crucified but risen Christ remains effective on earth in his followers.[294] Schillebeeckx claims that it is not the Christian interpretation of reality, but Christianity's continuation of Christ's praxis that is co-redemptive.[295] Importantly, Schillebeeckx understands Christ's praxis as not primarily directed at the restoration of creation, but at the initiation of people's contact to God.[296] The restoration of creation is only the necessary means for the latter. All of Christian praxis must be motivated by redemption in this way.[297] The church's orthopraxis serves to make apparent that the salvation and liberation experienced by people brings them into contact with the reality of God.[298]

In this way, the church is an integral part of Jesus's identity, one which exceeds that which Jesus has concretely done.[299] Schillebeeckx speaks of an 'ecclesial brotherhood [*sic*]' that represents redeemed humanity in Christ on earth.[300] Schillebeeckx stresses that the source of this community is the relationship of each member with Christ.[301] However, since all of reality has been redeemed in Christ, all worldly peace is now understood as eternally persistent, which means that the boundaries between church and world are blurred.[302] Christians can read any worldly peace as participating in Christ's redemption of reality. They are then called to celebrate and align themselves with these concrete manifestations of peace.[303]

In brief, the second reason why Schillebeeckx's understanding of the political relevance of Christian theology conflicts with public theology's as well as with Radical Orthodoxy's apologetic defences of theology's political relevance concerns his understanding of theology's specific engagement with reality as that of

293. Schillebeeckx, 'De Toegang tot Jezus van Nazaret', *Tijdschrift voor Theologie*, 39; Schillebeeckx, *Jesus*, 31 [47–8].

294. Schillebeeckx, *Christ*, 792–3 [796]; Schillebeeckx, *Church*, 128 [129–30].

295. Schillebeeckx, *Church*, 166 [167–8]. Orthodoxy is intrinsic to orthopraxis, but Schillebeeckx lays the emphasis on the concrete praxis. Stephan van Erp might be the theologian who is presently most concerned to develop Schillebeeckx's emphasis on orthopraxis into a new fundamental theology (Stephan van Erp, 'World and Sacrament: Foundations of the Political Theology of the Church', *Louvain Studies* 39 (2016): 109).

296. Schillebeeckx, *Jesus*, 172 [195–7].

297. Schillebeeckx, *Christ the Sacrament*, 151 [257–9].

298. Schillebeeckx, *Jesus*, 13–14 [30–2].

299. Schillebeeckx, *Christ*, 798 [802].

300. Schillebeeckx, 'The Church and Mankind', *World and Church*, 94 [121–2]; Schillebeeckx, *Jesus*, 554 [593–4].

301. Schillebeeckx, 'The Church and Mankind', *World and Church*, 95 [123–4].

302. Ibid., 96 [124–5].

303. Schillebeeckx, *Jesus*, 554 [593–4].

thankful and prayerful celebration.[304] Theology only enhances and perfects the secular world indirectly, insofar as human life is neither meaningful without this addition of thankful celebration, nor is it possible without complete gratuity.[305] Only in this indirect way is Christianity's '*service to God*, also a *service to men* [*sic*]'.[306] The gratuitous joy of the Christian relationship with God must be evident in Christian lives; to argue for it would be to mischaracterize this joy. Moreover, Christian theology is politically relevant insofar as a human life that '*dwell[s] upon* the personal mystery' retains a degree of independence from the majority opinion by way of acknowledging God as final judge over reality.[307] Significantly, however, Christianity's political relevance is not related to any ability on the part of theologians to solve the whole society's political problems.

Insofar as Schillebeeckx does conceive of Christianity as adequately mediating God's grace to the world, Christianity must exceed this surplus of positivity to the world. To this end, Schillebeeckx claims, in agreement with Radical Orthodoxy, that Christian theology must express the mystery and reality in which everyone exists, and thus be the interpretation of the whole of reality.[308] Its specific activity is that of prophetic naming; Milbank turns this Christian interpretation of the whole of reality into an apologetic defence of theology's political relevance by arguing that his Christian ontology translates into a particular social order that is presented as solution to certain problems inherent in its secular counterpart.[309] According to Schillebeeckx, to the contrary, Christian theology is not directly politically useful in the way that Radical Orthodox authors present it as being.[310] Schillebeeckx's stress on the superabundant positivity of grace implies that theology does not fulfil any particular function that could be fully explained in secular terms.[311] A secular

304. Schillebeeckx, 'Secularization and Christian Belief in God', *God the Future of Man*, 51–52 [82–5].

305. Schillebeeckx, 'Secular Worship and Church Liturgy', *God the Future of Man*, 57 [95–7]; Schillebeeckx, 'Correlation between Human Question and Christian Answer', *The Understanding of Faith*, 79 [90–1].

306. Schillebeeckx, *Christ*, 773 [775]. Schillebeeckx speaks of 'religions'.

307. Schillebeeckx, 'Secularization and Christian Belief in God', *God the Future of Man*, 49 [79–81]; Schillebeeckx, 'The New Image of God', *God the Future of Man*, 123 [200–1].

308. Schillebeeckx, 'Secularization and Christian Belief in God', *God the Future of Man*, 51 [82–4]; Schillebeeckx, 'Revelation, Scripture, Tradition and Teaching Authority', *Revelation and Theology*, 4 [4–6]; Schillebeeckx, 'Revelation-in-Reality and Revelation-in-Word', *Revelation and Theology*, 33 [48–50].

309. Milbank, 'The Body by Love Possessed', in *The Future of Love*, 81.

310. Schillebeeckx, 'Correlation between Human Question and Christian Answer', *The Understanding of Faith*, 79 [90–1].

311. Schillebeeckx, *Christ*, 768–73 [771–5]; Schillebeeckx, 'Secular Worship and Church Liturgy', *God the Future of Man*, 57 [95–7]. For a more detailed explanation of Christianity's gratuitous character see Edward Schillebeeckx, 'Christelijk antwoord op een menselijke vraag? De oecumenische betekenis van de "correlatiemethode"', *Tijdschrift voor Theologie* 10

solution must be found to all political problems and Christian theology should, then, celebrate the grace which made this answer possible. Whereas the world unconsciously owes its existence to the life, death and Resurrection of Christ, the church is the place where this reality is celebrated in thankfulness.[312] In this way, Christianity would mediate grace as the reality that exceeds the sum total of all natural positivity, that is, of all already existing solutions to political problems.[313]

Thus, if the Christian imitation of Christ was rendered into a promise to contribute positively to society, then this would erroneously downplay the sinfulness of the church on the one hand, and the reality of redemption which allows the church to exist nonetheless, on the other. Since Christians are primarily called to imitate Christ in joyfully thanking God for God's faithful bestowal of grace, Christian theologians should remind the church of the graces by which it is surrounded and upon which it depends. The church's joyful celebration of these received graces then, develops into an orthopraxis for the preservation and further distribution of these graces. If the primary focus was on the church's ethical duty to increase the world's redemption and to resolve all that which is still problematic, the church would risk overlooking the grace which already surrounds it. It is the call to imitate Christ that obliges theologians not to focus primarily on that which is still lacking perfection, but on the grace that is already mediated. Only in this way can theology build further upon the work of redemption that has already begun and avoid chasing its own utopian illusions.[314] Any theological promise to society must acknowledge how eternity begins to take shape in the depths of the present.[315]

c) Mediating God's Forgiveness: Mercifully Criticizing Non-Christian Solutions

Regarding the criticism that such a theology of grace might render Christian theology politically superfluous and uncritical, it should not be concluded from the above discussion that no consequences would be entailed by Schillebeeckx's theology for a Christian politics. But, a theologically informed criticism of alternative political positions should accord with the way in which Christians believe that all remaining sin is overcome in Christ, and in this way Christian

---

(1970): 1–22, in which Schillebeeckx criticizes Protestant correlation theologies for exaggerating the world's sinfulness and evil in order to highlight its need for redemption in Christ.

312. Schillebeeckx, 'Secularization and Christian Belief in God', *God the Future of Man*, 51 [82–4].

313. Schillebeeckx, 'Secular Worship and Church Liturgy', *God the Future of Man*, 69 [113–14].

314. Schillebeeckx opposes any apocalyptic interpretations of the present on the basis of an idealized understanding of the future (Schillebeeckx, 'The Interpretation of the Future', *The Understanding of Faith*, 7 [7–8]).

315. Ibid., 9 [10–11].

theology can contribute to the completion of the world's redemption, without promising to solve the world's political problems. The church mediates redemption by being the distinct community that shows mercy towards every human being, in spite of their sinfulness, and bears witness to the God who loves even sinful humankind.[316] The most important law for Christians is to be merciful and gracious in the imitation of God.[317] Believing that God's gracious love is stronger than any human rejection of that love, and that the whole world has already been redeemed in this sense,[318] Christians must follow Jesus in not focusing on other people's sinful rejection of God's love as much as on their potential for the future.[319] Conversion is not initiated by confronting people with their sins, but with the redemption that already surrounds them and can be theirs if only they were to accept it.[320]

Following Schillebeeckx's emphasis on mercy, it is precisely God's unconditional acceptance of people into the reality of redemption which calls sinners to repentance and transforms them. In other words, grace heals sinful nature whenever people realize that they are fundamentally accepted by God, despite their shortcomings.[321] The transformation from sinful to redeemed human nature does not commence with the human recognition of their own shortcomings, but with the recognition that they have a legitimate place in the reality of redemption despite these shortcomings. To follow their natural inclination towards grace, humans have to put all their trust not in themselves or other humans but in the reality of God.[322] Those who accept the Christian faith in God's trustworthy mercifulness are then granted the further grace of a heightened affinity with graced reality.[323] A redeemed human life is then superhuman in the sense that grace lives within that life.[324] The Christian faith might help people to trust in grace more than in their own ability to further the good, or to solve persisting political problems.

Consequently, Christianity is most crucially distinct from purely immanent outlooks through its faith in the possibility of the humanly impossible.[325] Whereas

---

316. Schillebeeckx, *Interim Report*, 91; 96; 112 [103–4; 108–9; 128–9].

317. Schillebeeckx, *Jesus*, 209 [236].

318. Ibid., 124 [144–5].

319. Ibid., 125 [145–6]. Schillebeeckx adds that 'such an attitude obviates all frantic searching for self-identity' (125 [146]).

320. Ibid., 151 [173–4]. This contrasts Schillebeeckx's theology of grace with that of Ward who argues that the recognition of one's sinfulness is 'a first step towards turning to God' (Ward, *How the Light Gets In*, 184, n.10).

321. Schillebeeckx, *Church*, 117 [118–19].

322. Schillebeeckx, *Jesus*, 600 [637–8].

323. Schillebeeckx, 'The Bible and Theology', *Revelation and Theology*, 121 [187–8].

324. Schillebeeckx, 'The Non-Conceptual Intellectual Element', *Revelation and Theology*, 261 [64–5].

325. Schillebeeckx, 'The New Image of God', *God the Future of Man*, 123 [200–1].

Milbank, following de Lubac, associates modern atheism with Christianity's failure to demonstrate sufficiently that the Christian faith is relevant for secular life and critical of the surrounding society, Schillebeeckx associates modern atheism with the churches' failure to nurture people's ability to trust in God's mercy. This is why, for Schillebeeckx, Christian theology's primary task is not to criticize non-Christian politics for their shortcomings, but theologians must highlight that God's grace transcends all human failures. Christian theology should not be presented as the solution to the human failure of sin, and in this way as the answer to contemporary societal problems. Instead, Christian theology must be presented in such a way that people understand that God's love and grace are not diminished by human sin.[326] In other words, Christian theology must present the reality of God, not Christian theology, as that which is most important in and for human life.[327] In a sense, Christian theologians are called to show that even those contemporaries who are regarded as most sinful and whose ideas are viewed as most problematic, are invited to join the church's prayerful relationship with God.

On the basis of his theology of merciful grace, Schillebeeckx's response to oppressive regimes then differs slightly from that of Yoder. Both are in agreement that such a response must be non-violent.[328] However, while Yoder claimed that Christ's cruciform redemption imposes upon Christians the ethical duty to endure the oppression for the sake of the world's further redemption non-violently, Schillebeeckx shifts the focus away from the Christian ethical duty to the graced environment.[329] Christians should primarily bear witness to the reality of a redemption that is brought about gratuitously by God, and not by human strength.[330] There is, thus, not primarily a Christian duty to redeem the world through the non-violent resistance to oppression, but oppressors, just as all other people, must be brought to recognize that all of reality is graced and that everyone has an equal share in this grace.[331] A Christian response to oppression is meant to manifest that 'God's mercy is greater than all evil in the world'.[332] Christians must not primarily follow an ethics that promises to counter the evil of oppression, but Christians must be merciful to the sinful and, thus, make manifest that 'human and divine justice evidently go their separate ways'.[333] This again is based on the trust that good and evil are not on the same ontological level but that only the

---

326. Schillebeeckx, *Jesus*, 601 [638–9]; Schillebeeckx, *Interim Report*, 96; 111 [108–9; 127–8].

327. Schillebeeckx, *Jesus*, 599 [636–7].

328. However, Schillebeeckx admits that this might sometimes involve compromises (Schillebeeckx, 'The New Image of God', *God the Future of Man*, 121 [198–9]).

329. Schillebeeckx, *Church*, 123; 133 [124–5; 134–5].

330. Ibid., 123 [124–5].

331. Ibid., 123; 133 [124–5; 134–5].

332. Schillebeeckx, *Christ*, 592 [600].

333. Ibid., 627 [637].

good will persist, whereas evil will annihilate itself.[334] Christianity should manifest that God's grace is revealed in the powerlessness of the servant Christ.[335] 'Although God always comes in power, divine authority knows no use of force, not even against people who are crucifying his Christ. But the kingdom of God still comes, despite human misuse of power and human rejection of the kingdom of God.'[336]

This returns us once again to the question why Schillebeeckx does not advocate this theological vision of how sin is overcome through God's forgiveness, as the best solution to the political problems of post-Christendom societies. One could be tempted to appropriate Schillebeeckx's theology of grace to promise to attain the further reconciliation among conflicting parties. In order to understand why Schillebeeckx refrained from making such a promise to society, we should direct our attention to how Schillebeeckx himself received the grace that has been mediated in his contemporary context into his theology. In the following chapter, I will trace the way in which Schillebeeckx received insights from atheist outlooks of his time through the hermeneutic of mercy that has been outlined above. The theological significance of these atheist positions consisted partly in reminding Schillebeeckx of the impacts of sin upon his own theological vision, which rendered it ultimately impossible for him to promise that he could, as a Christian theologian, solve the whole society's political problems.

Conclusion

This chapter showed that Schillebeeckx's reconciliatory approach towards atheism was remarkable throughout. Moreover, it was striking that Schillebeeckx understood Christianity and atheism to be entangled in the same structural sin. He believed this structural sin could be overcome through theology's redirecting of Christianity towards God in acknowledgement of the atheist criticism of the church. Nevertheless, Schillebeeckx refrained from apologetically defending theology's public relevance by offering this as the best solution to the whole society's political problems. He acknowledged that atheists, despite their entanglement in structural sin, are moved by God's abundant grace in ways unknown to Christian theologians, and that therefore they might be equally able to find such a solution. In the 1970s Schillebeeckx further mitigated any theological promises concerning the solution of current political problems, when explicitly stressing that Christian theologians lack the vision of how society's contemporary problems are best solved.

Common interpretations of this development either criticize Schillebeeckx, for being naively optimistic regarding atheism, and his increasing accommodation of Christian theology to atheist thought, or they praise Schillebeeckx's understanding

---

334. Schillebeeckx, *Church*, 124; 136 [125–6; 138].
335. Schillebeeckx, *Theologisch geloofsverstaan anno 1983*, 20.
336. Schillebeeckx, *Church*, 119 [120–1].

of creation as allowing him to adopt a particularly amicable stance towards atheism, which should inspire similar engagements with non-Christians in contemporary contexts. I have offered an alternative to both of these interpretations by way of arguing that Schillebeeckx's reception of atheism and his understanding of creation only make sense within his theology of redemption, evidenced in his simultaneous upholding of a grace optimism and a pessimistic anthropology. His optimism with regard to atheism does, thus, not come at the expense of neglecting the seriousness of human sin. Instead, it was motivated by Schillebeeckx's conviction that the world's sinfulness is overcome precisely by being confronted with God's forgiveness, which is more powerful than any human shortcoming. Moreover, Schillebeeckx's interpretation of the Resurrection highlights the mediated character of grace, which explains why he evaluated the theological significance of non-Christian responses to certain political problems to a much higher degree than any of the other theologians introduced in this book. Schillebeeckx thus invites political theologians to discern the reality of redemption, in their contemporary context, instead of promising to solve contemporary political problems by resourcing anew the Christian tradition. Hence, Schillebeeckx rejects apologetic defences of Christianity's political relevance by way of pointing to the church's positive influence on society, because this would risk denying the church's sinfulness and erroneously present the church as an ethical community, rather than as the community that joyfully celebrates God's forgiveness. Also Schillebeeckx's theologically informed social critique corresponds to his understanding of redemption, most prominently manifesting the conviction that sin is overcome through forgiveness.

This chapter's argument, as a whole, might suggest that Schillebeeckx did not promise to solve the whole society's political problems, because, believing in the superabundance of grace, non-Christian solutions could be equally good. An examination of the way in which Schillebeeckx's theology was shaped by what he conceived of as contextual mediations of grace will help to explain his acknowledgement of the impairment of his own theological vision through sin towards the end of his career. Together, this then allows me to speculate more explicitly about the significance of Schillebeeckx's theology or the question of theology's political role in the contemporary post-Christendom context.

Chapter 5

WITHOUT PROMISE: A NON-DOMINATING POLITICAL THEOLOGY FOR POST-CHRISTENDOM SOCIETIES

In the previous chapter, the Christological rationale for Schillebeeckx's remarkably unapologetic approach to those who opposed Christianity at his time was made apparent. Indicative of an extraordinary appreciation of the mediated character of grace, his Christology suggests that theologians should be preoccupied with understanding how grace is mediated in their contexts, so that the church might celebrate the world's redemption in Christ. Far from being naively optimistic and apolitical, Schillebeeckx's grace optimism is paired with a particularly pessimistic anthropology, thus corresponding to a specific understanding of how sin is overcome by Christ. Having low expectations regarding humanity's own capacities, Schillebeeckx focuses on God's ever-forgiving offer of grace. This highlighting of God's prevailing grace is political insofar as utopian promises to society are prevented. The divine promise, not the human efforts to respond thereto, gives Christians the continuous courage to prevail in their political activities, as well as the flexibility to change the political course of action in the event that previous projects appear to be flawed.[1] Contemporary mediations of redemption are understood as God's merciful forgiveness of the continuous failures of ecclesial and non-Christian political projects, and as a promise for a better future.

The relevance and appropriateness of Schillebeeckx's unapologetic approach to atheism, for answering the question concerning theology's political role in the contemporary post-Christendom context, remains to be investigated. Having exhibited the Christological underpinnings of Schillebeeckx's theology, I will now turn to the other side of the argument, explaining how Schillebeeckx's theology is already influenced by what he perceived of as contextual mediations of grace. This chapter helps to understand how Schillebeeckx's realistic grace optimism led him to respond to his surrounding in a very particular way. A contemporary employment of his hermeneutic of the primacy of God's mercy would entail changing certain emphases in response to new specific contextual mediations of grace. Having argued that Schillebeeckx's Christology predisposed him to transform his theology

---

1. Schillebeeckx, *Church*, 141 [143–4]; Schillebeeckx, *Interim Report*, 110 [126–7].

in accordance with contemporary mediations of grace, this chapter returns to the public theological focus on the contexts of post-Christendom and pluralism. I will examine what specific insights Schillebeeckx gained from the ways in which he believed grace to be mediated particularly in these contexts. This then paves the way to introduce a second reason as to why Schillebeeckx has refrained from using a problem-centred approach to political questions.

5.1 Developing Schillebeeckx's Theological Approach: Adopting a Hermeneutics of Mercy

If I want to advance the argument that Schillebeeckx's theology developed through the reception of what he understood as non-Christian mediations of grace in his own context, it is important to reconsider two criticisms. From the one side, Schillebeeckx has been criticized for failing to respect the true distinctiveness of non-Christian positions, and from the other side, he has been criticized for failing to uphold the distinctiveness of Christian theology. This returns us to the criticism of accommodation to the surrounding culture, voiced by certain post-liberal theologians in the direction of public theology. In what follows, I will show that in between both these criticisms lies a particularly subtle alternative of interpreting Schillebeeckx's distancing of his Christian theology from non-Christian positions, as it is marked by a merciful critique.[2] It is this subtle distinction which I seek to maintain in my updating of Schillebeeckx's theology for new contexts.

a) Objections: Overwriting Atheism's and Theology's Distinctiveness

From a postmodern theological perspective, Schillebeeckx's thought has recently been criticized for assuming too much continuity between Christian and non-Christian world views.[3] It has been claimed that, in order to suit the contemporary postmodern context, Schillebeeckx's theology would have to be updated in accordance with the postmodern assumption of irreducible particularities, instead of assuming with modernity that different positions share some underlying sameness. This objection concurs with de Lubac's much earlier criticism that Schillebeeckx's optimism, regarding atheism, insufficiently considers the historical connection between atheism's positive aspects and the Christian heritage on which

2. My interpretation of the way in which Schillebeeckx's theology of grace influenced his engagement with non-Christian positions, follows a similar trajectory as that pursued by Erik Borgman, 'Alle dingen nieuw: Theologie uit genade', *Tijdschrift voor Theologie* 52 (2012): 201–25.

3. Boeve, 'Experience According to Edward Schillebeeckx', in *Divinising Experience*, 222.

these might depend.[4] Schillebeeckx is said to ignore the actual influences that Christianity has had upon the sentiments, morals and legislation of European societies, which might explain why Christian theologians detect Christ-like elements in atheism too. Both criticisms, thus, reproach that Schillebeeckx naively assumes an underlying harmonious continuity between Christianity and atheism.[5] The correction proposed is either to re-establish the lost harmony between atheism and Christianity (de Lubac and later Milbank) or to abandon any assumptions about Christianity's harmony with non-Christian positions, updating Schillebeeckx's theology to postmodernity's prioritization of irreducible particularity over unity (Boeve).[6]

Alternatively my reading of Schillebeeckx's theology suggests that Schillebeeckx has never been as naively modern as these critics claim. To the contrary, my stress on the difference between a grace optimism and a pessimistic anthropology in Schillebeeckx's thought suggests that he argues for the harmonious continuity between Christianity and atheism not due to any presupposed general human nature in the way a modern theologian might uphold it.[7] Instead, the underlying harmony between atheism and Christianity is assumed due to Schillebeeckx's conviction that the whole of reality has been redeemed in Jesus Christ and that both Christians, as well as atheists, live in this reality. The claim that everyone continues to receive God's merciful bestowal of grace does not presuppose any intrinsic commonality except that from being sinners who fall short in their responses to their graced environments.[8] Like de Lubac and Boeve, Schillebeeckx also rejects the view of modern atheism as being implicitly Christian.[9] However,

---

4. De Lubac, *A Brief Catechesis on Nature and Grace*, 218. Concretely, de Lubac doubts Schillebeeckx's optimism with respect to the modern project of humanization (196).

5. Boeve, 'Experience According to Edward Schillebeeckx', 224.

6. Boeve claims that in a pluralist context, marked by 'irreducible plurality', the particularity of Christianity becomes constitutive of Christianity's meaning and truth, which has to be conceived of in relation to the meaning and truth claims of other religions and world views without relativizing one's own claims (and the other's) or this plurality from the very outset' (ibid., 222); for another argument that Schillebeeckx's assumption about a fundamental continuity underneath all cultural discontinuities might conflict with postmodern sensibilities (see Thompson, 'Schillebeeckx on the Development of Doctrine', 320).

7. The claim that Schillebeeckx's Christology relies on the assumption of a universal human nature is advanced by Rochford, 'The Theological Hermeneutics of Edward Schillebeeckx', 254.

8. This accords with Christian Bauer's interpretation that Schillebeeckx's optimism, with regard to atheistic secularity, is not so much based on his optimism concerning an anonymous Christianity as to his optimism concerning an anonymous God whose grace cannot be comprehended (Christian Bauer, 'Heiligkeit des Profane? Spuren der "école Chenu-Schillebeeckx" (H. de Lubac) auf dem Zweiten Vatikanum', in *Edward Schillebeeckx: Impulse für Theologien im 21. Jahrhundert*, 76).

9. Schillebeeckx, 'Op zoek naar Gods afwezigheid', 280–2.

unlike de Lubac's suggestion that atheism resembles Christianity due to some historical influences, Schillebeeckx argues that Christians might detect Christ-like elements in atheists due to their own influence upon them. Since commonalities are most likely gained from a shared environment in which both Christians and atheists live, not from some inner principle, the appearance of a good Christian in the atheist's environment can effect the best of the latter to come to the fore. The same would also hold for influences of atheists upon Christians.

The same criticism, concerning the assumption of too much commonality between Christianity and atheism, has also been voiced from the other side. Here, Schillebeeckx has been criticized for undermining theology's distinctiveness in favour of embracing atheist ideology critiques too wholeheartedly.[10] It has been argued that, in his later work, Schillebeeckx abandoned the traditional theological interest in understanding God for a primary interest in finding a theological contribution to Critical Theory, and in analysing how ideology critiques challenge traditional theological thought.[11] In his later theology, Schillebeeckx supposedly constructed an inductive metaphysics in the sense that he reasoned from human experience to God, and resisted providing definitive answers.[12] In a similar vein, Schillebeeckx is being criticized for entirely conflating God's saving activity with

10. William Portier, 'Edward Schillebeeckx as Critical Theorist: The Impact of Neo-Marxist Social Thought on his Recent Theology', *The Thomist* 48(3) (1984): 345; 363–4; William Hill, 'Schillebeeckx's New Look at Secularity: A Note', *The Thomist* 33 (1969): 169. However, Portier later argues that the overriding interest throughout Schillebeeckx's work was to help contemporary people to recognize the reality of Christ (Portier, 'Interpretation and Method', in *The Praxis of the Reign of God*, 27). Boeve also criticizes Schillebeeckx from this side, when he argues that Schillebeeckx's focus on the universal human ritualization of life risks overlooking the importance of the particular way in which the Christian tradition ritualizes human life (Lieven Boeve, 'The Sacramental Interruption of Rituals of Life', *The Heythrop Journal* XLIV (2003): 401–17).

11. Portier, 'Edward Schillebeeckx as Critical Theorist', *The Thomist*, 342–3; 349; 353–4. In an earlier article, Portier argues that Schillebeeckx's overall hermeneutical framework remains the theological quest for the absolute, but that he adopts insights from Enlightenment traditions into this endeavour (William L. Portier, 'Schillebeeckx' Dialogue with Critical Theory', *The Ecumenist* 21 (1983): 22). However, in the same article, Portier maintains a critical distance towards Schillebeeckx's supposed reconfiguration of Christian orthodoxy in his engagement with Critical Theory (26).

12. Steven M. Rodenborn, *Hope in Action: Subversive Eschatology in the Theology of Edward Schillebeeckx and Johann Baptist Metz* (New York: Fortress Press, 2014), 172–5. However, Rodenborn continues to argue that Schillebeeckx did not ontologize the mixture of good and evil that he observed in history (177). This means that Schillebeeckx only discerned in how far his optimistic ontology had to be refined through attendance to history (176). In other words, Schillebeeckx might have *refined* his metaphysics inductively but the ontological framework with which he assessed reality remained continuous.

human liberation movements.[13] This strand of criticisms resonates with the critiques mentioned in the previous chapter regarding Schillebeeckx's supposed tendency to naturalize grace and to be overly optimistic with regard to atheism.

As alternative to this criticism, I maintain that Schillebeeckx's overarching interest in his engagement with ideology critiques remained theological. Schillebeeckx engaged with ideology critiques, like other atheist thought, through his hermeneutic of God's abundant offer of mercy. Although the critics are right that, in his later theology, Schillebeeckx emphasized that the Christian faith in God's merciful forgiveness of human failures cannot be *deduced* from purely secular experiences, he maintained this faith nonetheless.[14] Yet, as will become clear in this chapter, Schillebeeckx modified his theology continuously in accordance with the specific graces being mediated in his own context, which some might view as the simplistic accommodation of theology to the cultural mainstream. However, I do not interpret these modifications as capitulation of theology to atheism, but as concurrent with Schillebeeckx's call on theologians to discern how the reality of redemption manifests itself in their contemporary contexts.[15]

b) Appreciating Subtle Distinctions: Mercifully Criticizing Atheism's Shortcomings

Both criticisms overlook the way in which Schillebeeckx maintains a subtle distinction between Christian theology and non-Christian positions. This subtlety derives from Schillebeeckx's *merciful* critique of atheism. Thus, both critiques overlook that Schillebeeckx rejects modern secularity's assumed neutrality.[16] Schillebeeckx antecedes Radical Orthodoxy in calling modernity a mythology if it generalizes that everyone lives in a secularist world, that is, if it disguises the fact that it upholds a culturally conditioned all-encompassing ontology.[17] This is

---

13. Portier, 'Edward Schillebeeckx as Critical Theorist' *The Thomist*, 363–5; see also Portier, 'Schillebeeckx' Dialogue with Critical Theory', *The Ecumenist*, 25; Hill, 'Schillebeeckx's New Look at Secularity', *The Thomist*, 163–6 or Anthony J. Godzieba, 'God, the Luxury of our Lives: Schillebeeckx and the Argument', in *Edward Schillebeeckx and Contemporary Theology*, 28–9; 31 for a more contemporary argument that Schillebeeckx fails to distinguish between secular liberation and supernatural grace, and to speak positively about the importance of God.

14. Schillebeeckx, 'Secularization and Christian Belief in God', *God the Future of Man*, 49 [79–81]; Schillebeeckx, *Jesus*, 600–1 [637–9].

15. See also Robert J. Schreiter, 'Schillebeeckx and Theology in the Twenty-First Century', in *Edward Schillebeeckx and Contemporary Theology*, 254; 259, who argues similarly that Schillebeeckx's inductive focus concerns his interest in the historical reception of God's grace.

16. Schillebeeckx, *Church*, 159–61 [160–3].

17. Schillebeeckx, 'The New Image of God' *God the Future of Man*, 105–6 [174--177]. This could be read as a critique of Boeve's conception of the continuity and discontinuity between Christian particularity and human universality (Boeve, 'The Sacramental Interruption of Rituals of Life' *The Heythrop Journal*, 401–17). Boeve conceives of continuity in

why Schillebeeckx seeks a way to accept modern secularization without rendering it absolute.[18] He claims that this is possible if secularization is celebrated within the framework of a theocentric world view, which is akin to the later Radical Orthodox projects. The overall structure of Schillebeeckx's merciful criticisms of atheist positions consists, however, of a primary interest in learning from atheism's good aspirations, while elaborating only secondarily on atheism's shortcomings.[19]

This is why I do not want to update Schillebeeckx's theology by simply accepting postmodernity's postulation of irreducible particularity, as though this claim was a self-evident truth about reality to which all members of contemporary West European societies assent.[20] Contrary to those who want to update Schillebeeckx's

---

terms of general categories (i.e. religious rituals) and of discontinuity in terms of the particularity of each faith tradition as that which shapes this category differently (412–4). This assumption of general categories, of which different faith traditions are particular instantiations, can be criticized for being a specifically modern Western invention, which assimilates non-Christian faith traditions *a priori* to the Christian world view (Cavanaugh, 'The Invention of the Religious-Secular Distinction' in *At the Limits of the Secular*, 105–28).

18. Schillebeeckx, 'Secularization and Christian Belief in God', *God the Future of Man*, 46 [75–6].

19. This structure of criticizing secularism, but still emphasizing its underlying good intuition, is recurrent throughout Schillebeeckx's work. See, for example, Schillebeeckx's claim that Christian theology should receive all that is good in Enlightenment reason, without also adopting Enlightenment reason's limitations (Schillebeeckx, *Jesus*, 555 [594]). The liberation of the modern subject should be celebrated without sliding into modern subjectivism (Schillebeeckx, *Church*, 47 [48–9]); or, Schillebeeckx's celebration of secular phenomenology's focus on historicity, while highlighting that the human transcendence of historicity, should not be lost from view (Schillebeeckx, 'The New Trends in Present-Day Dogmatic Theology', *Revelation and Theology*, 294; 313; [113–15; 143–5]). Schillebeeckx also criticizes atheist metaphysics mercifully, insofar as he integrates them into Christian theology, not due to their supposed neutrality but because he is convinced that atheist philosophies also respond to the reality of God's grace (Schillebeeckx, 'Correlation Between Human Question and Christian Answer', *The Understanding of Faith*, 85 [97–8]). Regarding relativism, Schillebeeckx denies the neutrality of the statement that the absolute truth can, by necessity, not be accessed from a historical perspective (Schillebeeckx, 'The Concept of "Truth"', *Revelation and Theology*, 190 [6–7]). Not elaborating on this shortcoming, but mediating God's mercy towards it, Schillebeeckx integrates the relativistic critique into his Christian theology and uses it as an aid by which to prevent idolatry (Schillebeeckx, *Christ*, 66 [79]). This means that relativism is not accepted as the final truth about the world, but relativism within the world is accepted in order to uphold the Christian faith in God as the only absolute (Schillebeeckx, *Church*, 166 [167–8]).

20. Boeve, 'Experience According to Edward Schillebeeckx', 222. For Boeve's own justification of why he appreciates postmodernity's appreciation of particularity, see Lieven Boeve, 'Religion after Detraditionalization: Christian Faith in a Post-Secular Europe', *Irish Theological Quarterly* 70 (2005): 99–122. His disagreement with Schillebeeckx on this point

thought to fit the postmodern current, Schillebeeckx is dubious of any purely formal acknowledgement of pluralism and the concomitant endeavour to position Christianity as one group within this pluralist landscape.[21] Such a position assumes a total vision that dissolves true pluralism into merely an epiphenomenal plurality of instantiations of metaphysical univocity: Each societal subgroup is regarded as but one more instantiation of one's overall assumption of radical plurality. Correcting the shortcomings of this secularist understanding of pluralism mercifully, Schillebeeckx does not elaborate on this criticism but focuses instead on his contemporaries' preference for plurality over unity without accepting their ontologization of this preference.[22]

Consequently, Schillebeeckx seeks a way in which pluralism will be continuously overcome without being dissolved.[23] It must be overcome in order to focus on God as the sole absolute reality, but not dissolved because this would ignore how Schillebeeckx's contemporaries' preference for plurality over unity manifests the reality of redemption in his context. If the particularity of each group celebrated by postmodern philosophy would be established as the sole point of departure for dialogue,[24] then the pluralist ontology would be consolidated rather than overcome. This is why Schillebeeckx presupposes the underlying harmonious reality in which any plurality participates. On the basis of this assumption, Christian theology can be challenged and expanded through a plurality of insights from non-Christians which are received as mediations of mercy.[25] In other words, Christianity breaks

---

might explain why Boeve relies, in his theological engagement with a postmodern context via the concept of 'interruption', on Johann Baptist Metz, not on Edward Schillebeeckx (Lieven Boeve, *God Interrupts History: Theology in a Time of Upheaval* (New York and London: The Continuum International Publishing Group, 2007). My argument has shown that the assumption that Christians and atheists participate in the same graced reality does not presuppose any consensus between them. This is a standard by which Boeve seems to measure the question about unity or particularity (Lieven Boeve, 'Zeg nooit meer correlatie: Over christelijke traditie, actuele context en onderbreking', *Collationes: Vlaams Tijdschrift voor Theologie en Pastoraal* 34 (2004): 204). The dividing issue between Boeve's and my suggestion of how to correct or develop Schillebeeckx's theology, seems to be that Boeve assumes that there is a consensus among inhabitants of contemporary post-Christendom societies that the pluralist societies in which we live are radically particularized (215). Doubting this consensus, I suggest that, as a Christian, I can only describe the context of plurality through a Christian theological lens, and this lens suggests to me that the plurality can be thought of as harmonious, rather than as radically particularized. However, I do not thereby assume that non-Christians agree with me on this description of the context in which we live.

21. Schillebeeckx speaks of 'a cheap form of tolerance' (Schillebeeckx, *Church*, 161 [163]).

22. Ibid.

23. Schillebeeckx, 'Theological Criteria', *The Understanding of Faith*, 48–9 [53–5].

24. Boeve, 'Experience According to Edward Schillebeeckx', in *Divinising Experience*, 222.

25. In 5.2, I will further elaborate upon the specific insights Schillebeeckx has gained from his contemporaries' preference of plurality.

with the postmodern assumption of radical particularity, insofar as it understands its own particularity as called to unify all particularities within itself. However, Christian theology is not meant to convert postmodern particularism to a Christian understanding of unity in difference, because true Christian unity must somehow embrace rather than exclude also this particular outlook.

Also in the case of ideology critique, Schillebeeckx interprets the shortcomings of this atheist outlook mercifully. Overall, Schillebeeckx assesses positively his contemporary atheists' fundamental faith that human beings are created for freedom.[26] However, Schillebeeckx rejects the 'fictitious concept of absolute freedom' underlying the ideological critiques with which he engages.[27] Again, Schillebeeckx denies the neutrality of ideology critique, and highlights its culturally specific foundations.[28] Schillebeeckx warns against any absolutization of the critical negativity of ideology critique, because this negativity itself becomes ideological if it is secretly used as an overarching vision of reality, and believed to be able to direct *all* human action.[29] This is why Schillebeeckx completes ideology critique's understanding of freedom with an acknowledgement of the origins on which freedom must build on the one hand, as well as of the end towards which freedom must be directed on the other.

Concerning freedom's origins, Schillebeeckx combines the insights of ideology critique with a hermeneutic theology that seeks not only to deconstruct current structures, but also to preserve insights gained in the past.[30] What has already been achieved must not be opposed as such, but just the tendency to perpetuate these achievements as the sole reality, as a result of which the realization of further possibilities would be foreclosed.[31] For example, theologians should admit that their insights might be incomplete and that a contemporary manifestation of the reality of redemption might lead them in a different direction. Used in this way, ideology critique is not nihilistic, but acts solely negatively against the human imaginative closure against further real possibilities.[32] Regarding freedom's end, the Christian understanding of liberation and the negativity of ideology critique also converge without being identical.[33] The Christian understanding of freedom is

---

26. Schillebeeckx, 'The New Critical Theory and Theological Hermeneutics', *The Understanding of Faith*, 110 [125–6].

27. Ibid., 111; 128 [126–7; 146–7].

28. Ibid., 105; 109–110 [120–1; 124–6].

29. Schillebeeckx, 'The New Critical Theory', *The Understanding of Faith*, 105 [120–1].

30. Schillebeeckx, 'The New Critical Theory and Theological Hermeneutics', *The Understanding of Faith*, 111-113 [126–9].

31. Schillebeeckx, 'The New Critical Theory', *The Understanding of Faith*, 105 [120–1].

32. Ibid., 105 [120–1].

33. Schillebeeckx, 'The New Critical Theory and Theological Hermeneutics', *The Understanding of Faith*, 122 [139–40].

not merely negative, but oriented to the liberation of others into the same freedom from oppression for a faithful following of God.[34]

Instead of criticizing Schillebeeckx for insufficiently distinguishing between Christian theology and non-Christian positions, and of then updating Schillebeeckx's theology by way of repairing this alleged shortcoming, I maintain that Schillebeeckx kept a very fine distinction between Christian theology and non-Christian positions recognizable in the merciful way in which he theologically corrected whatever he regarded as erroneous in non-Christian positions, without thereby denigrating the latter. Schillebeeckx's theology is precisely most distinct through its focus on how non-Christian positions always already participate in God's grace, despite their sinful shortcomings. Also a contemporary public theology could follow Schillebeeckx, in its theological approach, in manifesting to non-Christians that 'God loves us without conditions or limits: for our part undeservedly and boundlessly'.[35]

5.2 Receiving the End of Christendom as Grace: Redirecting Theology Towards God

A third suggestion of how Schillebeeckx's theological engagement with atheism should be updated, picks up on the critical distance he maintained to atheism, but overstretches it, thereby equally missing the subtlety of Schillebeeckx's merciful critique. The similarity of Schillebeeckx's criticism of atheism's feigned neutrality to that of Radical Orthodoxy has led some to claim that Schillebeeckx showed great respect for secular humanism, but sought 'to rescue it from its atheism'.[36] This interpretation overlooks Schillebeeckx's argument that Christian theologians themselves continuously fail to manifest adequately the reality they are meant to confess, and that his overall intention is not to overcome atheism's shortcomings, but to learn from atheism in order to overcome theology's entanglement in sin.[37] Schillebeeckx is concerned about the problems with any advocacy of Christian theology as playing the most central political role in post-Christendom societies, more than he is concerned about any theological rescuing

---

34. Schillebeeckx, *Christ*, 500 [513].

35. Schillebeeckx, *Church*, 121 [122–3].

36. William Cavanaugh, 'Return of the Golden Calf: Economy, Idolatry and Secularization since *Gaudium et spes*', *Theological Studies* 76 (2015): 710.

37. Schillebeeckx, *Church*, 4 [4]. Also Martin Poulsom has recently observed that Schillebeeckx rarely rejects opposing views but 'tends to affirm those aspects of them that he thinks are true, in order to invite them to move on together with him' (Poulsom, *The Dialectics of Creation*, 121). I would qualify this observation by arguing that Schillebeeckx did not primarily aim at convincing atheists, but at correcting Christianity.

of society from its atheism.[38] Schillebeeckx is convinced that, in the current post-Christendom context, efforts to re-establish a society in which Christianity was the unanimously accepted, all-encompassing world view must be rejected.[39] This is no naive accommodation of the Christian faith to secular trends and expectations. Schillebeeckx's rejection of Christian dominance is not motivated by any desire to defend Christianity's relevance in a secular age, but it is based on his evaluation of the post-Christendom critique as a new mediation of mercy which should redirect Christianity towards God.[40]

a) *Theological Appreciation of Post-Christendom: Encountering God in Atheism*

Concerning the theological significance of the post-Christendom context, Schillebeeckx thinks that Christian theology can no longer serve as the necessary basis for societal values and politics.[41] God's grace would be belittled if it was believed that separating values from their Christian roots would diminish the grace mediated by these values. The abundance of God's grace is revealed precisely in the fact that these values can develop in more than one positive direction. In this vein, Schillebeeckx reads his surrounding society's capacity to self-organization as constituting a further refinement and development of the Christian values that once underpinned a monolithic Christian culture.[42] This reception of the theological significance of the post-Christendom context can, thus, be read as an objection to Max Stackhouse's public theology[43] as well as to Radical Orthodox's triumphant presentations of Christian theology as rescuing society from all of the problems associated with atheism.

Far from downplaying the issue of human sinfulness, but also not primarily interested in correcting *atheism's* sinfulness, Schillebeeckx seeks to understand how the atheist post-Christendom critique reveals Christianity's sinfulness. Schillebeeckx, thus, discerns the way in which God's mercy over Christianity's shortcomings is being mediated in this criticism from outside. Schillebeeckx argues that the churches are now liberated from erroneous political alliances, a

---

38. Schillebeeckx, *Church*, 159–61 [160–3]; Schillebeeckx, 'The Church as the Sacrament of Dialogue', *God the Future of Man*, 79–80 [130–3]; Schillebeeckx, *Theologisch geloofsverstaan anno 1983*, 9. Contributions of the church to public politics can consist in not only collaboration, encouragement, confirmation or help, but also criticism and protest (Schillebeeckx, 'The Church as the Sacrament of Dialogue', *God the Future of Man*, 81–2 [133–5]).

39. Schillebeeckx, *Interim Report*, 4 [4–5].

40. Schillebeeckx, 'The Church as the Sacrament of Dialogue', *God the Future of Man*, 78 [128–30]; Schillebeeckx, *Jesus*, 16 [33–4]. Others have also observed that Schillebeeckx's theology shifted from an earlier focus on humankind's directedness to God to a later focus on God's approach to humankind (Maas, 'Stem & Stilte', *Tijdschrift voor Theologie* (2010): 58–60).

41. Schillebeeckx, *Interim Report*, 4–5 [5–6].

42. Ibid.,

43. See for example Stackhouse, *Globalization and Grace*, 85.

contention resembling Yoder's positive evaluation of the end of Christendom to some extent.[44] Like Yoder, Schillebeeckx stresses that established alliances between church and state can limit the church's focus on the gospel, but, in contrast to Yoder, Schillebeeckx also stresses that these alliances restrict the theological awareness of extra-ecclesial mediations of God's grace.[45] In other words, post-Christendom critiques of Christianity's cultural and political dominance are received as a mercy that redirects Christian theology's attention to the church's dependence on the reality of redemption in which it always already exists. In this sense, Schillebeeckx regards the diaspora situation of a post-Christendom church as a purification of Christianity.[46]

Schillebeeckx's position is distinct from Yoder's insofar as Schillebeeckx does not elaborate upon the critique in order to discard the concept of Christendom as a whole.[47] Schillebeeckx does not diagnose a principle contradiction between Christendom and truthfully following Christ. Instead, he laments that in the particular history of Christendom in the West, Christian theologians have downplayed the importance of Christianity's God-centredness.[48] At this point, Schillebeeckx is in agreement with both Radical Orthodoxy and John Howard Yoder, that a purely immanent world view has been consolidated during the history of Christendom, which must be regarded as insufficient in comparison to the Christian theocentric world view.[49] In agreement with Yoder, Schillebeeckx contends that an immanentist outlook cannot account sufficiently for the sacrifices that might, at times, be demanded from Christians for the sake of God's Kingdom.[50] However, whereas Yoder argued that this is the case because the logic of the Cross and Resurrection runs counter to immanent efficacy, Schillebeeckx laments the unintelligibility of prayer within a purely immanent ontology.[51] He stresses that

---

44. Schillebeeckx, 'Church, Magisterium and Politics', *God the Future of Man*, 87 [145–6].

45. Schillebeeckx, 'The New Trends in Present-Day Dogmatic Theology', *Revelation and Theology*, 315 [146–8]. Schillebeeckx mentions social revolutions against the established state politics in particular as potentially mediating people's desire for the Kingdom of God.

46. Ibid., 314 [145–6].

47. Contrary to Yoder, Schillebeeckx claims that Christ can be followed better without the external pressures of state persecution (Schillebeeckx, *Interim Report*, 50 [58–9]).

48. Instead of understanding the church as a service to God, God had been functionalized for the amelioration of the secular world (Schillebeeckx, 'The New Trends in Present-Day Dogmatic Theology', *Revelation and Theology*, 314 [145–6]). The church was preoccupied with its own self-interest (Schillebeeckx, 'The Church as the Sacrament of Dialogue', *God the Future of Man*, 79–80 [130–3]).

49. Schillebeeckx, 'The New Trends in Present-Day Dogmatic Theology', *Revelation and Theology*, 314 [145–6].

50. Schillebeeckx, 'Secular Worship and Church Liturgy', *God the Future of Man*, 68 [112–13].

51. Schillebeeckx, 'The New Trends in Present-Day Dogmatic Theology', *Revelation and Theology*, 314 [145–6].

these spiritual sacrifices are only properly conceived of in light of people's prayerful communion with God.[52] The preoccupation with worldly wealth in Christendom was limiting, because immanent beings were too narrowly assessed in reference to some present enjoyment. Christian theology, to the contrary, must conceive of all immanent affairs as intrinsically open to God, which makes prayer to God about these issues intelligible.[53]

Schillebeeckx then retrieves, from the post-Christendom critique primarily the incentive to remind the church of the significance of praying to God. According to Schillebeeckx, the most decisive difference between Christianity and atheism is that for Christianity the worldly reality is no longer simply the object of philosophical analysis, but also the subject of God's personal dialogue with humankind.[54] Christian theology must always be based on God's address to humankind, and in this way surpasses atheist philosophies that do not consider this prayerful relationship.[55] Against any philosophical disavowal of this interpersonal relationship as idolatrous conception of God as one being among beings, Schillebeeckx stresses that the interpersonal relationship between God and people in prayer does not fall short of, but transcends a human interpersonal relationship.[56] Despite all of the inequality between humans and God, despite God's independence from creation, Christians believe that God, in God's mysterious absoluteness, really offers reciprocity to humankind.[57] It is not up to theologians to protect God's absoluteness argumentatively, but to confess the mysterious reality of the reciprocity between God and humankind, and to thus motivate Christians to pray.[58]

However, instead of triumphantly presenting theology's appreciation of prayer over the atheist disavowal of prayer, Schillebeeckx's reception of the post-Christendom critique as incentive for Christian theology to re-appreciate the gift of prayer is precisely why he is not concerned with any triumphant presentation of Christian theology as something that promises to rescue society

52. Schillebeeckx, 'Secular Worship and Church Liturgy' *God the Future of Man*, 68 [112–13].

53. Schillebeeckx, 'The New Trends in Present-Day Dogmatic Theology', *Revelation and Theology*, 314 [145–6].

54. Schillebeeckx, 'Revelation-in-Reality and Revelation-in-Word', *Revelation and Theology*, 27 [39–40].

55. Schillebeeckx, *Church*, 14 [14–15]. This does not mean that Schillebeeckx would discount the importance of philosophy for theology. To the contrary, he argues that purely metaphysical thought does reveal some truth about reality (Schillebeeckx, *'Theologia* or *Oikonomia?', Revelation and Theology*, 286–7 [102–5]).

56. Schillebeeckx, *Christ*, 812–13 [817].

57. Schillebeeckx, 'De zin van het mens-zijn van Jezus', *Tijdschrift voor Theologie* 2 (1962): 133; Schillebeeckx, *Christ*, 78; 82–3 [89; 94].

58. Schillebeeckx, 'De zin van het mens-zijn van Jezus', *Tijdschrift voor Theologie*, 132; Schillebeeckx, *Christ*, 77 [88].

from its atheism. Instead of countering atheism, Schillebeeckx is concerned with prayerfully relating to God through all of creation, including the atheism of many of his contemporaries.[59] Prayer refers Christians back to the world which can now be interpreted as the context in which God reveals Godself. Schillebeeckx primarily re-appreciates that 'the genuine life of faith ... remains magnetized by a prayerful longing for encounter with God'.[60] It is, consequently, Christian prayer which stimulates the church to an active commitment in the world without ever identifying this commitment as the goal at which it could find rest.[61] Atheist political contributions do not have to be countered, despite all of their shortcomings, because knowing itself to be addressed by the reality of God in Christ, the church is freed from any natural fear in its political engagement.[62] In prayer, Christians know that their own as well as non-Christian political efforts are bound to remain imperfect on the one hand, but also that these shortcomings do not endanger the ultimate victory of God's grace on the other. In this sense, Schillebeeckx calls prayer Christianity's most critical element that can really change the face of the world. 'Prayer – and I think only prayer – gives Christian faith it's [*sic*] most critical and productive force.'[63]

b) Theological Appreciation of Pluralism: Expanding the Theological Vision Non-triumphantly

This reception of the post-Christendom critique as theologically significant, thus further elucidates why, despite exhibiting certain similarities with Milbank's criticism of atheist secularism as ideological, Schillebeeckx's rejection of the postmodern atheist interpretation of pluralism also remains distinct from the Radical Orthodox critique. Schillebeeckx also evaluates pluralism from a particularly Christian perspective, still positing God as the all-encompassing framework within which he assesses pluralism, while equally denying the neutrality of atheist understandings of pluralism. However, for Schillebeeckx, this means that atheist interpretations of pluralism are not to be replaced triumphantly, but theology must discern the way in which the atheist appreciation of pluralism, despite its shortcomings, mediates a grace for theology. Atheist interpretations of

---

59. Schillebeeckx, *Christ*, 805–6 [809–10].

60. Schillebeeckx, 'Secularization and Christian Belief in God', *God the Future of Man*, 50 [81–2].

61. This is why it has recently been aptly stated that, for Schillebeeckx, mysticism and politics stand in a mutually productive tension with each other (David Ranson, *Between the 'Mysticism of Politics' and the 'Politics of Mysticism': Interpreting New Pathways of Holiness within the Roman Catholic Tradition* (Hindmarsh: ATF Theology, 2014), 107). The secular realm of politics is identified as an important locus for Christian spirituality (217). See also Poulsom, *The Dialectics of Creation*, 121–6.

62. Schillebeeckx, *Interim Report*, 52 [61–2].

63. Schillebeeckx, *Christ*, 813 [817].

pluralism thus are not interpreted primarily as a cultural problem in need of a theological solution. Instead, Schillebeeckx receives this appreciation of pluralism as a merciful reminder for Christian theology that God's grace is mediated in plural ways.[64] He receives the secular celebration of pluralism as new positive incentive to examine critically and enlarge Christian theology through dialogue with others.[65] Dialogue with non-Christians must be entered into in order to understand the reality of redemption.[66] This means that Christian theologians must assess the goodness of every non-Christian insight in reference to the revelation of God in Christ.[67] In this way, Christian theology can show how the transcendent unity of all world views in God can be dimly seen in analogical relations within the world.[68]

Identifying God as pure positivity, Schillebeeckx understands the reality of God to be really mediated in all instances of goodness and as opposed by all instances of evil.[69] All worldly goodness directly participates in God and is, as such, revelatory of God's own Being.[70] The theological endeavour of understanding the Christian God better, thus, demands that the theologian attends to the positivity of human history. At the same time, when relating all this-worldly goodness into one coherent vision of reality, it must be respected that God's transcendent positivity surpasses

---

64. Schillebeeckx, *Church*, 165 [166–7].

65. Schillebeeckx, 'Theological Criteria', *The Understanding of Faith*, 48 [53–4]; Schillebeeckx, 'The Church as the Sacrament of Dialogue', *God the Future of Man*, 76–7 [125–8]; Schillebeeckx, 'The New Trends in Present-Day Dogmatic Theology', *Revelation and Theology*, 315 [148–148]. Schillebeeckx argues that 'in order to communicate, [the church] must also *receive from* and *listen to* what comes to her from the world as 'foreign prophecy', but in which she nonetheless recognizes the well-known voice of the Lord' (Schillebeeckx, 'The Church as the Sacrament of Dialogue', *God the Future of Man*, 76 [125–7]). Also Roger Haight has recently argued that in his theocentrism, Schillebeeckx did not fall short of, but went further than, an inclusive Christianity with regard to religious pluralism (Haight, 'Engagement met de wereld als zaak van God', *Tijdschrift voor Theologie* 50 (2010): 84). However, Haight relates this to Schillebeeckx's theology of creation instead of redemption.

66. Schillebeeckx, *Theologisch geloofsverstaan anno 1983*, 9.

67. At this point, Schillebeeckx admits to be involved in an inescapable hermeneutical circle, which cannot be resolved prior to the eschaton (Schillebeeckx, *Church*, 161 [162–3]).

68. Ibid., 165 [166–7].

69. Ibid., 73 [75–6]. In Schillebeeckx's context, human liberation was an instance of grace and human enslavement was an instance of evil.

70. Schillebeeckx, *Interim Report*, 110 [126–7]. This indicates that, in agreement with Radical Orthodoxy, Schillebeeckx affirms that God's ontological otherness from creation must be thought of in analogical, not in equivocal terms (Schillebeeckx, *Church*, 55–6 [56–7]). Schillebeeckx also claims that an equivocal understanding of God's otherness would render Christianity politically irrelevant. (Schillebeeckx, 'Secularization and Christian Belief in God', *God the Future of Man*, 43 [70–1]). Doctrinally, Schillebeeckx relates the analogical understanding of God and world to the Incarnation (Schillebeeckx, *Church*, 125 [126–7]).

that which has already been mediated.[71] Although theology can somehow already see the harmonious whole, this total vision slips 'from our grasp into depths unfathomable.'[72] At this point, Schillebeeckx refrains from elevating his theological interpretation of pluralism triumphantly over and above its atheistic counterparts in order to acknowledge God's transcendence over his own theological vision. Schillebeeckx stresses that precisely because Christian theology relates all mediated goodness into one coherent vision of *God*, it must at the same time 'slide into mysticism'.[73] Christian theology cannot be presented as something superior to other interpretations of reality, because it must bear witness to the God who remains greater than the Christian integration of all worldly positivity into one coherent vision.

Although God cannot be known independently from any ontological framework, theology must somehow evidence in its conceptual ontology that the abundant reality of God can never be adequately captured by any vision of reality.[74] As has already been observed by others, because the superior power of grace is affirmed as true, independent of human responses to this reality, Christianity would wrongly focus on itself instead of on God if it claimed that Christian theology is necessary in order to construct a better society.[75] To affirm the reality of redemption means precisely that Christian theologians must be able to discover true goodness, also in non-Christian interpretations of reality.[76] Because of the real superabundance of grace, Christian theology can never be demonstrated conclusively to be the best interpretation of reality.[77] Consequently, Christian theology is concerned with the totality of reality, but should not be totalizing.[78] Christian theologians must win their own vision of reality over and over again precisely as one that is not totalizing, for such totalization would be a disacknowledgement of the superabundance of grace. In this sense, 'the theologian is ... a custodian of transcendence but he [*sic*] does not guard it like a treasure'.[79] Theology should not be concerned with securing a respectable position in public dialogue, but it should be entirely outward-looking, precisely because Christian

71. Schillebeeckx, *Church*, 73–4 [75–6].

72. Schillebeeckx, *Jesus*, 16 [33–4].

73. Schillebeeckx, *Interim Report*, 51 [60–1].

74. Schillebeeckx, 'Theological Criteria', *The Understanding of Faith*, 57–8 [63–5].

75. Borgman, 'Retrieving God's Contemporary Presence', in *Edward Schillebeeckx and Contemporary Theology*, 238.

76. Schillebeeckx, 'Correlation between Human Question and Christian Answer', *The Understanding of Faith*, 84–5 [96–8].

77. Schillebeeckx, 'The New Critical Theory and Theological Hermeneutics', *The Understanding of Faith*, 135 [154–5].

78. Schillebeeckx, *Jesus*, 566 [602–4]. Schillebeeckx speaks of 'religion' instead of Christianity.

79. Schillebeeckx, 'The New Critical Theory and Theological Hermeneutics', *The Understanding of Faith*, 135 [154–5].

theology should be primarily preoccupied with discovering how other world views might redirect Christianity towards God.[80]

5.3 Receiving Ideology Critique as Grace: Confessing Theology's Entanglement in Sin

This rejection of any Christian triumphalism returns us to the above-mentioned issue of Schillebeeckx's relation to ideology critique. If my argument from the previous chapters has suggested that Christian theologians might be advised to be more modest in their promises of contributing positively to post-Christendom politics, and less eager in their attempts at identifying societal problems in need of theological solutions, it is now time to introduce a second reason, next to Schillebeeckx's grace optimism, as for why such a problem-centred approach to politics might be theologically inaccurate.

a) A Theological Appreciation of Ideology Critique: Confessing the Impairment of Theology's Vision

According to my reading, Schillebeeckx discerned also how the secular ideology critiques of his day mediated a mercy that reoriented Christian theology towards God, and consequently incorporated these insights into his theology. Still upholding theology's aspiration to form an overarching vision of reality, Schillebeeckx receives from ideology critique the distinction between legitimate and distorted ontologies.[81] An overarching ontology is not objectionable as such, but ideology critique shows that an ontology becomes problematic when it is used in order to consolidate the interests of a dominating group in society.[82] Consequently, Schillebeeckx calls on Christian theologians to use ideology critique in order to be faithful to God, not to ideological human interpretations of God.[83] In receiving ideology critique as a mediation of mercy, Schillebeeckx distinguishes between the Christian gospel, which escapes the criticism of only being a defective referent to the absolute truth, and theology's previous proclamation of the gospel, which

---

80. Schillebeeckx, *Church*, 182 [183–4].

81. Schillebeeckx, *Theologisch geloofsverstaan anno 1983*, 17.

82. Ibid. This invalidates the argument that, in his later theology, Schillebeeckx broke with De Petter's metaphysics, because to presuppose Christianity as overarching ontology was no longer socially acceptable in the 1960s (Kerr, *Twentieth Century Catholic Theologians*, 59).

83. Schillebeeckx, *Theologisch geloofsverstaan anno 1983*, 18; Schillebeeckx, *The Understanding of Faith*, xxi [xi-xii]; Schillebeeckx, 'The New Critical Theory and Theological Hermeneutics', *The Understanding of Faith*, 111 [126–7]. Schillebeeckx understands ideology as the absolutization of a relative conceptualization of reality (Schillebeeckx, 'The Church as the Sacrament of Dialogue', *God the Future of Man*, 82 [134–5]).

must now be acknowledged as partial and sometimes erroneous.[84] The universal truth of the Christian gospel must still be affirmed, but, reflecting Schillebeeckx's pessimistic anthropology, the Christian interpretation of this universal truth must be relativized.[85]

It is significant for this discussion that Schillebeeckx's engagement with ideology critiques led him to reject attempts, such as that of Radical Orthodoxy, which sought to devise a renewed theology in order to successfully overcome the problems of Christendom imperialism.[86] Receiving ideology critique as a criticism of Christianity's imperialist past also means acknowledging the impairment of the theological vision at present. Although Christian theology can legitimately draw upon resources from the past tradition, a purely speculative theology tends to forget that these past insights have not been accompanied by a concrete liberating practice. Schillebeeckx's argument suggests that the sinful shortcomings of theologians from the past cannot be separated from their theologies in such a way that contemporary theologians could draw upon traditional texts as though these coincided with the truth about reality. This means that Schillebeeckx understands all of Christian theology to be entangled in sin to some extent. This sin is not overcome through constructing an ideal which resolves the impasses and problems of the contemporary situation.

Theology's entanglement in sin is solely overcome by the superior power of God's grace as it forgives theology at present. Faith in the reality of God's forgiving mercy should help theologians to admit their own, as well as their ancestors' errors, and to trust in the superior power of God's grace, despite these failures.[87] Schillebeeckx's reception of ideology critique does not result in an abandonment of his theology, but it refines his combination of a grace optimism with a pessimistic anthropology: God's grace is sufficiently powerful to persist, despite theological distortions. 'The power to realise this *humanum* and to bring about an individual and collective peace is reserved for God, the power of love.'[88] Ideology critique helped Schillebeeckx to see more clearly that Christian theologians should not exempt themselves from their own understanding of human sinfulness, erroneously siding with God's unique power to overcome human sin.

84. Schillebeeckx, *Church*, 186 [188–9]. Schillebeeckx laments the church's 'obsession with being right'.

85. Schillebeeckx, *Christ*, 66 [79].

86. Schillebeeckx, 'The New Critical Theory and Theological Hermeneutics', *The Understanding of Faith*, 125 [142–3].

87. Schillebeeckx, *Theologisch geloofsverstaan anno 1983*, 18–19; Schillebeeckx, 'The New Critical Theory and Theological Hermeneutics', *The Understanding of Faith*, 122 [139–40].

88. Schillebeeckx, 'Correlation between Human Question and Christian Answer', *The Understanding of Faith*, 81 [92-93].

b) *Merciful Distancing from Ideology Critique: Theology's Distinct God-Centredness*

This, then, also shows how Schillebeeckx's theology remains distinct from atheist ideology critique: Schillebeeckx grounds faith in a better future theologically, whereas ideology critique does so anthropologically. Schillebeeckx's combination of an optimistic ontology with a pessimistic anthropology is evidenced when he stresses that a Christian conception of freedom is not based on trust in human capacities. Quite the contrary, the human liability to failure renders any hope placed in a purely human redemption of the world impossible.[89] Christian hope rests on the faith that humans are accepted by God despite their sin.[90] Humans are not so much free by their own strength, as they are free due to God's forgiveness, which continuously draws them away from self-enclosure towards the realization of new possibilities. Consequently, theology's political contributions to post-Christendom societies should not be limited to humanly realizable projects.[91] Instead, Christian theology must direct its attention to the impossible as it is mediated in surprising ways in the public sphere.[92] From Schillebeeckx's Christian theological perspective, grace is not always realized in planned political projects, but it arrives as the entirely new and previously inconceivable, sometimes in spite of that which was humanly planned.

Some interpret Schillebeeckx's theologically motivated engagement with ideology critique as a critique of atheism, inasmuch as the human devotion to secular liberation is only meaningful and fully accounted for where the superior power of grace over evil is acknowledged.[93] Schillebeeckx indeed argues that Christian theology is able to explain that humanity's continuous trust in the superior power of goodness, also evidenced in non-Christian political engagement ultimately makes sense on the basis that grace has overcome all evil at Christ's Resurrection.[94]

89. Schillebeeckx, *Jesus*, 582 [620-621]; Schillebeeckx, 'Correlation between Human Question and Christian Answer', *The Understanding of Faith*, 81 [92–3].

90. Schillebeeckx, *Church*, 130 [131–2].

91. Schillebeeckx, 'Church, Magisterium and Politics', *God the Future of Man*, 97 [160–1].

92. Schillebeeckx, 'The New Critical Theory and Theological Hermeneutics', *The Understanding of Faith*, 129–31 [147–50]. Schillebeeckx here associates ideology critique with the Pelagian error of assuming that humankind can redeem itself.

93. Boeve, 'The Enduring Significance and Relevance of Edward Schillebeeckx?', in *Edward Schillebeeckx and Contemporary Theology*, 12. See also Hilkert, 'Grace-Optimism': *Spirituality Today* 43 (1991): 220–39, for an earlier argument that, without the perspective of faith, Schillebeeckx did not see any hope for the future of humanity. This insight is still relevant for contemporary public theological discussions insofar as Jeffrey Stout has been criticized precisely for not sufficiently accounting for his optimism regarding the achievement of better democracies (Cornel West, 'Pragmatism and Democracy: Assessing Jeffrey Stout's *Democracy and Tradition*', *Journal of the American Academy of Religion* 78 (2010), ed. Jason Springs: 418).

94. Schillebeeckx, 'Secularization and Christian Belief in God', *God the Future of Man*, 46 [75–6]; Schillebeeckx, *Interim Report*, 51 [60–1]; Schillebeeckx, *Jesus*, 601–2 [638–41];

However, Schillebeeckx ends his engagement with ideology critique, not on the note of criticizing the shortcomings of a purely atheistic outlook, but by way of reminding the church that everyone who chooses goodness over evil can be regarded as already implicitly affirming the reality of redemption.[95] He appreciates that, in spite of all evidence to the contrary, these 'people, …, refuse to be shaken in their conviction that it is not evil but goodness which has the last word.'[96] Significantly, Schillebeeckx appreciates that atheism's seemingly unaccounted trust in the meaningfulness of good actions mediates the superior power of God's grace over evil.[97] Consequently, Schillebeeckx, unlike Radical Orthodox thinkers, does not argue that secular ontologies fail to make consistent sense of reality. Instead, he makes the positive claim that theology's overarching view of the positivity of reality frees Christians from despair, for they know that all evil that is encountered will not ultimately last.[98]

5.4 Receiving Contextual Mediations of Grace: Restoring the Theological Vision

Thus far, I have presented Schillebeeckx's hermeneutic of God's merciful forgiveness as an alternative proposal to an adequate update of Schillebeeckx's engagement

---

Schillebeeckx, 'Correlation between Human Question and Christian Answer', *The Understanding of Faith*, 86 [98–9]; Schillebeeckx, *Theologisch geloofsverstaan anno 1983*, 20; Schillebeeckx, *Christ*, 795 [799].

95. Schillebeeckx, 'Secularization and Christian Belief in God', *God the Future of Man*, 45 [73–4]; Schillebeeckx, 'Correlation between Human Question and Christian Answer', *The Understanding of Faith*, 84 [96–7]. As Lieven Boeve stresses, in contradistinction to Tillich's correlational method, Schillebeeckx does not understand the Christian revelation as a solution of the meaninglessness of human life, but as meaningfulness of Christianity that must be correlated with that which is already meaningful in secularity (Boeve, 'Experience According to Edward Schillebeeckx', in *Divinising Experience*, 203–4).

96. Schillebeeckx, 'Secularization and Christian Belief in God', *God the Future of Man*, 45 [73–4]; Schillebeeckx, 'Correlation between Human Question and Christian Answer', *The Understanding of Faith*, 85–6 [96–9], Schillebeeckx, *Christ*, 787–8; 819–20 [791; 824].

97. Schillebeeckx, *Church*, 5–6 [5–7]; Schillebeeckx, 'Church, Magisterium and Politics', *God the Future of Man*, 95 [157–8]; Schillebeeckx, 'Theological Criteria', *The Understanding of Faith*, 58 [64–5]. For a succinct presentation of Schillebeeckx's theological appreciation of non-Christian humanism, see Erik Borgman, 'Deus humanissimus: Christelijk geloof als excessief humanisme bij Edward Schillebeeckx', in *Humanisme en Religie: Controverses, Bruggen, Perspectieven*, eds Joachim Duyndam, Marcel Poorthuis, and Theo de Wit (Delft: Eburon, 2005), 229–46.

98. Schillebeeckx, *Church*, 130 [131–2]. Schillebeeckx claims that the eschaton is exclusively positive, and that all that which remains evil will simply vanish, for God alone will have the last word (137).

with atheism. Importantly, Schillebeeckx was the only theologian introduced in this book who was able to confess the impairment of theology's own vision, which, as I will argue in the following section, renders him more hesitant than others to advocate Christian theology as being best able to solve contemporary political problems. This exposition of how Schillebeeckx modified his response to the question of theology's political role in post-Christendom societies will then pave the way for my application of Schillebeeckx's hermeneutics of mercy in response to contemporary political questions.

a) Recognizing Grace in Unexpected Places: Re-appreciating the Cruciformity of Grace

If we ask how Schillebeeckx modified his response to the question concerning theology's political role in post-Christendom societies, in accordance with the grace that he perceived to be mediated in the atheist ideology critiques of his day, then this modification presents Schillebeeckx's introduction of a second reason as to why Christian theologians cannot promise to solve political problems better than non-Christian philosophers. The first reason concerned the superabundant reality of redemption, which can never be captured exhaustively by theological concepts. The notion of the implicit intuition allowed Schillebeeckx to conceive of a noetic knowledge of the concrete reality of redemption, which always surpasses the human conceptual grasp of reality. The continuous reorientation towards one's external environment serves to continuously expand upon and correct the theological understanding of the reality of redemption. On this basis, Christian theologians would have to admit that non-theological concepts and world views could equally, but differently, be able to give expression to the same abundant reality of redemption, which explains why their political projects could be equally good as Christian theological ones.[99]

Receiving the theological significance of ideology critique, this argument is now being complexified, insofar as Schillebeeckx must admit, on the one hand, that theological statements, just as well as any other, could also deviate from the superabundant truth about reality.[100] On the other hand, he also admits that

---

99. For an explanation of how Schillebeeckx's endeavour, of deciphering the way in which God's grace is present in his surrounding context, relates to his metaphysics of the implicit intuition, and of how this is different from Milbank's position, see Stephan van Erp, 'Implicit Faith: Philosophical Theology after Schillebeeckx', in *Edward Schillebeeckx and Contemporary Theology*, 209–23.

100. In this sense, I agree with Philip Kennedy who denies that Schillebeeckx's later theology fundamentally breaks from his earlier thought, arguing that just as Schillebeeckx's early theological reception of De Petter's philosophy is based on his underlying conviction that God can be known through human experience, so is his later reception of Critical Theory (Kennedy, 'Continuity underlying Discontinuity', *New Blackfriars* 70 (1989): 275–6). However, I investigate how, on the basis of this persisting conviction, Schillebeeckx

empirical reality itself is shot through with sinful imperfections, which renders it impossible to prove on the basis of any noetic contact with one's environment that the reality we live in has been definitely redeemed in Christ.[101] And yet, contrary to his critics who argue that Schillebeeckx consequently abandoned this theological claim, concerning the Christian understanding of reality as redeemed, Schillebeeckx continues to interpret the world from the perspective of this conviction.[102]

Schillebeeckx now nuances his theology inasmuch as he modifies his notion of the implicit intuition of reality's abundant positivity in light of his atheist contemporaries' heightened attention to all evil in the world. Using the notion of the negative contrast experience, he now argues that the superior power of grace over all evil is not only intuited through experiences of meaning and goodness, but that the final victory of grace can also be anticipated in the confrontation with suffering and evil.[103] Christian theologians are now called upon to discern God's offer of grace not in spite of, but in the fragmentary realization of goodness amid evil.[104] His contemporary atheists' pessimism has, thus, helped Schillebeeckx to pay heightened attention to the theological truth of the cruciformity of the reality of redemption, which might have been downplayed in his earlier thought.[105]

Thus, for Schillebeeckx, Christian theologians bear witness to the reality of redemption, not by seeing how all evil can be overcome by Christian theology in a Radical Orthodox manner, or how societal problems are being solved by Christian theology *pace* public theology and Kathryn Tanner, but through sharpening their perception of the reality of redemption even when it appears in no obvious manner.[106] Accordingly, whereas Radical Orthodox authors argue that the

modified his theology in accordance with the new experience of God to which Critical Theory pointed him.

101. Schillebeeckx, *Church*, 5 [5–6]; Schillebeeckx, 'Secularization and Christian Belief in God', *God the Future of Man*, 45–6 [73–6]; Schillebeeckx, *Interim Report*, 5 [5–6]; Schillebeeckx, *Christ*, 774–5 [777]. This understanding that secular experiences of reality can only be interpreted as referring to Christianity if interpreted from the perspective of Christian theology, means that those critics who claim that Schillebeeckx assumes that there is a secular experience which would compel people to believe in Christianity are actually mistaken (Antoon Vergote, 'Ervaringsgeloof and geloofservaring', *Streven* 52 (1985): 891–903, cit. by Boeve, 'Experience According to Edward Schillebeeckx', in *Divinising Experience*, 219, who criticizes Vergote for the same reason, 221).

102. Schillebeeckx, *Jesus*, 570 [608]. More precisely, Schillebeeckx rejects anthropological foundations for theology. This opposition to purely inductive reasoning from nature to God is the point at which Schillebeeckx displays a Thomist sense of fideism (Kennedy, 'Continuity underlying Discontinuity', *New Blackfriars* 70 (1989): 266).

103. Schillebeeckx, *Jesus*, 7 [23–4].

104. Schillebeeckx, *Church*, 94; 175 [96–7; 176–7].

105. Ibid., 5 [5–6].

106. Schillebeeckx, *Theologisch geloofsverstaan anno 1983*, 20.

Christian ontology can further expand upon or complete the world's redemption, and promise a better future than any atheist social order, Schillebeeckx abstains from these promises, because due to human sin the Christian vision of the whole of reality also remains fragmentary.[107] On the one hand, the acknowledgement that history is interwoven with sinful elements means that Christian theologians can only see the reality of redemption beneath sin, but they cannot rationally formulate how everything is interconnected into one meaningful whole. On the other hand, this inability can be explained in relation to theology's own entanglement in sin, which is why the theological resources from the past are not entirely reliable in paving the way into a better future. Redemption can, thus, only be promised insofar as grace is shown to be mediated *in* the remaining evil in the world and insofar as people believe that this grace will win in the end.[108]

At this point, Schillebeeckx then conceives of a plurality of positive political projects to overcome the remaining evil in the world.[109] He suggests that a communal discussion about the best political path to overcome the evil should commence once a plurality of groups agrees that a certain situation is problematic. Christian theologians must not be too concerned about presenting their own solution as being superior to others.[110] Instead, Christian theologians must strike the right balance between witnessing to God as sole ruler of reality and to the faith that humankind freely participates in this rule.[111] Christian theologians must show that humans are the active subjects of history in their public engagement, but they should not be the dictators who think that they have grasped the truth about the world and humankind.[112] The positive solution chosen should be acknowledged

107. Schillebeeckx, 'Correlation between Human Question and Christian Answer', *The Understanding of Faith*, 83 [95–6]. Hilkert relates Schillebeeckx's break with De Petter's metaphysics in *Jesus* to Schillebeeckx's acknowledgement of the suffering and meaninglessness in the world, which led him to question the proposition of a meaningful whole (Mary Catherine Hilkert, 'St. Thomas and the appeal to experience: A response to Kenneth L. Schmitz', *CTSA Proceedings* 47 (1992): 23–4).

108. Schillebeeckx, 'The New Critical Theory and Theological Hermeneutics', *The Understanding of Faith*, 117 [133–4].

109. Schillebeeckx, 'Theological Criteria', *The Understanding of Faith*, 58 [64–5].

110. This restraint, regarding admitting the superior insight into the concrete path that should be taken, has been criticized (Hill, 'Schillebeeckx's New Look at Secularity', *The Thomist*, 168–9). Hill claims that Schillebeeckx focuses too much on negative protest in order to prevent ideological distortions, and suggests that faith in the Resurrection would imply that more concrete positive insights into the divine reality must be acknowledged. However, my reading challenges Hill's insofar as I interpret Schillebeeckx as suggesting that due to the Resurrection, all positive solutions to suffering must be acknowledged as grace. The problem for Christian theology is not the lack of positive insights, but the acknowledgement that there is an abundance of equally positive insights.

111. Schillebeeckx, *Christ*, 784–5 [788].

112. Ibid.

to be decisive for the course of a society's future, but it must not be dictated by Christian theology.

b) *The Contemporary Relevance of Schillebeeckx's Position: Receptive Openness Instead of Promising Solutions*

If we ask how we might retrieve Schillebeeckx's hermeneutics of mercy for contemporary theology, I first summarize the distinctiveness of Schillebeeckx's theology in comparison to all of the others. Most importantly, public theologians, as well as Kathryn Tanner and Radical Orthodoxy, all associate theology's political relevance with theological attempts to solve the surrounding society's problems. Yoder rejects this approach in order to respect society's alleged freedom to reject Christ, that is, to be sinful. All of the theologians introduced have, thus, shared a reliance on Christianity's surrounding societies to be relatively unredeemed in order to distinguish theology from atheist positions, and to highlight theology's distinct political relevance with reference to its ability to solve problems in the surrounding society or to further the world's redemption, even while the surrounding society continues to reject these efforts. Schillebeeckx showed a different way of theologically informed political engagement, summarized in his warning not to follow the present tides of a 'cultural pessimism'.[113] If public theology, post-liberal Protestant theologies and Radical Orthodoxy associate theology's political relevance with Christianity's task to further realizing the world's redemption, they are likely to rely on the world's problematic state in order for theology to be politically relevant.

To reiterate Graham Ward's pessimism, mentioned previously in Chapter 2: 'We can all see that the world is fucked up but we're all still hoping for something that can stop it from being so fucked up.'[114] By stressing theology's superior role in overcoming the world's problems even more, Milbank similarly expresses his pessimism in the reactive hope 'that in the current century this [the Catholic] project will be able to recover and rethink the Western tradition in a way that could even (in the face of increasing global catastrophe) prove universally pervasive.'[115] For Ward and Milbank alike, discontent with the present functions as something fundamental for the theologically informed promise of deliverance. With Schillebeeckx, we could ask whether it is really as self-evident that the world is primarily marked by problems. The particular Christian interpretation of reality could, instead, suggest learning anew to perceive the reality of redemption, amid and underneath all political problems.[116] The focus on this realized redemption

---

113. Ibid., 817–18 [822].

114. Warlick, 'An Interview with Graham Ward', *Radical Orthodoxy: Theology, Philosophy, Politics* Vol. 1 (2012): 337.

115. John Milbank, 'Foreword', in Antonio López, *Gift and the Unity of Being* (Eugene, OR: Cascade Books, 2014), xiv.

116. Schillebeeckx, *Christ*, 817–18 [822].

prevents Christian hope from becoming utopian on the one hand, and, it prevents theology from becoming circular in the sense of inventing problems in society that it then promises to solve, on the other. This is not to suggest that there are not enough political problems in the world, but Schillebeeckx reminds us that theologians should trust that the future will be a better place only if we first notice 'the log in our own eye before we see the speck in the eyes of our neighbours' (Mt. 7:3). Christian theology's real political problem might be even more profound than public or Radical Orthodox theologians dare to acknowledge, namely, that we cannot even see what precisely is problematic in the contemporary post-Christendom context. Christian theology's specific contribution might not so much be to detect problems, which atheists do not see, but to rely on atheists' detection of problems as well as their proposed solutions, and to discern signs of redemption in their activity.[117] Christians are invited to respond to these signs of redemption by collaborating with them, and by entering or strengthening through them their prayerful relationship to God.

It is important to consider that Schillebeeckx has once more been criticized for being too naively optimistic in this regard, and updating Schillebeeckx's theology has been proposed for the contemporary context once more through a correction of this shortcoming. Schillebeeckx's trust that the surrounding society will react against evil has been criticized for insufficiently considering that social sin can blur a whole culture's vision of evil and render it apathetic.[118] The adequate update proposed of Schillebeeckx's theology would, then, once more point in the direction of Radical Orthodoxy, criticizing the shortcomings of the surrounding culture and assigning to theology the task of opening up everyone's eyes to the miserable state of the world. My interpretation of Schillebeeckx's theology points in a different direction: if contemporary society's vision is too blurred to recognize evil, Christian theologians should not exempt themselves from this impairment.

If there is, at present, a certain observable apathy regarding political engagement for a better future, who then tells us that this is the result of indifference? Schillebeeckx's interpretation of atheism would rather suggest that atheism's cultural pessimism might have led to apathy because people have despaired over

---

117. It might be objected that the contemporary context significantly differs from Schillebeeckx's own insofar as some forms of atheism have become more oppressive and intolerant with regard to the existence of any faith tradition (Stephan van Erp, 'Incarnational Theology – Systematic Theology After Edward Schillebeeckx', in *Edward Schillebeeckx: Impulse für Theologien im 21. Jahrhundert – Impetus Towards Theologies in the 21st Century*, eds Thomas Eggensperger, Ulrich Engel and Angel F. Méndez Montoya (Ostfildern: Matthias Grünewaldverlag, 2008), 64). My interpretation of Schillebeeckx suggests, however, that this should not lead Christian theologians to think about how to overcome the shortcomings of contemporary atheism, but to look more closely in order to perceive the grace mediated by this atheism, despite its shortcomings, and to reformulate Christian theology accordingly.

118. Rodenborn, *Hope in Action*, 321–4.

the evil which, at times, seems overpowering, not because they are indifferent to it. Christian theology's role is not to overcome atheism's political apathy, but to receive this apathy as an offer of God's forgiveness for the church. Theologians could learn that, due to their overall optimistic Christian outlook, they might have continuously proposed solutions to evils when atheists might have seen more clearly, and acknowledged more honestly, that the negativity of evil cannot be resolved. The contemporary political apathy observed should then not be 'healed' by an overzealous Christian theology, but Christians should learn from this apathy to face evil in all its gravity and negativity. And yet, Christian theologians should maintain a critical distance to the atheist outlook precisely in not despairing, but in interpreting the atheist despair over evil itself as a mediation of God's mercy towards Christianity and, as such, as a sign of hope. Christian theologians should trust that this present state of political apathy is not the last word about reality, and is not determinative for a perpetual degradation of West European societies' political fate. Again, Christians could be assured that neither the church's past sin of overzealous activity and its downplaying of the seriousness of evil, nor the apathy of certain contemporaries in the face of evil, place an obstacle to enter a prayerful relationship with God. One's own alliance with evil can be lamented to God, and one can trust that, at an appropriate time, one's eyes will be opened to recognize the emergence of a solution to Christianity's problematic engagement with evil.

Yet, what would such a public theological approach imply more concretely? Let us consider the current political disputes in Europe concerning the degree of hospitality with which refugees should be welcomed. Contemporary theologians might be inclined to side with all those who favour open borders and engage in rendering Europe more hospitable. This is laudable and Christian theologians should indeed not discard the grace that is clearly mediated by all those who welcome those in need. Christians can thank those who are hospitable, and collaborate with them. They can thank God for the encounters, the new relationships between hosts and refugees that are being created in this situation. These relationships can be regarded as a foreshadowing of the eschatological feast in the contemporary context. Christians should not underestimate how wonderful it is that this world allows for encounters and friendships even among people who have been born far apart from each other.

But, how to respond to those who refuse any hospitality, and who would like to close Europe's borders in order to shield themselves against any influence from non-European cultures? Instead of one-sidedly accusing them for being sinful and evil, Christian theologians could interpret their refusal to join the community of hosts and refugees as a tragic reminder that we are not yet celebrating the eschatological feast. Their closedness interrupts any feasting at present with the dreadful anticipation of the judgement day. This does not mean that those who refuse to offer hospitality will be eternally condemned, but that their not joining the celebratory community at present calls the redemption of this very community into question – their not joining does not remain external to the community of the feasting. There is not a community of the redeemed that exists apart from those individuals who remain outside. Christians must ask themselves in how far the existing community is exclusive of some. There is no joyful rest for the Christian, no self-congratulation, and no condemnation of others, until all of humankind lives in an all-embracing community, including also those who refuse any hospitality to refugees, all those who do not want to be united with the whole of the human race.

This means that Christian theologians cannot apologetically advocate their reconciliatory stance, and their aspiration towards unity, as one that should be adopted by everyone involved in the current disputes about European immigration. This outlook should not be mistaken to suggest that those who refuse to enter the community between Europeans and refugees are the political problem and that Christianity's striving towards unity can be presented as the solution. Theologians should confess that, if parts of a society want to close their countries' borders, it would be simplistic to understand these people as being entirely sinful, as problems that need to be overcome, and those in favour of an open border policy as entirely graced and as already possessing the solution that needs to be adopted by everyone. Instead, theologians should confess that the entire society is implicated in the problem that leads some to refuse any hospitality towards refugees. Christian theologians cannot promise to redeem the world from its present disharmony, because the theologian lives in the middle of the disharmony, not besides it. Being themselves entangled in the sinfulness of the conflict, theologians would have to confess that they cannot see any resolution. Only if all are united in one community, can we all see clearly the solution to the current political problem. In this sense, the refusal of some to join casts a dark shadow on any ecclesial celebration at the moment. The celebration of community is at the same time also the occasion to mourn all those who refuse to join the celebration. The post-Christendom context's disunities remind the church that there is no fulfilled joy before the eschatological feast, as any anticipatory joy in a disharmonious world is someone else's misery. At the moment, from their position in the conflict, Christian theologians should learn to see a surplus of grace in conflicting outlooks, and heal with it our own impaired vision. At the same time, theologians should turn to the church and investigate the extent to which the church is itself part of the problem that has led some contemporaries to be so anxious about the supposed dangers of an open border policy, perhaps reminding the church of how deeply it has failed to unite humankind in the past.

Moreover, the church should be welcoming to those presently wounded. It must somehow strive to build a community even with those who refuse community, without demanding them to abandon their refusal prior to the collaborative task. Theologians should admit that they cannot understand those people's political opinions on a purely conceptual level before they have accompanied them in their concrete lives. Treading the path to a more integral community, inclusive of all, Christians should spend some time with those people who refuse community and discern how far they, even in their overall mistaken refusal of entering the community between hosts and refugees, mediate a grace that we would not have otherwise seen. Instead of demanding those people to abandon their hurts, their fears and their rage for the sake of a community that they find little attractive, Christians should seek to understand these people's anxieties, and should re-form the existing community with them in such a way that the wounds of the excluded can be assuaged.

Conclusion

If my explanation of Schillebeeckx's Christology, from the previous chapter, might still have been close to presenting Schillebeeckx's openness to non-Christian positions as, universally, the best solution for the peaceful coexistence of a pluralist society, I have highlighted in this chapter that Schillebeeckx's position is always already the response to a specific Christian theological mistake or one-sidedness in the past that can be corrected by way of attending to the way in which God's forgiveness is mediated in the surrounding context. Schillebeeckx's hermeneutic of mercy cannot be universalized, because it is the result of the specific dialogue between a Christian theologian and Christianity's critics and is, thus, aimed at overcoming theological problems that might not be present in other positions. Yet, this merciful engagement with the surrounding society shows forth an alternative public theological sensibility, one that is more hesitant to offer theological solutions to political problems. Public theologians are challenged to learn to recognize how God's grace is mediated in the surrounding society's politics, and discern how they reveal the church's sinful shortcomings as well as how they nourish new hope that these might not ultimately foreclose a better future. This is not to distinguish Christianity and atheism as two entirely self-enclosed systems, each with their own problems. Christianity's problems will exhibit similarities with atheism's problems. However, if Christian theologians trust that sin is overcome through God's forgiveness, and not by focusing on the other's failures, but by showing to them the best version of themselves, then it is not the theologian's duty to point out atheism's problems before having removed the log in our own eye.

CONCLUSION

If we ask how political theology can contribute to the enhancement of the political life of post-Christendom societies, contemporary theologians will nearly unanimously respond by promising to solve currently existing political problems. Not many might be inclined to object to what appears as such a laudable willingness to enhance the public sphere through solving its problems with theological resources. Yet, I have called into question the very starting point of such an endeavour. Whereas these heroic defenders of the contemporary relevance of Christian theology begin their political thinking with identifying what is lacking or what is problematic in their surroundings, I have revisited Edward Schillebeeckx's Christology in order to ask whether it might not just as well be possible to build political theology more firmly on the graces that already surround us. This is not to deny the reality of political problems at present, but, having learnt the Radical Orthodox lesson, it is an invitation to look at these problems from a different perspective, calling into question the unspoken consensus that describing certain phenomena as problematic is *all* that can be said about them.

Yet, are we not, as Christians, called to imitate, complete or exceed Christ's work of redemption – models which all translate Christ's redemptive work into the Christian task of solving contemporary political problems?, some Christians might be inclined to ask. Underneath this consensus of associating the political implications of the Christian faith in Christ's redemption of the world, with an ethical duty to imitate Christ, I have found the alternative to uphold Christ as unique redeemer of the world, whose work of redemption no human being yet has been able to fully enjoy. Acknowledging Christ as unique redeemer allows Christian theologians to commence their political thinking with grace, but, in the contemporary post-Christendom context, it also calls on us to confess that we are primarily sinful beneficiaries of graces which are most often mediated in spite of ourselves.

When associating political theology with the task of solving also a post-Christendom society's problems, theologians will tend to interpret as a hindrance to their undertaking any secularist opposition to explicitly Christian contributions to public politics. This opposition is then identified as a further problem for political theology, in need of an apologetic solution. But, precisely, in their very eagerness to defend Christian theology's political relevance apologetically, these contemporary public and Radical Orthodox theologians might be prematurely rejecting the grace God offers. A political theology built on grace does not need to interpret such strong secularist opposition to theologically motivated political engagement as a threat. Instead, this opposition can be welcomed as a reminder of Christianity's Christendom past, in which Christians intruded into different cultures, promising redemption and, thus, providing solutions to problems that these cultures might never have dreamed of.

In other words, when suggesting that theology's political role in post-Christendom societies consists in solving the entire society's political problems, those theological heroes risk overlooking the problem that Christian theology itself could present to secular politics. An acknowledgement of being ourselves in the very midst of the problems we so sincerely hope to overcome, might invite us Christian theologians, living and working in post-Christendom contexts, to confess that our entanglement in sin blinds our theological vision of a commendable solution. The primary task of contemporary political theology would, then, consist of discerning God's forgiveness offered to theology in the contemporary context. At this moment in history, we might be well advised to confess that, looking back at a long and often painful history of Christendom, many of us still suffer from the long-lasting effects of Christianity's sinful disobedience to God during its imperialist past, which tore our societies apart. How do we reconcile these societies? How do we show that our Christian faith convinces us that we still belong to our brothers and sisters who have left the church?

I do not wish to advocate Schillebeeckx's merciful approach to atheism, and my political theology of forgiving grace built upon it, as being the best remedy to reconciling a pluralist society that seems, at times, to be more marked by its many disputes and conflicts than by its harmony and peace. I cannot promise that reading one's contemporary situation through a hermeneutics of mercy will reconcile conflicting positions. I simply suggest to my Christian readers that they may reconsider the graces they have received and thank God and the ones who mediated them, before they lament about all that which they are still lacking. I appeal to them to sharpen their sights in order to see the grace mediated by another person's outlook, which they might otherwise simply reject as being entirely mistaken. What I offer up for thought is that, perhaps, it is time for Christian theologians to confess publicly that the best we can do is look around for signs of God's forgiveness as it is offered to us at present, and thereby receive our non-Christian contemporaries' insights as welcome signs of hope. When accepting this forgiveness, Christian theologians might, one day, be reconciled with God and with the surrounding society.

BIBLIOGRAPHY

Albinus, Lars, 'Radical Orthodoxy and Post-Structuralism: An Unholy Alliance', *Neue Zeitschrift für Systematische Theologie und Religionsphilosophie* 51 (2009): 340–54.

Ayres, Lewis, 'Review of Theology and Social Theory: Beyond Secular Reason, by John Milbank', *Scottish Journal of Theology* 45 (1992): 125–26.

Baker, Anthony D., 'Convenient Redemption: A Participatory Account of the Atonement', *Modern Theology* 30 (2014): 96–113.

Barber, Daniel, 'The Particularity of Jesus and the Time of the Kingdom: Philosophy and Theology in Yoder', *Modern Theology* 23 (2007): 63–89.

Barbieri Jr., William A., 'Introduction', in *At the Limits of the Secular: Reflections on Faith and Public Life*, ed. William A. Barbieri Jr. (Grand Rapids, MI: Eerdmans, 2014), 1–25.

Barbieri Jr., William A, 'The Post-Secular Problematic', in *At the Limits of the Secular: Reflections on Faith and Public Life*, ed. William A. Barbieri Jr. (Grand Rapids, MI: Eerdmans, 2014), 129–61.

Barthes, Roland, *Mythologies*, translated by Annette Lavers (London: Vintage Books, 2000).

Bauer, Christian, 'Heiligkeit des Profanen? Spuren der "école Chenu-Schillebeeckx" (H. de Lubac) auf dem Zweiten Vatikanum', in *Edward Schillebeeckx: Impulse für Theologien im 21. Jahrhundert – Impetus Towards Theologies in the 21st Century*, ed. Thomas Eggensperger, Ulrich Engel and Angel F. Méndez Montoya (Ostfildern: Matthias Grünewaldverlag, 2008), 67–83.

Bauerschmidt, Frederick Christian, 'The Word Made Speculative? John Milbank's Christological Poetics', *Modern Theology* 15 (1999): 417–32.

Bender, Kimlyn J., 'Christ, Creation and the Drama of Redemption: "The Play's the Thing."', *Scottish Journal of Theology* 62 (2009): 149–74.

Bergin, Helen, 'The Death of Jesus and its Impact on God – Jürgen Moltmann and Edward Schillebeeckx', *The Irish Theological Quarterly* 52 (1986): 193–211.

Berkhof, Hendrikus, *Christ and the Powers* (Scottdale, PA: Herald, 1962).

Bertschmann, Dorothea, 'The Rule of Christ and Human Politics – Two Proposals: A Comparison of the Political Theology of Oliver O'Donovan and John Howard Yoder', *The Heythrop Journal* LVI (2015): 424–40.

Boeve, Lieven, 'The Sacramental Interruption of Rituals of Life', *The Heythrop Journal* XLIV (2003): 401–17.

Boeve, Lieven, 'Experience According to Edward Schillebeeckx: The Driving Force of Faith and Theology', in *Divinising Experience: Essays in the History of Religious Experience from Origen to Ricoeur*, ed. Lieven Boeve and Laurence P. Hemming (Leuven: Peeters, 2004), 199–225.

Boeve, Lieven, 'Zeg nooit meer correlatie. Over christelijke traditie, actuele context en onderbreking', *Collationes. Vlaams Tijdschrift voor Theologie en Pastoraal* 34 (2004): 193–219.

Boeve, Lieven, 'Religion after Detraditionalization: Christian Faith in a Post-Secular Europe', *Irish Theological Quarterly* 70 (2005): 99–122.

Boeve, Lieven, *God Interrupts History. Theology in a Time of Upheaval* (New York and London: The Continuum International Publishing Group, 2007).

Boeve, Lieven, 'Introduction: The Enduring Significance and Relevance of Edward Schillebeeckx? Introducing the State of the Question in Medias Res', in *Edward Schillebeeckx and Contemporary Theology*, ed. Lieven Boeve, Frederiek Depoortere and Stephan van Erp (London: T&T Clark, 2010), 1–24.

Borgman, Erik, 'Deus humanissimus: Christelijk geloof als excessief humanisme bij Edward Schillebeeckx', in *Humanisme en Religie: Controverses, Bruggen, Perspectieven*, ed. Joachim Duyndam, Marcel Poorthuis and Theo de Wit (Delft: Eburon, 2005), 229–46.

Borgman, Erik, *Edward Schillebeeckx: A Theologian in His History*, translated by John Bowden (London: Bloomsbury T&T Clark, 2006).

Borgman, Erik, 'als het ware een sacrament – Naar een theologische visie op de reëel bestaande kerk', in *Trouw an Gods toekomst – De blijvende betekenis van Edward Schillebeeckx*, ed. Stephan van Erp, Tijdschrift voor Theologie (2010), 123–143.

Borgman, Erik, 'Retrieving God's Contemporary Presence: The Future of Edward Schillebeeckx's Theology of Culture', in *Edward Schillebeeckx and Contemporary Theology*, ed. Lieven Boeve, Frederiek Depoortere, and Stephan van Erp (London: T&T Clark, 2010), 235–51.

Borgman, Erik, 'Alle dingen nieuw: Theologie uit genade', *Tijdschrift voor Theologie* 52 (2012): 201–25.

Borgman, Erik, 'Edward Schillebeeckx's Reflections on the Sacraments and the Future of Catholic Theology', in *Sacramentalizing Human History: In Honour of Edward Schillebeeckx (1914-2009)*, ed. Erik Borgman, Paul D. Murray and Andrés Torres Queiruga (London: SCM Press, Concilium, 2012), 13–24.

Bourne, Richard, 'Witness, Democracy and Civil Society: Reflections on John Howard Yoder's Exilic Ecclesiology', *Ecclesiology* 3, no. 2 (2007): 195–213.

Breitenberg Jr., Harold E., 'What Is Public Theology?' in *Public Theology for a Global Society: Essays in Honor of Max L. Stackhouse*, ed. Deirdre Hainsworth and Scott R. Paeth (Cambridge: William B. Eerdmans Publishing Company, 2010), 3–20.

Breyfogle, Todd, 'Is There Room for Political Philosophy in Postmodern Critical Augustinianism?' in *Deconstructing Radical Orthodoxy: Postmodern Theology, Rhetoric and Truth*, ed. Wayne J. Hankey and Douglas Hedley (Aldershot: Ashgate, 2005), 31–48.

Brown, Malcolm, Stephen Pattison and Graeme Smith, 'The Possibility of Citizen Theology: Public Theology After Christendom and the Enlightenment', *International Journal of Public Theology* 6 (2012): 183–204.

Buckley, James J., Review of *Christ the Key*, by Kathryn Tanner, *Modern Theology* 27 (2011): 698–701.

Burrus, Virginia, 'Radical Orthodoxy and the Heresiological Habit', in *Interpreting the Postmodern: Responses to 'Radical Orthodoxy'*, ed. Rosemary Radford Ruether and Marion Gau (London: T&T Clark, 2006), 36–55.

Carter, Craig A., *The Politics of the Cross: The Theology and Social Ethics of John Howard Yoder* (Grand Rapids, MI: Brazos Press, 2001).

Casarella, Peter, 'Public Reason and Intercultural Dialogue', in *At the Limits of the Secular: Reflections on Faith and Public Life*, ed. William A. Barbieri Jr. (Grand Rapids, MI: Eerdmans, 2014), 51–84.

Cavanaugh, William, T., 'Church', in *Blackwell Companion to Political Theology*, ed. Peter Scott and William T. Cavanaugh (Oxford: Blackwell Publishing 2004), 393–406.

Cavanaugh, William, T., 'The Invention of the Religious-Secular Distinction', in *At the Limits of the Secular: Reflections on Faith and Public Life*, ed. William A. Barbieri Jr. (Grand Rapids, MI: Eerdmans, 2014), 105–28.

Cavanaugh, William, T., 'Return of the Golden Calf: Economy, Idolatry, and Secularization since *Gaudium et spes*', *Theological Studies* 76 (2015): 698–717.

Chapman, Mark, 'The Common Good, Pluralism, and the Small Church', *Political Theology* 16 (2015): 61–77.

Clack, Beverley, 'Radical Orthodoxy and Feminist Philosophy of Religion', in *Interpreting the Postmodern: Responses to 'Radical Orthodoxy'*, ed. Rosemary Radford Ruether and Marion Gau (London: T&T Clark, 2006), 215–30.

Coakley, Sarah, 'Why Gift? Gift, gender and Trinitarian relations in Milbank and Tanner', *Scottish Journal of Theology* 61 (2008): 224–35.

Coles, Romand, 'Storied Others and Possibilities of *Caritas*: Milbank and Neo-Nietzschean Ethics', *Modern Theology* 8 (1992): 331–51.

Crisp, Oliver, *Revisioning Christology: Theology in the Reformed Tradition* (Farnham: Ashgate, 2011).

Davies, Oliver, 'Revelation and the Politics of Culture: A Critical Assessment of the Theology of John Milbank', in *Radical Orthodoxy? – A Catholic Enquiry*, ed. Laurence Paul Hemming (Aldershot: Ashgate, 2000), 112–25.

De Gruchy, John W., 'Public Theology as Christian Witness', *International Journal of Public Theology* 1 (2007): 26–41.

DeHart, Paul, 'On Being Heard but Not Seen', *Modern Theology* 26 (2010): 243–77.

DeHart, Paul, 'f (S) I/s: The Instance of Pattern, or Kathryn Tanner's Trinitarianism', in *The Gift of Theology: The Contribution of Kathryn Tanner*, ed. Rosemary P. Carbine and Hilda P. Koster (Minneapolis: Fortress Press, 2016), 29–55.

De Lubac, Henri, *A Brief Catechesis on Nature and Grace* (San Francisco: Ignatius Press, 1984).

De Lubac, Henri, 'The Total Meaning of Man and the World', *Communio* 35 (2008): 613–41.

Dengerink Chaplin, Adrienne, 'The Invisible and the Sublime: From Participation to Reconciliation', in *Radical Orthodoxy and the Reformed Tradition: Creation, Covenant, and Participation*, ed. James K. Smith and James H. Olthuis (Grand Rapids, MI: Baker Academic, 2005), 89–106.

Derksen, Kevin, 'Milbank and Violence: Against a Derridean Pacifism', in *The Gift of Difference: Radical Orthodoxy, Radical Reformation*, ed. Chris H. Huebner and Tripp York (Winnipeg, MB: CMU Press, 2010), 27–49.

Doak, Mary, 'The Politics of Radical Orthodoxy: A Catholic Critique', *Theological Studies* 68 (2007): 368–93.

Doerksen, Paul G., *Beyond Suspicion: Post-Christendom Protestant Political Theology in John Howard Yoder and Oliver O'Donovan* (Milton Keynes: Paternoster, 2009).

Duffy, Stephen J., *The Graced Horizon: Nature and Grace in Modern Catholic Thought* (Collegeville, MN: The Liturgical Press, 1992).

Dunn, David J., 'Radical Sophiology: Fr. Sergej Bulgakov and John Milbank on Augustine', *Studies in East European Thought* 64 (2012): 227–49.

Dupré, Louis, 'Experience and Interpretation: A Philosophical Reflection on Schillebeeckx' *Jesus* and *Christ*', *Theological Studies* 43, no. 1 (1982): 30–51.

East, Brad, 'An Undefensive Presence: The Mission and Identity of the Church in Kathryn Tanner and John Howard Yoder', *Scottish Journal of Theology* 68 (2015): 327–44.

Ford, David A., Review of *God and Creation in Christian Theology. Tyranny or Empowerment?*, by Kathryn Tanner, *Religious Studies* 26 (1990): 550–2.

Galvin, John P., 'The Death of Jesus in the Theology of Edward Schillebeeckx', *The Irish Theological Quarterly* (1983): 168–180.

Gardener, Lucy, 'Listening at the Threshold: Christology and the "Suspension of the Material,"' in *Radical Orthodoxy? - A Catholic Enquiry*, ed. Laurence P. Hemming (Aldershot: Ashgate, 2000), 126–46.

Gerber Koontz, Gayle, 'Confessional Theology in a Pluralistic Context: A Study of the Theological Ethics of H. Richard Niebuhr and John H. Yoder', unpublished doctoral dissertation (Boston University, 1985).

Godzieba, Anthony J., 'God, the Luxury of Our Lives: Schillebeeckx and the Argument', in *Edward Schillebeeckx and Contemporary Theology*, ed. Lieven Boeve, Frederiek Depoortere and Stephan van Erp (London: T&T Clark, 2010), 25–35.

Graham, Elaine L., 'Power, Knowledge and Authority in Public Theology', *International Journal of Public Theology* 1 (2007): 42–62.

Graham, Elaine L., 'Health, Wealth or Wisdom? Religion and the Paradox of Prosperity', *International Journal of Public Theology* 3 (2009): 5–23.

Graham, Elaine L., *Between a Rock and a Hard Place: Public Theology in a Post-Secular Age* (London: SCM Press, 2013).

Graham, Elaine L., 'The Unquiet Frontier: Tracing the Boundaries of Philosophy and Public Theology', *Political Theology* 16 (2015): 33–46.

Grimsrud, Ted, 'Jesus to Paul', in *John Howard Yoder: Radical Theologian*, ed. J. Denny Weaver (Eugene, OR: Cascade Books, 2014), 187–206.

Grumett, David, 'Radical Orthodoxy', *The Expository Times* 122, no. 6 (2011): 261–70.

Gunton, Colin, '"Until He Comes": Towards an Eschatology of Church Membership', *International Journal of Systematic Theology* 3 (2002): 187–200.

Habermas, Jürgen, 'Dialogue: Jürgen Habermas and Charles Taylor', in *The Power of Religion in the Public Sphere*, ed. Eduardo Mendieta and Jonathan Vanantwerpen (New York, Chichester and West Sussex: Columbia University Press, 2011), 60–9.

Hackett, Chris, 'Review Essay: What's the Use of a Skeleton Key for Christian Theology?: A Report on an Essential Problematic in Kathryn Tanner's *Christ the Key*', *Radical Orthodoxy: Theology, Philosophy, Politics* 2 (2014): 191–221.

Haight, Roger, *The Future of Christology* (New York and London: Bloomsbury, 2005).

Haight, Roger, 'Engagement met de wereld als zaak van God: Christologie & Postmoderniteit', *Tijdschrift voor Theologie* 50 (2010): 73–94.

Hainsworth, Deirdre and Scott R. Paeth, 'Introduction', in *Public Theology for a Global Society: Essays in Honor of Max L. Stackhouse*, ed. Deirdre Hainsworth and Scott R. Paeth (Cambridge: William B. Eerdmans Publishing Company, 2010), viii–xx.

Hankey, Wayne J., '*Theoria Versus Poesis*: Neoplatonism and Trinitarian Difference in Aquinas, John Milbank, Jean-Luc Marion and John Zizioulas', *Modern Theology* 15 (1999): 387–415.

Healy, Nicholas M., 'Practices and the New Ecclesiology: Misplaced Concreteness?' *International Journal of Systematic Theology* 5 (2003): 287–308.

Healy, Nicholas J., 'Henri de Lubac on Nature and Grace: A Note on Some Recent Contributions', *Communio* 35 (2008): 535–64.

Hedley, Douglas, Review of *Radical Orthodoxy. A New Theology*, by John Milbank, Catherine Pickstock and Graham Ward, *Journal of Theological Studies* 51 (2000): 405–8.

Hefling, Charles, 'Review Article Christologies and Philosophies', *Anglican Theological Review* 93, no. 4 (2011): 693–703.

Heilke, Thomas, 'Yoder's idea of Constantinianism: An Analytic Framework Toward Conversation', in *A Mind Patient and Untamed: Assessing John Howard Yoder's Contributions to Theology, Ethics, and Peacemaking*, ed. Ben C. Ollenburger and Gayle Gerber Koontz (Telford, PA: Cascadia Publishing House, 2004), 89–125.

Helmer, Christine, 'A Systematic Theological Theory of Truth in Kathryn Tanner's *Jesus, Humanity and the Trinity*', *Scottish Journal of Theology* 57 (2004): 203–20.

Hemming, Laurence P., 'Introduction: Radical Orthodoxy's Appeal to Catholic Scholarship', in *Radical Orthodoxy? - A Catholic Enquiry*, ed. Laurence P. Hemming (Aldershot: Ashgate, 2000), 3–19.

Hemming, Laurence P., 'What Catholic Theologians Have to Learn from Radical Orthodoxy: What Radical Orthodoxy Has to Learn from Catholic Theology', *Louvain Studies* 28 (2003): 232–9.

Hemming, Laurence P., '*Analogia non Entis sed Entitatis*: The Ontological Consequences of the Doctrine of Analogy', *International Journal of Systematic Theology* 6 (2004): 118–28.

Henreckson, David, P., 'Possessing Heaven in Our Head: A Reformed Reading of Incarnational Ascent in Kathryn Tanner', *Journal of Reformed Theology* 4 (2010): 171–84.

Hershberger, Nathan, 'Patience as Hermeneutical Practice: Christ, Church and Scripture in John Howard Yoder and Hans Frei', *Modern Theology* (2015): 547–72.

Higton, Mike, 'Review of *Radical Orthodoxy: A Critical Introduction*, by Steven Shakespeare', *International Journal of Systematic Theology* 12 (2010): 240–2.

Hilkert, Mary Catherine, '"Grace-Optimism": The Spirituality at the Heart of Schillebeeckx's Theology', *Spirituality Today* 43 (1991): 220–39, http://www.spiritualitytoday.org/spir2day/91433hilkert.html.

Hilkert, Mary Catherine, 'St. Thomas and the Appeal to Experience: A Response to Kenneth L. Schmitz', *CTSA Proceedings* 47 (1992): 21–5.

Hilkert, Mary Catherine, 'Experience and Revelation', in *The Praxis of the Reign of God*, ed. Mary Catherine Hilkert and Robert J. Schreiter (New York: Fordham University Press, 2002), 59–77.

Hilkert, Mary Catherine, 'Responses to Tanner's Jesus, Humanity and the Trinity', cit. by Jean Donovan, *CTSA Proceedings: Anthropology Group* 58 (2003): 157–8.

Hilkert, Mary Catherine, 'The Threatened Humanum as Imago Dei: Anthropology and Christian Ethics', in *Edward Schillebeeckx and Contemporary Theology*, ed. Lieven Boeve, Frederiek Depoortere and Stephan van Erp (London: T&T Clark, 2010), 127–41.

Hill, William, 'Schillebeeckx's New Look at Secularity: A Note', *The Thomist* 33 (1969): 162–70.

Hübenthal, Christoph, 'Apologetic Communication', *International Journal of Public Theology* 10 (2016): 7–27.

Huebner, Chris K., 'Can a Gift Be Commanded? Theological Ethics Without Theory by Way of Barth, Milbank, and Yoder', *Scottish Journal of Theology* 53 (2010): 472–89.

Huebner, Chris K., 'Radical Orthodoxy, Radical Reformation: What Might Milbank and Mennonites Learn from Each Other?' in *The Gift of Difference: Radical Orthodoxy, Radical Reformation*, ed. Chris H. Huebner and Tripp York (Winnipeg, MB: CMU Press, 2010), 205–17.

Huebner, Harry J., 'The Christian Life as Gift and Patience: Why Yoder Has Trouble with Method', in *A Mind Patient and Untamed: Assessing John Howard Yoder's Contributions to Theology, Ethics, and Peacemaking*, ed. Ben C. Ollenburger and Gayle Gerber Koontz (Telford, PA: Cascadia Publishing House, 2004), 23–38.

Huebner, Harry J., 'Participation, Peace, and Forgiveness: Milbank and Yoder in Dialogue', in *The Gift of Difference: Radical Orthodoxy, Radical Reformation*, ed. Chris H. Huebner and Tripp York (Winnipeg, MB: CMU Press, 2010), 180–204.

Hughes, Carl S., '"Tehomic" Christology? Tanner, Keller, and Kierkegaard on Writing Christ', *Modern Theology* (2015): 257–83.

Hughes, Kevin L., 'The Ratio Dei and the Ambiguities of History', *Modern Theology* 21 (2005): 645–61.

Hyman, Gavin, *The Predicament of Postmodern Theology: Radical Orthodoxy or Nihilist Textualism?* (Louisville, KY: Westminster John Knox Press, 2001).

Insole, Christopher, 'Against Radical Orthodoxy: The Dangers of Overcoming Political Liberalism', *Modern Theology* 20 (2004): 213–41.

Jacobsen, Eneida, 'Models of Public Theology', *International Journal of Public Theology* 6 (2012): 7–22.

Kennedy, Philip, 'Continuity underlying Discontinuity: Schillebeeckx's Philosophical Background', *New Blackfriars* 70 (1989): 264–77.

Kennedy, Philip, 'Human Beings as the Story of God: Schillebeeckx's Third Christology', *New Blackfriars* 71 (1990): 120–31.

Kennedy, Philip, *Schillebeeckx* (London: Geoffrey Chapman, 1993).

Kennedy, Philip, 'God and Creation', in *The Praxis of the Reign of God*, ed. Mary Catherine Hilkert and Robert J. Schreiter (New York: Fordham University Press, 2002), 37–58.

Kerr, Fergus, *Twentieth-Century Catholic Theologians* (Oxford: Blackwell Publishing, 2007).

Kerr, Nathan, 'Transcendence and Apocalyptic: A Reply to Barber', *Political Theology* 10 (2009): 143–52.

Kim, Sebastian, *Theology in the Public Sphere: Public Theology as a Catalyst for Open Debate* (London: SCM Press, 2011).

Kim, Sebastian, 'Editorial', *International Journal of Public Theology* 1, no. 1–4: (2007): 147–50.

Kim, Sebastian, 'Editorial', *International Journal of Public Theology* 3 (2009): 137–43.

Kim, Sebastian, 'Editorial', *International Journal of Public Theology* 4 (2010): 131–4.

Kim, Sebastian, 'Editorial', *International Journal of Public Theology* 6 (2012): 131–5.

Kim, Sebastian, 'Editorial', *International Journal of Public Theology* 8 (2014): 121–9.

King, James, 'Theologizing the State: What Hauerwas Could Have Learned From Yoder', *International Journal of Public Theology* 8 (2014): 313–29.

Koster, Hilda P., 'Book Forum', *Theology Today* 68 (2011): 310–47.

Koster, Hilda P., 'Questioning Eco-Theologyical *Panentheisms*: The Promise of Kathryn Tanner's Theology of God's Radical Transcendence for Ecological Theology', *Scriptura* 111 (2012: 3): 385–94.

Krasevac, Edward, 'Salvation "Thanks to" or "In Spite of" the Cross?' *New Blackfriars* 93 (2011): 572–9.

Kroker, Travis, 'Is a Messianic Political Ethic Possible? Recent Work by and about John Howard Yoder', *Journal of Religious Ethics* 33 (2005): 141–74.

LaFountain, Philip N., 'Theology and Social Psychology: Pluralism and "Evangel" in the Thought of Peter Berger and John Howard Yoder', *Theology Today* 69 (2012): 18–33.

Larsen, Sean, 'The Politics of Desire: Two Readings of Henri de Lubac on Nature and Grace', *Modern Theology* 29 (2013): 279–310.

Lash, Nicholas, 'Where Does Holy Teaching Leave Philosophy? Questions on Milbank's Aquinas', *Modern Theology* 15 (1999): 433–44.

Little, Joyce A., 'Review of *The Church with a Human Face*, by Edward Schillebeeckx', *The Thomist: A Speculative Quarterly* 52, no. 1 (1988): 158–65.

Lösel, Steffen, 'Book Forum', *Theology Today* 68 (2011): 310–47.

Maas, Frans, 'Stem & Stilte: Waarheid en openbaring bij Schillebeeckx', *Tijdschrift voor Theologie* (2010): 51–72.

Marenbon, Jon, 'Aquinas, Radical Orthodoxy and the Importance of Truth', in *Deconstructing Radical Orthodoxy: Postmodern Theology, Rhetoric and Truth*, ed. Wayne J. Hankey and Douglas Hedley (Aldershot: Ashgate, 2005), 49–64.

Martinez, Gaspar, *Confronting the Mystery of God: Political, Liberation and Public Theologies* (New York and London: Continuum, 2001).

Mast, Gerald J., 'Deconstructing Karl Barth', in *John Howard Yoder: Radical Theologian*, ed. J. Denny Weaver (Eugene, OR: Cascade Books, 2014), 167–85.

Masterson, R. R., Review of *God and Man*, by Edward Schillebeeckx, *The Thomist: A Speculative Quarterly Review* 34, no. 1 (1970): 131–3.

Mathewes, Charles., *A Theology of Public Life* (Cambridge: Cambridge University Press, 2007).

McDowell, John C., 'Theology as Conversational Event: Karl Barth, the Ending of "Dialogue" and the Beginning of "Conversation"', *Modern Theology* 19 (2003): 483–509.

McManus, Kathleen, 'Suffering in the Theology of Edward Schillebeeckx', *Theological Studies* 60 (1999): 476–91.

McPartlan, Paul, *The Eucharist Makes The Church: Henry de Lubac and John Zizioulas in Dialogue* (Edinburgh: T&T Clark, 1993).

Milbank, John, *Theology and Social Theory: Beyond Secular Reason*, 2nd edn (Oxford: Blackwell Publishing, 1990, 2006).

Milbank, John, 'The End of Dialogue', in *Christian Uniqueness Reconsidered: The Myth of a Pluralistic Theology of Religions*, ed. Gavin D'Costa (Maryknoll and New York: Orbis Books, 1992), 174–91.

Milbank, John, 'History of the One God', *The Heythrop Journal* XXXVIII (1997): 371–400.

Milbank, John, *The Word Made Strange: Theology, Language, Culture* (Oxford: Blackwell Publishers, 1997).

Milbank, John, 'Truth and Vision', in *Truth in Aquinas*, ed. John Milbank and Catherine Pickstock (Abingdon, Oxon: Routledge, 2001), 17–51.

Milbank, John, 'Beauty and the Soul', in *Theological Perspectives on God and Beauty*, ed. John Milbank, Graham Ward, and Edith Wyschogrod (London: Trinity Press International, 2003), 1–34.

Milbank, John, *Being Reconciled: Ontology and Pardon* (Oxon: Routledge, 2004).

Milbank, John, 'Alternative Protestantism: Radical Orthodoxy and the Reformed Tradition', in *Radical Orthodoxy and the Reformed Tradition: Creation, Covenant, and Participation*, ed. James K. Smith and James H. Olthuis (Grand Rapids, MI: Baker Academic, 2005), 25–42.

Milbank, John, *The Suspended Middle: Henri de Lubac and the Debate Concerning the Supernatural* (London: SCM Press, 2005).

Milbank, John, 'Only Theology Saves Metaphysics: On the Modalities of Terror', in *Belief and Metaphysics*, ed. Peter M. Candler Jr. and Conor Cunningham (London: SCM Press, 2007), 452–500.

Milbank, John, *The Future of Love: Essays in Political Theology* (London: SCM Press, 2009).

Milbank, John, 'Foreword', in *The Gift of Difference: Radical Orthodoxy, Radical Reformation*, ed. Chris H. Huebner and Tripp York (Winnipeg, MB: CMU Press, 2010), xi–xviii.

Milbank, John, 'The New Divide: Romantic versus Classical Orthodoxy', *Modern Theology* 26 (2010): 26–38.

Milbank, John, 'Hume *Versus* Kant: Faith, Reason and Feeling', *Modern Theology* 27 (2011): 276–97.

Milbank, John, *Beyond Secular Order: Critique on Modern Ontology* (Oxford: Blackwell Publishing, 2013).

Milbank, John, 'Foreword', in *Gift and the Unity of Being*, Antonio López (Eugene, OR: Cascade Books, 2014).

Milbank, John, Catherine Pickstock and Graham Ward, eds, *Radical Orthodoxy: A New Theology* (London: Routledge, 1999).

Milbank, John and Creston Davis, eds, *The Monstrosity of Christ: Paradox or Dialectic?* (Cambridge, MA: MIT Press, 2011).

Murphy, Francesca A., 'De Lubac, Grace, Politics and Paradox', *Studies in Christian Ethics* 23 (2010): 415–30.

Newell, Christopher, 'Communities of Faith, Desire, and Resistance: *A Response to Radical Orthodoxy's Ecclesia*', in *The Poverty of Radical Orthodoxy*, ed. Lisa Isherwood and Marko Zlomislic (Eugene, OR: Wipf and Stock, 2012), 178–95.

Nichols, Aidan, 'Henri de Lubac: Panorama and Proposal', *New Blackfriars* 93 (2012): 3–33.

Norman, Ralph, 'Review of *Christ and Culture*', by Graham Ward, *International Journal of Systematic Theology* (2007): 242–5.

Nugent, John C., 'The Politics of YHWH: John Howard Yoder's Old Testament Narration and Its Implications for Social Ethics', *Journal of Religious Ethics* 39 (2011): 71–99.

Ormerod, Neil, 'The Grace-Nature Distinction and the Construction of a Systematic Theology', *Theological Studies* 75 (2014): 515–36.

Parler, Branson L., *Things Hold Together: John Howard Yoder's Trinitarian Theology of Culture* (Harrisonburg: Herald Press, 2012).

Phillips, Elizabeth, 'We've Read the End of the Book: An Engagement with Contemporary Christian Zionism through the Eschatology of John Howard Yoder', *Studies in Christian Ethics* 21 (2008): 342–61.

Phillips, Peter, 'Schillebeeckx's Soteriological Agnosticism', *New Blackfriars* 78 (1997): 76–84.

Pickstock, Catherine, *After Writing: On the Liturgical Consummation of Philosophy* (Oxford: Blackwell Publishing, 1997).

Plantinga Pauw, Amy, 'Ecclesiological Reflections on Kathryn Tanner's Jesus, Humanity and the Trinity', *Scottish Journal of Theology* 57 (2004): 221–7.

Portier, William, 'Schillebeeckx' Dialogue with Critical Theory', *The Ecumenist* 21 (1983): 20–7.

Portier, William, 'Edward Schillebeeckx as Critical Theorist: The Impact of Neo-Marxist Social Thought on his Recent Theology', *The Thomist* 48, no. 3 (1984): 341–65.

Portier, William, 'Interpretation and Method', in *The Praxis of the Reign of God*, ed. Mary Catherine Hilkert and Robert J. Schreiter (New York: Fordham University Press, 2002), 9–36.

Poulsom, Martin, *The Dialectics of Creation: Creation and the Creator in Edward Schillebeeckx and David Burell* (London: Bloomsbury, 2014).

Ranson, David, *Between the 'Mysticism of Politics' and the 'Politics of Mysticism':* *Interpreting New Pathways of Holiness within the Roman Catholic Tradition* (Hindmarsh: ATF Theology, 2014).

Reno, R. R., 'The Radical Orthodoxy Project', *First Things* (February 2000), http://www.firstthings.com/article/2000/02/the-radical-orthodoxy-project.

Reynolds, Terrence, 'A Closed Marketplace: Religious Claims in the Public Square', *International Journal of Public Theology* 8 (2014): 201–22.

Richardson, Graeme, 'Integrity and Realism: Assessing John Milbank's Theology', *New Blackfriars* 84 (2007): 268–80.

Roberts Skerrett, Kathleen, 'Desire and Anathema: Mimetic Rivalry in Defense of Plenitude', *Journal of the American Academy of Religion* 71 (2003): 793–809.

Rochford, Dennis, 'The Theological Hermeneutics of Edward Schillebeeckx', *Theological Studies* 63 (2002): 251–67.

Rodenborn, Steven M., *Hope in Action: Subversive Eschatology in the Theology of Edward Schillebeeckx and Johann Baptist Metz* (New York: Fortress Press, 2014).

Root, Michael, 'The Wrong Key: A Review of *Christ the Key* by Kathryn Tanner', *First Things* (December 2010), http://www.firstthings.com/article/2010/12/the-wrong-key.

Ryan, Robin, 'Holding on to the Hand of God: Edward Schillebeeckx on the Mystery of Suffering', *New Blackfriars* 89 (2007): 114–25.

Sachs, John R., 'Responses to Tanner's Jesus, Humanity and the Trinity', cit. by Jean Donovan, *CTSA Proceedings: Anthropology Group* 58 2003: 157–8.

Schillebeeckx, Edward, 'Christelijke Situatie III. – Naar een oplossing: Bovennatuurlijk Exclusivisme', *Kultuurleven* (1945): 585–611.

Schillebeeckx, Edward, 'Op zoek naar Gods afwezigheid: Ontkerstening of een historische genadekans', *Kultuurleven* 24 (1957): 276–91.

Schillebeeckx, Edward, 'De betekenis van het niet-godsdienstige humanisme voor het hedendaagse katholicisme', in *Modern nietgodsdienstig humanism*, ed. W. Engelen (Nijmegen: Utrecht, 1961), 74–112.

Schillebeeckx, Edward, 'De zin van het mens-zijn van Jezus, de Christus', *Tijdschrift voor Theologie* 2 (1962): 127–72.

Schillebeeckx, Edward, 'Theologische reflexie op godsdienstsociologische duidingen in verband met het hedendaagse ongeloof', *Tijdschrift voor Theologie* 2 (1962): 55–76.

Schillebeeckx, Edward, 'De ascese van het zoeken naar God', *Tijdschrift voor Geestelijk Leven* 20 (1964): 149–58.

Schillebeeckx, Edward, 'Herinterpretatie van het geloof in het licht van de seculariteit. Honest to Robinson', *Tijdschrift voor Theologie* 4 (1964): 109–50.

Schillebeeckx, Edward, 'Kerk en mensdom', *Concilium* 1 (1965): 63–86.

Schillebeeckx, Edward, 'Leven in God en Leven in de Wereld', in *God en Mens* (Bilthoven (Holland): Uitgeverij H. Nelissen, 1965), 66–149.

Schillebeeckx, Edward, 'Dialoog met God en Christelijke Seculariteit', in *God en Mens* (Bilthoven (Holland): Uitgeverij H. Nelissen, 1965), 150–66.

Schillebeeckx, Edward, 'Het leed der ervaring van Gods verborgenheid', *Vox Theologica* 36 (1966): 92–104.

Schillebeeckx, Edward, 'Persoonlijke openbaringsgestalte van de Vader', *Tijdschrift voor Theologie* 6 (1966): 274–89.

Schillebeeckx, Edward, 'Christelijk geloof en aardse toekomstverwachtingen', in *De kerk in de wereld van deze tijd. Schema dertien. Tekst en commentaar* [Vaticanum II, 2] (Hilversum, Antwerpen 1967), 78–109.

Schillebeeckx, Edward, 'Zwijgen en spreken over God in een geseculariseerde wereld',
   Tijdschrift voor Theologie 7 (1967): 337-58.
Schillebeeckx, Edward, 'Het nieuwe Godsbeeld, secularisatie en politiek', *Tijdschrift voor
   Theologie* 8 (1968): 44-65.
Schillebeeckx, Edward, 'Enkele hermeneutische beschouwingen over de eschatologie',
   Concilium 5 (1969): 38-51.
Schillebeeckx, Edward, 'Het Evangelie als appél in onze geseculariseerde wereld (1)', in *Het
   Evangelie als appél* [Groepsgesprek van de religieuzen; 28] (Mechelen, 1969), 5-17.
Schillebeeckx, Edward, 'Christelijk antwoord op een menselijke vraag? De oecumenische
   betekenis van de "correlatiemethode"', *Tijdschrift voor Theologie* 10 (1970): 1-22.
Schillebeeckx, Edward, 'Leven ondanks de dood in heden en toekomst', *Tijdschrift voor
   Theologie* 10 (1970): 418-52.
Schillebeeckx, Edward, 'The Critical Status of Theology', *World Congress 'The Future of the
   Church'* (Brussels 12-17 September, 1970).
Schillebeeckx, Edward, 'Kritische theorie en theologische hermeneutiek: confrontatie',
   Tijdschrift voor Theologie 11 (1971): 113-39.
Schillebeeckx, Edward, 'Naar een verruiming van de hermeneutiek: de "nieuwe kritische
   theorie"', *Tijdschrift voor Theologie* 11 (1971): 30-50.
Schillebeeckx, Edward, 'De Toegang tot Jezus van Nazaret', *Tijdschrift voor Theologie* 12
   (1972): 28-60.
Schillebeeckx, Edward, 'The Christian and Political Engagement', *Doctrine and Life* 22
   (1972): 118-27.
Schillebeeckx, Edward, 'Stilte, Gevuld Met Parables', in *Politiek of Mystiek? Peilingen naar
   de verhouding tussen religieuze ervaring en sociale inzet* (Utrecht and Brugge, 1972),
   69-81.
Schillebeeckx, Edward, 'Crisis van de geloofstaal als hermeneutisch probleem', *Concilium* 9
   (1973): 33-47.
Schillebeeckx, Edward, 'De vrije mens Jezus en zijn conflict', *TGL* 29 (1973): 145-55.
Schillebeeckx, Edward, 'Kritische theorieën en politiek engagement van de christelijke
   gemeente', *Concilium* 9 (1973): 47-61.
Schillebeeckx, Edward, 'Ons heil: Jezus' leven of Christus de verrezene', *Tijdschrift voor
   Theologie* 13 (1973): 145-65.
Schillebeeckx, Edward, 'Arabisch-Neoplatoonse Achtergrond van Thomas' Opvatting over
   de Ontvangelijkheid van de Mens voor de Genade', *Bijdragen* 35 (1974): 298-308.
Schillebeeckx, Edward, *Jezus. Het verhaal van een levende* (Bilthoven (Holland): Uitgeverij
   H. Nelissen, 1974).
Schillebeeckx, Edward, 'De "God van Jezus" en de "Jezus van God"', *Concilium* 10 (1974):
   100-15.
Schillebeeckx, Edward, 'De vraag naar de universaliteit van Jezus', in *De vraag naar de
   universaliteit van Jezus*, Openingswoord en inleidingen gehouden voor het congres van
   de Werkgroep voor Moderne Theologie op 20 oktober 1975 te Utrecht (Utrecht, 1975),
   15-26.
Schillebeeckx, Edward, 'Mysterie van ongerechtigheid en mysterie van erbarmen',
   Tijdschrift voor Theologie 15 (1975): 3-24.
Schillebeeckx, Edward, 'Jezus en de menselijke levensmislukking', *Concilium* 12 (1976):
   86-96.
Schillebeeckx, Edward, *Gerechtigheid en liefde : genade en bevrijding* (Bilthoven (Holland):
   Uitgeverij H. Nelissen, 1977).

Schillebeeckx, Edward, 'Godsdienst van en voor mensen. Naar een criteriologie voor godsdienst en religie', *Tijdschrift voor Theologie* 17 (1977): 353–70.

Schillebeeckx, Edward, 'Waarom Jezus de Christus?' *TGL* 33 (1977): 338–53.

Schillebeeckx, Edward, 'God, Society and Human Salvation', in *Faith and Society. Acta Congressus Internationalis Theologici Lovaniensis* 1976 [Bibliotheca Ephemeridum Theologicarum Lovaniensium XLVII] (Gembloux, 1978), 87–99.

Schillebeeckx, Edward, 'Op weg naar een christologie', *Tijdschrift voor Theologie* 18 (1978): 131–56.

Schillebeeckx, Edward, Jezus voor wie vandaag gelooft', *Kultuurleven* 46 (1979): 887–901.

Schillebeeckx, Edward, 'Openbaringsdichtheid van menselijke ervaringen en moderne geloofsmogelijkheden', *Verbum* 46 (1979): 14–29.

Schillebeeckx, Edward, 'Wezen en grenzen van het christendom', *De Vrij-Katholiek* 54 (1979): 8–9.

Schillebeeckx, Edward, 'Het theologisch zoeken naar katholieke identiteit in de twintigste eeuw', in *De identiteit van katholieke wetenschapsmensen* [Annalen van het Thijmgenootschap 68/II] (Baarn, 1980), 175–89.

Schillebeeckx, Edward, 'Wereldlijke kritiek op de christelijke gehoorzaamheid en christelijke reactie daarop', *Concilium* 16 (1980): 17–29.

Schillebeeckx, Edward, 'Ingekeerd of naar de wereld toegewend?' *TGL* 37 (1981): 652–68.

Schillebeeckx, Edward, 'Op zoek naar de heilswaarde van politieke vredespraxis', *Tijdschrift voor Theologie* 21 (1981): 232–43.

Schillebeeckx, Edward, 'Christelijke identiteit en menselijke integriteit', *Concilium* 18 (1982): 34–42.

Schillebeeckx, Edward, *Theologisch geloofsverstaan anno 1983*, Afscheidscollege gegeven op vrijdag 11 februari 1983 door Mag. dr. Edward Schillebeeckx o.p. hoogleraar Systematische Theologie en Geschiedenis van de Theologie, Nijmegen (januari 1958 tot 1 september 1982) (Baarn: Nelissen, 1983).

Schillebeeckx, Edward, 'Spreken over God in een context van bevrijding', *TGL* 40 (1984): 7–24.

Schillebeeckx, Edward, 'Christelijke spiritualiteit als ziel en bevrijding van de ethiek', *TGL* 41 (1985): 407–18.

Schillebeeckx, Edward, *Als politiek niet alles is. Jezus in onze westerse cultuur*, Abraham Kuyper-lezingen 1986 (Baarn: Ten Have, 1986).

Schillebeeckx, Edward, *Jesus in Our Western Culture: Mysticism, Ethics and Politics* (London: SCM Press, 1986).

Schillebeeckx, Edward, "Gij zijt een verborgen God'. Jesaja 45,15. Een vastenmeditatie', *TGL* 43 (1987): 27–30.

Schillebeeckx, Edward, 'Vanzelfsprekendheid van een eigentijds geloof', in *Zijn de Middeleeuwen nu echt voorbij? Over verschuivingen in een katholiek paradigma* (Nijmegen, 1987), 39–44.

Schillebeeckx, Edward, 'Vergebung als Modell menschlicher Autonomie und die Gnade Gottes', in *Die Widerspenstige Religion: Orientierung für eine Kultur der Autonomie?*, ed. Toine van den Hoogen, Hans Küng and Jean-Pierre Wils (Kampen: Pharos, 1997), 128–57.

Schillebeeckx, Edward, 'Christelijke identiteit, uitdagend en uitgedaagd: Over de rakelingse nabijheid van de onervaarbare God', in *Ons rakelings nabij: Gedaanteveranderingen van God en geloof. Ter ere van Edward Schillebeeckx*, ed. M. Kalsky e.a. (Nijmegen/Zoetermeer, 2005), 13–32.

Schillebeeckx, Edward, 'Letter from Edward Schillebeeckx', in *Edward Schillebeeckx and Contemporary Theology*, ed. Lieven Boeve, Frederiek Depoortere and Stephan van Erp (London: T&T Clark, 2010), xiv–xvi.

Schillebeeckx, Edward, *Christ the Sacrament of the Encounter with God*, translated by Paul Barret, N. D. Smith, *CW* vol. 1 (London: Bloomsbury T&T Clark, 2014).

Schillebeeckx, Edward, *Revelation and Theology*, translated by N. D. Smith, *CW* vol. 2 (London: Bloomsbury T&T Clark, 2014).

Schillebeeckx, Edward, *God the Future of Man*, translated by N. D. Smith, *CW* vol. 3 (London: Bloomsbury T&T Clark, 2014).

Schillebeeckx, Edward, *World and Church*, translated by N. D. Smith, *CW* vol. 4 (London: Bloomsbury T&T Clark, 2014).

Schillebeeckx, Edward, *The Understanding of Faith: Interpretation and Criticism*, translated by N. D. Smith, *CW* vol. 5 (London: Bloomsbury T&T Clark, 2014).

Schillebeeckx, Edward, *Jesus: An Experiment in Christology*, translated by John Bowden, *CW* vol. 6 (London: Bloomsbury T&T Clark, 2014).

Schillebeeckx, Edward, *Christ: The Christian Experience in the Modern World*, translated by John Bowden, *CW* vol. 7 (London: Bloomsbury T&T Clark, 2014).

Schillebeeckx, Edward, *Interim Report on the Books Jesus and Christ*, translated by John Bowden, *CW* vol. 8 (London: Bloomsbury T&T Clark, 2014).

Schillebeeckx, Edward, *Church: The Human Story of God*, translated by John Bowden, *CW* vol. 10 (London: Bloomsbury T&T Clark, 2014).

Schillebeeckx, Edward, 'Schillebeeckx and Theology in the Twenty-First Century', in *Edward Schillebeeckx and Contemporary Theology*, ed. Lieven Boeve, Frederiek Depoortere and Stephan van Erp (London: T&T Clark, 2010), 252–64).

Schreiter, Robert J., 'Indicators of the Future of Theology in the Works of Edward Schillebeeckx', in *Edward Schillebeeckx: Impulse für Theologien im 21. Jahrhundert – Impetus Towards Theologies in the 21st Century*, ed. Thomas Eggensperger, Ulrich Engel and Angel F. Méndez Montoya (Ostfildern: Matthias Grünewaldverlag, 2008), 21–38.

Schwarz-Boennecke, Bernadette, , Die Widerständigkeit der Wirklichkeit als erstes Moment des Erfahrens', in *Edward Schillebeeckx: Impulse für Theologien im 21. Jahrhundert – Impetus Towards Theologies in the 21st Century*, ed. Thomas Eggensperger, Ulrich Engel and Angel F. Méndez Montoya (Ostfildern: Matthias Grünewaldverlag, 2008), 94–109.

Shakespeare, Steven, *Radical Orthodoxy: A Critical Introduction* (London: SPCK, 2007).

Sider, Alexander, *To See History Doxologically: History and Holiness in John Howard Yoder's Ecclesiology* (Grand Rapids, MI: Eerdmans, 2014).

Smit, Dirkie, 'Notions of the Public and Doing Theology', *International Journal of Public Theology* 1 (2007): 431–54.

Smith, Graeme, 'Pluralism and Justice: A Theological Critique of Red Toryism', *Political Theology* 13 (2012): 330–47.

Smith, James K., *Introducing Radical Orthodoxy: Mapping a Post-Secular Theology* (Grand Rapids, MI: Baker Academic, 2004).

Smith, James K., 'Will the Real Plato Please Stand Up? Participation versus Incarnation', in *Radical Orthodoxy and the Reformed Tradition: Creation, Covenant, and Participation*, ed. James K. Smith and James H. Olthuis (Grand Rapids, MI: Baker Academic, 2005), 61–72.

Southern, Richard William, *Western Society and Church in the Middle Ages* (Middlesex: Penguin Books, 1970).

Stackhouse, Max, 'Public Theology and Ethical Judgment', *Theology Today* 54 (1997): 165–79.

Stackhouse, Max, 'Introduction', in *Christ and the Dominions of Civilization. God and Globalization: Theological Ethics and the Spheres of Life*, vol. 3, ed. Max L. Stackhouse and Diane B. Obenchain (Harrisburg: Trinity Press International, 2002).

Stackhouse, Max, *Globalization and Grace: A Christian Public Theology for a Global Future. God and Globalization: Theological Ethics and the Spheres of Life*, vol. 4. London (New York: Continuum, 2007).

Stackhouse, Max, 'Reflections on How and why we Go Public', *International Journal of Public Theology* 1 (2007): 421–30.

Stackhouse, Max, 'Commentary: Public Theology and Democracy's Future', 2004 Templeton Lecture, *The Review of Faith & International Affairs* 7, no. 2 (2009): 7–11.

Stassen, Glen H., 'A Nonviolent Public Ethic', in *John Howard Yoder: Radical Theologian*, ed. J. Denny Weaver (Eugene, OR: Cascade Books, 2014), 244–67.

Storrar, William, '2007: A Kairos Moment for Public Theology', *International Journal of Public Theology* 1 (2007): 5–25.

Storrar, William, 'The Naming of Parts: Doing Public Theology in a Global Era', *International Journal of Public Theology* 5 (2011): 23–43.

Stout, Jeffrey, *Democracy and Tradition* (Princeton: Princeton University Press, 2003).

Stout, Jeffrey, 'Pragmatism and Democracy: Assessing Jeffrey Stout's *Democracy and Tradition*', *Journal of the American Academy of Religion* 78 (2010), ed. Jason Springs: 413–48.

Surin, Kenneth, ,Atonement and Christology', *Neue Zeitschrift für Systematische Theologie und Religionsphilosophie* 24 (1982): 131–49.

Tanner, Kathryn, *God and Creation in Christian Theology: Tyranny or Empowerment?* (Minneapolis, MN: Fortress Press, 1988).

Tanner, Kathryn, 'Respect for Other Religions: A Christian Antidote to Colonialist Discourse', *Modern Theology* 9 (1993): 1–18.

Tanner, Kathryn, *Theories of Culture: A New Agenda for Theology.* (Minneapolis, MN: Fortress Press, 1997).

Tanner, Kathryn, 'Justification and Justice in a Theology of Grace', *Theology Today* 55 (1999): 510–23.

Tanner, Kathryn, *Jesus, Humanity and the Trinity: A Brief Systematic Theology* (Minneapolis: Fortress Press, 2001).

Tanner, Kathryn, 'Incarnation, Cross, and Sacrifice: A Feminist-Inspired Reappraisal', *Anglican Theological Review* 86, no. 1 (2004): 35–56.

Tanner, Kathryn, 'The Church and Action for the World: A Response to Amy Pauw', *Scottish Journal of Theology* 57 (2004): 228–32.

Tanner, Kathryn, *Economy of Grace* (Minneapolis: Fortress Press, 2005).

Tanner, Kathryn, Review of *Christ and Culture*, by Graham Ward, *Modern Theology* 23 (2007): 482–4.

Tanner, Kathryn, *Christ the Key* (Cambridge: Cambridge University Press, 2010).

Tanner, Kathryn, 'How My Mind Has Changed: Christian Claims', *The Christian Century* (2010): 40–5.

Tanner, Kathryn, 'Is Capitalism a Belief System?' *Anglican Theological Review* 92, no. 4 (2010): 617–35.

Tanner, Kathryn, 'Shifts in Theology over the Last Quarter Century', *Modern Theology* 26 (2010): 39–44.

Tanner, Kathryn, 'Book Forum', *Theology Today* 68 (2011): 310–47.

Tanner, Kathryn, 'Article Review: David Brown's Divine Humanity', *Scottish Journal of Theology* 68 (2015): 106–13.

Tanner, Kathryn and John Howard Yoder, 'Radical Orthodoxy and the Future of British Theology', *Scottish Journal of Theology* 54 (2001): 385–404.

Tavard, George H., Review of *Interim Report on the Books Jesus and Christ*, by Edward Schillebeeckx, *Journal of Theological Studies* 32 (1981): 573–4.

Thiemann, Ronald F., *Constructing a Public Theology: The Church in a Pluralistic Culture* (Louisville, KY: Westminster/ John Knox Press, 1991).

Thompson, Daniel P., 'Schillebeeckx on the Development of Doctrine', *Theological Studies* 62 (2001): 303–21.

Tonstad, Linn Marie, *God and Difference: The Trinity, Sexuality, and the Transformation of Finitude* (New York and London: Routledge, 2016).

Van de Walle, A. R., 'Theologie over de werkelijkheid: Een betekenis van het werk van Edward Schillebeeckx', *Tijdschrift voor Theologie* 14 (1974): 461–90.

Van Erp, Stephan, 'Incarnational Theology – Systematic Theology after Edward Schillebeeckx', in *Edward Schillebeeckx: Impulse für Theologien im 21. Jahrhundert – Impetus Towards Theologies in the 21st Century*, ed. Thomas Eggensperger, Ulrich Engel and Angel F. Méndez Montoya (Ostfildern: Matthias Grünewaldverlag, 2008), 53–66.

Van Erp, Stephan, 'Implicit Faith: Philosophical Theology after Schillebeeckx', in *Edward Schillebeeckx and Contemporary Theology*, ed. Lieven Boeve, Frederiek Depoortere and Stephan van Erp (London: T&T Clark, 2010), 209–23.

Van Erp, Stephan, 'Incessant Incarnation as the Future of Humanity: The Promise of Schillebeeckx's Sacramental Theology', in *Sacramentalizing Human History: In Honour of Edward Schillebeeckx (1914-2009)*, ed. Erik Borgman, Paul D. Murray and Andrés Torres Queiruga (London: SCM Press, Concilium, 2012), 92–105.

Van Erp, Stephan, 'The Sacrament of the World: Thinking God's Presence Beyond Public Theology', *ET Studies* 6, no. 1 (2015): 119–34.

Van Erp, Stephan, 'World and Sacrament: Foundations of the Political Theology of the Church', *Louvain Studies* 39 (2016): 100–18.

Velloso Ewell, Rosalee C., 'The Word Made Silent: Reflections on Christian Identity and Scripture', in *The Gift of Difference: Radical Orthodoxy, Radical Reformation*, ed. Chris H. Huebner and Tripp York (Winnipeg, MB: CMU Press, 2010), 67–86.

Vergote, Antoon, 'Ervaringsgeloof and geloofservaring', *Streven* 52 (1985): 891–903.

Waltner Goossen, Rachel, 'The Failure to Bind and Loose: Responses to Yoder's Sexual Abuse', *The Mennonite* (1 December 2015), https://themennonite.org/feature/failure-bind-loose-responses-john-howard-yoders-sexual-abuse/.

Ward, Graham, *Barth, Derrida, and the Language of Theology* (Cambridge: Cambridge University Press, 1995).

Ward, Graham *Theology and Contemporary Critical Theory*, second edition (London: MacMillan Press, 1996, 2000).

Ward, Graham, *Cities of God* (London: Routledge, 2000).

Ward, Graham, 'Radical Orthodoxy and/as Cultural Politics', in *Radical Orthodoxy? – A Catholic Enquiry*, ed. Laurence Paul Hemming (Aldershot: Ashgate, 2000), 97–111.

Ward, Graham, *Christ and Culture* (Oxford: Blackwell Publishing, 2005).

Ward, Graham, *Cultural Transformations and Religious Practice* (Cambridge: Cambridge University Press, 2005).

Ward, Graham, 'Response to: Rivera, Joseph M., "Review: Ward, Graham, Christ and Culture"', *Conversations in Religion & Theology* 6 (2008): 24–36.

Ward, Graham, *The Politics of Discipleship: Becoming Postmaterial Citizens* (Grand Rapids, MI: Baker Academic, 2009).

Ward, Graham, 'Transcorporeality: The Ontological Scandal', in *The Radical Orthodoxy Reader*, ed. John Milbank and Simon Oliver (London: Routledge, 2009), 287–307.

Ward, Graham, 'History, Belief and Imagination in Charles Taylor's *A Secular Age*', *Modern Theology* 26 (2010): 337–84.

Ward, Graham, 'The Weakness of Believing: A Dialogue with de Certeau', *Culture, Theory and Critique* 52 (2011): 233–46.

Ward, Graham, 'Affect: Towards a Theology of Experience', *Radical Orthodoxy: Theology, Philosophy, Politics Vol.* 1 (2012): 55–80.

Ward, Graham, 'De Certeau and an Enquiry into Believing', in *Between Philosophy and Theology: Contemporary Interpretations of Christianity* (Farnham: Ashgate, 2014), 73–86.

Ward, Graham, 'Receiving the Gift', *Modern Theology* 30 (2014): 74–88.

Ward, Graham, 'The Myth of Secularism', *Telos* 167 (2014): 162–79.

Ward, Graham, *Unbelievable: Why We Believe and Why We Don't* (London and New York: I. B. Tauris, 2014).

Ward, Graham, *How the Light Gets In: Ethical Life I* (Oxford: Oxford University Press, 2016).

Ware, Robert C., 'Review of *God and Man*, by Edward Schillebeeckx', *Theological Studies* 31, no. 2 (1970): 320.

Warlick, Ian, 'Post-Secularity, Hegel and Friendship: An Interview with Graham Ward', *Radical Orthodoxy: Theology, Philosophy, Politics* 1 (2012): 333–48.

Weaver, Alain Epp, 'After Politics: John Howard Yoder, Body Politics, and the Witnessing Church', *The Review of Politics* 61 (1999): 637–73.

Weaver, J. Denny, 'Introduction', in *John Howard Yoder: Radical Theologian*, ed. J. Denny Weaver (Eugene, OR: Cascade Books, 2014), 1–25.

West, Cornel, 'Pragmatism and Democracy: Assessing Jeffrey Stout's *Democracy and Tradition*', *Journal of the American Academy of Religion* 78 (2010), ed. Jason Springs: 413–48.

Williams, Rowan, 'Saving Time: Thoughts on Practice, Patience and Vision', *New Blackfriars* 73 (2007): 319–26.

Wisse, Maarten, 'Introduction to the Thinking of Graham Ward', in *Between Philosophy and Theology: Contemporary Interpretations of Christianity*, ed. Lieven Boeve and Christophe Brabant (Farnham: Ashgate, 2010), 65–72.

Wood, William, 'Review of *Christ the Key*, by Kathryn Tanner', *Scottish Journal of Theology* 66 (2013): 364–7.

Yoder, John Howard, *The Politics of Jesus* (Grand Rapids, MI: Eerdmans, 1972, 1994).

Yoder, John Howard, *The Priestly Kingdom: Social Ethics as Gospel* (Notre Dame: University of Notre Dame Press, 1984).

Yoder, John Howard, 'Meaning after Babble: With Jeffrey Stout beyond Relativism', *Journal of Religious Ethics* 24 (1996): 125–39.

Yoder, John Howard, 'Jesus – A Model of Radical Political Action', in *Faith and Freedom: Christian Ethics in a Pluralistic Culture*, ed. David Neville and Philip Matthews (Hindmarsh, SA: ATF Press, 2003), 163–9.

Yoder, John Howard, 'Three Unfinished Pilgrimages', in *Faith and Freedom: Christian Ethics in a Pluralistic Culture*, ed. David Neville and Philip Matthews (Hindmarsh, SA: ATF Press, 2003), 126–36.

York, Tripp, 'The Ballad of John and Anneken', in *The Gift of Difference: Radical Orthodoxy, Radical Reformation*, ed. Chris H. Huebner and Tripp York (Winnipeg, MB: CMU Press, 2010), 50–66.

Ziegler, Philip, 'God and Some Recent Public Theologies', *International Journal of Systematic Theology* 4 (2002): 137–55.

Zimbelman, Joel, 'The Contribution of John Howard Yoder To Recent Discussions in Christian Social Ethics', *Scottish Journal of Theology* 45 (1992): 367–99.

Zimmerman, Earl, 'Sixteenth-Century Anabaptist Roots', in *John Howard Yoder: Radical Theologian*, ed. J. Denny Weaver (Eugene, OR: Cascade Books, 2014), 89–116.

Zimmerman, Earl, 'Oscar Cullmann and Radical Discipleship', in *John Howard Yoder: Radical Theologian*, ed. J. Denny Weaver (Eugene, OR: Cascade Books, 2014), 145–66.

INDEX